Economics of Banking

Economics of Banking

Hans Keiding

First published 2016 by
PALGRAVE

Palgrave in the UK is an imprint of Macmillan Publishers Limited, registered in England, company number 785998, of 4 Crinan Street, London N1 9XW.

Palgrave Macmillan in the US is a division of St Martin's Press LLC, 175 Fifth Avenue, New York, NY 10010.

Palgrave is the global imprint of the above companies and is represented throughout the world.

Palgrave® and Macmillan® are registered trademarks in the United States, the United Kingdom, Europe and other countries.

ISBN 978–1–137–45304–4 paperback

This book is printed on paper suitable for recycling and made from fully managed and sustained forest sources. Logging, pulping and manufacturing processes are expected to conform to the environmental regulations of the country of origin.

A catalogue record for this book is available from the British Library.

A catalog record for this book is available from the Library of Congress.

Printed in China

Contents

Preface

The economic theory of banks, or more generally, financial intermediation, has a long history, almost as long as the banks themselves, but as a subject of university courses, with appropriate textbooks, it is much more recent. A coherent body of theory dealing with financial intermediation arose in the 1980s, fostered by the development of models of economic behaviour subject to uncertainty and asymmetric information, and the appearance of the textbook by Freixas and Rochet [2008] signaled the entrance of the field into the university curriculum. Later textbooks, including the present one, owe much to this landmark in the development of the field, and their organization of the material basically remains the same.

A closer study of the way in which banks behave, as well as in the way they should behave, is important for several reasons. Banks matter much for the economic life of society, as shown by their share in the national product as well as the incomes obtained by top management in large banks. But more important perhaps, and in particular in view of the recent financial crisis, if the banks perform improperly or fail, then it has important consequences for the economic well-being of society as a whole. The consequences of the financial crisis of 2007–8 have been very serious, bringing downturn or stagnation for almost a decade to a large part of the world. This has had an impact on the prestige of banks and bankers, felt even in university teaching, where student excitement over finance and banking has faded over recent years. Even so, it remains important to understand what is going on in financial intermediation because a thorough understanding of the functioning of this sector remains the best basis for its regulation.

The specific object of study in the economic theory of banking is the role of the *intermediary*, and therefore we must cover the basic functions of the intermediary as well as consequences that these functions will have on the economic environment. On the other hand, it also means that some topics, which intuitively come close to banking, nevertheless fall outside because no intermediation is involved. Thus, the theory of money and monetary policy is not touched upon in this book, and in our treatment of central banks, we concentrate on their role as lenders of last resort, as intermediaries for interbank payments, and possibly as financial supervisors. The remaining roles are outside our scope.

Banking is an activity where regulation matters very much, and the regulation of the financial sector has been growing in detail and complexity over the last few decades, to the extent that banks have separate departments which are concerned with adapting to the

The financial crisis of 2007–8: What contributed to bringing it about? In the literature about the crisis and how it emerged, several points stand out:

The rise and subsequent fall in house prices: For several years preceding the crisis, house prices had been moving upwards consistently, by more than 10% per year, until they peaked in late 2006. The steadily increasing prices of houses led to an expansion of credit, because even notoriously bad borrowers would be able to pay back their loans given that their houses had increased in value.

New methods of financial engineering: The already existing methods of transferring bank credit to marketable securities had been extended to include financial derivatives of growing complexity, leading to a situation where the methods for assessing the risk of the new securities were insufficient, so large parts of the securities in the market were overvalued.

Deregulation: From the late nineties and onwards, most countries liberalized controls of the financial sector, allowing the banks to engage in new activities and relaxing the restrictions pertaining to risk taking and use of borrowed funds.

Artificially low interest rates: Monetary policy had been concerned with keeping interest rates low at least from 2001, in the beginning due to a fear of deflation and recession. The low interest rates contributed significantly to keeping house prices high, and the easy access to credit fostered the development of new financial products.

Increasing leveraging: The possibility of buying up securities using money borrowed through contracts using these very securities as collateral meant that very little capital was needed to command large funds, but even small changes in the value of the collateral might – and eventually did – cause a default which then would have repercussions on other agents.

In the course of this book, we shall return to most of these phenomena, each of which, taken in isolation, might constitute a risk to a healthy financial system. It will also emerge that they are closely interrelated, so e.g. the rise and subsequent fall in house prices was not so much an isolated phenomenon causing a financial crisis, but rather a result of an imperfectly functioning financial system.

rules of the regulators. These rules, and in particular the responses of the sector to the rules and the changes of rules, matter for the understanding of the workings of financial intermediation, and this can also be seen in the chapters of this book, where, in particular, the Basel rules show up from the first to the last chapters. In connection with this, the basics of risk management have been given a more detailed treatment than what is usual, because this is one of the key activities in contemporary financial intermediation and therefore a necessary part of the overall picture. Clearly, in a context where more specialized courses in risk management are available for students, these chapters may be skipped.

The chapters of the book are organized as follows: We begin with what could be considered the basics of financial intermediation, explaining why intermediaries perform an important activity in the economy; this is dealt with in the first two chapters, and in Chapter 3 we introduce risk management in general, followed in the next chapter by a detailed treatment of market risk. After this introductory part of the book come two chapters dealing with the loan contract (Chapter 5) and the problems of credit rationing (Chapter 6). Following up on these chapters, where creditworthiness and repayment are central topics, it is natural to treat credit risk management, and this is done in Chapter 7.

The following chapters discuss some of the newer aspects of financial intermediation, such as securitization in Chapter 8, investment banking in Chapter 9 and payments in Chapter 10. Then we return to more mainstream topics; in Chapter 11, we consider competition in the banking sector and in particular its impact on risk taking. Then Chapter 12 deals with what may be considered as unwanted phenomena of the banking sector, followed by a chapter on operational risk. The final part of the book is concerned with the cases where banks get into trouble; liquidity problems and bank runs are treated in Chapter 14, followed by two chapters treating the special institutions which are geared to assist the banks in such situations, namely deposit insurance (Chapter 15) and lenders of last resort (Chapter 16). Chapter 17 deals with the cases where a bank may have to be closed down. Finally, we conclude with Chapter 18, collecting previous material on regulation and adding some specific theoretical viewpoints on capital regulation of banks.

The book has grown out of lecture notes from different courses and with differing audiences; some of them more experienced in economic theory than others. The book is intended for a reader with some acquaintance with mathematically formulated economic theory, but no particular background knowledge of mathematics is required, and whenever the formalism becomes overwhelming, it can be sidestepped without much damage to the understanding. The problems provided at the end of each chapter emphasize the interpretation and applications of the theory rather than its formal and academic aspects. On the other hand, the formal theory is presented in the text, so the reader can get the full picture and possibly be captured by the purely academic aspects of the financial sector, which may be fascinating also for other reasons than the large incomes falling upon some of its participants.

The text has benefited greatly from the suggestions of many generations of students. In its final version, valuable assistance and advice was provided by Bodil O. Hansen, for which I am grateful.

Hans Keiding

Chapter 1

Why Are There Banks?

1.1 Introduction: Key competences of banks

In this and all the chapters to follow, we shall be concerned with banks, their activity and their impact on society. The treatment of banks, the way in which they interact with other agents and the way in which they manage their business will take us through many different aspects of economics and involve many different types of economic theory.

As a starting point for the discussion, it may be appropriate to consider the economic role of banking, or more generally, *financial intermediation*, in the economy. Banks are engaged in borrowing and lending, receiving deposits from the public and offering credit to industry and consumers; also they are increasingly engaged in other financial activities such as trading securities, administrating financial assets and restructuring the financial structure of business firms. Nowadays, banks and insurance companies tend to overlap in their business activities, so banking goes far beyond the classical banking activities of taking deposits and extending credit. In this book, we shall use the terms 'bank' and 'banking' in this broad sense, comprising all relevant forms of financial intermediation (though some of these will be studied more extensively than others).

This is all very well in the sense that it underlines the need for a closer study of financial intermediation, but with the broad view of banking comes some disadvantages as well; in particular, it is far from obvious which kind of economic activities should be accepted as banking and which should not. Or, to put it differently, what are the characteristic features of financial intermediation that makes it a specific field of research?

Even for the more restricted field of classical banking, questions of this type may arise. Indeed, it might be asked why there should be specific institutions (banks) to take care of borrowing and lending. Why is this not left to the (money) market? In a perfectly competitive economy, borrowers would issue debt certificates to be bought by the public at some price, and there would be no obvious need for a bank. We may show this using a simple formal model.

Consider an economy with one consumer, one producer and a bank. There are two periods of time, $t = 0, 1$, and one good which cannot be stored from one period to the next. The consumer has an endowment ω of the good at $t = 0$ and wants to carry out consumption in both periods, choosing a bundle $(x_0, x_1) \in \mathbb{R}_+^2$ so as to maximize utility $u(x_0, x_1)$ under the budget constraint

$$x_0 + b^c + s \leq \omega$$

$$px_1 \leq (1 + r)b^c + (1 + r_D)s + \pi^p + \pi^b.$$

Here b^c is the amount of bonds bought by the consumer in period 0, to be sold again in period 1, and s denotes saving in the form of deposits in the bank. The price of the commodity is normalized to 1 in period 0, and it is p in period 1. Finally, r denotes the bond interest rate; r_D is the interest rate on deposits in the bank; and π^p and π^b are the profits of the firm and the bank, assumed to be owned by the consumer. Because the consumer maximizes utility (assumed to be increasing in both x_0 and x_1), she will use the most advantageous form of financing period 1 consumption so that $s = 0$ if $r_D < r$.

The producer invests z of the commodity in period 0 and obtains output $y = g(z)$ in period 1. The investment is financed by issuing bonds b^p and taking a loan l in the bank at the interest rate r_L so that $z = b^p + l$, and the producer chooses so as to maximize profit

$$\pi^p = pg(b^p + l) - (1 + r)b^p - (1 + r_L)l.$$

Again, we have only the most advantageous way of financing the investment being used. In particular, if $r_L > r$, then $l = 0$.

The bank extends credit to the amount of l, which is funded by deposits s and bond issue b^b, so $l = s + b^b$. Profit is given by

$$\pi^b = (1 + r_L)l - (1 + r)b^b - (1 + r_D)s,$$

and $\pi^b = 0$ unless either $r < r_L$ or $r_L < r_D$ (assuming that the bond market is in balance, $b^c = b^p + b^b$). But in the first case we have seen that $l = 0$, and in the second case we would have $s = 0$. So, if the bank has any business at all, it must charge the same interest rate for lending and borrowing, namely the bond market rate. This means that the bank only mimics the bond market, playing no role of its own, and it is superfluous in the economy considered.

The result, that there is no use for banks, is, of course, not a statement about banks in general, but about our particular model, which clearly is deficient in some respect because financial intermediation has no essential role to play. We must add some features which make banking a meaningful activity.

One might be tempted to point to the absence of uncertainty as the main shortcoming of the model. Adding uncertainty will, however, not immediately solve the problem.

EXAMPLE 1.1 Suppose that the consumer has utility function

$$u(x_0, x_1) = 4 \ln x_0 + 2 \ln x_1,$$

and that the firm transforms input z into output y using a production function

$$y = g(z) = \sqrt{z}.$$

The initial endowment ω consists of 1 unit of the good in period 0.

The unique Pareto optimal allocation is obtained when the consumer's utility is maximized under the constraint that second period consumption, x_1, must be produced from what is left over of the initial endowment, $1 - x_0$, using the production function. Inserting the latter into the utility function and maximizing with regard to (w.r.t.) x_0, we get the first-order condition

$$\frac{4}{x_0} - \frac{1}{1 - x_0} = 0,$$

which is satisfied at $(x_0, x_1) = (0.8, 0.447)$, with 0.2 units of the good used as input in period 0.

The price p of the good in period 1 (as seen in period 0) is found as

$$p = \frac{1}{g'(0.2)} = 2\sqrt{0.2} = 0.894.$$

This corresponds to an interest rate of $r = 0.118$ (since $1 + r = \dfrac{1}{p} = 1.118$). Thus, 1 unit of the good given up in period 0 should be compensated with 1.118 units of the good in period 1.

The model is well known as an illustration of *decentralization using prices*: The consumer sells an endowment to the producer against a promise of delivery of the good in the next period. Such a contract for future delivery can be arranged in several ways; the producer may issue a paper promising to deliver the good in the next period, and if the price of the good is set to 1 in each period, this will give us the loan with an interest rate of 0.118. Alternatively, the consumer may use an intermediary for performing the investment, delivering the good in period 0 to the agent as a saving, with the right to get it back in the next period together with interest. Either way, the basic transaction is the same.

Uncertainty could be handled by insurance markets (markets for contingent commodities, to be delivered only if some uncertain event happens), and the only change in the model would be that the number of commodities becomes larger, which clearly matters little for the main reasoning. So, even if uncertainty is intuitively important for the functioning of financial intermediation, it is not enough. One needs to proceed one step further, adding *asymmetric information* in the sense that the borrowers and lenders have unequal access to relevant information. We shall consider several cases of asymmetric information below.

1.2 Liquidity transformation

One of the first contributions to the new theory of financial intermediation is the *liquidity insurance* model proposed by Diamond and Dybvig [1983]. Here the uncertainty pertains to sudden need for liquidity, and the information asymmetry arises in connection with contracts where an investor wants to withdraw from a project as a result of this need for liquidity.

More specifically, suppose that there is a single investment project available, by which 1 unit of money invested gives a certain payoff of R. However, once the investment is carried out, and until the payoff is received, the money invested is bound and can be taken out only at a cost, described as a liquidation payoff L of the investment with $L < 1 < R$. Because we are interested in situations where investors need money before the investment matures, we shall work with three periods of time, namely $t = 0$ (investment is carried out), $t = 1$ (need for liquidity may or may not arise) and $t = 2$ (payoff is received).

The investor has an initial endowment of 1 unit (of the single good available in the economy), and a consumption plan considered at $t = 0$ is a pair (c_1, c_2), where c_1 is consumption in the case that liquidity is needed at $t = 1$, where the consumer is 'impatient', and c_2 is consumption without such liquidity needs, where the consumer is 'patient'. The consumer is assumed to choose so as to maximize expected utility

$$\mathsf{E}u(c_1, c_2) = \pi u(c_1) + (1 - \pi)u(c_2),$$

where π is the probability of being impatient. Here u is the (von Neumann-Morgenstern (vNM)) utility of consumption, assumed to be the same whether the consumer is patient or not. We assume independent risks in the sense that the individuals will become impatient independent of each other.

The choice of investment, and thereby of consumption in the two alternative states, will depend on the institutions available. We begin with the simplest possible case:

(a) Investment on your own. In this case, also known as *autarchy*, there are no possibilities of carrying out financial transactions with other individuals. The consumer maximizes $\mathsf{E}u$ under the constraints

$$c_1 = 1 - I + LI,$$

$$c_2 = 1 - I + RI,$$

saying that in the case of impatience, the consumer can get only what is not invested together with the invested amount times the liquidation payoff, and in the other case the consumer gets a similar outcome, but this time with the full payoff. Collecting terms, we get that

$$c_1 = 1 - I(1 - L),$$

$$c_2 = 1 + I(R - 1),$$

and it is seen that $c_1 \leq 1$, with equality only for $I = 0$, and similarly that $c_2 \leq R$ with equality only in the case that $I = 1$. In particular, the consumption (c_1, c_2) obtained under autarky is inferior to the bundle $(1, R)$.

(b) Using a money market. Adding a bond market will improve the situation. We assume that the impatient consumer can sell the right to the ultimate payoff in a market by formally writing a bond on the future payoff and selling this bond in the market at the price p (per unit of future payoff). The buyers of the bond are the patient consumers who have no need for the unused part of the investment. The constraints now become

$$c_1 = 1 - I + pRI,$$

$$c_2 = \frac{1-I}{p} + RI = \frac{1}{p}(1 - I + pRI).$$

We now need to determine the bond price which clears the market. For this we first notice that if $p = 1/R$, then $c_1 = 1$ and $c_2 = R$. If $p > 1/R$, then each consumer would prefer to set $I = 1$, because then $c_1 > 1$ and $c_2 = R$, but if all consumers invest everything, then there would be no buyers of the bonds, so the bond market cannot be in equilibrium. Similarly if $p < \frac{1}{R}$; here it will be best to choose $I = 0$ and then buy bonds in the case of impatience, giving $c_1 = 1$ and $c_2 > R$, but again this is not an equilibrium, because there would be no bond issuers. We conclude that $p = \frac{1}{R}$ is the only equilibrium price.

When a bond market is added to the model, the consumers are doing better than under autarchy because now they realize the bundle $(c_1, c_2) = (1, R)$. However, there is still room for some improvement.

EXAMPLE 1.2 Suppose that the utility function u has the form

$$u(z) = \ln(\ln(10x))$$

for $x \geq \frac{1}{10}$ (we are not concerned with values outside the domain of definition), and $\pi = \frac{3}{4}$, giving

$$\mathsf{E}u(c_1, c_2) = \frac{3}{4}\ln(\ln 10c_1) + \frac{1}{4}\ln(\ln 10c_2),$$

and that $R = 1.2$, $L = 0.5$. With no access to money markets and no banks, the consumer faces the constraints

$$c_1 = 1 - 0.5I, \quad c_2 = 1 + 0.2I,$$

and $\mathsf{E}u(1 - 0.5I, 1 + 0.2I)$ takes its maximal value 0.8340 at $I = 0$, so $(c_1, c_2) = (1, 1)$. This result is inferior to what could be obtained using a money market, namely $(c_1, c_2) = (1, 1.2)$, which gives expected utility 0.8530.

EXAMPLE 1.2 CONTINUED
The social optimum must satisfy the equations

$$\frac{1}{c_1 \ln(10c_1)} = 0.2 \frac{1}{c_2 \ln(10c_2)}$$

$$0.75c_1 = 1 - \frac{0.25}{0.2} c_2,$$

with solution $(c_1, c_2) = (1.013, 1.152)$ and expected utility 0.8802.

The consumption in case of impatiency exceeds 1, whereas c_2 is smaller than 1.2, as was to be expected. The utility function is such that

$$zu'(z) = z \frac{1}{\ln(10z)} \frac{1}{z} = \frac{1}{\ln(10z)}$$

is indeed decreasing in z so that the consumer has considerable risk aversion.

(c) Sustaining a social optimum. In order to see this, we maximize expected utility (which is the same for all) $\mathsf{E}u(c_1, c_2)$ under the constraints

$$\pi c_1 = 1 - I,$$
$$(1 - \pi)c_2 = RI.$$

The constraints can be interpreted as expressing the way that society must meet the needs of the impatient (which by the law of large numbers constitutes a fraction π of all consumers) and the impatient (which make up the remaining fraction $(1 - \pi)$ of all).

Assuming differentiability of u, we can find the first-order conditions for a maximum by inserting the expressions for c_1 and c_2 in the utility function to obtain

$$\mathsf{E}u(c_1, c_2) = \pi u\left(\frac{1 - I}{\pi}\right) + (1 - \pi)u\left(\frac{RI}{1 - \pi}\right),$$

which after taking derivatives w.r.t. I yields the condition

$$u'\left(c_1^0\right) = Ru'\left(c_2^0\right),$$

to be satisfied by the social optimum (c_1^0, c_2^0).

Comparing now with the solution $(c_1, c_2) = (1, R)$ obtained using a bond market, we see that the latter is optimal only if

$$u'(1) = Ru'(R);$$

something which will happen only as an exception, because u is an arbitrarily given function and R an arbitrary parameter. In other words, the market solution will typically *not* be Pareto optimal. We can also see what should be done in order to improve the market solution, at least in the case where the utility function u satisfies the condition that $z \mapsto zu'(z)$ is decreasing, because in that case we get from $R > 1$ and $c_2^0 \leq R$ that

$$Ru'(R) < 1 \cdot u'(1) = u'(1),$$

and consequently c_1^0 must be greater than 1 in the optimum.

(d) The deposit contract. At this point, we introduce a bank which can sustain the social optimum by offering a contingent deposit contract to the public: Every consumer deposits 1 unit in the bank, and the bank delivers c_1^0 at time $t = 1$ if the customer is impatient and c_2^0 at time $t = 2$ otherwise. Clearly, this contract is feasible, in the sense that the bank has an investment program which secures that it has enough liquidity to pay all the impatient customers and yields a payoff which exactly corresponds to what the patient customers expect to get.

We have thus presented a first argument for the presence of banks in the economy – they provide services which could not be obtained otherwise; in particular, those the money market could not allocate in a satisfactory way.

Upon a closer look, the arrangement obtained is not without flaws. Intuitively, all is well as long as only the genuinely impatient customers turn up and want their money at $t = 1$. But if some of the patient customers also present themselves at $t = 1$, the bank will run out of liquidity, and a bank run has happened. One might then ask why the patient customers should want their money at $t = 1$, and the model as stated here gives no answer to this. We shall return to the matter later, when we discuss bank runs and banking crises (in Chapter 14); for the moment it suffices to say that such behaviour may be rational if we add expectations to the model: If the patient customers expect the bank to be insolvent at $t = 2$, they will prefer to obtain as much cash as they can at $t = 1$ – which means that the bank cannot pay at $t = 1$ and defaults. Thus, the solution that we have come up with is somewhat fragile and depends on the right expectations for its feasibility.

1.3 Monitoring borrowers

Although the liquidity insurance argument emphasized the deposit side of banking business, there are other justifications for banks or financial intermediaries which have their origin in the other aspect of classical banking, lending. The main element of uncertainty in a credit contract comes from the possibility that the borrower does not or cannot fulfil her obligations. This uncertainty is also a source of information asymmetry because in most cases the borrower has more detailed knowledge of her ability to pay than has the lender, even if more information can be obtained by monitoring the borrower. We shall return to this possibility of monitoring borrowers on many occasions.

1.3.1 Cost-saving monitoring of borrowers

Monitoring tends to be incomplete and – what is more important at present – costly. Consider an example where m investors each place 1 unit of money in each of n firms. The outcome of these investments is subject to uncertainty, and we formalize this by letting the outcome be a random variable $\tilde{y}$ which is identically and independently distributed among firms. We assume expected outcome $\bar{y} = E\tilde{y}$ is big enough to cover the monitoring cost K and still make investment in firms more attractive than the money market,

$$\bar{y} - K > 1 + r,$$

where r is the money market interest rate.

If investors are risk averse, they will prefer to spread their investment among firms, something which will expand the need for monitoring, but even with risk-neutral investors, the cost of monitoring can be substantial, as shown in Fig. 1.1. If each investor incurs a cost K, the total monitoring cost with n firms and m investors in each firm will be nmK. The goal of our analysis is to propose a scheme for reducing this monitoring cost.

Introducing a single monitoring agent instead of m investors acting independently reduces the cost of monitoring investment from mnK to nK, and this can be a quite considerable cost reduction when m is large. The diagrams in Fig.1.1(a) and (b) support this intuition, but in particular Fig.1.1(b) shows that our argumentation is yet incomplete: It is correct that monitoring firms has become much simpler, but what about monitoring the new centralized monitoring agent? Here we run into incentive problems – if the agent is paid a fee, then we cannot be sure that the necessary monitoring effort will be forthcoming, and it may not be easy to check that the effort is satisfactory.

We therefore propose to add an incentive scheme: The new monitoring agent runs an independent business, taking the investments as deposits and offering a fixed deposit

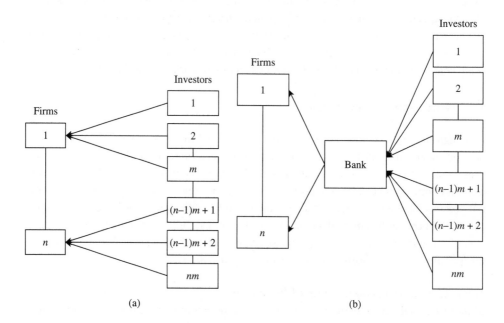

(a)   (b)

Figure 1.1 Individual versus delegated monitoring of investment. In (a), all m investors of each firm must monitor the firm receiving their investments, whereas in (b), only the agent monitors the firms.

interest rate, to be paid from the outcome of the investments. Thus, we have transformed the monitoring agent into a bank. Because the outcome is random and the bank has promised the depositors a fixed interest rate, it may go bankrupt, which will happen if

$$\sum_{j=1}^{n} \tilde{y}_j - nK < (1 + r_D)n$$

(the bank's total receipts from investments minus its monitoring cost is insufficient for the fulfillment of its obligations towards depositors), and we assume that in this event the depositors get what is left but incur an auditing cost of γ. Expected bankruptcy cost with n firms is therefore

$$C_n = \gamma P \left\{ \sum_{j=1}^{n} \tilde{y}_j - nK < (1 + r_D)n \right\}, \tag{1}$$

which does not depend on m, the number of investors (here and in the sequel, we use the notation $P\{A\}$ for the probability of the event A). If C_n is small enough, then it seems plausible that there will be a cost saving for society. We will check that this is indeed so.

EXAMPLE 1.3 Assume that investment projects are such that for each unit invested, either a payoff of 3 is obtained, which happens with probability 1/2, or the investment is lost. All investors have 1 unit for investment, and the monitoring cost is 0.3 per firm. Investors have logarithmic utility and a wealth of 5 units. The expected utility of the investor is then

$$\frac{1}{2} \ln(5 - 1 - 0.3) + \frac{1}{2} \ln(5 + 2 - 0, 3) = 1.6052$$

if investing and $\ln(5) = 1.6094$ if nothing is invested.

If two investors pool their investments and choose two different projects, then the monitoring cost becomes 0.6, but both investments fail only with probability 0.25. With probability 0.5, the pooled investment gives a gain to each of $(3 - 0.6)/2 = 1.2$, so the expected utility of this arrangement is

$$\frac{1}{4} \ln(5 - 1 - 0.3) + \frac{1}{2} \ln(5 + 0.5 - 0.3) + \frac{1}{4} \ln(5 + 2 - 0, 3) = 1.6269.$$

If the two investors cannot agree to perform in this cooperative way, there is room for a financial intermediary. Suppose that a bank proposes to perform investments using the funds of the individuals. If it promises to pay a deposit interest rate of 165%, then it will retain the remaining 5% in the case of success of both investments. In the remaining cases, the bank will default on its obligations, and the depositors will take over the estate after paying an additional 0.05. Expected utility for the depositors will be

$$\frac{1}{4} \ln(5 - 1 - 0.3 - 0.05) + \frac{1}{2} \ln(5 + 0.5 - 0.3 - 0.05) + \frac{1}{4} \ln(5 - 1 + 2.65) = 1.6168,$$

which is again better than individual investment.

First of all, we need to know the size of r_D, the deposit rate offered to investors. Assuming that there is a money market with interest rate r, the expected return on deposits must equal this interest rate,

$$\mathsf{E}\left[\min\left\{\sum_{j=1}^{n}\frac{\tilde{y}_j}{n} - K, 1 + r_D\right\}\right] = 1 + r. \tag{2}$$

We now let n become large. By the law of large numbers, the average outcome $\sum_{j=1}^{n}\frac{\tilde{y}_j}{n}$ will converge (almost surely) to the mean value $\bar{y}$, and because $\bar{y} > 1 + r + K$ by our assumption, $1 + r_D$ converges to $1 + r$ for n increasing. Moving to (1), we get that

$$\frac{C_n}{n} = \gamma\,\mathsf{P}\left\{\frac{\sum_{j=1}^{n}\tilde{y}_j}{n} - K < 1 + r_D\right\}$$

goes to 0 when n becomes large. But this means that the cost to society of the banking solution (per unit invested) satisfies

$$K + \frac{C_n}{n} < mK$$

for large n when $m > 1$, or, multiplying on both sides by n,

$$nK + C_n < mnK,$$

which shows that the banking solution is indeed cost saving.

1.3.2 Moral hazard and monitoring

The advantages of monitoring borrowers may take other forms than that considered above. In the following case, the possibility of monitoring borrowers, something which presumably requires some professional skill, may change a situation where no investment funds are forthcoming to one where savings may indeed be channelled into productive use.

The model is a simple case of *moral hazard*, and it will be used repeatedly in the sequel. We assume that there are two investment projects available, namely I_B and I_G; investment is carried out for borrowed money, and only the investors can observe whether the funds are used for I_B or for I_G.

The two feasible investment projects will either succeed or fail (and this event will be observable). In the case of success, investment project I_B yields outcome B, and its probability of success is π_B; similarly, for I_G we have an outcome G occurring with probability π_G. In the case of failure, outcome is 0 in both projects. We assume that $B > G$ but $\pi_G > \pi_B$ and

$$\pi_B B < 1 < \pi_G G,$$

so the expected outcome with I_B is worse than just keeping the funds (we assume that the discount factor is 1 for simplicity), whereas I_G is advantageous on average.

Assume that the money market interest rate is such that the repayment rate is R. Then investors will choose I_G if

$$\pi_G(G - R) \geq \pi_B(B - R)$$

or

$$R \leq R^* = \frac{\pi_G G - \pi_B B}{\pi_G - \pi_B}.$$

If this is not the case, the investors will be better off choosing I_B. But if investors choose I_B, then the savers will lose money on average; consequently they will prefer to keep the funds uninvested. The result is that the market breaks down.

We can find conditions for this to happen: Savers will demand that lending money is at least as good as storing it, and because this will never happen if I_B is chosen, we must have $\pi_G R \geq 1$, and since $R \leq R^*$ when the market works, we have

$$\pi_G R^* \geq 1,$$

or alternatively,

$$\pi_G G - \pi_B B \geq 1 - \frac{\pi_B}{\pi_G},$$

showing that the moral hazard must not be too important. If this condition is not satisfied, the market cannot work.

Assume now that a bank can monitor investors, thereby securing that the funds are used for project I_G. Monitoring has a cost C, which must be covered before the depositors can be paid off, so the funding condition for the bank is

$$\pi_G R \geq 1 + C. \tag{3}$$

Assuming zero profit in banks (which may be caused by competition among banks), (3) will be satisfied with =, so R is determined by

$$R = \frac{1 + C}{\pi_G}.$$

There is still a bound on R, namely $R \leq G$, which is the condition for any project (and in that case a good one because choice is monitored) to be undertaken, which with the expression for R may be rewritten as

$$\pi_G \geq \frac{1 + C}{G}.$$

If this inequality is satisfied, then the bank can be funded, and investment can be carried through, even though we may have that $\pi_G < 1/R^*$, so investment could not be financed through the money market. We thus have another case where financial intermediaries can achieve something which could not be obtained through ordinary markets.

1.4 Banks as coalitions of borrowers

Although our attention in the preceding sections has been on servicing savers-investors, either by liquidity insurance or by monitoring the borrowers, we shall now take a different point of view, looking at the specific problems of the borrowers. Assume that the potential borrowers are all endowed with an investment project, the outcome $\tilde{y}(\theta)$ of which is normally distributed with mean θ and variance σ^2. Although the variance is the same for all investors, they may have different means, and moreover, this mean is individual information and not observable to others.

Investor-borrowers are assumed to be risk averse, so they would prefer to sell their projects and obtain a fixed amount of money instead of taking on a risky project. We assume that they assess their own project in such a way that their expected utility is

$$\mathsf{E}u(W + \tilde{y}(\theta)) = u\left(W + \theta - \frac{1}{2}\rho\sigma^2\right).$$

Here W is the initial wealth of the investor, and the quantity $\theta - \frac{1}{2}\rho\sigma^2$ is the *certainty equivalent* of the risky project $\tilde{y}(\theta)$, that is its the money value to the investor; ρ is a constant. For the following, we need only that the expected utility has this expression. It is shown in Box 1.4 (p. 14) that this holds for a suitable specification of the utility function. Because we are dealing with borrower-lender relationships rather than with purchase or sale of investment projects, we interpret the sale of the project as a transfer of the investment project to a lender who will assume all the risk; we shall have a closer look at risk sharing between borrower and lender in a later chapter.

The problem with selling the project is that the market has no information about project quality, that is, θ, so there is a common price P for all projects. Clearly, the investor will sell only if the price is at least as good as the certainty equivalent, or equivalently, if

$$\theta \leq P + \frac{1}{2}\rho\sigma^2. \tag{4}$$

We thus have a case of *adverse selection*: The good projects are not offered in the market because the price obtained is too low.

Given that only the lower end of the projects are in the market, this must also be reflected in the equilibrium price. Indeed, we must have

$$P = \mathsf{E}[\theta \mid \theta \leq \theta^*],$$

where θ^* is given by the right-hand side of (4).

For simplicity, we assume from now that there are only two types of project, with $\theta_1 < \theta_2$, occuring with probability π_1 and $\pi_2 = 1 - \pi_1$. If both types of project are set for sale, then $P = \pi_1 \theta_1 + (1 - \pi_1) \theta_2$, and by (4) we must have that

$$\pi_1 \theta_1 + (1 - \pi_1) \theta_2 + \frac{1}{2} \rho \sigma^2 \geq \theta_2,$$

from which we get that

$$\pi_1 (\theta_2 - \theta_1) \leq \frac{1}{2} \rho \sigma^2.$$

Here the right-hand side is the risk premium, and the left-hand side is the expected gain to the low-quality types, expressing the size of adverse selection, which must not be too big.

If the adverse selection is sufficiently important, the good projects are held back from the market. Consequently, the price in the market equals the value of the bad project, $P = \theta_1$, and the investors with good projects will have to develop them by themselves, notwithstanding their risk aversion.

In order to improve their situation, the owners of good projects may want to signal quality to the market. This must be done so as to prevent owners of bad projects from sending similar signals. A possible way of doing this is to sell only *part* of the project. The signal of quality is then the participation of the project owner. If the fraction α is retained, then the signal is trustworthy when owners of bad projects would lose money by pretending to sell a good project (and participating), that is, when

$$u(W + \theta_1) \geq u \left(W + (1 - \alpha) \theta_2 + \alpha \theta_1 - \frac{1}{2} \rho \alpha^2 \sigma^2 \right)$$

(the risk premium is computed on the fraction α of the project). Since utility is monotonically increasing, this is equivalent to

$$\theta_1 \geq (1 - \alpha) \theta_2 + \alpha \theta_1 - \frac{1}{2} \rho \alpha^2 \sigma^2$$

or

$$\frac{\alpha^2}{1 - \alpha} \geq \frac{2 (\theta_2 - \theta_1)}{\rho \sigma^2}. \tag{5}$$

Because the left-hand side is an increasing function of α, there is a smallest value for which this inequality is satisfied, actually with an equality sign, and this value $\hat{\alpha}$ is the one preferred by the seller.

Box 1.4

In the model, we have used an explicit expression for expected utility of a random variable $\tilde{y}$ which is normally distributed with mean θ and variance σ^2. We show here that this expression arises when the vNM utility function is given by

$$u(w) = -e^{-\rho w},$$

so

$$\mathsf{E}[-e^{-\rho y}] = -e^{-\rho\left(\theta - \frac{1}{2}\rho\sigma^2\right)}.$$

Because $\tilde{y}$ is normally distributed, we can find the expectation of $e^{-\rho\tilde{y}}$ using the standard formula for expectation,

$$\mathsf{E}[-e^{-\rho y}] = \int_{-\infty}^{+\infty} -e^{-\rho y}\left[\frac{1}{\sqrt{2\pi}\sigma}\exp\left(-\frac{(y-\theta)^2}{2\sigma^2}\right)\right]dy,$$

where the quantity inside the brackets is the density function of the normal distribution with mean θ and variance σ^2.

We note that

$$\left(y - \left(\theta - \rho\sigma^2\right)\right)^2 = y^2 + \left(\theta - \rho\sigma^2\right)^2 - 2y\left(\theta - \rho\sigma^2\right)$$

$$= y^2 + \theta^2 + \rho^2\sigma^4 - 2\theta\rho\sigma^2 - 2y\theta + 2y\rho\sigma^2,$$

so

$$-\frac{\left(y - \left(\theta - \rho\sigma^2\right)\right)^2}{2\sigma^2} = -\frac{y^2 + \theta^2 - 2y\theta}{2\sigma^2} - \frac{2y\rho\sigma^2}{2\sigma^2} + \frac{2\theta\rho\sigma^2 - \rho^2\sigma^4}{2\sigma^2}.$$

The first two terms on the right-hand side can be found as exponents in the integral above, whereas the last is missing. Therefore, we insert the exponential of this term,

$$\exp\left(-\frac{2\theta\rho\sigma^2 - \rho^2\sigma^4}{2\sigma^2}\right),$$

together with its inverse, into the integral, which of course is not changed by this, and after reduction the integral becomes

$$\mathsf{E}[-e^{-\rho y}] = -\int_{-\infty}^{+\infty}\left[\exp\left(-\frac{2\theta\rho\sigma^2 - \rho^2\sigma^4}{2\sigma^2}\right)\right]\left(\frac{1}{\sqrt{2\pi}\sigma}\exp\left(-\frac{(y-(\theta-\rho\sigma^2))^2}{2\sigma^2}\right)\right)dy$$

$$= -\left[\exp\left(-\frac{2\theta\rho\sigma^2 - \rho^2\sigma^4}{2\sigma^2}\right)\right]\int_{-\infty}^{+\infty}\frac{1}{\sqrt{2\pi}\sigma}\exp\left(-\frac{(y-(\theta-\rho\sigma^2))^2}{2\sigma^2}\right)dy$$

$$= -\exp\left(-\frac{2\theta\rho\sigma^2 - \rho^2\sigma^4}{2\sigma^2}\right) = -e^{-\rho\left(\theta - \frac{1}{2}\rho\sigma^2\right)},$$

where we have used that integrating the density of the normal distribution gives 1.

Box 1.5

Building societies and mortgage credit. Credit institutions which are associations of borrowers have a long history, and from the very beginning their basic principle has been the reduction of risk obtained when several borrowers band together and assume joint liability. The obvious purpose of the loan transactions was financing investment in private housebuilding, so the associations became known as *building societies*.

The first building societies, founded in the late eighteenth century in England, were organized by a number of citizens paying a subscription. The money obtained in this way could be used for housebuilding, after which the society could obtain loans using the already constructed houses as collateral. The society was dissolved when all members had obtained a house (and the loans were paid back). Permanent building societies arose in around 1830.

Other countries had a similar development of mortgage credit institutions. In Denmark, the first borrower-owned credit institutions were organized around 1850, but they had a predecessor in the form of a mortgage credit institution founded in 1797 following one of the big fires in Copenhagen. Credit was based on joint liability even though the bank was owned by lenders rather than borrowers; the interest in mortgage operations came from an interest rate ceiling of 4% p.a., which was quite insufficient to compensate for credit risk of other commercial ventures, so the financial intermediaries were interested in engagements with a very small level of risk.

As was the case with many other types of organizations, the building societies were transformed into ordinary financial institutions in the course of the financial liberalizations of the 1990s.

The market now functions with two prices, namely θ_1 for bad projects and θ_2 for good projects, which are sold only with owner participation $\hat{\alpha}$. The loss (or financing cost) to the project owner, as compared with an ideal (and indeed unrealizable) situation, where the project could be sold for full value θ_2, is the risk premium

$$C_f = \frac{1}{2}\rho\hat{\alpha}^2\sigma^2. \tag{6}$$

This loss depends (among other things) on σ^2, the variance of the underlying normal distribution.

It is this dependence on the variance that makes it possible to achieve cost savings by creating a bank. Indeed, if n owners of good projects get together and create an investment pool, then the variance of the pooled project with outcome $\frac{1}{n}\sum_{j=1}^{n}\tilde{y}_j(\theta)$ is $\frac{\sigma^2}{n}$. We show that this reduction of variance leads to a reduction of the financing cost, something which is not quite evident from (6) because also $\hat{\alpha}$ depends on σ^2. We have, however, from (5) that

$$C_f = \frac{1}{2}\rho\hat{\alpha}^2\sigma^2 = (\theta_2 - \theta_1)(1 - \hat{\alpha}), \tag{7}$$

and, again from (5), that $\hat{\alpha}$ is a decreasing function of σ^2. It now follows from (7) that C_f decreases with σ^2.

In the present model, the bank has arisen as a coalition of borrowers, who can reduce their financing cost by getting together. Actually, the model is not a merely formal construct but illustrates the background of an important class of financial intermediaries, namely mortgage credit institutions, which historically arose as coalitions of borrowers.

1.5 Can financial intermediation induce cycles?

In the previous sections, we have considered several cases where financial intermediation played a positive role because it permitted an allocation which was better than what could have been achieved without it. To provide some contrast, we consider here a case with another message, namely that financial intermediation may give rise to phenomena which are unwanted and which would not have occurred otherwise.

The model, taken from Banerji et al. [2004], is one of overlapping generations. In each time period $t = 1, 2, \ldots$, there is an old generation as well as a young generation living also in the next period; generations have a constant large number of members (we shall need the law of large numbers at a later stage); we choose units such that this number is 1. All members of generations born at $t \geq 1$ have the same utility function

$$U(c^y, c^o) = u(c^y) + v(c^o),$$

specifying the utility of consumption when young (c^y) and when old (c^o). Consumers are risk averse in the sense that v is concave.

The initial old generation has a capital stock K_1, the members of the generations born at $t \geq 1$ have 1 unit of labour when young, and they supply this unit at the price w_t prevailing in the labour market.

The technology available is such that if investment is made at some date t, then output is obtained (if at all) only at date $t + 1$. Let K_{t+1} be the investment made at date t (the reason for our notation will become clearer as we proceed). Now uncertainty intervenes because this investment survives to the next date $t + 1$ only with a probability $p(K_{t+1})$. Given that it survives, it may be used together with labour to produce output. We assume constant return to scale in capital goods *and* labour, and let $f(x)$ be the output obtained when inserting 1 unit of labour and x units of goods.

Given that the investment survives, the entrepreneur will hire labour so as to maximize profit. With competitive markets the remuneration of factors exhausts the production result, so

$$f(x_{t+1}) - f'_{t+1} x_{t+1} = w_{t+1}, \tag{8}$$

where

$$x_{t+1} = p(K_{t+1}) K_{t+1}. \tag{9}$$

The equation (8) determines the wage level at time $t + 1$ once we know the investment K_{t+1} at time t; we write this as

$$w_{t+1} = \psi(K_{t+1}). \tag{10}$$

With the set-up as described, there is room for financial intermediaries who can provide risk and consumption smoothing, taking deposits from young consumers and lending to entrepreneurs. Assuming that each financial intermediator has many borrowers, the law of large numbers is at work, and the financial intermediator may offer a riskless return to depositors. Now the young consumer at time t has income w_t and may borrow B_t from the financial intermediator, and this amount is used for consumption when young c_t^y, investment K_{t+1}, and deposits with the financial intermediator D_t, under the budget constraint

$$c_t^y = w_t + B_t - K_{t+1} - D_t.$$

For consumption in the next period, there are two possibilities: If the investment succeeds (the good state), the consumer-entrepreneur gets not only the sure return on deposits but also the output of production, but then the loan has to be repaid at a rate R_{t+1}, giving a budget constraint

$$c_{t+1}^{o,g} = r_{t+1}D_t + f'(x_{t+1})K_{t+1} - R_{t+1}B_t,$$

whereas in the case of failure (the bad state), the budget constraint is

$$c_{t+1}^{o,b} = r_{t+1}D_t.$$

We assume that the financial intermediaries are created by the young consumers and act on their behalf, so the contract specifies D_t, K_{t+1}, B_t and R_{t+1} so as to maximize entrepreneur expected utility

$$u\left(c_t^y\right) + (1 - p(K_{t+1}))v\left(c_{t+1}^{o,b}\right) + p(K_{t+1})v\left(c_{t+1}^{o,g}\right) = u(w_t + B_t - K_{t+1} - D_t)$$

$$+ (1 - p(K_{t+1}))v(r_{t+1}D_t) + p(K_{t+1})v(r_{t+1}D_t + f'(x_{t+1})K_{t+1} - R_{t+1}B_t) \tag{11}$$

subject to the financial intermediators break-even constraint

$$p(K_{t+1})R_{t+1} = r_{t+1}. \tag{12}$$

Without formally deriving first-order conditions for the maximum of (11) under the constraint (12), we can see that in the optimum, the deposit rate must equal the marginal return of capital, taking into consideration that the probability of survival of investment depends on the size of investments,

$$r_{t+1} = r(K_{t+1}) = p(K_{t+1}) f'(x_{t+1}) [1 + \eta(K_{t+1})], \tag{13}$$

where $\eta(K) = Kp'(K)/p(K)$ is the elasticity of success w.r.t. investment. The equation (13) defines r_{t+1} as a function $r(K_{t+1})$ of K_{t+1}. Also, we must have that the total repayment of debt, which is B_tR_{t+1}, must be equal to the income from investment, $f'(x_{t+1})K_{t+1}$, or

$$B_t = \frac{f'(x_{t+1})K_{t+1}}{R_{t+1}}, \tag{14}$$

so ratio of loan to investment equals ratio of marginal product of capital to loan rate.

Now we need only one more condition to close the model, namely the financial market equilibrium condition that the deposits D_t in the optimal contract should equal the amount B_t borrowed by entrepreneurs,

$$D_t = D(w_t, r_{t+1}, K_{t+1}) = B_t. \tag{15}$$

If we insert (10) and (13) on the left-hand side and (14) on the right-hand side, and in addition use (9), then (15) can be written as

$$D(\psi(K_t), r(K_{t+1}), K_{t+1}) = B(K_{t+1}). \tag{16}$$

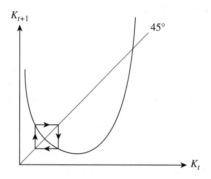

Figure 1.2 Two-period cyclical movements in an overlapping generations model with financial intermediation. The figure shows a possible form of the graph of Φ which connects equilibrium investments in each period.

Now, (16) determines K_{t+1} implicitly as a function of K_t

$$K_{t+1} = \Phi(K_t), \ t = 1, \ldots$$

Given K_1, we then obtain a sequence $(K_t)_{t=1}^{\infty}$ describing the way in which the economy evolves over time.

What is of interest in this context is whether the equilibrium sequence $(K_t)_{t=1}^{\infty}$ is stationary and displays cyclical movements; something which will depend on the initial capital endowment. If the utility functions u and v, the production function f, as well as the failure function p, are specified, one may plot the function Φ which gives K_{t+1} as a function of K_t (the forward dynamics). For suitable specification of u, c, $f(\cdot)$ and $p(\cdot)$, one may get a functional relationship as shown in Fig. 1.2. Here there are two stationary solutions (the intersections with the 45° line), but there is also a two-period cycle. With other specifications one may get cycles of higher periodicity.

Why does this happen? If there had been no financial intermediaries, then each entrepreneur would have had to take matters into her own hands, choosing K_{t+1} so as to maximize expected utility

$$u\left(c_t^Y\right) + p\left(K_{t+1}\right) v\left(c_{t+1}^{o,g}\right) + [1 - p(K_{t+1})] v\left(c_{t+1}^{o,b}\right)$$

under the constraints

$$c_t^y = w_t - K_{t+1}, \; c_{t+1}^{o,g} = \rho_{t+1} K_{t+1}, \; c_{t+1}^{o,b} = 0,$$

where ρ_{t+1} is the return on investment (disregarding possibility of failure), which is taken as given by the entrepreneur. In equilibrium, we must have $\rho_{t+1} = f'(x_{t+1})$ and $w_t = w(x_t)$, with $x_t = p(K_t)K_t$. With simple specifications of the technology, this gives rise to a unique equilibrium path. Thus, without financial intermediation, there are no cycles.

The point is that financial intermediation opens up the possibility of borrowing more or less than what is invested so that the entrepreneur may transfer value to the second life year also in the case that the investment fails. This insurance aspect of the financial intermediation may improve expected utility, at least for some generations, but because the direct link between savings and investment has been relaxed, some other features such as cycles come in as a by-product.

1.6 Exercises

1. In the general equilibrium model of Section 1.1, suppose that issuing debt in the money market is costly, so the debtor incurs a cost cd when issuing debt d. Explain how this provides the possibility for financial intermediation.

2. Consider an economy with many investors, each having two investment options, namely a *good* project with payoff G obtained with probability π_G (otherwise payoff is 0) and a *bad* project with payoff B obtained with probability π_B. As in Section 1.3.2, we assume that $B > G$ but $\pi_G G > \pi_B B$. For all the projects, success or failure are independent events, and at the time of contracting loans, the type of project cannot be observed.

We now introduce *joint responsibility* in the model: Investors get together in groups of size k, and the repayment of the loan is made for the group as a whole. How does this change the results of investor choices?

3. Consider the following simple dynamical extension of the Diamond-Dybvig model: In each period $t = 1, 2, 3, \ldots$, the newborn young consumers have a wealth of 1 which can be invested or stored. If invested at date t, it will yield R units a date $t + 2$. However, the consumer may be impatient with probability π, in which case she wants to consume at $t + 1$; otherwise, she consumes at $t + 2$.

Formulate the model and check that the banking solution to the investment problem constitutes a steady-state optimum in the model.

Suppose that at some date t, the fraction of (genuinely) impatient consumers is greater than π. To meet the liquidity demand, the bank can use its liquid reserves, but it may also use the deposits of the generation born at $t + 1$. Check whether this option is actually feasible in the sense of not giving rise to a default at a later date, even when the fraction of impatient consumers has returned to its normal state, and if so, how much can the fraction of impatient consumers exceed π?

4. In the Diamond-Dybvig model, suppose that at date $t = 1$ there will be an additional investment project available, with a stochastic repayment rate $\tilde{\rho}$ such that

$$
\tilde{\rho} = \begin{cases} \bar{\rho} > R & \text{with probability } \dfrac{1}{2}, \\[2mm] 0 & \text{with probability } \dfrac{1}{2}. \end{cases}
$$

Is financial intermediation feasible in this case, and how should the contracts be formulated?

5. A new branch of industry based on modern technology is characterized by the existence of both a traditional way of production and a more risky one. The financial institutions providing credit to the industry cannot observe the investor's choice of technique; they can observe only the success or failure of the investment project.

The firms in the industry complain that they cannot obtain all the credit that they want, even though they are willing to pay an interest rate much higher than what is demanded by the banks. It is known from comparison with other fields of industry that higher interest rates will result in more credit. Give an explanation of this phenomenon.

6. In the moral hazard model of Section 1.3.2, suppose that the banks change to contracts that contain an *upside* in the sense that the borrower pays a share $0 < q < 1$ of the investment payoff rather than a fixed repayment.

How does this change affect the choices of investors and the workability of the loan market?

7. A bank has chosen as its specific line of business to obtain deposits from persons who have received large lump-sum payments from their pensions. These customers usually cannot find an immediate use for such sums and spend some time finding their favourite villa in Provence or something similar. In the meantime the bank can get a payoff from investing the money in modern art. If the deposits are required back before the artists, in the works of whom the bank has invested, have become famous, the bank will have a loss, but otherwise the bank can obtain a considerable interest payment for the customers waiting long enough.

Describe the efficient contract between bank and depositor in this situation. Explain why there is an inherent instability in this contract. Suggest what can be done to obtain efficient contracts if there are many banks of the type described.

1.7 Comments

The material in this chapter constitutes the standard basis of the contemporary theory of financial intermediation, such as e.g. Freixas and Rochet [2008]. For another exposition of what the theory of banking is about, see Bhattacharya and Thakor [1993].

The liquidity insurance model in Section 1.2 was introduced in Diamond and Dybvig [1983]. The delegated monitoring model of Section 1.2.1 is the work of Diamond [1984], and the simple moral hazard model in Section 1.2.2 is taken from Freixas and Rochet [2008]. The model in Section 1.4, with banks as coalitions of borrowers, was introduced by Leland and Pyle [1977].

Explaining business cycles has been a concern of economists since the nineteenth century, where economic downturns occurred almost regularly every eighth year, usually accompanied by spectacular bank defaults. Models giving rise to cyclical ups and downs can be obtained in many different ways, but there are few models where financial intermediation plays a crucial role, as is the case in the model of Section 1.5. We shall see another such model at a later stage.

Chapter 2

The Business Lines of a Bank

2.1 The many aspects of financial intermediation

In the previous chapter, we considered the theoretical reasons for the presence of financial intermediaries (FIs) in an economy, and our main finding was that informational incompleteness in some form would make a serious case for financial intermediation. Also, the situations considered called for FIs of different types, so it should come as no surprise that financial intermediation has many faces. As often happens, reality far surpasses theory, as can be seen by the following.

2.1.1 Types of financial intermediaries

There are many different ways of classifying financial intermediation, which can take different forms both between and inside each independent financial firm. One classical method of classification pertains to *types of services performed*, which at the root can be split into two different categories, *brokerage* and *quantitative asset transformation*, as shown in Table 2.1.

However, other ways of classifying FIs may be more useful, depending on the context. It matters whether the bank takes deposits from the public or not, because the latter type of bank, depositary FIs, are subject to special concern by keeping the savings of ordinary citizens. In any case, most financial intermediaries have been broadening their fields of business in recent decades, so the same firm may do traditional banking but also engage in insurance and brokerage. Listing different financial intermediaries therefore tends to be a backward-looking activity, and it is useful mainly in opening up discussion of the different lines of business which may be represented in any particular bank.

Commercial banks. These are the banks that receive deposits from savers and offer loans to business, and indeed the type of banks that most if not all of the subsequent chapters are dealing with. The reason that they figure as *commercial* banks is that they were formerly to be distinguished from *investment* banks (see below), at least in the United States, where the two types of banks were not allowed to be connected through ownership.

Thrifts and credit unions. These are different versions of savings banks and other financial institutions, mainly directed towards investment in mortgage loans. Historically they were subject to strict regulation as guarding the savings of the less wealthy, but regulations have gradually been weakened so as to completely abolish the distinction between savings banks and other commercial banks.

Savings banks are cooperatively owned, as are credit unions, which originated as coalitions of borrowers selling bonds against mortgages. Also, mortgage loans have largely been transferred to the ordinary banks in the course of the last two decades.

Table 2.1 Services Performed by Financial Intermediaries

Brokerage	**Qualitative Asset Transformation**
Transactions (buying/selling securities, safekeeping, etc.)	Monitoring (following a borrower's compliance with loan covenants)
Financial advice (portfolio management etc.)	Management expertise (venture capitalist running a firm)
Certification (bond ratings)	Guaranteeing (insurance company providing insurance)
Origination (initiating loan to borrower)	Liquidity creation/claims transformation (bank making illiquid loans and transforming them to liquid deposits)
Issuance (taking security offer to the market)	
Funding (making a loan)	

Venture capitalists are investment companies offering capital to firms under development and taking an active role in the management of the borrowing firm. The venture capitalist not only provides funds but may also deliver expertise in conducting the business. This participation not only gives the lender a better insight into what happens to the loan but may create additional value. On the other side, the venture capitalist is running a much higher risk than would have been the case with an ordinary bank loan, because typically more capital is advanced, and the creditworthiness of the entrepreneur is such that ordinary bank financing is not available.

Finance companies have a background in non-financial enterprises creating a subsidiary to facilitate the sale of their products to consumers; prominent examples are General Electric Capital and General Motors Acceptance Corporation. Finance companies usually fund themselves by issuing commercial paper, and therefore they are not a matter of public concern to the same degree as commercial banks funded by deposits.

Since the finance companies are formally independent but nevertheless connected to and backed by a large non-financial enterprise, their possibility of attracting funds from what would otherwise have been a rather fragile source of finance (short-term commercial paper) has allowed them to develop into full-profile banks.

Insurance companies are in many aspects very close to ordinary banks, and indeed one of the basic functions of a bank is liquidity insurance, as we saw in the previous chapter. It is not surprising therefore that on the one hand many financial enterprises offer both standard banking services and insurance, and on the other hand that the regulation of insurance companies bears much resemblance to that of banks, with specified rules for accumulation of reserves against losses that can occur as the consequence of the activities.

Also, much of what will be said about banking in the following chapters is relevant for insurance as well, and in some cases it even originates in considerations of insurance contracts. However, insurance contains other aspects which are well outside our scope.

Pension funds may be considered as specialized insurance companies, but usually they have a narrower business purpose and are government subsidized and regulated, in particular pension funds have rather strict limitations in their choices of financial assets.

Mutual funds have had a considerable increase in market share for financial intermediaries, in particular in the United States. A mutual fund is a financial firm whose assets are securities and who are financed by shares, which may be traded separately and consequently can be valued differently from the shares in which the fund has invested. The funds are often managed by large fund management companies, charging fees on the funds. Nevertheless, there may still be good reasons to invest in such funds, either for risk diversification or because of the confidence in the abilities of the fund managers.

In recent years, the role of mutual funds has been increasing steadily, and they now play an important role in the context of *shadow banking*, see Section 2.5 below.

Hedge funds are private investment pools which are actively managed, typically using non-conventional investment strategies such as taking short positions in a range of securities. Regulation of hedge funds has in most countries been lenient, and hedge funds are allowed a high degree of leverage so that they can fund their activities by debt. The name comes from the original purpose of the hedge fund, namely to invest in securities while using leverage and short selling to hedge the movements in security prices.

Investment banks specialize in financial contracts, typically related to buying and selling firms, creation of new ownership capital, introduction of a firm on the stock exchange, etc. In the United States, investment banking was formerly separated by law (the Glass-Seagal Act from the 1930s) from commercial banking, so there were two separate systems of banks; the commercial banks with access to (subsidized) customer deposits, but restricted choice of assets, and investment banks with no access to deposits, but almost unlimited choice of assets; a feature which had no counterpart in other countries and has now been abolished.

Box 2.1

Large banks. Because there has been a trend over the last few decades of a move towards larger banks, either through growth or as a result of mergers, it should come as no surprise that some of the largest banks have a considerable size.

A list of the largest banks (world- as well as countrywise) is regularly collected and published by relbanks (at http://www.relbanks.com). Measuring the size of a bank is not a straightforward matter, because size may be reflected in either the *total amount of assets* or alternatively in its *market capitalization,* the total value of its shares.

The resulting ranking of banks according to size turns out to be quite different in the two cases. If total assets are used, then the biggest five banks are

1. Industrial and Commerical Bank of China (China)
2. HSBC Holdings (UK)
3. China Construction Bank Corporation (China)
4. BNP Paribas (France)
5. Mitsubishi UFJ Financial Group (Japan)

with asset values ranking from 3,182 to 2,500 billions of US$. On the other hand, using market cap, other banks appear in the list:

1. Wells Fargo & Co. (USA)
2. Industrial and Commerical Bank of China (China)
3. J.P. Morgan Chase & Co. (USA)
4. China Construction Bank Corporation (China)
5. Bank of America (USA)

with market capitalizations in the range 188–284 billions of US$ (rankings in both cases reflect the situation at April 2014).

Gambling may be considered as reversed insurance, where the individual aims at obtaining a large gain in events occurring with low probability. Gambling firms may therefore also be considered as financial intermediaries, and because gambling in some sort or another has an important role in the economy, they are by no means the least interesting financial intermediaries. It may be added that gambling activities are closely related to other activities in the economy and that gambling is one of the classic ways of money laundering (see Chapter 12).

Pawn brokers. At the lower end of the range of financial intermediaries, we find the pawn brokers who have a long historical record but nowadays play a minor role. This should not lead us into forgetting that the basic method of transaction, namely offering credit against collateral, which in this case is actually in the possession of the lender, is well known and widespread also in the more prestigious parts of the financial sector, and we shall have much more to say in later chapters about the advantages of using collateral.

Loan sharks. Here we are moving into the informal or illegal part of the financial system, often connected with organized crime, and using methods for securing repayments of loans which are beyond what we shall be considering.

Government participation. The degree of government presence in the financial sector varies between countries. State-owned commercial banks are widespread, although their role is diminishing, and many have been privatized in recent years. However, the government may have its own pension funds, and it may be actively engaged in gambling, reserving for itself several types of popular lotteries. Even when the government is not formally involved, it may well be perceived by the public as backing a particular financial institution.

In the United States, prominent examples of institutions with unclear government involvement are Fannie Mae and Freddie Mac, supplying loans or loan guarantees for housing, funded by marketable securities. Fannie Mae (Federal National Mortgage Association) was founded in 1938 as a government agency but privatized in 1968, and another government agency was created for guaranteeing government-issued mortgages. Freddie Mac (Federal Home Loan Mortgage Corporation) was set up in 1970 in order to establish competition in the market.

The two agencies earn money by charging a guarantee fee on loans which they securitize into marketable papers. There is no underlying government guarantee, but the market has generally had the expectation that there would be some government intervention if the two agencies were held to fulfil guarantees beyond their ability, something which eventually turned out to be correct.

2.2 Banking business

Even though banks come in many versions, some of them not even resembling our intuitive conception of a bank, there are still many common traits, due to which it makes sense to treat banking as a single topic rather than splitting it into separate theories of money lending, deposit care, security trading, corporate financing, insurance, etc.

When it comes to financial reporting, all financial intermediaries are similar if approached in sufficient generality. The balance statement of a bank (which nowadays will not be reported in this form but still can be figured as shown) is outlined in Table 2.2.

Table 2.2 Simplified Balance Sheet

Assets	**Equity and Liabilities**
Cash	Short-term debt
Lending	Deposits
Financial assets	Financial liabilities
Fixed assets	Long-term debt
	Equity
Off-balance sheet (contingencies received)	Off-balance sheet (contingencies given)

The bank holds assets in different degrees of liquidity, and similarly the outside world has claims on the bank as shown in the liability side of the balance.

What attracts attention is not so much the usual items, but rather the so-called *off-balance sheet items*, which, as indicated by their name, are not taken into the balance as ordinary assets or liabilities but nevertheless have considerable and increasing importance. This is a result of the steadily increasing complexity of banking activity, where traditional loans are replaced by financial constructs of various types, some of which will be commented upon later when we look at securitization. The bank negotiates the loan, collects the initiating fees, and then packs this and other loans into special securities which are sold to the general public. As a result, the loan disappears from the books of the bank. However, there may still rest some obligations with the bank that may have guaranteed some of the payments on the securities, and such obligations of the bank should in principle appear among the off-balance items.

For completeness, we also add a stylized income statement of the bank (see Table 2.3). This table shows only what is obvious, namely that the income of a bank comes from the interest margin, the difference between deposit and loan rates, *plus* the fees that the bank gets from performing various other services. The long-term trend in bank earnings shows a shift towards fees as the main source of income, caused both by the low interest rates that have prevailed over the last decade but also reflecting the changes in banking activity already mentioned. When the activities shift towards financial services other than deposits and loans, this must show up in the income statement.

Table 2.3 Income Statement and Earnings

Interest margin and fees
Capital gains and losses
– Operating costs
Operating income (EBITD)
– Depreciation
– Provisions
– Tax
Net income

The item shown under the name 'depreciation' contains also the losses on loans that are not repaid. The amount of such losses depends, of course, on both external factors as the general business conditions and on the quality of work done by the credit officers of the bank, both when initiating the loan and in renegotiating non-performing loans. In subsequent chapters, we shall have much to say about credit risk, defaulting borrowers, and repayment of loans in general. In our theoretical discussion, a default on a loan will typically mean that the full amount of the loan is lost to the bank. In reality, however, loans that are not repaid according to the contract are not necessarily lost and may even be fully recovered after some negotiation.

2.3 Business lines

Inside the bank, the activities are classified according to the type of financial intermediation that is carried out.

Private banking or retail banking consists of banking services offered to private consumers and small businesses, either in the form of taking deposits or in providing loans, often in connection with housing. Private banking may, however, contain business contracted with firms of considerable size, up to the servicing of the corporate sector, which belongs to the next category. In the field of private banking we shall find most of what will concern us in the chapters to follow. However, the fact that banks typically do other kinds of business – and get much of their earnings from this – means that we will have to make occasional detours into other fields of finance.

Commercial banking. The terminology is not altogether fixed, and in some contexts commercial banking means all banking business which does not fall into the realm of investment banking (buying and selling firms, arranging mergers and acquisitions). However, we shall use it in the more common meaning of providing banking services (funding arrangements and other banking business) for corporate firms. It is clear from this description that only banks of sufficient size are engaged in commercial banking.

Investment banking (corporate finance). As mentioned already, investment banking deals with problems of long-term financing of the corporate sector, either through purchases of firms by others or through introduction of firms to the stock exchange (so-called IPOs, initial public offerings, to be dealt with in Chapter 9). Although the individual business transactions are often very lucrative for the bank, the amount of business is highly volatile and subject to cyclical movements.

Payment and settlement. Financial intermediaries are increasingly involved in payment services, both national and international, and although the fee to be gained from any single transaction is small, the total sums transferred are such that the earnings are interesting. We shall return to specific banking problems related to payments in a later chapter.

Asset management takes care of the placement of large sums of money in securities as well as the task of matching the payments of assets and liabilities. The asset management department charges a fee which depends on the size of the fortune which is taken care of, and again this activity may be an important part of the total earnings of a bank.

Trading is the buying and selling of securities in the market for a commission. Trading is done on behalf of customers or for the bank itself, and the bank charges a commission fee for this.

Retail brokerage is a brokerage service for customers who are retail investors rather than institutional investors.

Agency services are more specialized financial services where the bank acts on behalf of its customer in a given context.

It goes without saying that any particular bank can have some, but not necessarily all, of the above-mentioned departments, and it may have others depending on its business profile. Also, the bank may have several general purpose departments (known as the *back office*) which do not deal with the above specified tasks.

Box 2.2

What is the 'value added' of an FI? Over the last few decades, the financial sector has not only been consolidated into larger units, but its size in the economy as a whole has increased. The size of the financial sector varies between European countries, cf. Fig. 2.1.

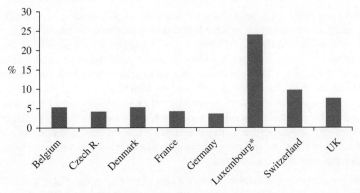

* 2013. Source: OECD statistics (http://stats.oecd.org).

Figure 2.1 Percentage share of financial intermediation in GDP, 2014.

These shares have changed over the years, with an increasing trend in the decades preceding the financial crisis around 2008. However, some peculiar features emerge from a closer look at the shares over recent years. As noticed in Maer and Broughton [2012], the share in gross value added in UK banks, increasing slowly from around 6% to around 8% in the years before the financial crisis, suddenly rose to 10.4% in 2009 and stayed above 9% in the following years.

It may seem strange that the contribution of the financial sector to the total value added in the United Kingdom should be so great in the years of financial crisis. How can this be explained?

To see what is behind it, one has to look at the way in which value added is computed for an FI, say a bank. What should be measured is the difference between the value of input to the bank and value of output from the bank. However, measuring input and in particular output is not a simple matter; even defining output in this context may be troublesome.

Basically, the bank contributes to the value added in society by

- receiving and managing deposits;
- providing payment services, e.g. debit cards;
- making loans; and
- offering financial advice to businesses.

Box 2.2 CONTINUED

This corresponds to what can be found in the guidelines of FISIM (Financial Intermediation Services Indirectly Measured), introduced in 1993 by the UN System of National Accounts. But many of these activities are not identified in the process of providing financial services, and in practice the value added must be based on loans and deposits. Here FISIM uses what is called a 'reference rate' of interest, which functions as a measure of the cost of funding. So, a loan of €1,000 with 9% interest and a reference rate of 4% gives rise to a value added of

$$€1,000 \times (0.09 - 0.04) = €50.$$

Similarly, a deposit of €1,000 with a 2% deposit rate gives a value added of €20.

This seems straightforward, but many complications creep in: Market rates tend to move quite quickly, and therefore value added should be based on fixed prices to make sense, but the methods for transforming current prices to fixed prices are at best ad hoc. What may be more damaging is that there are also conceptual problems involved, in particular the problem of *risk bearing*: The loan rates of the banks reflect the risk of the relevant credit engagements, so the value added as computed by FISIM also covers an element of risk bearing by banks. However, this should not figure as a contribution of the FI to value added, as risk taking by private individuals is not considered as contributing to the GDP (gross domestic product) of society. It is therefore to be expected that in periods of economic downturn, where loans become more risky and banks increase loan rates, the value added becomes inflated by the increased risk.

For other possible biases in measuring value added of banks, see e.g. Haldane et al. [2010]. A recalculation performed for Ireland by Everett et al. [2013] gives a GDP share of Irish-owned banks in 2009 of 0.63% instead of the 3.08% which emerges from the current approach.

2.4 Relationship banking

2.4.1 Traditional and newer methods of banking

We have seen in the previous sections that financial intermediation has become a broad field consisting of very different services offered to customers. In particular, the last two decades have witnessed a considerable change in the position and role of the FI, as indicated in Fig. 2.2. From the original role as intermediaries using household deposits to finance small and medium-size businesses, banks have developed into multifaceted institutions providing not only loans but also insurance and risk sharing in a broader sense.

Even though the models of the previous chapter gave several possible explanations of why there should be financial intermediation and what kind of task would be undertaken by financial intermediators, there is still much left to be explained, given the multitude of different types of financial intermediators and the complexity of the intermediation as such. In this and the following section, we consider some of the extensions which have come as a partial answer to the many questions posed by the development of the financial industry.

The first one, known as *relationship banking*, points to the specific information about the customer (in our discussion, a borrower) which the bank obtains in the course of their business relationship. Such information may be useful to the bank as well as to the customer: It may allow the bank to assess the risks in a better way, and it may also be advantageous to the customer who defaults on the repayment, because a bank may choose to renegotiate the loan rather than initiating a liquidation. This latter aspect of the bank's function, the ability to deal with engagements which are not fulfilled, has to some extent been overlooked, not only in theory but also in practice, but it may be argued that banks are distinguished by their ability to carry out investment projects, if not as good as the entrepreneur then better than the ordinary investor.

2.4.2 The intuition behind relationship banking

We begin with a simple case, following Allen and Gale [1999]. Suppose that an investor wants to hedge the risk of an income which is subject to random fluctuations. The investor has a utility function u and income $w(s)$, where s is the uncertain state of nature. There is also a security market with a security f, which pays the return $f(s)$ in state s. If the investor adds this security to the portfolio, the net income will be $f(s) + w(s)$ in state s, so expected utility is

$$\mathsf{E}[u(f + w)] = \sum_s \pi(s)u(f(s) + w(s)),$$

where $\pi(s)$ is the probability of state s.

So far for using the market. If instead the investor contacts a financial intermediary, then the latter may set up a contract g specifying income transfers $g(s)$ to the investor in state s. This contract should provide hedging to the customer and at the same time yield maximal expected utility to the intermediary. If the latter has a utility function v, then the contract must solve the problem

$$\max_g \mathsf{E}[v(-g)]$$

$$\text{s.t.} \quad \mathsf{E}[u(w + g)] \geq \mathsf{E}[u(w + f)].$$

So the financial intermediary has a role to play designing a security which is better for the investor than what could be obtained in the market.

There is nothing new in this situation, which was essentially covered in the previous chapter. The new aspects come in when we add that the financial intermediary and the customer meet not only in this single instance but may enter a long-term relationship. Let $t = 1, 2, \ldots,$ and suppose that at each date t a state s_t is realized; for simplicity the states are assumed to be independent and identically distributed with probabilities $\pi(s_t)$. The investor has a *written* contract g with the financial intermediary, being paid $g(s_t)$ if state s_t occurs at date t, and this gives expected utility $\mathsf{E}_{s_t}[u(w + g)]$ at date t; the financial intermediary has $\mathsf{E}_{s_t}[v(-g)]$. But the question now arises as to whether the customer and the intermediary could improve by entering an *implicit* risk-sharing arrangement.

Let h be such an implicit arrangement, according to which the intermediary pays the investor $h(s_t)$ in state s_t. For such an arrangement to be sustainable, it must be

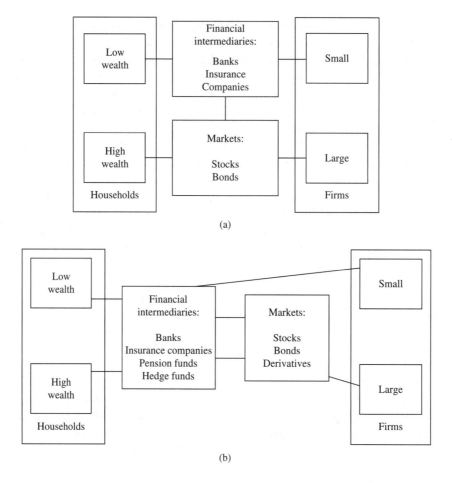

(a)

(b)

Figure 2.2 The changing ways of banking. In panel (a), illustrating traditional banking, the financial intermediaries mainly serve smaller businesses (loans) and low wealth households (deposits), whereas large businesses and wealthy households use the market. In *contemporary banking*, shown in panel (b), the financial intermediaries offer specific services not only to low income households but also to businesses, using their easier access to the capital market.

self-enforcing in the sense that none of the parties has an incentive to default on its obligations. For the investor, this may be expressed as follows: Let u^* be expected utility when the obligations of the implicit arrangement are being honored,

$$u^* = \mathsf{E}[u(w + g + h)],$$

and let u^{**} be expected utility if the implicit arrangement is *not* carried out,

$$u^{**} = \mathsf{E}[u(w + g)].$$

Then the incentive compatibility constraint for the implicit arrangement can be written as

$$u(w(s_t) + g(s_t) + h(s_t)) + \frac{u^*}{r} \geq u(w(s_t) + g(s_t)) + \frac{u^{**}}{r}, \text{ each } s_t,$$

where on the left-hand side we have utility at date t plus utility in all future periods if the implicit arrangement is adhered to, and on the right-hand side the same quantity in the case that the implicit arrangement terminates.

It is seen that if the written contract is not already optimal for either of the parties, then there is certain room for improvement, limited by the incentive compatibility constraints on both sides. The particular nature of this constraint can be exploited to provide some insight into the role of competition among banks: If there are many financial intermediaries willing to enter implicit arrangements, then the expected future utility of the investor (after switching bank) is close to u^*, in which case the constraint tells us that $h(s_t) \geq 0$, so there is little or no room for implicit risk sharing. If neither the market nor written contracts can provide efficient risk sharing so that implicit arrangements are important, then competition among financial intermediaries may lower overall efficiency.

Much of the above clearly hinges upon the existence of limitations in choice of either market securities or written contracts in providing efficient risk sharing. This can be substantiated by lack of knowledge of the market on the side of customers, the cost of setting up formal contracts, etc. Such phenomena make it plausible that customers can obtain benefit from a long-term relationship with their bank, tailored to their specific needs, thereby sustaining the development of the banking sector towards its more modern structure, as depicted in Fig. 2.2. It also provides some explanation of the stability of customer-bank relationships observed even after liberalization of the sector.

2.4.3 Loan pricing under relationship banking

In the following, we present some other features of relationship banking, using the approach of Freixas [2005]. The point of departure will be the model introduced in Section 1.3.2, where there are two technologies yielding outcomes G and B, respectively, with $B > G$, with probabilities π_G and π_B, satisfying $\pi_G G > 1 > \pi_B B$. We assume here that firms have individual and possibly different π_G (and π_B). These probabilities, which express the risk characteristics of the firm, may be assessed through credit ratings, but the choice of technology cannot be observed. However, banks can monitor their borrowers at a cost C for each firm. Because relationship banking has to do with a bank-customer relationship, which necessarily develops over time, the model needs more than one period, but this will come later. We shall assume that the specific ability of banks to deal with non-performing loans yields a benefit V to the firm.

As was seen in Section 1.3.2, firms will choose the technology G for their investment projects if financed through the market with a repayment

$$R \leq \frac{\pi_G G - \pi_B B}{\pi_G - \pi_B}.$$

The repayment, which occurs only in the case of success, corresponds to an expected repayment $\pi_G R$. Assuming for simplicity that the market interest rate is 1, we have that there is a value $\bar{\pi}_G$ of π_G such that market financing is possible if $\pi_G > \bar{\pi}_G$, and repayment corresponding to π_G is $1/\pi_G$, because expected repayment must be at least 1.

The bank offers debt contracts with a (nominal) repayment R_m. Because bank contracts yield a benefit V to the borrower in the case of non-fulfilment, R_m should be larger than the financial market repayment R, but firms may accept this for two reasons: Either their probability of success π_G is so small that they cannot finance their investment through the financial markets, or the firm prefers the additional services provided by the bank (in the case of financial distress); in this case we say that there is *horizontal differentiation.*

Suppose that the rate R_m set by the bank is set in such a way that expected repayment should cover the market rate, which is 1, plus the cost C of monitoring, together with a mark-up ρ which reflects the competitiveness of the banking sector, so expected payoff for a firm with risk characteristics π_G is

$$\pi_G R_m(\pi_G) = (1 + C)(1 + \rho),$$

from which

$$R_m(\pi_G) = \frac{1 + m + \rho}{\pi_G}, \tag{1}$$

where $m = (1 + \rho)C$.

Consider a firm with risk characteristics $\pi_G \geq \bar{\pi}_G$, which is big enough to allow for financing via the market. If the firm nevertheless chooses the bank so that there is horizontal differentiation of firms, we must have that

$$\pi_G \left(G - \frac{1}{\pi_G} \right) \leq \pi_G(G - R_m(\pi_G)) + (1 - \pi_G)V. \tag{2}$$

The particular value π_G^* of π_G for which the firm is indifferent between the two sources of finance, so (2) holds with equality, can be found as

$$\pi_G^* = 1 - \frac{\rho + m}{V}, \tag{3}$$

so horizontal differentiation occurs when $\bar{\pi}_G < \pi_G^* < 1$ or equivalently $(1 - \pi_G)V > \rho + m$.

Already here, we have some segmentation of the borrowers, namely that which follows the credit rating given by π_G. Assuming that small firms have a bad rating, they may be unable to obtain credit even through the banks, namely if

$$\pi_G < \frac{1 + m + \rho}{V}.$$

Large firms with $\pi_G < \pi_G^*$ will use the money market, whereas firms in the intermediate interval will use banks as a source of credit even though the market is open for them.

2.4.4 Consequences for the pricing of credit

Now we move on to consider relationship banking in the present context, and for that we must extend the model to deal with at least two periods. Let $R_{n,t}$, $t = 0, 1$ be the nominal repayments for a borrower with risk characteristics π_G in periods 0 and 1, respectively, and let $R_{r,1}$ be the repayment for a borrower whose loan is renewed in period 1 (under the conditions that the borrower did not fail in period 0). If the expected net return on bank lending is ρ then the bank can extract a repayment for renewal which is as large as the cost to the borrower of obtaining a new loan in a competing bank, so that

$$R_{r,1} = R_{n,1}, \; \pi_G R_{n,1} = (1 + \rho)(1 + C),$$

or

$$R_{r,1} = R_{n,1} = \frac{1 + m + \rho}{\pi_G}. \tag{4}$$

For the repayment rate in the first year, the expected return on a loan, which is $1 + \rho + m$, should be equal to $\pi_G(R_{n,0} + \pi_G R_{r,1}) = \pi_G(R_{n,0} + 1 + m + \rho)$, so

$$R_{n,0} = \frac{1 + (1 - \pi_G)m + \rho}{\pi_G}.$$

The result that $R_{i,1} > R_{n,0}$, $i = n, r$, may seem counter-intuitive, because the established borrower-lender relationship might be expected to result in some advantages to the renewed borrower. This does not happen, because the bank exploits its (restricted) monopoly power in order to collect payment for monitoring which is relevant only to new customers. On the other hand, first-period price is lower than second-period price because new customers at $t = 0$ have a future of possible renewed borrowing at lower cost.

This asymmetry over periods is partly due to the closedness of our model, which does not go beyond the two periods considered, as can be seen from (4), where the new contract is expected to last only for one period. If instead we consider the contracting as something which goes on in an indefinite future, but keep the simple structure of two-period contracts, then again we would have that the repayment at renewal equals that of new contracts at this period, so there is only one repayment rate for firms with risk characteristics π_G. If this repayment rate R is to be constant over time, it must satisfy the equation

$$\pi_G R + \pi_G^2 R = (1 + \pi_G + C)(1 + \rho),$$

because total expected receipts should equal total outlays plus overhead, with solution

$$R = \frac{(1 + \pi_G)(1 + \rho) + m}{\pi_G + \pi_G^2}. \tag{5}$$

It may be checked that the repayment rate in (5) is smaller than that of the one-period model. Thus, the advantages of relationship which come from the once-and-for-all nature of monitoring is spread evenly among new and old customers, but it is not confined to one side of the market.

Needless to say, the model is so simple, and the information that the bank obtains in the course of a borrower-lender relationship so modest, that it can only catch some of the features of relationship banking, but it serves as a warning that the consequences of the more detailed intercourse between bank and customer may have consequences other than those that are immediately obvious.

2.5 Shadow banking

In the previous section, we were concerned with personal relationships in the financial sector and its possible consequences. Here we shall have a (first) look of what might be seen as the opposite – impersonal – side of financial intermediation, where both the deposit and the loan businesses take the form of trading in securities. This is the field known as 'shadow banking' (cf. Gorton and Metrick [2010]), which in recent years has become increasingly important, transacting funds of a size comparable to those of traditional banking.

One of the reasons for this development can be found in the way that traditional banking functions, as discussed in Chapter 1. Banks receive liquid deposits and use the funds for illiquid investment, an arrangement which works well under usual circumstances, but which, however, is vulnerable to panics – if depositors for some reason doubt that their deposits are safe in the bank, they will demand them back, and if many depositors do so, there will be a run on the bank. We shall have much to say about bank runs in later chapters; at the present stage it suffices to remark that the most widely adopted method for preventing bank runs is to establish a system of *deposit insurance* so that depositors will get their money back even in the case that the bank should fail.

Most systems of deposit insurance have an upper limit, large enough to make the system work for ordinary private depositors, but possibly inconvenient for larger scale money market institutions (in the following, called MMMFs, money market mutual funds) which may want to place considerable sums on demand. Because such deposits cannot be made in a safe way using ordinary deposits with banks, another approach had to be invented, and this was found in the *repo* market.

In a repo (repurchase) trade between an MMMF and a bank, the MMMF buys an asset (a security) of the bank at some price p_0 with the condition that the bank buys it back at some agreed future time (which may be the next day) at the price p_1, so that the interest rate on this arrangement is $(p_1 - p_0)/p_0$. The bank provides collateral v in the form of the asset concerned; thereby the contract will correspond to depositing p_0 with the bank, and this deposit is safe if enough collateral is provided, meaning that $v > p_0$. One defines the *haircut* for this repo trade as $(v - p_0)/v$. If the bank fails before the repurchase is carried out, the MMMF is left with the collateral, which under usual circumstances is enough to ensure that no money is lost. For the bank, the arrangement has the

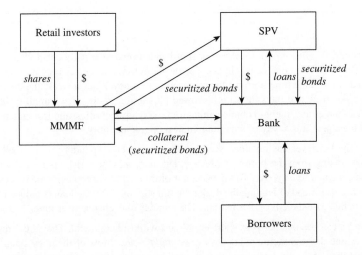

Figure 2.3 Schematic illustration of shadow banking. The investors buy shares in an MMMF, which transfers the funds to the bank using repos. The bank uses the funds for loans which are transferred to an SPV, transforming them to securities, some of which are used as collateral in the repo trade.

advantage that the amount deposited takes the form of a sale of an asset, and the promise to buy it back is an off-balance item, so the results of this activity are largely absent from the balance of the bank.

This, however, is only part of the story. Because the repo trade involves the use of securities, there is an increased need for securities to be used as collateral, and creating securities is another advantageous line of business for the bank. The bank collects loans already negotiated and sells them to a specifically created firm, a *special purpose vehicle* (SPV), which sells securities backed by the loans. The SPVs have no other functions, they have no offices nor employees, but technically the loans are sold off from the bank, and if the borrowers do not fulfil their obligations, the losses must be covered by the owners of the securities and not by the bank originating the loans.

The method allows for a considerable degree of tailoring securities to the demand. A given pool of loans can be transformed into several tranches of securities, differing in the underlying risks of the assets, and in this way the loans can be transformed into papers which can attract a large variety of investors.

Adding this phenomenon of *securitization* to the replacement of deposits by repo trade, we get the basic structure of shadow banking, as illustrated in Fig. 2.3. The bank is only present in the initial phase of the lender-borrower relationship; after originating the loans these are transformed into securities which can then be used as collateral in the repo transactions with MMMFs. Shadow banking performs all the basic tasks of ordinary banks: It transforms illiquid investments to liquid assets, and changes maturity from long to short

---

Box 2.3

Repo trades. A *repurchase agreement*, or shorthand, a *repo*, is usually concluded between a securities dealer and one of its clients. The dealer delivers securities for say, $100, for a week and at the same time borrows the same sum of money. After a week, the dealer gets the securities back and pays the sum borrowed plus a little more, for example $105. The dealer uses the arrangement to obtain capital for buying up securities, and from the point of view of the client, it is a way of obtaining interest on idle liquidity.

Because the borrower has obtained securities for a sum corresponding to the loan, there is no risk arising from the borrower (dealer), but there may be a risk connected with the securities, a *counterparty risk*. To take account of this risk, the repo agreement uses a so-called *haircut:* Instead of lending the dealer the full sum of $100, the loan is reduced to e.g. $90, so in this case there is a 10% haircut. The haircuts may change over time.

Repo trades can be considered as short-term loans with full collateral. They are often concluded as one-day transactions, known as *overnight repos*. Most of them are open in the sense that they are continued automatically until one party decides to exit. But repos may also be concluded for longer terms (the so-called *term repos*), typically around three months.

---

or even very short time intervals. Because the funds are placed outside banks in a large number of SPVs, it becomes much more difficult to monitor and regulate shadow banking than ordinary banking, which already is no simple matter.

2.6 Exercises

1. Usury occurs when the interest rate in a borrower-lender contract is exorbitantly high. Usury has been considered immoral since ancient times, and it is illegal in most countries. However, it is not quite so easy to define in exact terms.

Which arrangements can be made on the individual level (between borrower and lender) or for society as a whole to avoid usury?

2. P2P lending: In recent years, a new type of financial intermediation has emerged: Direct contact between borrowers and lenders is achieved by an intermediary using an internet portal, and all transactions are online. Loans are unsecured but take the form of securities that can be sold to other lenders. The intermediary verifies borrower identity and characteristics, and filters out unqualified borrowers; and it also services the loans.

How does this method of financial intermediation fit into the theoretical framework of this and the previous chapter? Are there new markets which can be opened up by P2P lending? How much competition will it entail for the traditional banking sector?

(P2P lending started in 2005 and has made considerable progress in recent years, but its turnover is still very small in comparison with traditional financial intermediation.)

3. Suppose that in a country, the share of capital in value added and the rate of return on assets in financial intermediation and in business in general are as follows:

	Capital Share in Value Added (%)	Internal Rate of Return on Fixed Assets (% p.a.)
Financial intermediation:		
Net of risk-free return	60	16
Net of risk-adjusted return	40	6
Private sector	42	10

Do these figures show that ordinary economic activity is more profitable than financial intermediation when risk bearing is removed?

4. A *credit default swap* (CDS) is a security protecting lenders if the borrower defaults, transferring this risk in return for periodic payments.

Suppose that A holds a 10-year bond issued by a company with a nominal value of €1,000 and a coupon interest amount of €100 each year. To protect herself, A enters into a CDS with B, paying a premium of €20 a year. In return, A agrees to pay B the €1,000 par value of the bond together with the remaining interest on the bond (€100 times number of remaining years).

It turns out that the company may default with probability 0.1 in each of the years. Who gets positive expected profits from this CDS?

5. In a repo transaction, 5-year German government bonds of a nominal value of €10,000,000 are sold for €10,157,671. After a week, the seller repurchases the bonds for €10,161,819. Comment on this transaction: What is the interest rate paid in this agreement? Is there a haircut, and if so, how large?

6. Suppose that a shadow bank has sold securities for $100,000,000 with a haircut of 20% so that the buyer in the repo transaction paid only $80,000,000. Due to the increased uncertainty about the securities, the haircut is changed to 30%. What are the consequences for the bank if the deposit is to be continued?

2.7 Comments

The listing of different forms of financial intermediation – including some with a shattered reputation – is inspired by the treatment in Greenbaum and Thakor [2007]. For another treatment along the same lines, see Heffernan [2005]. The brief treatment of value added by financial intermediation merely scratches the surface of the discussion, which opens up more subtle questions of how to measure value and value added. For further material, see e.g. Fixler and Zieschang [2010].

Relationship banking was a phenomenon which received much attention in the 2000s, but despite its intuitive appeal – it matters that a borrower is known by the bank – not many new insights have emerged. For a treatment emphasizing the role of relationship banking in relation to banks' competition and their pricing decisions, see Besanko and Thakor [2004] or the survey in Boot [2000].

The model in Section 2.4.3, which as mentioned is taken from Freixas [2005], has the advantage of being explicit on a possible additional advantage of financial intermediation, namely that banks can provide a more acceptable exit for a borrower in the case of a default than if only the market is used for funding.

We shall have much more to say about shadow banking in later chapters, so the present section serves only as an introduction, which seems appropriate when dealing with the diversity of financial intermediation. For another introduction to shadow banking, see Pozsar et al. [2010].

Chapter 3

Basic Concepts of Risk Management

3.1 Introduction

As has been seen repeatedly in the previous chapters, the business of a financial intermediary is closely interwoven with risk, indeed the bank is earning a considerable part of
its income by taking on specific forms of risk. It follows that the success or failure of the
bank is connected with its ability to handle risk, both the basic forms of risk, on which
it earns money, and the less easily identified forms of risk which were not contemplated
in the basic business transactions. Not surprisingly also, the regulation of banks has to do
with the risk that banks are running – and how to control it.

In the present chapter, we begin the systematic treatment of assessing and managing
risk, starting with the common features of the discipline. As we shall see presently, the
bank faces different types of risk, some of which are connected with the type of business
transactions that the bank is engaged in, whereas others are specific in their nature but
concern every type of financial intermediary. In later chapters, we deal with the specific
aspects of such forms of risk.

Risk management has several aspects. To control risk one must be able to *measure* it, so
risk measurement is an important building block. Next, having measured the relevant risk,
one must take action, and such action can take different forms, ranging from eliminating
causes at one extreme (changing the type of business transacted or the way in which it is
carried out) to offsetting the risk by other transactions (hedging).

Risk management is an important part of what a bank does, but it is also an aspect of
banking which is closely interrelated with the control and regulation of banks. It matters
for society that banks are managed in a proper way, in particular that they do not run
excessive risks, and with the Basel regulations from 1988 onwards – about which we shall
have much to say as we proceed – this has resulted in a considerable expansion of the
efforts in measuring and managing risk.

3.1.1 Types of risk in banking

Just as banking consists of several different business activities, there are several main types of risk occuring in financial intermediation. Some of these are connected with the specific business lines; others are common to all of them.

Liquidity risk. This is the risk that the financial institution will not be able to meet its obligations at a designated point of time, although it has the necessary assets. Liquidity risk typically arises as *withdrawal risk*. Depositors may claim back their assets at short notice, often for reasons which are not connected with the way in which the bank is managed, and if the number of withdrawals is large enough, it takes the form of a run on the bank.

We have already considered the role of a financial institution in transforming liquidity; taking on highly liquid obligations and covering the obligations by illiquid assets is a central feature of banking, so liquidity risk cannot be avoided, but it is fundamental for the functioning of the bank that it can foresee and control its liquidity.

The liquidity of a given asset has to do with whether there are well-functioning markets for this specific type of asset. If such markets exist, the asset can be disposed of at market prices, and no liquidity problem arises; of course, the bank may lose money due to the development of market prices, but this is another problem (and the associated risk is of another type). If markets do not open regularly so that there is no quoted market price of the asset, then there may be a considerable difference between the value of the asset if evaluated on the basis of future earnings on one side, and the proceeds from a sale here and now on the other. One speaks of a *bid-ask spread* in this case, and it may be so large as to make the value of all assets smaller than the value of liabilities, causing solvency problems for the bank.

Interest rate risk. Interest rates move up and down, and the fluctuations of interest rates can give rise to considerable losses for a bank engaged in asset and liability management. If the assets of a bank earn a fixed rate of interest while the liabilities are subject to variable (market) interest, then an upwards movement of the market rate of interest will mean that the net earnings of the bank, taken as the difference between interest earned on assets and interest payments on liabilities, will decrease. This is, however, only the very simplest version of the problem, because in practice one has to take into consideration that assets and liabilities have different maturities, and that the borrowers may have the option of converting their debt to another one with a different structure if the interest rate changes. We return to interest rate risk in Section 3.3 below.

Market risk. Interest rates are closely related to the net present value of interest bearing assets, and therefore interest rate risk can be considered as a special case of risk derived from changes in the price of marketable assets, i.e. market risk. Among such assets the most important are derived securities such as futures contracts and in particular options, which will play a certain role in our discussion of risk management and even of other topics in banking theory. An option is a right to sell or buy an asset at a specified price and under specified conditions. We shall review the theory of option pricing in Chapter 4.

Exchange rate risk is another specific form of market risk, where the risk is related to exchange rates. Because there is little new here as compared to other risk types, at least from a theoretical point of view, we shall not discuss it further.

Credit risk. Because the bank is traditionally concerned with offering credit, the risk that a borrower does not pay back or pays back only partially is at the very heart of banking business. Because each loan transaction is to some extent individual, the specific circumstances of the transaction must enter into the consideration of the associated risk. There is no unique way of doing this, and as we shall see later, when we go into the details of credit risk measurement and management, the methods to be chosen will depend considerably on the kind of banking business transacted and the type of customers that the bank is servicing.

Credit and market risk are the 'oldest' types of risk in the sense that they have been considered in connection with solvency requirements for banks from the beginning. The history of capital regulation is anyway quite short, going back only to the Basel I agreement from 1988.

Operational risk is risk which is related to the overall performance of business activity which does not belong to the previously mentioned categories. Examples of events leading to operational risk are fraud, litigation and IT breakdowns. With the increase in magnitude and scope of banking transactions, the importance of operational risk has grown, and this has been emphasized by its incorporation in the capital regulation as specified in Basel II from 2002.

As we shall see when dealing with operational risk, its causes are manifold and diverse, and there is still some need for theoretical underpinning for the methods applied to assess operational risk.

3.1.2 The loss function and its distribution

The point of departure for our discussion of risk management in banking is a *portfolio* to be considered over some time, where it is subject to uncertain changes. Letting $\widetilde{V}(s)$ be the (random) value of the portfolio at time s (the value of which we may observe at s), we are interested in its value after an interval Δ of time, and the *loss* of the portfolio over the period $[s, s + \Delta]$ is then

$$\widetilde{L}_{[s,s+\Delta]} = -\left(\widetilde{V}(s + \Delta) - \widetilde{V}(s)\right). \tag{1}$$

Here $\widetilde{L}_{[s,s+\Delta]}$ is clearly a random variable, and as such it has a distribution, the *loss distribution* with which we shall be much concerned in the following.

The formulation here has been in continuous time, and the value may be considered as a continuous time stochastic process. When going into details in the assessment of, for example, credit risk, this way of looking at the portfolio value is useful, because one may then apply known results such as the Black-Scholes option price formula. At present it is, however, more appropriate to consider models with discrete time so that intervals always have fixed length 1, and we may write (1) as

$$\widetilde{L}_{t+1} = \widetilde{L}_{[t\Delta,(t+1)\Delta]} = -\left(\widetilde{V}_{t+1} - \widetilde{V}_t\right).$$ (2)

So far, nothing has been said as to what determines the (random) values of $\widetilde{V}$, not surprising because the portfolio may consist of loan contracts (credit risk) or marketable securities (market risk) or even other assets. However, the standard approach in risk management is to assume that $\widetilde{V}$ is a function of time and of some underlying *risk factors*, the latter represented as a random vector $\widetilde{z}_t = (\widetilde{z}_{t,1}, \ldots, \widetilde{z}_{t,d})$ with d components, so

$$\widetilde{V}_t = f(t, \widetilde{z}_t).$$ (3)

The risk factors in $\widetilde{z}_t$ are assumed to be observable at time t. The expression (3) is called the *risk mapping* and is derived from the model of the underlying risk in the given case. Below we consider some examples of risk mappings.

With the fixed time intervals, it may be useful to shift attention from absolute values (of portfolios and risk factors) to *changes* in these values. Let $\widetilde{x}_t = \widetilde{z}_t - \widetilde{z}_{t-1}$; then (2) can be rewritten using (3) as

$$\widetilde{L}_{t+1} = -(f(t+1, z_t + \widetilde{x}_{t+1}) - f(t, z_t)).$$ (4)

Here z_t is observed at time t, so the loss distribution is determined by the vector of risk factor changes $\widetilde{x}_{t+1}$. Defining the *loss operator* $l_{[t]}$ as the function from $\mathbb{R}^d$ to $\mathbb{R}$ taking risk factor changes x to losses,

$$l_{[t]}(\widetilde{x}) = -(f(t+1, z_t + \widetilde{x}) - f(t, z_t)),$$ (5)

then clearly $\widetilde{L}_{t+1} = l_{[t]}(\widetilde{x}_{t+1})$.

Assuming that f is differentiable, we can approximate $\widetilde{L}_{t+1}$ by a Taylor series expansion taking only first-order terms,

$$\widetilde{L}_{t+1} = -\left(f_t'(t, z_t) + \sum_{i=1}^{d} f_{z_i}'(t, z_t)\widetilde{x}_{t+1,i}\right),$$ (6)

where f_y' denotes the partial derivative of f w.r.t. the variable y (the Δ-notation used here refers to the length of time interval, used when we move to a discrete model of losses over time). The advantage of (6) over (4) is, of course, that we now have a linear expression rather than a general functional form. The similar linear version of the loss operator is

$$l_{[t]}(\widetilde{x}) = -\left(f_t'(t, z_t) + \sum_{i=1}^{d} f_{z_i}'(t, z_t)\widetilde{x}_{t+1,i}\right).$$ (7)

The expressions on the right-hand side in (6) and (7) are, of course, the same, and the advantage of considering a *loss operator* as in (7) rather than just finding the loss is mainly conceptual: In risk management, we are concerned with the assessment of the risk which a bank faces as a consequence of its business activities. This assessment depends crucially on the correct identification of risk factors as well as on adequate quantitative information about these risk factors. Therefore, the risk managers will want to see the losses in their functional dependence of risk factors rather than as a single number, or, in our context, they will prefer (7) to (6).

Once we have expressed the losses as a function of the risk factor changes, we can find the *loss distribution* F_L from the (presumably known) distribution of these changes,

$$F(\lambda) = \mathsf{P}\{x_{t+1} \,|\, l_{[t]}(x_{t+1}) \le \lambda\},$$

for $\lambda \in \mathbb{R}$. The loss distribution contains all the relevant information about the risk of the bank, and it will be the basis for the further analysis.

EXAMPLE 3.1 **Losses on a portfolio of stocks.** Suppose that the portfolio consists of d stocks, let $S_{t,i}$ denote the price of stock i at date t, and let α_i be the number of stocks of type i in the portfolio. The value at date t of the portfolio is

$$V_t = \sum_{i=1}^{d} \alpha_i S_{t,i}.$$

The possible losses are caused by price changes, but because rates of change of prices are more natural in the context of stocks than absolute price changes, we write stock prices as

$$S_{t,i} = e^{z_{t,i}},$$

taking $z_{t,i} = \ln S_{t,i}$ as risk factors instead of $S_{t,i}$, we get the loss operator

$$l_{[t]}(\mathbf{x}) = -\left(\sum_{i=1}^{d} \alpha_i e^{z_{t+1,i}} - \sum_{i=1}^{d} \alpha_i e^{z_{t,i}} \right) = -V_t \sum_{i=1}^{d} \omega_{t,i} \left(e^{x_{t,i}} - 1 \right),$$

where we have introduced the relative portfolio weights

$$\omega_{t,i} = \frac{\alpha_i S_{t,i}}{V_t}.$$

Numerical example. Suppose that there are two different stocks, with $S_{t,1} = 750$, $S_{t,2} = 130$, and that the portfolio contains the two stocks in the ratio 1:3. If the rates of change in stock prices are -0.1 and -0.05, respectively, then we get a loss of size

$$L_{[t]} = -1120 \left(0.6579(e^{-0.1} - 1) + 1.0263(e^{-0.05} - 1) \right) = 90.392.$$

3.2 Risk measures

3.2.1 What is risk?

In the previous section, we looked at the loss connected with the business of a bank and models for finding (approximate) loss distributions. The next question is what to measure, how to select the quantities to be computed and to be used in decision making; using the loss distributions as such is not a feasible solution because they are typically found only numerically and anyway are too complex as the basis for day-to-day decisions.

There are at least four different approaches which may be taken (and which have been used in practice):

(1) *Notional-amount approach.* This is the less sophisticated approach to risk measurement; here the risk of a portfolio is defined as the sum of the (notional) values of the individual securities in the portfolio, possibly multiplied by a weight factor which represents riskiness of the particular class of assets to which the security belongs. The approach is much used in practice, even if not as the only measure of risk, and it is indeed the way of measuring risk which is behind the Cooke ratio (8% of assets should be held as equity) and the Basel rules for regulation of banks.

Although its main advantage is its simplicity (no assumptions made, no complicated calculations needed), it has several drawbacks from an economic point of view, for example that it cannot take diversification of portfolios into account, and, more technically, that the notional value of some assets, in particular derivatives, can differ widely from their 'real' value.

(2) *Factor-sensitivity measures.* Here, one measures the change in portfolio value which follows a given change in the underlying risk factors, which amounts to finding partial derivatives (or possibly elasticities if one measures percentage changes) of the loss function. We saw in the examples of the previous section that such partial derivatives are important and useful, for example in determining the impact on overall losses of changes in risk factors for options. The information provided by sensitivity measures pertain to the robustness of the portfolio against changes in risk factors.

On the other hand, sensitivity measures also have several drawbacks. Thus, there is no simple way of aggregating sensitivities with respect to different risk factors, and also it is not easy to aggregate over different types of assets (related to different markets) to obtain a measure of overall riskiness, which after all is what matters. This means that although useful, such measures can hardly stand alone.

(3) *Risk measures based on loss distributions.* Although the two previous approaches largely neglect the statistical aspects of the portfolio, modern measures of risk are based on the loss distribution. Examples of such measures are *Value at Risk* (VaR) and *expected shortfall*, to be considered in more detail below.

It is obvious that working with a particular statistic such as VaR means neglecting many other aspects of the distribution, but the advantage of going for this type of measurement is that the whole of the distribution must in principle be available, and more information can be had if needed, whereas for much standard business the simple statistics such as VaR are sufficient.

One of the drawbacks of the loss distribution approach is that the estimation of this distribution is based on past observation and therefore reflects the past rather than the future, which is important in decisions. This is, of course, an objection which can be raised against most statistical methods and there is little one can do about it, except, of course, by taking certain specific circumstances into account whenever possible.

(4) *Scenario-based risk measures.* Here the basic idea is to find the worst possible case for a given set of risk factor changes. Let $C = \{x_1, \ldots, x_n\}$ be such a set, and let $w = (w_1, \ldots, w_n)$ be a vector of weights, with $w_j \in [0, 1]$ for each j. The risk of a portfolio (with its associated loss operator $l_{[t]}(\cdot)$) is then

$$\psi_{[C,w]} = \max\{w_1 l_{[t]}(x_1), \ldots, w_n l_{[t]}(x_n)\}.$$

Many risk measures used in practice have this form.

The approach can be given a theoretical interpretation: Assume that $l_{[t]}(0) = 0$ (so the vector of no changes in risk factors gives a zero loss). The expression $w_j l_{[t]}(x_j)$ can be seen as the expectation of $l_{[t]}(\cdot)$ with respect to the probability distribution which assigns the mass w_j to the point x_j and $1 - w_j$ to the point 0 (no changes in risk factors; so $l_{[t]}(0) = 0$). This probability distribution has the form $w_j \delta_{x_j} + (1 - w_j)\delta_0$, where δ_x is the (degenerate) probability distribution which assigns a mass of 1 to x, and if we introduce the set

$$\mathcal{P}_{[C,w]} = \{w_1 \delta_{x_1} + (1 - w_1)\delta_0, \ldots, w_1 \delta_{x_n} + (1 - w_1)\delta_0\}$$

of such distributions, then we have that

$$\psi_{[C,w]} = \max\left\{ \mathsf{E}_P[l_{[t]}(\tilde{x})] \,\middle|\, P \in \mathcal{P}_{[C,w]} \right\},$$

so the scenario-based risk measure can be found by taking the maximum of expected loss, when the probability distribution over which expectation is taken is of a special type as specified above.

When the family of probability distributions takes more general forms, one speaks of *generalized scenarios*, and they play a certain role in the discussion of risk measures.

3.2.2 Value at Risk (VaR) and related measures

Given that we have computed the loss distribution F_L, we would like to extract some information from this distribution in order to get an impression of the possible losses which we may experience. An obvious candidate for such a measure would be the maximal possible loss, but in many cases the distribution has no upper bound, and a maximal loss makes no sense.

EXAMPLE 3.2 **VaR for some simple loss distributions.** If F_L is normal with mean μ and variance σ^2, then

$$\mathrm{VaR}_\alpha = \mu + \sigma \Phi^{-1}(\alpha), \; \mathrm{VaR}_\alpha^{mean} = \sigma \Phi^{-1}(\alpha).$$

The simplicity of the formula is, of course, a consequence of the properties of the normal distribution (or rather the family of normal distributions which differs only by location and scale). If the loss distribution is such that the standardized loss $(L - \mu)/\sigma$ has a (Student) t distribution with ν degrees of freedom, then

$$\mathrm{VaR}_\alpha = \mu - \sigma t_\nu^{-1}(\alpha),$$

where t_ν is the distribution function of the t distribution with ν degrees of freedom, available in most statistics packages (together with its inverse).

However, a way out almost suggests itself: Although the distribution may have no upper bound, the large losses will typically have a very small probability, so it seems reasonable to choose a certain confidence level $\alpha < 1$ and restrict attention to losses less than a certain size, so losses higher than that have probability $\leq 1 - \alpha$. This is exactly what is done by VaR; we define

$$\mathrm{VaR}_\alpha = \inf \{l \in \mathbb{R} \mid F_L(l) \geq \alpha\}. \tag{8}$$

In terms of probability theory, VaR is a *quantile* of the loss distribution. Typical values of α are 0.95 or 0.99.

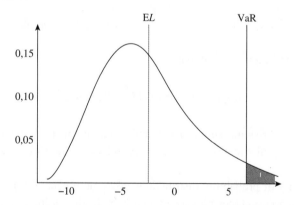

Figure 3.1 An example of a loss distribution with 95% VaR given as a vertical line and average loss (which here fortunately is negative) as a dashed line.

VaR is illustrated in Fig. 3.1, where we have drawn the density of a loss distribution. VaR is found such that the area under the density on the right-hand side is 5%. Note that because we have drawn a *loss* (rather than a profit) distribution, the mean will typically be ≤ 0.

Mean VaR. If we denote the mean of the loss distribution by μ, then it may be reasonable in some cases to consider the statistic $\mathrm{VaR}_\alpha^{mean} = \mathrm{VaR}_\alpha - \mu$ instead of ordinary VaR; this measure is often termed *earnings at risk*. Whether it makes sense to correct for the mean loss depends on the type of risk investigated; in considerations of market risk it is less relevant because μ is close to 0 when the relevant time horizon (usually a day) is taken into account. However, for credit risk it may be more relevant, and indeed it is used in connection with the determination of *economic capital* needed as a buffer against unexpected losses in a loan portfolio.

Expected tail loss. For this measure, we first define the *quantile function* associated with the probability distribution F as the map q_F, which to each α assigns the α-quantile of F,

$$q_F(\alpha) = \inf\{x \in \mathbb{R} \mid F(x) \geq \alpha\}$$

(for strictly increasing probability distributions, $q_F(\alpha)$ is just the inverse of F), and then we define the *expected tail loss*, ETL, at confidence level α as

$$\mathrm{ETL}_\alpha = \frac{1}{1-\alpha} \int_\alpha^1 q_{F_L}(u) f_L(u)\, du,$$

where f_L is the density function of the loss distribution. Using the formula for VaR, which, as we saw, is just a quantile, we see that

$$\mathrm{ETL}_\alpha = \frac{1}{1-\alpha} \int_\alpha^1 \mathrm{VaR}_u f_L(u)\, du.$$

It may be shown that what is computed is (at least for well-behaved loss distributions) the conditional expectation of the losses given that they are above the α-quantile; intuitively, ETL_α will be large if the probability density goes very slowly to 0 when it has passed the α-quantile, so this measure gives more detailed information than does VaR_α.

3.3 Interest rate risk

3.3.1 The term structure of interest rates

As a first example of the approach outlined in the previous sections, we consider the assessment of risk on a portfolio of *bonds*. We shall assume for the time being that the bonds are default-free, meaning that the risk associated with a portfolio of bonds can arise only from changes in the market rates of interest, so we have a case of pure interest rate risk.

The simplest bond is a zero-coupon bond, which gives a payoff 1 at date T, which is called the maturity of the bond. At any date $t > T$, this bond is priced in the market at $p(t, T)$. From the price of the zero-coupon bond we can find its *yield to maturity* $y(t, T)$ as

$$p(t, T) = e^{-(T-t)y(t,T)},$$

EXAMPLE 3.3 **Expected tail loss for some well-known distributions.** If F_L is normal with mean μ and variance σ^2, then

$$\text{ETL}_\alpha = \mu + \sigma \text{E} \left[\frac{L - \mu}{\sigma} \, \middle| \, \frac{L - \mu}{\sigma} \geq q_\Phi(\alpha) \right],$$

where we have just turned to the standardized loss with distribution function Φ, and we get

$$\text{ETL}_\alpha = \frac{1}{1 - \alpha} \int_{\Phi^{-1}(\alpha)}^{\infty} l \phi(l) \, dl,$$

where ϕ is the density of the standardized normal distribution. Since

$$\phi(l) = \frac{1}{\sqrt{2\pi}} e^{-\frac{l^2}{2}},$$

we get that $\phi'(l) = -l\phi(l)$ for all l, and inserting this we get that

$$\text{ETL}_\alpha \left(\frac{L - \mu}{\sigma} \right) = \frac{1}{1 - \alpha} \left[-\phi(l) \right]_{\Phi^{-1}(\alpha)}^{\infty} = \frac{\phi \left(\Phi^{-1}(\alpha) \right)}{1 - \alpha}$$

for the standardized loss, so

$$\text{ETL}_\alpha = \mu + \sigma \frac{\phi \left(\Phi^{-1}(\alpha) \right)}{1 - \alpha}.$$

so $y(t, T)$ is the interest rate at which we would get the present value $p(t, T)$ of an amount 1 to be paid at date T. Then $p(T, T) = 1$. The map $T \mapsto y(t, T)$ (or rather, its graph) is known as the *yield curve* at time s (showing how interest rate and maturity are connected).

Consider a portfolio of d default-free (zero-coupon) bonds with maturity T_i and prices $p(t, T_i)$ (at time t given maturity T_i). We let λ_i denote the number of bonds with maturity T_i in the portfolio. Taking the yields $y(t, T)$ as risk factors, we may now write the model of profits and losses as

$$V_t = \sum_{i=1}^{d} \lambda_i p(t, T_i) = \sum_{i=1}^{d} \lambda_i e^{-(T_i - t) y(t, T_i)},$$

and the linearized version of the loss L_{t+1} is

$$L_{t+1} = - \sum_{i=1}^{d} \lambda_i p(t, T_i) \left(y(t, T_i) - (T_i - t) x_{t+1, i} \right),$$

where $x_{t+1, i} = y(t + 1, T_i) - y(t, T_i)$ is the risk factor change for type i.

3.3.2 Notional measures: Gap analysis

Starting with the simplest possible measures of interest rate risk, we are taken into the so-called *gap analysis*. In general, gaps arise when comparing relevant parts of the asset and the liability side of the balance; thus, if considering liquidity problems, it is natural to check the number of liquid assets and compare these to the amount of liabilities which may be demanded immediately. Similarly, for a first study of interest rate exposure, one would look at two types of gap:

- *fixed interest rate gap* (for a given period), found as the difference between fixed interest (in this period) assets and fixed interest liability, and

- *variable interest rate gap*, which is the difference between assets and liabilities with a flexible interest rate. The variable interest rate gap may be subdivided into gaps relating to particular variable interest rates such as 1 month LIBOR, 3 months LIBOR, etc.

The sum of the fixed and the variable interest rate gaps will be zero if assets are equal to liabilities, which is, of course, always the case ex post. But gap analysis is intended as a forward-looking tool, and in that case it may well be that assets exceed liabilities, giving rise to a *liquidity gap* (about which we shall have more to say in a later chapter). It is, however, convenient to assume here that the liquidity gap is zero, so we need only work with the variable interest rate gaps, the other one having just the opposite sign.

It goes without saying that the time horizon is important, because in the long run, all assets and liabilities have a variable interest rate. Therefore, interest rate gaps measure, though in a very crude way, the differences in time between the change of composition of the asset and the liability side.

Clearly, the variable interest margin gives a first impression of the exposure to interest rate changes. Letting the amount of variable interest rate assets be A^v and variable interest rate liabilities L^v, the changes $\triangle Y$ in the earnings from interest payments, the *interest margin*, arising from a change $\triangle i$ in the interest rate is

$$\triangle Y = (A^v - L^v)\triangle i, \tag{9}$$

where the quantity $A^v - L^v$ is identified as the variable interest rate gap.

The main advantage of the gap approach is its simplicity. The gap provides an intuitive description of the risk exposure, and it is also suggestive of the measures than can be taken to reduce it, either by changing the composition of assets and liabilities, or by suitable hedging activities. It has drawbacks, however. Among these, one usually mentions the following:

- The gap analysis neglects uncertainties pertaining to volume and maturity and measures only the static picture of the composition between fixed and variable rates.

- Gaps give no information about assets and liabilities which are either implicit options (in-balance) or other types of guarantees (off-balance).

- The gap measures tend to neglect the many different types of interest rate connected with the individual assets and liabilities.
- The gaps neglect the flows within the time limits set (the fixed rate assets and liabilities may balance from a one-month perspective, giving a zero gap, but the assets may expire a few days after the beginning of the month and the liabilities only at the end of the month, thus creating an imbalance for almost a month).

The deficiencies will, of course, have to be remedied by additional analyses, going beyond the gaps, and in any case, the gap analysis should be seen only as a very first step to obtain an overview of the situation. For a better measurement of the risk, one needs to carry out the calculation not for a deterministic interest rate change, but for a menu of alternative future interest rates, possibly following a prescribed probability distribution. We return to this in a later section.

3.3.3 Sensitivity measures: Duration and convexity

The background for introducing duration is the need for a simple measure of the riskiness of an interest bearing security, typically a bond, with respect to changes in interest levels. The time to maturity certainly matters: The longer it is, the more one will lose by keeping it if the market level of interest is rising. On the other hand, looking only at time to maturity means that the time profile of the cash flow is disregarded. Instead, the security should be seen as a portfolio of different bonds, each with its time to maturity, and then take the correspondingly weighted average of those maturities. This is exactly what is done by computing duration, but it may be more instructive to take a slightly different approach, as we do below.

Consider a market where the interest rate y is constant over time. The market value at time t_1 of a bond with maturity t_n is then

$$V = \sum_{t=t_1}^{t_n} Y_t (1+y)^{-t}$$

where Y_t is the payment at time t. Differentiating with respect to the rate of interest y (or equivalently with respect to the payoff $1 + y$), we get

$$\frac{\partial V}{\partial y} = - \sum_{t=t_1}^{t_n} t Y_t (1+y)^{-(t+1)}. \tag{10}$$

Using a linear Taylor approximation of V as a function of y we get

$$\Delta V \sim \frac{\partial V}{\partial y} \Delta y.$$

We now define the (Macaulay) duration D as the elasticity of V with respect to the payoff rate $1 + y$:

$$D = -\frac{\partial V}{\partial y} \frac{1+y}{V}.$$

Using (10), we get that

$$D = -\left[\sum_{t=t_1}^{t_n} tY_t(1+y)^{-(1+t)}\right]\frac{1+y}{V} = \frac{1}{V}\sum_{t=t_1}^{t_n} tY_t(1+y)^{-t} = \sum_{t=t_1}^{t_n} tw_t,$$

where

$$w_t = \frac{Y_t(1+y)^{-t}}{V}.$$

The duration gives a first expression of the sensitivity of present value to changes in the rate of interest. The higher duration, the more sensitive is the bond. Using the first-order (linear) Taylor approximation means that we consider the market value as a linear function of the interest rate, which for changes which are not very small will give rise to errors. This leads to consideration of better approximations, and the obvious first idea is to include the second-order term in the Taylor approximation.

The curvature of the function giving V as depending on y is expressed by its second derivative

$$\frac{\partial^2 V}{\partial y^2} = \sum_{t=t_1}^{t_n} t(t+1)Y_t(1+y)^{-(t+2)}$$

$$= V(1+y)^2 \sum_{t=t_1}^{t_n} \frac{(t^2+t)Y_t(1+y)^{-t}}{V} = V(1+y)^{-2}\sum_{t=t_1}^{t_n}(t^2+t)w_t$$

Now the (Macaulay) *convexity* is defined as

$$K = \sum_{t=t_1}^{t_n}(t^2+t)w_t,$$

and we get that

$$\frac{\partial^2 V}{\partial y^2} = \frac{VK}{(1+y)^2},$$

and the second-order Taylor approximation gives the change in value derived from a change in interest rates as

$$\Delta V = \frac{\partial V}{\partial y}\Delta y + \frac{1}{2}\frac{\partial^2 V}{\partial y^2}(\Delta y)^2 = -\frac{VD}{1+y}\Delta y + \frac{1}{2}\frac{VK}{(1+y)^2}(\Delta y)^2.$$

The convexity has a natural interpretation as the sensitivity of the duration with respect to changes in the interest rate. Both duration and convexity are rather simple concepts. Because they are defined on the basis of the interest rate of a given bond, and different bonds have different (effective) interest rates, it does not immediately make sense to compare durations of different bonds. This will work only in situations with flat yield curves and where changes in the interest rate take the form of parallel shifts of the yield curves, a somewhat unrealistic situation. On the other hand, these measures are simple and easy to work with, at least compared to what would have to be used otherwise.

Box 3.4

Duration in a continuous time model. Consider the *special case* where the yield curve is flat, and $y(s, T) = y(s)$ independently of T, so that movements in interest rate come as parallel shifts in the yield curve, $y(t + 1, T) = y_t + \delta$ for all T (this is a very unrealistic case but often used in practical computations). Then (6) may be rewritten as

$$L_{t+1} = -V_t \left(y_t - \sum_{i=1}^{d} \frac{\lambda_i p(t, T_i)}{V_i} (T_i - t)\delta \right) = -V_t(y_t - D\delta),$$

where

$$D = \sum_{i=1}^{d} \frac{\lambda_i p(t, T_i)}{V_i} (T_i - t),$$

the duration, is a weighted sum of times to maturity $T_i - t$ of the different cash flows in the portfolio, with weights proportional to the NPV (net present value) of the cash flows.

3.3.4 Duration matching

Consider an asset and liability management (ALM) institution which plans over a (long) horizon of T years. There are assets A_j with maturity t_j, $j = 1, \ldots, m$, and liabilities L_k with maturity t_k, $k = 1, \ldots, n$, respectively. Until maturity, the interest rates are r_j and r_k, and after renewal, they are i_j and i_k, respectively. We shall assume that the horizon has length 1, so the maturities t_j and t_k are numbers between 0 and 1 (this is convenient in the computation and can always be obtained by redefining units of time). We look first at the assets. At time 1, the value of the assets has increased to

$$V_A^1 = \sum_{j=1}^{m} A_j(1 + r_j)^{t_j}(1 + i_j)^{1-t_j}.$$

Assume now that the interest rate structure has a parallel lift of size λ. For small values of this shift, the effect on asset value at time 1 can be found as

$$\frac{\partial V_A^1}{\partial \lambda} = \sum_{j=1}^{m} A_j(1 + r_j)^{t_j}(1 - t_j)(1 + i_j)^{-t_j} = \sum_{j=1}^{m} \frac{A_j(1 + r_j)^{t_j}}{(1 + i_j)^{t_j}}(1 - t_j) = V_A(1 - D_A),$$

where V_A is the value of the assets at time 0, and D_A is the duration of the assets. Repeating the computation for the liabilities, we get that

$$\frac{\partial V_L^1}{\partial \lambda} = \sum_{k=1}^{n} L_k(1 + r_k)^{t_k}(1 - t_k)(1 + i_k)^{-t_k} = V_L(1 - D_L),$$

with V_L the value of the liabilities at time 0 and D_L their duration. It follows that the portfolio is immune against shifts in the interest rate structure if

$$V_A(1 - D_A) = V_L(1 - D_L),$$

which is the principle of *duration matching* known as a first principle when coping with interest rate risk.

The reservations against the concept of duration which were stated above are, of course, still in force, so duration matching as a tool must be considered as only a guideline rather than the basic principle in asset-liability management.

3.4 Coherent risk measures

In the previous section, we introduced risk measures, which were numbers designated to capture the essential features of riskiness, and some examples (in particular the widely used VaR) were considered. Here we take a closer look at the theoretical underpinnings of risk measures. The exposition is based on Artzner et al. [1999], which has initiated a lively field of research in risk measures, their properties and the implication of using them.

When discussing measures of risk, one is almost immediately led to a consideration of the very nature of risk, a concept which is less simple than it appears. In particular, it is not obvious that risk is necessarily related to probability theory; a vast literature on human decisions under uncertainty has shown that perceptions of risk and decisions involving uncertainty cannot easily be reduced to notions of probability, such as is done in the classical theory of expected utility (a theory which nevertheless remains useful as a first approach to understanding many phenomena). All this means that we need a more basic approach and that it should involve as few complicated notions as possible, at least at the outset.

3.4.1 Risks and acceptance sets of risks

We assume that the basic problem amounts to assessing different investment opportunities. Each such is called a *risk* and defined as a function from a given fixed set Ω of possible future states of the world to the real numbers. We shall assume here that Ω is a finite set with n elements, so a risk X can be considered as a vector with n components. We let G be the set of all risks; a measure of risk is then a map ρ from G to the real numbers, which to each risk $X \in G$ assigns its risk $\rho(X)$.

Before we discuss properties that a reasonable measure of risk should have, it is useful to introduce another notion. Because we want a measure which should be useful to decision makers in financial institutions, we may be more explicit on this. A decision maker or regulator would not consider just any risk (in the form of an investment chosen by some employee of the bank) as acceptable, because some of them are far too 'risky' (whatever that means), whereas other investments (risks) are very desirable. The simplest possible way of subsuming this information (about what the decision makers or regulators consider as acceptable) is by defining a subset $\mathcal{A}$ of $\mathcal{G}$ consisting of all such risks, called the *acceptance set*.

Clearly, an acceptance set must be a strict subset of $\mathcal{G}$ (excluding, for example, risks which result in losses for the bank, no matter which state will materialize). Below are some properties of acceptance sets which may be considered as reasonable:

AXIOM 1.   *The acceptance set $\mathcal{A}$ contains $\mathbb{R}_+^n$.*

Since in our interpretation of the formalism, a risk in $\mathbb{R}_+^n$ is one which pays something ≥ 0 in every state, this is a reasonable property, as no bank would object to investments which give a sure profit. In a similar vein, we can assume (as mentioned above) that investments with a sure loss are inacceptable:

AXIOM 2.   *The acceptance set $\mathcal{A}$ does not intersect $\mathbb{R}_{--}^n = \{X \in \mathcal{G} \mid X(\omega) < 0,\ all\ \omega \in \Omega\}$.*

The following axiom is perhaps less intuitive; it may be considered a reflection of some kind of risk aversion, saying that mixing two acceptable risks (by taking, for example, half of each) still gives a risk in the acceptance set.

AXIOM 3.   *The acceptance set $\mathcal{A}$ is convex.*

Finally, a fourth property has to do with scales of investment: If X belongs to the acceptance set, then so does the risk which is a portfolio of 2 X's – or 3, or 10, or a third of X; formally, any λX, for $\lambda > 0$, is in the acceptance set.

AXIOM 4.   *The acceptance set $\mathcal{A}$ is a cone (i.e. $[X \in \mathcal{A},\ \lambda \geq 0] \Rightarrow \lambda X \in \mathcal{A})$.*

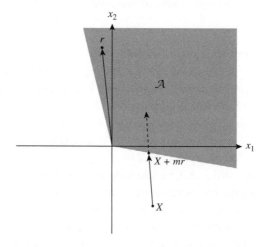

Figure 3.2   A coherent risk measure. Given the set $\mathcal{A}$ of acceptable risks and a designated risk r, the risk of an arbitrary portfolio X can be measured as the quantity of r that must be added to the portfolio in order to make it acceptable.

The axiom is perhaps less innocent than is apparent from a superficial look; in particular it rules out that the decision maker or regulator can have reservations which pertain to the size of the transactions taken on apart from the transactions themselves. In practice, regulators tend to be concerned about size of transactions, but such aspects of risk assessment are not part of our approach.

3.4.2 Acceptance sets and risk measures

Having defined acceptance sets as simple formalizations of standards of conduct for prudent bank managers, we may now measure risk as distance to the acceptance set; thus, acceptable risks have risk measure ≤ 0; risks that are far away from the acceptance set get a numerically large measure. However, we still have to find a way of defining the distance to the acceptable set.

An approach which fits well to the present context is the following: Let r be a fixed *reference investment* (such as gold or US government bonds); then the non-acceptability of a risk X may be expressed as the number of reference investments (number of bonds or gold bars) that we would need as a payment to take on the risk X, in the sense that the portfolio consisting of the risk together with the specified number of reference investments would be a risk in the acceptance set. We define therefore

$$\rho_{\mathcal{A},r}(X) = \inf\{m \mid mr + X \in \mathcal{A}\}.$$

Conversely, given a function ρ assigning numbers to any risk X, we can define an associated acceptance set

$$\mathcal{A}_\rho = \{X \mid \rho(X) \leq 0\}.$$

If $\rho = \rho_{\mathcal{A},r}$, where $\mathcal{A}$ satisfies the axioms 1 to 4 above, then ρ is well defined (in the sense that the set of numbers on which we take the infimum is never empty nor unbounded from below). Also, ρ inherits some properties, namely the following:

TRANSLATION INVARIANCE (T). *For all $X \in G$ and all $\alpha \in \mathbb{R}$, we have $\rho(X + \alpha r) = \rho(X) - \alpha$.*

This is a direct consequence of the definition, because

$$\inf\{m \mid mr + \alpha r + X \in \mathcal{A}\} = \inf\{m \mid mr + X \in \mathcal{A}\} - \alpha.$$

The property gives us that changing the portfolio by adding or removing reference investments changes the riskiness in the obvious way (because riskiness now is defined in terms of the compensating amount of the reference investment).

SUBADDITIVITY (S). *For all $X, Y \in G$, $\rho(X + Y) \leq \rho(X) + \rho(Y)$.*

The subadditivity property is once again a way of expressing risk aversion – the portfolio containing both X and Y has a risk which is no greater than the combined risks of X and Y (because in some cases losses in one of the investments may be offset by gains in another).

To see that it follows from the axioms on $\mathcal{A}$, we note that if $m_1 r + X \in \mathcal{A}$ and $m_2 r + Y \in \mathcal{A}$, then by Axioms 3 and 4 we get that $(m_1 + m_2)r + (X + Y) \in \mathcal{A}$ ($\mathcal{A}$ is a convex cone, so if $Z_1, Z_2 \in \mathcal{A}$, then so is $Z_1 + Z_2 = 2(\frac{1}{2}Z_1 + \frac{1}{2}Z_2)$), and property S is now an immediate consequence.

POSITIVE HOMOGENEITY (P). *For all $\lambda \geq 0$ and $X \in \mathcal{G}$, $\rho(\lambda X) = \lambda \rho(X)$.*

This property tells us that scaling up and down a given investment will give the same scaling up and down of the risk as measured by ρ. It follows easily from the definitions and Axiom 4 because by the latter $mr + X \in \mathcal{A}$ implies that $\lambda(mr + X) = (\lambda m)r + \lambda X \in \mathcal{A}$.

MONOTONICITY (M). *If $X, Y \in \mathcal{G}$ and $X \leq Y$, then $\rho(Y) \leq \rho(X)$.*

An investment which gives more (which for negative outcomes means that the losses are smaller) in any state is less risky. To show that this holds, we let $mr + X \in \mathcal{A}$ and show that also $mr + Y \in \mathcal{A}$; indeed, we have that $Y - X \geq 0$ and therefore belongs to $\mathcal{A}$ by Axiom 1, and therefore $mr + Y = (mr + X) + (Y - X) \in \mathcal{A}$ by Axioms 3 and 4.

At this point, one may wonder whether the axioms on acceptance sets have other implications for the resulting measure of risk. As a matter of fact, they have not, because we have the following result, the first part of which has been shown already, but the second part of which is a converse:

PROPOSITION 1: *Let $\mathcal{A}$ be an acceptance set satisfying Axioms 1–4. Then $\rho_{\mathcal{A},r}$ is a risk measure satisfying properties T, S, P and M. Conversely, if ρ satisfies T, S, P and M, then $\mathcal{A}_\rho$ satisfies Axioms 1–4.*

PROOF: As already mentioned, we need only prove the second part. So assume that ρ satisfies T, S, P and M, and let $\mathcal{A} = \mathcal{A}_\rho$. We have $\rho(0) = 0$ by P, and therefore $\rho(X) \leq 0$ for $X \geq 0$ by M, so $\mathcal{A}$ satisfies Axiom 1.

Assume next that $X \in \mathbb{R}^n_{--}$; if $\rho(X) < 0$, then we must have $\rho(0) \leq \rho(X) < 0$ by M, a contradiction. If $\rho(X) = 0$, then there is $\alpha > 0$ sufficiently small so that $X + \alpha r \in \mathbb{R}^n_{--}$, but then by T we have that $\rho(X + \alpha r) = \rho(X) - \alpha = -\alpha < 0$, and we would still have some $X' \in \mathbb{R}^n_{--}$ with $\rho(X') < 0$, a contradiction. We conclude that $\mathbb{R}^n_{--} \subset \{X \mid \rho(X) > 0\}$, which is Axiom 2.

Axiom 3 follows directly from S, and finally Axiom 4 is a consequence of P. □

In view of this result, it seems reasonable to concentrate attention on risk measures satisfying the four properties M, S, P and M. Such risk measures are called *coherent*.

3.4.3 Coherent and non-coherent risk measures: Examples

Although the approach so far has had no reference to any underlying probability distribution over states, most practical examples of risk measures are defined with reference to such a probability distribution. Suppose now that there is given such a probability distribution P (so that the probability of any event (subset of Ω) B is $P(B)$). Given the probability distribution (and, as previously, the reference instrument), we may define *Value at Risk* at level α as

$$\text{VaR}_\alpha(X) = -\inf\{y \mid P(\{\omega \mid X(\omega) \le yr\}) > \alpha\},$$

which, except for the change from losses l to gains y and the explicit reference to a reference instrument, is the same as that in (8).

The risk measure VaR_α satisfies T, P and M. However, it does not, in general, satisfy the subadditivity axiom. To see this, consider the following example: An individual may sell an obligation (A) to pay in the next period 1,000 if a given security attains an upper level U; the price at which this obligation may be sold today is u; similarly, it is possible to sell another obligation, where 1,000 has to be paid if the security gets below a certain level $L < U$, and the price of this is l.

If the reference investment is the simplest possible, namely that yielding 1 in all future states, then we may compute VaR using the formula. Assume that $\alpha = 1\%$ and that the probability that the security rises above U is $0,008$; then

$$\text{VaR}_\alpha(A) = -u$$

(the payoff of A is the price u which is paid for the obligation minus the 1,000 to be paid if the security gets above U, but this happens with probability less than 1%), which is negative, so A belongs to the acceptance set. Similarly, we find that

$$\text{VaR}_\alpha(B) = -l.$$

Consider now the portfolio $A + B$; here one gains the combined price $u + l$ unless the underlying security gets either above U or below L, and in this case the gain is $u+l-1000$. But the latter payoff occurs with probability $> 1\%$, and therefore

$$\text{VaR}_\alpha(A + B) = 1000 - (u + l) > \text{VaR}_\alpha(A) + \text{VaR}_\alpha(B),$$

contradicting subadditivity. We see also that the acceptance set is not convex, because the risk $\frac{1}{2}A + \frac{1}{2}B$ has positive VaR. This is, of course, no surprise given the connection between coherent risk measures and acceptance sets.

Although VaR fails to satisfy the subadditivity property and therefore is not a coherent measure of risk, it is by far the most widely used. On the other hand, rather small changes will improve the situation; it may be shown that the expected shortfall measure is coherent (for a given underlying probability measure).

We close this short discussion by returning to the general case where there is no given probability on the states of nature. In such a case we would expect scenario-based risk measures (mentioned in Section 3.2.1(4) above) to be the best approach. This is supported by the theory; it may be shown that there is a rather close connection between coherence and (generalized) scenario-basedness: If ρ is coherent w.r.t. r, then there is a family $\mathcal{P}$ of probability measures on Ω such that

$$\rho(X) = \sup \left\{ \mathbb{E}_{\mathbb{P}} \left[-\frac{X}{r} \right] \middle| \mathbb{P} \in \mathcal{P} \right\}.$$

3.5 Exercises

1. A bank has assets in the form of buildings and other real estate facilities. Design a model for the losses which can be ascribed to such fixed assets: Identify risk factors, describe the dependence of profits or losses on these risk factors and find the loss function.

2. Give examples of notional-amount risk measures for a bank dealing extensively with foreign exchange. Identify possible risk factors and consider the possibility of using factor sensitivity measures in the given case.

3. A small investor holds a portfolio consisting of €1,000,000 of stock A, €500,000 of stock B, and €1,500,000 of stock C. The rates of change in the stock values are independent and uniformly distributed in the interval $[-0.1, 0.1]$.

Find the loss distribution and determine VaR at the 0.99 level.

4. Gap analysis (from Bessis [2002]). Consider a bank with assets and liabilities as follows:

Fixed assets	10	Equity	20
Fixed interest rate assets	75	Fixed interest rate liabilities	30
Variable interest rate assets	35	Variable interest rate liability	40

Find the liquidity and the fixed interest rate gap. What will happen to the bank if the market rate of interest changes by 1%?

5. A small bank engaged in asset and liability management has used duration matching for some years and has been satisfied with the results. However, following the financial crisis and the fall in market interest rates, the bank has experienced rather big losses for which they were not prepared. Explain how this could happen, and suggest how the bank should arrange its interest risk management.

6. Suppose that an investor must choose between different risky projects, all characterized by their payoff in two future states s_1 and s_2. The investor finds that investments are satisfactory if a negative outcome in one of the states is compensated by at least 5 times as large a positive outcome in the other state. Among these satisfactory investments there is a particular one which pays 10 in state one but gives a loss of 1 in state 2.

Is the set of satisfactory investments an acceptance set (satisfying Axioms 1–4 of Section 3.4? Show that one may define a coherent risk measure ρ using the particular investment described above.

Find $\rho(X)$ for $X = (-4, 6)$, $X = (5, -5)$, $X = (2, -3)$.

7. Is the standard deviation a coherent measure of risk?

3.6 Comments

The general model of risk management, which may be considered as a common framework for computing risk measures and assessing risk of all the different types, was proposed in Embrechts et al. [2005]. The standard textbook for risk management is Jorion [2006]; see also Bessis [2002].

Value at Risk entered financial risk management in the 1980s, although some earlier attempts at finding a simple numerical measure of risk came close. The use of VaR has been criticized for many shortcomings, but it remains by far the most widely used measure.

The Macaulay duration was introduced by Frederick Macaulay in 1938. Contemporary asset and liability management has moved beyond sensitivity measures.

Coherence of risk measurement is a concept of considerable theoretical interest but has not yet found many practical applications. The coherence properties, in particular that of subadditivity, may also be less relevant in relation to capital requirements, cf. for example Dhaene et al. [2008].

Chapter 4

Market Risk and Value at Risk Analysis

4.1 Introduction: Prices of marketable securities

Market risk is the risk connected with marketable assets, whose prices in the market may change and thus create changes in the balance of the financial institution. In the context of markets where prices are volatile and where the number of transactions carried out is enormous, changes in market values may occur which can have very serious effects on the enterprise as a whole, even causing its insolvency. It is clear that keeping track of the value of the portfolio of marketable securities is very important and crucial for the survival of the institution.

In order to model the changes in the market value of a portfolio, one needs a theory of pricing of the securities involved. We shall have a brief look at the basic theoretical framework for the determination of prices of financial assets.

4.1.1 The capital asset pricing model

Consider a market where n securities are traded. These securities have random returns $\widetilde{r_i}$ with mean r_i and they are assumed to have covariance matrix $\Sigma = (\sigma_{ij})_{i=1}^{n} {}_{j=1}^{n}$. A portfolio is a vector $x = (x_1, \ldots, x_n)$, where x_i is the amount invested in security i (here x_i may be positive, negative or 0). If an investor with initial wealth W_0 chooses a portfolio $x = (x_1, \ldots, x_n)$, then wealth in the next period will be

$$\widetilde{W} = \left(W_0 - \sum_{i=1}^{n} x_i \right) r + \sum_{i=1}^{n} x_i \widetilde{r_i}$$

(where r is the risk-free rate of interest), with mean

$$\mu(x) = \mathsf{E}\widetilde{W} = \left(W_0 - \sum_{i=1}^{n} x_i \right) r + \sum_{i=1}^{n} x_i r_i = W_0 r + \sum_{i=1}^{n} x_i (r_i - r)$$

and variance

$$\sigma^2(x) = \text{Var} \widetilde{W} = x^t \Sigma x,$$

where $\cdot^t$ stands for 'transpose'.

We assume now that the investor's utility of portfolios depend only on mean and variance; this is quite restrictive as a general assumption, but it does hold if securities are (jointly) normally distributed or if the von Neumann-Morgenstern utility functions of investors are of a special type. In the following, we shall take the first approach, assuming normality of the distribution of securities.

Because only mean and variance matter for the utilities, we may restrict attention to portfolios maximizing a utility function of the type $U(\mu(x), \sigma^2(x))$, with first-order conditions

$$U'_\mu \frac{\partial \mu(x)}{\partial x_i} + U'_{\sigma^2} \frac{\partial \sigma^2(x)}{\partial x_i} = U'_\mu(r_i - r) + 2U'_{\sigma^2} \sum_{j=1}^{n} \sigma_{ij} x_j = 0$$

for $i = 1, \ldots, n$, or, in matrix notation,

$$-\gamma \rho^t + \Sigma x = 0,$$

where

$$\gamma = -\frac{U'_\mu}{2U'_{\sigma^2}}$$

can be identified as the marginal rate of substitution between mean and variance (the two aspects of the payoff which matter for the decision maker), and where $\rho = (r_1 - r, \ldots, r_n - r)$; and because Σ as a covariance matrix is symmetric and positive definite, it has an inverse Σ^{-1}, so we can write the optimal portfolio as

$$x^t = \gamma \Sigma^{-1} \rho.$$

The important property of this solution is that, except for the scalar γ, which depends on the utility function, the solution is independent of the particular investor, so all investors in the market choose portfolios which are proportional to each other and consequently also proportional to the *market portfolio*, which is defined as the total amount of each of the securities held by all investors. This is the property of *two-fund separation*: All portfolios can be conceived as a mixture of one particular (composite) security, namely the market portfolio, and the risk-free asset.

4.1.2 Option pricing

We take the simplest possible example of options, a European call option on a non-dividend-paying security R with maturity date T and exercise price K (that is, a right to buy the security at date T at price K. The value of this option is described by the *Black-Scholes option pricing formula* (which we are not going to derive here – we use it several times in other contexts)

$$V^{BS}(s, R, r, \sigma, K, T) = R\Phi(d_1) - Ke^{-r(T-s)}\Phi(d_2).$$

Here $\Phi(\cdot)$ is the distribution function of the standardized normal distribution, r is the risk-free rate of interest, σ the volatility of the underlying security (technically, it is assumed to follow a geometric Brownian motion with standard deviation σ) and where

$$d_1 = \frac{\ln\left(\frac{R}{K}\right) + \left(r + \frac{\sigma^2}{2}\right)(T - s)}{\sigma \sqrt{T - s}}, \quad d_2 = d_1 + \sigma \sqrt{T - s}.$$

It would seem natural to choose the price – or perhaps its logarithm – of the underlying security as a risk factor, but in practice one adds two more factors, namely r and σ, because they tend to vary quite a lot, whereas in the Black-Scholes model they are considered as given and fixed.

Let $\widetilde{z}_t = (\ln R_r, r_t, \sigma_t)$ be the vector of risk factors, with associated vector of risk factor changes

$$\widetilde{x}_{t+1} = (\widetilde{x}_{t,1}, \widetilde{x}_{t,2}, \widetilde{x}_{t,s}) = (\ln R_{t+1} - \ln R_t, r_{t+1} - r_t, \sigma_{t+1} - \sigma_t);$$

using the Black-Scholes formula to describe the dependence on risk factors, we get the linearized loss

$$L_{t+1}^{\Delta} = -\left(V_s^{BS}\Delta + V_R^{BS}R_t\widetilde{x}_{t+1,1} + V_r^{BS}\widetilde{x}_{t+1,2} + V_{\sigma}^{BS}\widetilde{x}_{t+1,3}\right).$$

The partial derivatives of the Black-Scholes pricing formula are known as *Greeks*, with V_R^{BS} being the *delta*, or price, risk; V_s^{BS} the *theta*, or time decay, risk; V_{ρ}^{BS} the *rho*, or discount rate, risk of the option; and V_{σ}^{BS} the *vega*, or volatility, risk of the option.

In practice, the linear Taylor approximation of the loss is not very well functioning, and one might consider involving also higher order terms, such as the second derivative V_{RR}^{BS}, called the *gamma* of the option.

4.2 Basic issues: Value at Risk analysis

4.2.1 The mapping approach

The assessment of market risk begins with the individual positions, but what is at risk is the portfolio as a whole. As already noticed in the discussion of risk measures, adding a risky asset to a portfolio may change the overall risk of the portfolio in many different ways, depending on its correlation with those already in the portfolio. Therefore, it is crucial that risk is measured for the portfolio as a whole.

However, the portfolio to be assessed will in most cases consist of a very large number of different assets (or *instruments* as they are called in the literature), and it may therefore be convenient to select a few, hopefully representative, instruments and concentrate on them. This is the *mapping* approach, whereby the actual instruments are approximated by 'core' instruments with a typical behaviour. The choice of core instruments may be as follows:

(1) *equity* positions are represented by equivalent amounts following equity indices,

(2) *fixed income* positions are represented by combinations of cash flows of a limited number of specified maturities,

(3) *foreign exchange* positions are represented by relevant amounts in core currencies, and

(4) *commodity* positions are represented by selected standardized futures contracts traded in organized exchanges.

In this way, the portfolio will be reduced to another and much simpler one, which will behave in more or less the same way if the mapping has been chosen in the proper way. The disadvantage of approximation will in most cases be offset by the gain in tractability.

For the four main types of instruments, one may find VaR rather easily:

(1) To assess the risk of an equity, say of firm A, to the amount x_A, we assume that the return to equity r_A can be written as

$$\widetilde{r}_A = \alpha_A + \beta_A \widetilde{R}_m + \widetilde{\varepsilon}_A,$$

where α_A and β_A are firm-specific constants, R_m is the market return, and $\widetilde{\varepsilon}_A$ is a firm-specific random disturbance, independent of the other variables. The variance of the return is then

$$\sigma_A^2 = \beta_A^2 \sigma_m^2 + \sigma_{\varepsilon_A}^2,$$

where $\sigma_A^2, \sigma_m^2, \sigma_{\varepsilon_A}^2$ have the obvious meaning, showing that the variance has a market component as well as a firm-specific one. Assuming now that $\widetilde{r}_A$ is normally distributed with zero mean, we get that

$$\text{VaR}_A = -\alpha_{cl}\sigma_A x_A = -\alpha_{cl}x_A \sqrt{\beta_A^2 \sigma_m^2 + \sigma_{\varepsilon_A}^2},$$

with α_{cl} the confidence level chosen. Here β_A and σ_m^2 should be publicly available, and if data is available for $\sigma_{\varepsilon_A}^2$, VaR_A can be computed. If not, one may reason that with a well-diversified portfolio, the firm-specific risks will net out, so it can be set equal to 0, and we have

$$\text{VaR}_A = -\alpha_{cl}\sigma_A x_A = -\alpha_{cl}\beta_A \sigma_m x_A,$$

meaning that we map the equity risk to the market index using only the market volatility and the firm's beta.

For a portfolio of several assets, the same procedure can be followed. If the portfolio consists of equities of firms A and B, we get

$$\text{VaR}_{AB} = -(\alpha_{cl}\beta_A \sigma_m x_A + \alpha_{cl}\beta_B \sigma_m x_B).$$

Notice that there is no covariance term because the only risk factor present is that of the market portfolio. This makes the treatment of equity portfolios very straightforward.

(2) The simplest fixed income security is a zero-coupon bond, which here is assumed to have no default risk. However, there are many different zero-coupon bonds, depending on their maturity, and no data may be available on the particular bond considered, meaning

that such bond should be mapped to others using reference instruments for which data is available. The approach can be illustrated in a case where the reference instruments have maturity $t_1 < t_2$, and we consider a bond with maturity t, $t_1 < t < t_2$. Writing the cash flow of the combination as

$$I_t = \lambda I_{t_1} + (1 - \lambda)I_{t_2},$$

the problem reduces to finding values of λ for which I_t approximates the given instrument. We have

$$\sigma_t^2 = \lambda^2 \sigma_{t_1}^2 + (1 - \lambda)^2 \sigma_{t_2}^2 + 2\lambda(1 - \lambda)\rho_{t_1 t_2}\sigma_{t_1}\sigma_{t_2}$$

with $\rho_{t_1 t_2}$ the correlation coefficient of the two reference instruments. If all the other terms are known, this determines λ, but the original problem was that we did not know σ_t^2. One suggestion would be to use $\hat{\lambda}$ defined by

$$t = \hat{\lambda}t_1 + \left(1 - \hat{\lambda}\right)t_2,$$

that is using the maturities to determine the linear average. Solving for $\hat{\lambda}$ we can then find the VaR of the artificial bond from the maturity and volatility data of this bond.

(3) A basic foreign exchange (FX) position consists in holding non-interest-bearing foreign currency. If the current value of the exchange rate is e and its standard deviation σ_e, and assuming that e is normally distributed with mean 0 and standard deviation σ_e, we get

$$\text{VaR}^{FX} = -\alpha_{cl}\sigma_e ex.$$

(4) A basic forward or futures position (a forward contract is an agreement to buy at a specified future date and price, and a futures contract is a standardized forward contract traded in an organized exchange, but in the present context the difference is unimportant) gives a return which depends on the futures price. Given that we have x contracts worth F each, the VaR would be

$$\text{VaR} = -\alpha_{cl}\sigma_F xF,$$

again assuming normality with mean 0 and disregarding some minor details of the contract (such as collateral). However, this leaves us with the problem of mapping F itself, that is, finding some reference instruments which can be used in the assessment of its variance. In practice, one would use the same method as for bonds, so the futures position is mapped to linear combinations of reference assets, futures with selected maturities, for which data is available, in the same way as it was done for bonds.

Once the mapping has been defined on the basic instruments, one may proceed to more complex positions, writing the latter as linear combinations of the basic positions. Here are some examples:

- *Coupon-paying bonds* can be considered as a portfolio of zero-coupon bonds with different maturities.

- *Floating-rate instruments* are repriced with every coupon payment, so they can be treated as zero-coupon bonds whose maturity is equal to the period until the next coupon payment, and this bond can be mapped as any other zero-coupon bond.

- *Interest-rate swaps* are equivalent to portfolios which are long in a fixed-coupon bond and short in a floating-rate bond (or vice versa), and VaR can easily be found on such portfolios.

- *Commodity, equity and foreign exchange swaps* can also be split into several futures contracts.

Thus, more complex positions can be written as suitable linear combinations of a few basic instruments, something which considerably facilitates the task of assessing the riskiness of the portfolio. There are, however, limitations to this approach: The instruments considered are such where the loss is linear in the underlying risk factors, and even though approximation necessarily must be imprecise, the errors are not such as to cause problems. That may change if we consider options, or rather if options constitute a large part of the portfolio; here the lack of linearity may give rise to large errors when mapping to linear combinations of a few building blocks. It is usually recommended to reconsider the weights as often as possible in such cases.

4.3 Finding VaR and ETL

4.3.1 Non-parametric VaR and ETL

Consider a portfolio with amounts w_i invested in securities $i = 1, \ldots, m$, where the returns of the securities are $R_{i,t}$ at time t, so the total profit (or loss) at t is

$$\Pi_t = \sum_{i=1}^{n} w_i R_{it},$$

and we want to find VaR (or ETL). There are several ways to proceed, depending on the situation (type of asset, availability of data). We begin with the conceptually simplest:

Historical simulation. Here one makes use of the records of profits over the last n periods. The profit/loss data can be organized in a histogram showing the relative frequency of profit/loss in given chosen intervals. The resulting frequency distribution may then be used directly as an approximation of the loss distribution, and VaR at any confidence level (say 95%) may be read off the histogram as the loss size for which 95% of the cases display smaller loss. Also ETL may be computed (provided that the histogram allows this) using the simple approach mentioned in Section 4.1.

Weighted historical simulation. In the simple historical simulation, the observations of returns at any point of time will matter for the calculations (through the construction of the histogram) over the following n periods, and then it will disappear altogether. This may give rise to problems, for example if the period n is short so that it cannot cover possible seasonal variations.

Instead of the simple approach, where each observation, no matter how old, has the same weight in calculating VaR, up to the age of n periods, after which they disappear altogether, one might consider an age-weighted approach, using weights λ^t for observations dating t periods back. Other systems of weight are conceivable, such as using new information on volatility to update weights on all past observations.

4.3.2 Parametric VaR and ETL

Rather than working with historical data directly, one might want to fit data to a theoretical distribution of profits and losses. This has the obvious advantage of producing simple expressions for VaR and ETL, at least for families of distributions which are sufficiently well behaved.

The simplest case is that of a **normal distribution** with mean μ_A and variance σ_A^2, for which we find

$$\text{VaR}\left(\widetilde{A}\right) = -\alpha_{cl}\sigma_A - \mu_A$$

and

$$\text{ETL}\left(\widetilde{A}\right) = \sigma_A \frac{\phi\left(-\alpha_{cl}\right)}{\Phi\left(\alpha_{cl}\right)} - \mu_A,$$

where α_{cl} is the normal fractile corresponding to the confidence level, and ϕ (Φ) is the normal density (distribution) function. As in most cases mean and variance are not known, one will have to use their estimates, yielding estimated values of VaR and ETL.

We can extend this to a formula for arbitrary holding periods. The loss from the distribution over a period consisting of T unit intervals of time is the sum of T normal variables with mean μ_A and variance σ_A^2, which again is normal with mean $T\mu_A$ and variance $T\sigma_A^2$, so the risk measures over this holding period become

$$\text{VaR}\left(\widetilde{A};T\right) = -\alpha_{cl}\sqrt{T}\sigma_A - T\mu_A$$

and

$$\text{ETL}\left(\widetilde{A};T\right) = \sqrt{T}\sigma_A \frac{\phi\left(-\alpha_{cl}\right)}{\Phi\left(\alpha_{cl}\right)} - T\mu_A.$$

The formula shows that the effect of the holding period is ambiguous, and because the first term depends on the square root of T, which grows slower than T itself, both VaR and ETL will eventually become negative.

Although the assumption of a normal profit-loss distribution gives a simple and useful formula, it may be less attractive from the point of view of realism. Experience shows that profit and loss has another distribution, not as symmetrical as the normal distribution, and with more probability weight given to outcomes far away from the mean; this phenomenon will show up when one looks at the fourth moment of the distribution, which then is bigger than that of the normal distribution ('fat tails'). If we want to use the parametric approach, we must look for other suitable distributions.

If the problem is fat tails, then it might be appropriate to use **t-distributions** with v degrees of freedom, where v is not too big (the t-distribution tends to the normal distribution when v goes to infinity), because the kurtosis of a t-distribution is $3(v-2)/(v-4)$. For practical reasons, one works with a generalized distribution, which involves location and scale besides the one parameter v of the t-distribution, because this allows for fitting the distribution to the observed means and standard deviations. Thus, the generalized t-distributed variable has the form

$$\widetilde{A} = a + b\widetilde{A}_v,$$

where $\widetilde{A}_v$ is t-distributed with v degrees of freedom. Then $\widetilde{A}$ has mean a, variance $b^2 v/(v-2)$, skewness 0 (the t-distribution is symmetric) and kurtosis $3(v-2)/(v-4)$. One may now find the Value at Risk (VaR) over holding period T as

$$\text{VaR}\left(\widetilde{A}; T\right) = -\alpha_{cl,v} \sqrt{T\frac{v-2}{v}}\sigma_A - T\mu_A.$$

If skewness matters, then a possible choice would be the **lognormal distribution** (assuming that logarithmic losses or gains are normally distributed), in which case the value of risk becomes

$$\text{VaR}\left(\widetilde{A}; T\right) = P_{t-1} - e^{T\mu_A + \alpha_{cl}\sqrt{T}\sigma_A + \ln P_{t-1}},$$

where P_{t-1} is the initial value of the portfolio. Alternatively, one may use distributions which are explicitly derived from considerations of very big losses (the so-called extreme value theory). One example of this approach is the following, known as *peaks over threshold*: Assume that $\widetilde{X}$ is a random loss with distribution function $F(x)$ and that there is a given threshold u, after which losses are considered as serious. We can find the distribution of the excesses over u as

$$F_i(y) = \text{P}\left\{\widetilde{X} - u \geq y \mid \widetilde{X} \geq u\right\},$$

that is the conditional probability that $X - u$ is at least y, given that the loss exceeds u. When u gets large, this distribution converges to a **generalized Pareto distribution**

$$G_{\xi,\beta}(y) = \begin{cases} 1 - \left(1 + \xi\frac{x}{\beta}\right)^{-\frac{1}{\xi}} & \xi \neq 0, \\ 1 - e^{-\frac{x}{\beta}} & \xi = 0. \end{cases}$$

Here $\beta > 0$ is a scale parameter, and ξ is a parameter determining the tail of the distribution, typically assumed > 0 corresponding to fat tails. The value at risk (which, of course, is above the large threshold u) can be found as

$$\text{VaR}\left(\widetilde{X}\right) = u + \frac{\beta}{\xi}\left(\left[\frac{n}{N_u}(1 - cl)\right]^{-\xi} - 1\right),$$

where n is sample size and N_u the number of values exceeding u. The expected tail loss is found as

$$\text{ETL}\left(\widetilde{X}\right) = \frac{\text{VaR}\left(\widetilde{X}\right) + \beta - \xi u}{1 - \xi}.$$

4.3.3 Multivariate distributions

Since portfolios usually consist of many different positions, the overall portfolio profits or losses should be derived from those of the components. For this, we need to know something about the correlations of the individual losses.

The simplest case is that of a **multivariate normal distribution** with known mean μ (considered as an $(n \times 1)$-matrix) and covariance matrix Σ (which is an $(n \times n)$-matrix). The portfolio is given by the vector $\mathbf{w} = (w_1, \ldots, w_n)$ of *portfolio shares* (with $w_i \in [0, 1]$, $\sum_{i=1}^{n} w_i = 1$). The portfolio has expected value $\mathbf{w}\mu$ and variance $\mathbf{w}\Sigma\mathbf{w}$, and if the initial value of the portfolio is A_0, then we get

$$\text{VaR}\left(\widetilde{A}, T\right) = -\left(\alpha_{cl} \sqrt{T \mathbf{w}\Sigma\mathbf{w}^t} + T\mathbf{w}\mu\right) A_0$$

(where, as before, we use the notation $\cdot^t$ for transposition of matrices).

If the portfolio is *not* multivariate normal, one may apply methods for transforming the variables, at least approximately to others that are normal, so the straightforward approach used in the case of normal distributions may still be used. However, an alternative approach consists in using **copulas**: If the means of the individual positions in the portfolio are known, together with their marginal distributions, then one may choose a simultaneous distribution having these marginals and reflecting the known structure of correlations, by selecting a suitable copula. The approach is outlined in Section 4.7 below.

4.3.4 Approximations: The delta-gamma approach

As was seen above, the parametric approach is convenient in situations where positions are linear in risk factors. Unfortunately, this is not always the case. Non-linearity occurs if the portfolio contains options, but also in connection with fixed-income instruments, for example if the relationship between the price and the yield of a bond is non-linear. In such cases, the obvious way out is to look for linear approximations and then treat the approximated positions as if they were linear in risk factors. This is known as the *delta-normal* approach.

Consider the case of an option having value $\widetilde{V}$. As we know, this value depends on a number of factors (price of underlying stock, its volatility, the exercise price), but using the delta-normal approach one would disregard all except one of these factors and consider the linear approximation

$$\triangle\widetilde{V} \approx \delta\triangle R,$$

where δ is the option's delta (as introduced in Section 4.2 above) and R the equity value. If we deal with a short period of time where δ may be assumed constant, then

$$\mathrm{VaR}\left(\widetilde{V}\right) \approx \delta \mathrm{VaR}\left(\widetilde{R}\right),$$

so VaR of the option can be found once we know VaR of the underlying equity. If $\widetilde{R}$ is normally distributed, then we get that

$$\mathrm{VaR}\left(\widetilde{V}\right) \approx -\delta \alpha \sigma R,$$

where R is the current value, and σ is the volatility of $\widetilde{R}$. Clearly, this approach is attractive for its simplicity; there is no need for the introduction of new risk factors, and the volatility of the underlying stock is usually available for any traded option.

A particular case where this approach may be useful is when dealing with instruments having *embedded options*. Such embedded options arise if bond issuers have a repurchase option, that is, the possibility of buying them back before maturity at a specified price, or if the bonds are convertible so that they can be exchanged for equity at prespecified terms. Handling such instruments becomes easy when using the delta-normal approach; for a callable bond the price is

$$\widetilde{P}_B^{\,callable} = \widetilde{P}_B - \widetilde{C},$$

where $\widetilde{P}_B$ is the value of the bond without embedded options, and $\widetilde{C}$ is the option value. Assuming normality, one may proceed as above from here.

Although this linear approximation may be satisfactory in some cases, particularly when the holding period is short, it may be less so if the non-linearity of the position in the risk factors is considerable. One possibility is to improve the quality of the approximation by adding a quadratic term,

$$\Delta \widetilde{C} \approx \delta \Delta \widetilde{R} + \frac{\gamma}{2}\left(\Delta \widetilde{R}\right)^2,$$

where γ is the gamma of the option (see Section 4.2.1). This expression is known as the *delta-gamma approximation*. However, proceeding from this expression is less straightforward than it was before, due to the quadratic term.

As a first approach, one might regard the term $(\Delta \widetilde{R})^2$ as another normal variable, independent of $\Delta \widetilde{R}$. We then have a portfolio $\widetilde{\Pi}$ which is linear in two risk factors; its variance is

$$\sigma_{\widetilde{\Pi}}^2 = \delta^2 \sigma^2 + \frac{1}{4}\gamma^2 \sigma^4,$$

so VaR becomes

$$\mathrm{VaR}\left(\widetilde{C}\right) = -\alpha \sigma \widetilde{R} \sqrt{\sigma^2 + \frac{1}{4}\gamma^2 \sigma^2}.$$

This approach retains the simplicity of the delta-normal approximation but suffers from internal errors because the square of a normally distributed variable is χ^2 and *not* normal – and it definitely cannot be independent of the variable itself.

An alternative approach [Wilson, 1994] uses the ideas behind VaR: VaR is the maximal loss within a given level of probability, so an option with value $\widetilde{C}$ can be considered as the solution to the maximization problem

$$\max_{(\triangle \widetilde{R})} (-\triangle C)$$

under the constraint

$$\frac{(\triangle R)^2 \sigma_R}{\sigma^2} \leq \alpha^2.$$

Now using the delta-gamma approximation $\triangle C = \delta \triangle R + (\gamma/2)(\triangle R)^2$, we have that the maximum loss in the problem should occur for

$$0 \leq (\triangle R)^2 \leq \alpha^2 \sigma^2.$$

But in this case the maximum is attained at one of the endpoints of the feasible interval for $\triangle R$, that is, either at $\triangle R = \alpha \sigma$ or $\triangle R = -\alpha \sigma$, and we have that

$$\text{VaR}\left(\widetilde{C}\right) = \max\left\{\delta \alpha \sigma + \frac{\gamma}{4}\alpha^2 \sigma^2, -\delta \alpha \sigma + \frac{\gamma}{4}\alpha^2 \sigma^2\right\}.$$

In the more general case of a portfolio with more than one instrument, the same approach can be used, but the solution is now less straightforward, so one has to solve the maximization problem to find VaR. Even so, the approach remains a reasonably simple one. Unfortunately, it has not quite solved the inherent problem, because solving the maximization problem does *not* give the exact VaR: The constraint is formulated in the underlying stock but should have been defined in the value of the option. Thus, we have added another source of imprecision apart from the original delta-gamma approximation.

4.4 Stress testing and model risk

As many of the methods described above have involved approximations, with the associated implicit hypothesis that the differences between the variables modelled and those used as simplifying proxies are small, there is a need for occasional testing of the models on larger deviations. Such stress tests are particularly useful for detecting possible changes in the usual correlation assumptions and for the identification of sudden liquidity needs, and also they may be used to check the vulnerability to macroeconomic changes such as the financial crisis of 2008.

In a stress test, one computes the effects on the portfolio of a particular event, and as such it complements the analysis outlined in the previous sections, which is directed towards computation of VaR and as such reflects the most likely outcomes.

There are two main types of stress tests, namely *scenario analysis*, which aims at assessing the impact of some specific scenario on the portfolio, and *mechanical stress tests*, where a possibly large number of specified changes in the risk factors are analysed in order to find the most serious one for the value of the portfolio.

The need for stress testing points to the imperfectness of the models applied. Because the portfolios in financial institutions are getting still more complex, their modelling will be subject to an increasing number of potential misspecifications and omissions, so one may speak of a specific *model risk* giving rise to losses of its own. This risk is, however, difficult to quantify, and the best way of handling this risk is following some standard guidelines for risk managers, such as checking key assumptions, testing models on known problems, being aware that even small problems may grow into large ones and re-evaluating the models periodically.

4.5 Capital regulation for market risk

In the present section, we take a closer look at capital regulation (of the type prescribed in Basel II) for the case of a bank which is engaged solely in holding securities (in short or long positions). This restriction, which means that we disregard other banking activities, and more specifically other types of risk, allows us to use the standard model for portfolio analysis, the CAPM (capital asset pricing model). The analysis of market risk, and in particular the role of capital regulation, in the context of CAPM was initiated by Koehn and Santomero (1980) and Kim and Santomero (1988).

We use the version of the CAPM introduced in Section 4.1. We now assume that the particular investor considered is a bank whose sole business is holding portfolios of securities or, alternatively, the department of the bank specialized in this line of business. The bank has an initial capital K and chooses a portfolio x; in the next period, the capital has changed to

$$\widetilde{A} = K + \sum_{i=1}^{n} x_i \widetilde{r}_i.$$

For simplicity, we assume that the risk-free rate of interest is 0.

Whereas in the general formulation of the CAPM, portfolios may contain both long and short positions, we shall asssume here that $x_i \geq 0$ for all i. In the interpretation, this means that the bank has obtained the funding of the portfolio from sources which are not part of the model (such as deposits from the public). The random payoffs of the portfolio may lead to an increase or a decrease in its value. In the latter case, the result will be that some of the initial capital will be used for paying back the original funding of the portfolio. In our model as it stands, it may even be the case that more than K will be needed, which would mean that the bank has full responsibility for debts contracted, a somewhat unrealistic feature to which we return later.

If the bank maximizes a utility $U(\mu, \sigma^2)$ depending only on mean and variance of the portfolio, then we get, as previously, that the optimal portfolio has the form

$$x^* = \gamma \Sigma^{-1} \rho,$$

with

$$\gamma = -\frac{U'_\mu}{2U'_{\sigma^2}}.$$

We are now particularly interested in the event that losses on the portfolio are so big that A becomes negative. We have that

$$P\{A < 0\} = P\left\{\frac{A - \mu(x^*)}{\sigma(x^*)} < -\frac{\mu(x)}{\sigma(x)}\right\} = \Phi\left(-\frac{\mu(x)}{\sigma(x)}\right),$$

where $\Phi(\cdot)$ is the normal probability distribution function. Inserting $\mu(x) = K + x^t\rho$ and $\sigma(x) = \sqrt{x^t\Sigma x}$, we have therefore that

$$P\{A < 0\} = \Phi\left(-\frac{K + x^t\rho}{\sqrt{x^t\Sigma x}}\right).$$

We want to relate this probability to the solvency ratios used in regulation. In the standard approach to capital requirements, the *weighted assets* of the bank are computed, in accordance with a given system of weights, where less risky types of assets are given smaller weights than more risky ones. The quantity thus computed is then compared to the equity capital of the bank. In the present set-up, the capital ratio can be defined as

$$\kappa(x) = \frac{K}{\sum_{i=1}^n \alpha_i x_i},$$

where $\alpha = (\alpha_1, \ldots, \alpha_n)$ is the given weight vector.

To see that capital ratios are relevant, we show that the probability of ruin, $P\{A < 0\}$, is a decreasing function of κ. Indeed, if we normalize the portfolio by defining $\hat{x} = \frac{1}{\sigma(x)}x$, then we can write

$$P\{A < 0\} = \Phi\left(-\frac{K}{\sigma(x)} - \hat{x}^t\rho\right) = \Phi\left(-(\alpha^t\hat{x})\kappa(x) - \hat{x}^t\rho\right), \tag{1}$$

where we have used that

$$\kappa(x) = \frac{K}{(\alpha^t\hat{x})\sigma(x)}.$$

It is seen that the last expression in (1) is indeed a decreasing function of κ.

On the other hand, introducing capital requirements in the form of lower bounds on $\kappa(x)$ may have consequences for the workings of the market. If the bank has to choose x so as to maximize

$$U\big(\mu(x), \sigma^2(x)\big)$$

subject to the constraint

$$\kappa(x) \geq \bar{\kappa},$$

or, equivalently,

$$\alpha^t x\bar{\kappa} \leq K,$$

then first-order conditions for a maximum (where we assume that the constraint is binding) will be

$$U'_\mu \rho_i + 2U'_{\sigma^2} \sum_{j=1}^{n} \sigma_{ij} x_j - \lambda \alpha_i, \; i = 1, \ldots, n,$$

with solution

$$x^0 = \Sigma^{-1} \left(\gamma \rho + \hat{\lambda} \alpha \right), \tag{2}$$

where

$$\gamma = -\frac{U'_\mu}{2U'_{\sigma^2}}, \; \hat{\lambda} = \frac{\lambda}{2U'_{\sigma^2}}.$$

It is seen that the optimal portfolio is now a weighted sum of two vectors, with weights depending on the individual characteristics. As a consequence, the optimal portfolios of different market agents may differ, and moreover, the allocation in the market will no longer be efficient.

There is, of course, a possible remedy, namely that of making the weight vector α proportional to the vector ρ, $\alpha = k\rho$ for some $k > 0$, because in this case the expression (2) reduces to

$$x^0 = \Sigma^{-1} \left(\gamma + \hat{\lambda} k \right) \rho,$$

and proportionality of optimal portfolios has been restored. However, for practical regulation it seems unlikely that the weights to be used in the computation of solvency ratios can be prescribed in a sufficiently flexible way so as to follow the variations in expected payoff of the securities concerned.

4.6 Mathematical appendix

4.6.1 The Black-Scholes formula

Below is a brief derivation of the Black-Scholes formula, following the line of reasoning in the original paper by Black and Scholes [1973]; see also Hull [1997]. It is assumed that the price of the underlying asset S follows a geometric Brownian motion,

$$\frac{dS}{S} = \mu \, dt + \sigma \, dW, \tag{1}$$

where W is Brownian motion (so W_t has mean 0 and variance t).

The value V of the option depends on S, so $V_t = V(S, t)$. By Itô's lemma, we get

$$dV = \left(\mu \frac{\partial V}{\partial S} + \frac{\partial V}{\partial t} + \frac{1}{2} \sigma^2 S^2 \frac{\partial^2 V}{\partial S^2} \right) dt + \sigma S \frac{\partial V}{\partial S} dW. \tag{2}$$

Now we construct a portfolio (the composition of which will vary over time), which is short in 1 option and long in $\frac{\partial V}{\partial S}$ units of the asset at time t. The value Π of this portfolio is

$$\Pi = -V + \frac{\partial V}{\partial S} S,$$

and the change in value over a small (infinitesimal) interval dt is

$$d\Pi = -dV + \frac{\partial V}{\partial S}dS.$$

Inserting the expressions (1) and (2), we get

$$d\Pi = \left(-\frac{\partial V}{\partial t} - \frac{1}{2}\sigma^2 S^2 \frac{\partial^2 V}{\partial S^2}\right)dt.$$

Now the term involving dW has disappeared from the expression, so there is no uncertainty involved; in other words, the portfolio is a risk-free investment, and as such it must earn the risk-free rate of interest (here we have used that there are no arbitrage possibilities in the market). It follows that

$$d\Pi = r\Pi\,dt,$$

and inserting, we get that

$$d\Pi = r\left(-V + S\frac{\partial V}{\partial S}\right)dt = \left(-\frac{\partial V}{\partial t} - \frac{1}{2}\sigma^2 S^2 \frac{\partial^2 V}{\partial S^2}\right)dt,$$

which can be reduced to the partial differential equation

$$\frac{\partial V}{\partial t} + \frac{1}{2}\sigma^2 S^2 \frac{\partial^2 V}{\partial S^2} + rS\frac{\partial V}{\partial S} = 0. \tag{3}$$

To proceed from the differential equation, we must specify the type of option, so we assume that it is a call option, which then satisfies the boundary conditions

$$V(0,t) = 0, \text{ all } t, V(S,t) \to S \text{ for } S \to \infty, V(S,T) = \max\{S - K, 0\}.$$

Define the new variables

$$\tau = T - t, \ u = Ve^{r\tau}, \ x = \ln\left(\frac{S}{K}\right) + \left(r - \frac{\sigma^2}{2}\right)\tau.$$

Then equation (3) takes the form

$$\frac{\partial u}{\partial \tau} = \frac{1}{2}\sigma^2 \frac{\partial^2 u}{\partial x^2},$$

with the initial condition

$$u(x,0) = u_0(x) = K\left(e^{\max\{0,1\}} - 1\right).$$

The standard solution for an equation of this type is

$$u(x,\tau) = \frac{1}{\sigma\sqrt{2\pi\tau}} \int_{-\infty}^{\infty} u_0(y)e^{-\frac{(x-y)^2}{2\sigma^2\tau}}\,dy.$$

Rewriting this equation, one finally gets the expression

$$u(x, \tau) = Ke^{x+\frac{1}{2}\sigma^2\tau}N(d_1) - KN(d_2),$$

where

$$d_1 = \frac{\left(x + \frac{1}{2}\sigma^2\tau\right) + \frac{1}{2}\sigma^2\tau}{\sigma\sqrt{\tau}}, \quad d_2 = \frac{\left(x + \frac{1}{2}\sigma^2\tau\right) - \frac{1}{2}\sigma^2\tau}{\sigma\sqrt{\tau}}.$$

Inserting back the original variables will give the Black-Scholes equation.

4.6.2 Copulas

In many situations, one has several random variables $\tilde{x}_1, \ldots, \tilde{x}_n$, which presumably are correlated. The marginal distributions $F_1, \ldots, F_n$ are known, but the simultaneous distribution of all the variables is unknown or is known only in some general terms, so one needs a way of binding the marginal distributions together. This can be done using a *copula*.

We begin by considering the special case, where all the marginal distributions are the uniform distribution on $[0, 1]$ (so $F_i(u) = u$, all $u \in [0, 1]$). We then *define* an *n-dimensional copula* as a simultaneous distribution C on $[0, 1]^n$ such that all the marginal distributions are uniform.

An n-dimensional copula has the following properties:

(a) $C(u_1, \ldots, u_{i-1}, 0, u_{i+1}, \ldots, u_n) = 0$ for all i;

(b) $C(1, \ldots, 1, u, 1, \ldots, 1) = u$ for all $u \in [0, 1]$;

(c) if $a_i \leq b_i$, $i = 1, \ldots, n$, then $\mathsf{P}\{\tilde{u}_1 \in [a_1, b_1], \ldots, \tilde{u}_n \in [a_n, b_n]\}$ must be non-negative, and writing out this probability gives the *rectangle inequality*

$$\sum_{i_1=1}^{2} \cdots \sum_{i_n=1}^{2} (-1)^{i_1 + \cdots + i_n} C(u_{1,i_1}, \ldots, u_{n,i_n}) \geq 0,$$

where $u_{j,1} = a_j$, $u_{j,2} = b_j$, $j = 1, \ldots, n$ (in the special case of $n = 2$, the rectangle inequality becomes $C(b_1, b_2) - C(a_1, b_2) - C(b_1, a_2) + C(a_1, a_2)$).

We can use a copula to model a multivariate distribution when the marginal distributions are uniform. But copulas can be used quite generally; this follows from the result known as Sklar's theorem:

THEOREM 1 *If $F(x_1, \ldots, x_n) = \mathsf{P}\{\tilde{x}_1 \leq x_1, \ldots, \tilde{x}_n \leq x_n\}$ is the multivariate distribution of a random vector $(\tilde{x}_1, \ldots, \tilde{x}_n)$ with marginal distributions $F_i(x) = \mathsf{P}\{\tilde{x}_i \leq x\}$, $i = 1, \ldots, n$, then*

$$F(x_1, \ldots, x_n) = C(F_1(x_1), \ldots, F_n(x_n))$$

for some copula C, which is uniquely determined if the distribution functions F_i are continuous.

The converse of Sklar's theorem holds as well, in the sense that for any copula C and distribution functions $F_1, \ldots, F_n$, the composite $C(F(x_1), \ldots, F(x_n))$ defines an n-dimensional cumulative distribution function.

The most obvious example of a copula is obtained when starting from a multivariate normal distribution with covariance matrix Σ. This gives the Gaussian copula

$$C_{\Sigma}^{Gauss}(u_1, \ldots, u_n) = \Phi_{\Sigma}\big(\Phi^{-1}(u_1), \ldots, \Phi^{-1}(u_n)\big),$$

with Φ the distribution function of the standard normal distribution, and Φ_{Σ} the multivariate normal distribution with mean 0 and covariance matrix Σ. Other families of copulas can be obtained in a similar way (using Sklar's theorem), but with simpler functional expressions,

$$C(u_1, \ldots, u_n) = \psi\big(\psi^{-1}(u_1), \ldots, \psi^{-1}(u_n)\big),$$

where $\psi : \mathbb{R}_+ \to [0, 1]$ is a function with

$$(-1)^k \psi^{(k)}(u) \geq 0$$

for all u and for $k = 0, 1, \ldots, n - 2$, and with $(-1)^{n-2}\psi^{n-2}(u)$ non-increasing and convex. Examples of such functions are

$$e^{-u}, \quad (1 + u)^{-\frac{1}{\theta}} \text{ for } \theta > 0, \quad \frac{1 - \theta}{e^u - \theta} \text{ for } 0 < \theta < 1.$$

4.6.3 Cholesky factorization

The technique of Cholesky factorization is often mentioned in texts on risk management, but the explanations provided are not always very good (if there are any), and consequently it might sound like something very complicated, which it is not, as is hopefully clarified by the present note.

In risk management, the need arises when we want to generate n random variables $Y_1, \ldots, Y_n$ with a given covariance matrix. It is easy to generate independent random variables $X_1, \ldots, X_n$ using the random generator, but in order to simulate correlated random variables, we need to take the covariance matrix into account. The obvious way out would be to take suitable linear combinations of the random variables and then adjust the coefficents to get the right covariance matrix. Namely, if

$$Y_i = \sum_{j=1}^{n} a_{ij}X_j, \ i, j = 1, \ldots, n,$$

then the variance formula gives us

$$\mathrm{cov}(Y_h, Y_k) = \mathrm{cov}\left(\sum_{j=1}^{n} a_{hj}X_j, \sum_{j=1}^{n} a_{kj}X_j\right) = \sum_{i=1}^{n} a_{hi}a_{ik}\mathrm{var}(X_i)$$

using that the X_i are independent; so if $\mathrm{var}(X_i) = 1$ for all i, then the covariance matrix of $(Y_1, \ldots, Y_n)$ is the matrix AA^t (where A^t is the transpose of A). It remains only to choose the coefficents a_{ij} so that the matrix product AA^t becomes equal to the given covariance matrix.

This is where Cholesky factorization becomes useful. We try to write the given covariance matrix Σ as a product $\Sigma = AA^t$, with the additional condition that A is lower triangular with non-zero diagonal elements,

$$\begin{pmatrix} \sigma_{11} & \cdots & \sigma_{1n} \\ \vdots & & \vdots \\ \sigma_{n1} & \cdots & \sigma_{nn} \end{pmatrix} = \begin{pmatrix} a_{11} & 0 & \cdots & 0 \\ a_{21} & a_{22} & \cdots & 0 \\ \vdots & \vdots & & \vdots \\ a_{n1} & a_{n2} & \cdots & a_{nn} \end{pmatrix} \begin{pmatrix} a_{11} & a_{21} & \cdots & a_{n1} \\ 0 & a_{22} & \cdots & a_{2n} \\ \vdots & \vdots & & \vdots \\ 0 & 0 & \cdots & a_{nn} \end{pmatrix}$$

Solving for the elements of A, we get first from $\sigma_{11} = a_{11}^2$ that $a_{11} = \sqrt{\sigma_{11}}$, then $\sigma_{i1} = a_{i1}a_{11}$ that $a_{i1} = \sigma_{i1}/a_{11}$ for $i = 2,\ldots,n$, so now we have the first column of A. In general, we have

$$a_{ii} = \sqrt{\sigma_{ii} - \sum_{k=1}^{i-1} a_{ik}^2}$$

for the diagonal elements and

$$a_{ji} = \left(\sigma_{ji} - \sum_{k=1}^{j-1} a_{jk}a_{ik} \right) \Big/ a_{ii}$$

for the remaining elements of column i. For this to work, we need all the expressions under square roots to be positive, and this is indeed the case when A is symmetric and positive definite (as covariance matrices are). It is remarkable that the solution can be obtained recursively; there is no need for inversion of matrices.

EXAMPLE 4.1 We find a lower triangular decomposition of the matrix

$$\begin{pmatrix} 25 & 15 & -5 \\ 15 & 18 & 0 \\ -5 & 0 & 11 \end{pmatrix} = \begin{pmatrix} a_{11} & 0 & 0 \\ a_{21} & a_{22} & 0 \\ a_{31} & a_{32} & a_{33} \end{pmatrix} \begin{pmatrix} a_{11} & a_{21} & a_{31} \\ 0 & a_{22} & a_{32} \\ 0 & 0 & a_{33} \end{pmatrix}.$$

The first diagonal element a_{11} is 5. Then we go downwards to solve $a_{21}a_{11} = 15$ for a_{21}, giving 3, and $a_{31}a_{11} = -5$ for a_{31}, giving -1. We now have the first column and proceed to the second. The diagonal element a_{22} is found from $a_{12}a_{12} + a_{22}^2 = 18$, giving $a_{22} = 3$, and then a_{32} is found from $a_{31}a_{21} + a_{32}a_{22} = 0$, which has the solution $a_{32} = 1$. Now the last element a_{33} is found as the solution to $a_{31}a_{31} + a_{32}a_{32} + a_{33}^2 = 11$, or $a_{33} = 3$. We have thus found

$$\begin{pmatrix} a_{11} & 0 & 0 \\ a_{21} & a_{22} & 0 \\ a_{31} & a_{32} & a_{33} \end{pmatrix} = \begin{pmatrix} 5 & 0 & 0 \\ 3 & 3 & 0 \\ -1 & 1 & 3 \end{pmatrix}.$$

The Cholesky decomposition has other applications. Indeed, Cholesky developed the method in order to solve linear equations of the form

$$Dx = b$$

with $b \in \mathbb{R}^n$ and D an $(n \times n)$ matrix which is symmetric and positive definite. Writing $D = AA^T$, we see that the solution can be obtained by first solving the system

$$Az = b,$$

and then solving

$$A^t x = z.$$

The advantage of this approach over standard methods is that no matrix inversion is needed.

4.7 Exercises

1. The betas in CAPM: Because in equilibrium all traders have chosen the market portfolio, the ratio in which return can be traded against risk must be the same for all assets (and for the market portfolio), so

$$\frac{\bar{r}_i - r}{\beta_i} = \mu - r$$

for all i (where $\mu = \mu(x)$ is the return of the market portfolio). Here β_i is a constant expressing the change in risk which occurs when the weight of asset i is changed from that of the market portfolio.

Find an expression of β_i in terms of the data of the problem, and give an interpretation.

2. An investor contemplates holding a portfolio consisting of three securities A, B and C. The market portfolio has an expected return of 12% and its standard deviation is 16%. The risk-free rate of interest is 4%.

The following is known about the securities in the proposed portfolio:

Security	Beta (cf. Exercise 1)	Weight in portfolio
A	1.2	30
B	0.9	40
C	1.1	30

Find the expected return on the proposed portfolio.

3. Chebyshev's inequality, which holds for *any* probability distribution with mean μ and finite variance σ^2, says that

$$P\{|x - \mu| \geq k\sigma\} \leq \frac{1}{k^2}$$

for all $k > 0$. Use Chebyshev's inequality to give a suggestion for $\text{VaR}_{0.99}$ (99% VaR) for a portfolio of €1,500,000, given that it is known only that the loss distribution has mean 1% and standard deviation 2%, and that the distribution is symmetric.

Compare this result to the VaR which obtains if it is also known that the loss distribution is normal.

4. The VaR on a portfolio using a 1-day time horizon is €20 million. What is the VaR using a 10-day horizon? State the assumptions behind the result.

5. Consider a position consisting of a $100,000 investment in asset A and a $100,000 investment in asset B. Assume that the daily volatilities of both assets are 1% and that the correlation coefficient between their returns is 0.3. What is the 5-day 99% VaR for the portfolio?

6. A risk manager wants to find the 99% VaR on a portfolio valued at $1,200,000. Almost nothing is known about the theoretical loss distribution, but the historical data shown below for the previous 300 days is as follows (ranked from lowest to best):

Returns: −6.1%, −6%, −5.9%, −5.7%, −5.5%, −5.1%..........4.9%, 5%, 5.3%, 5.6%, 5.9%, 6%.

Find an estimate for $VaR_{0.99}$.

7. A money market fund has equity of size $1,000,000 and has borrowed $10,000,000 at the risk-free rate of interest, which is 2%. The capital is invested in the market portfolio, which has an expected return of 5% and a standard deviation of 8%.

Find the probability that the fund will have losses so large that it cannot pay back some of its creditors.

4.8 Comments

The capital asset model of portfolio selection was developed by Sharpe [1964] and Lintner [1965], and it marked the beginning of the theory of pricing of financial assets. It is widely used today both in practical application and in teaching.

The use of VaR, more specifically $VaR_{0.99}$ on a 10-day horizon, was introduced in the 1996 amendment of Basel I. Later revisions have added other measures, also based on VaR. Thus, an addition to Basel II appearing at the end of 2011 introduced the notion of *stressed VaR* (denoted sVaR), which is VaR based on a 250-day period of stressed market conditions, and the total capital charge is set to

$$\max\{VaR_{t-1}, m_c VaR_{avg}\} + \max\{sVaR_{t?1}, m_s sVaR_{avg}\},$$

where VaR_{t-1} and $sVaR_{t-1}$ are VaR and sVaR based on data from the previous day, and $VaR_{avg}, sVaR_{avg}$ are averages over the last 60 days (sVaR is found using a simulation based on the data from the stressed period). The constants m_c and m_s are determined by the financial supervisors but should at least be equal to 3.

There are several textbooks on measuring market risk, e.g. Dowd [2002], Jorion [2006] and Alexander [2009]. These texts cover a much broader field, including data collection and problems of estimating parameters.

The mathematical appendix, deriving the formula for pricing of options and briefly introducing copulas and Cholesky decomposition, has been inserted in order to provide some explanation of terminology used in the text. It may be skipped without serious consequences, because a deeper knowledge of how the formulas are derived is needed only occasionally (in Chapter 7 below) and as additional material.

Chapter 5

The Loan Contract

5.1 Introduction

In the present chapter, we shall look more closely at the loan contract, the agreement between bank and borrower. At first sight – and following our approach to the lender-borrower relationship taken so far – a loan contract specifies when and how much to repay for each unit of money borrowed.

However, the contract contains much more, either in terms of explicitly stated conditions or as rules of conduct implicitly agreed upon. This is indeed necessary because the contracts deal with transactions which are subject to risk. It may happen that the borrower is unable to pay the agreed amount at the termination of the contract, and the parties should know what will happen in such situations, that is, how much the lender can collect either in terms of cash repayment or through the appropriation of collateral. The contract may also specify that renegotiation takes place if the original terms of the contract are not fulfilled.

Since what matters when deciding upon the precise version of loan contract to be used in a given lender-borrower relationship is not so much the formulation as the behaviour which is to be expected given the contract, we shall be concerned with the incentives which the contract gives rise to. Among these, the most important one is the incentive to repay the amount borrowed, in particular in situations where the lender has few possibilities of penalizing the borrower for violations of the contract.

To discuss such matters in a unified context, we focus on a simple loan transaction, where a loan of the amount of 1 unit of money is to be repaid at a fixed date. We assume that the outcome of the borrower's investment project, out of which the repayment should be made, is a random variable $\tilde{y}$, and we introduce the *repayment function* $R(y)$, specifying the payment to the bank for each possible value y of $\tilde{y}$.

The intuitively most natural form of a repayment function is the one illustrated in Fig. 5.1, known as the *standard contract*,

$$R(y) = \max\{0, \min\{y, \overline{R}\}\}. \tag{1}$$

The borrower pays a fixed amount $\overline{R}$ whenever the outcome of the investment is big enough; if not, the bank gets the whole outcome. Although this repayment function is intuitive, it may not be the only – indeed not even the most reasonable – one, as we shall see in this chapter.

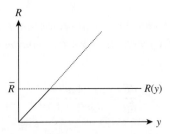

Figure 5.1 The standard contract: A fixed amount $\overline{R}$ is repaid unless investor's outcome y is insufficient, and in this case all of y is paid to the bank.

To see how the loan contract depends on the circumstances under which it is set up, we begin our study with the simplest possible case of a risky contract, namely the case where all relevant variables, which in our simple situation means y, are observable to both parties. Then we proceed in Section 5.3 to the more complicated cases of asymmetric information where the lender cannot observe y, opening up for possible opportunistic behaviour of the borrower. It may be useful to use additional instruments to provide the needed incentives to repay, and we consider the use of collateral in Section 5.4. In the last section, we discuss a particular case which has obtained some prominence, namely *microfinance*, which has as its purpose to provide credit to small communities in developing countries in a way which is commerciably viable in the sense that the loans are generally paid back.

5.2 Bank credit as risk sharing

In this section, we assume that the outcome y can be observed only by the borrower-investor, or, alternatively, the outcome may be observed but is not *verifiable*, which means that it cannot be used as a condition in legally enforceable contracts. The only problem that the borrower and lender face is that outcome is subject to risk, so the contract must indicate how this risk is born by the two parties, something which must depend on their respective attitudes towards risk. To investigate this, we need to introduce utility functions: The borrower is assumed to have a von Neumann-Morgenstern utility u of income, and the (von Neumann-Morgenstern) utility function of the lender is denoted by v. Expected outcomes are then

$$\mathsf{E}[u(\tilde{y} - R(\tilde{y}))] = \int u(y - R(y))f(y)\,dy, \quad \mathsf{E}[v(R(\tilde{y}))] = \int v(R(y))f(y)\,dy$$

for the borrower and the lender, respectively. Here we have assumed that the random outcome $\tilde{y}$ has a density $f(y)$.

We are interested in contracts which are *Pareto optimal* in the sense that none of the parties can be made better off by a change in the repayment function without the other party becoming worse off. Such optimal contracts have particular properties.

PROPOSITION 1: *Assume that both insured and insurer are risk averse with concave (von Neumann-Morgenstern) utility functions. Then the repayment function $R(\cdot)$ of a Pareto optimal contract satisfies*

$$\frac{dR}{dy} = \frac{\lambda_B u''}{\lambda_B u'' + \lambda_L v''},\tag{2}$$

for some weights $\lambda_B, \lambda_L > 0$.

PROOF: A Pareto optimal contract can be found by maximizing the expected utility of one of the parties, say the borrower, given that the expected utility of the other party, the lender, should retain a certain fixed value, which means that

$$\lambda_B \mathsf{E}[u(\tilde{y} - R(\tilde{y}))] + \lambda_L \mathsf{E}[v(R(\tilde{y}))]$$

is maximized for some positive numbers λ_B, λ_L.

If this is the case, then for each value y of the outcome, the quantity

$$\lambda_B u(y - R(y))f(y) + \lambda_L v(R(y))f(y)$$

cannot be increased by changing the repayment from $R(y)$ to $R(y) + z$, for some z, meaning that

$$\lambda_B u(y - R(y) - z)f(y) + \lambda_L v(R(y) + z)f(y)$$

is maximal for $z = 0$. The first-order condition for this maximum is

$$-\lambda_B u'(y - R(y))f(y) + \lambda_L v'(R(y))f(y) = 0,$$

which can be rewritten as

$$\lambda_B u'(y - R(y)) - \lambda_L v'(R(y)) = 0.\tag{3}$$

This expression gives $R(y)$ as a solution in R to an equation $F(R, y) = 0$ (where $F(R, y)$ is the left-hand side of (3)) for given y, that is, as an implicit function of y. Using the implicit function theorem, we get that R has derivative

$$\frac{dR}{dy} = -\frac{F'_y}{F'_R},$$

and inserting

$$F'_y = \frac{\partial F}{\partial y} = \lambda_B u'', \quad F'_R = \frac{\partial F}{\partial R} = -\lambda_B u'' - \lambda_L v'',$$

we obtain

$$\frac{dR}{dy} = \frac{\lambda_B u''}{\lambda_B u'' + \lambda_L v''},$$

which is (2). □

The characterization of Pareto optimal contracts obtained in Proposition 1 does not give us an exact functional form, but it gives some useful properties, which can be used in special cases. Also, it can be seen from expression (2) for the derivative of R that it is *not* that of the standard contract. Indeed, taking the simple case where the bank is risk neutral so that $v'' = 0$, we get that

$$\frac{dR}{dy} = 1,$$

which contrasts with the constant repayment (after a certain threshold) typical of the standard contract. Thus, the repayment function will be as shown in Fig. 5.2, where we show a case of a risk-neutral lender and a risk-averse borrower (left panel) and another case where both lender and borrower are risk neutral. The reason for this is that at present we have considered the loan contract *only* as a risk-sharing device. Actually, the above result is taken from the economic theory of insurance, where it pertains to the size of reimbursement by the insurance company of a loss experienced by the insured. The optimal contract involves risk sharing, and details of this risk sharing depend on the attitude towards risk of the two parties.

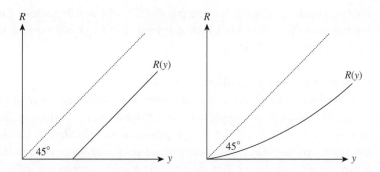

Figure 5.2 Two examples of repayment functions under full information: The left panel shows repayment when the borrower is risk averse while the lender is risk neutral – the lender bears all the risk and the borrower receives a fixed amount, at least when y is big enough. The right panel shows a repayment function in a case where both borrower and lender are risk averse.

Formula (2) can be reformulated slightly if we rewrite (3) as

$$\frac{\lambda_B}{\lambda_L} = \frac{v'(R(y))}{u'(y - R(y))}$$

(showing that the right-hand side is constant independent of y) and insert to get

$$\frac{dR}{dy} = \frac{\lambda_L v' \dfrac{u''}{u'}}{\lambda_L v' \dfrac{u''}{u'} + \lambda_L v''} = \frac{\rho_u}{\rho_u + \rho_v},$$

where we have introduced the coefficients of (absolute) risk aversion

$$\rho_u = -\frac{u''}{u,}, \ \rho_v = -\frac{v''}{v'},$$

which measure the curvature of the concave utility functions u and v.

5.3 Repayment under asymmetric information

Moving beyond simple risk sharing, we have to consider the impact of asymmetric information on the loan contract and particularly on the repayment function. When the lender cannot observe the outcome of the investment made by the borrower, she faces the problem that the outcome reported by the borrower may be different from the true outcome, and if repayment is increasing in outcome, a too low reported outcome is to be expected.

In the extreme case, where the borrower's situation is totally hidden to the lender, nothing prevents the borrower from reporting an outcome of 0. The lender-borrower relationship breaks down, because the lender cannot protect herself against opportunistic behaviour of the borrower. Many intermediate stages exist, however, where the lender may not observe outcome but still has some possibilities of extracting relevant information from the borrower. We shall have a look at several such cases, with special regard to the repayment function that will emerge.

5.3.1 Contracts with costly monitoring

If the realization of $\tilde{y}$ can be observed after an audit, the lender has a way of obtaining information, but this information acquisition method should be used with care because it is costly – we assume a fixed cost C for verifying the outcome obtained by the borrower-investor, and it is understood that C is rather large, so automatic verification of all reports by the borrower should be avoided. But the lender (bank) may try to discipline the borrower by using the verification in a suitable way. This amounts to setting up a mechanism, a set of rules for the borrower which will produce a reasonable result for the lender. Such a mechanism should satisfy some requirements in order to be acceptable to the lender, and this, in turn, has implications for the repayment function.

The mechanism is defined by a message space for the borrower, which we assume to be reports $\hat{y}$ about outcome, true or false (we consider a *direct* mechanism), and an outcome rule, which consists of two parts, namely a repayment rule determining the amount to be paid to the bank given the message $R(\hat{y})$, and an audit rule specifying the set of messages A which give rise to audit. Assuming that false messages are penalized heavily if detected, we may take it that the borrower will send the true messages if the latter is in the audit region A.

We want the mechanism to be incentive compatible in the sense that *truth-telling is optimal* for the borrower. This is not for ethical reasons; rather, we want the mechanism to correspond to realism in the sense that the repayment given any outcome y should be the repayment that results when the borrower chooses her optimal message (we use here the *revelation principle* known from game theory).

This puts some restrictions on the repayment function. First of all, if there are two messages y_1 and y_2 which are not audited, then we cannot have $R(y_1) < R(y_2)$, because in that case y_1 would be preferred as the message even if payoff was actually y_2. Thus, repayment is constant, say $R(y) = \overline{R}$, in the no-auditing region. Secondly, if y_1 is audited, and $R(y_2) < R(y_1)$, then also y_2 must be audited. In particular, this means that

$$R(y) = \overline{R}, \; y \notin A,$$
$$R(y) \leq \overline{R}, \; y \in A.$$

The condition of incentive compatibility thus puts several restrictions on the repayment function, but it still permits many different functional forms, as indicated in Fig. 5.3. To get a more detailed characterization of the repayment function, we need to add further conditions.

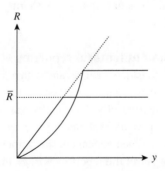

Figure 5.3 Contracts satisfying the incentive compatibility condition under costly monitoring. The standard contract satisfies incentive compatibility, but so do other repayment functions.

One such condition is *efficiency*: We assume that the contract maximizes the expected repayment over all incentive-compatible contracts with the same probability of an audit. This condition may not look very appealing at first sight, but it is a reformulation of the

condition that the probability of audit should be minimal for all incentive contracts with
the same expected repayment, and as such sounds like a reasonable demand of a repayment
function. We have then the following result:

PROPOSITION 2: *Let R be an incentive-compatible repayment rule under costly auditing
which is efficient in the sense that it maximizes expected repayment for a given probability
of audit. Then R has the form*

$$R(y) = \min\{y, \overline{R}\}$$

and the auditing region is A = {y | y ≤ $\overline{R}$}, for some $\overline{R}$ > 0.

PROOF: Let R' be another incentive-compatible repayment rule with auditing region A'
such that $E[R'(\tilde{y})] = E[R(\tilde{y})]$. Because R' is a repayment rule, it satisfies $R'(y) \leq y$ for
all y. Also, there is some $\overline{R}'$ such that $R'(y) = \overline{R}'$ for $y \notin A'$. Because $P(A) = P(A')$ and
$A = \{y \mid y \leq \overline{R}\}$, there must be some $y \in A$ which is not in A', but then

$$R'(y) = \overline{R}' < y = R(y) < \overline{R}.$$

It then follows that the $R(y) \geq R'(y)$ for all y, so $E[R(\tilde{y})] > E[R'(\tilde{y}]$, and R does not
maximize expected repayment.   □

It is seen that we have recovered the standard contract introduced in the previous section as one which emerges under the conditions stated in the proposition. This contract
differs markedly from pure risk-sharing arrangements because there is an upper bound to
the repayment. It should, of course, not come as a surprise that we get a different solution because we have explicitly disregarded any risk sharing by (implicitly) assuming risk
neutrality of the two parties involved.

5.3.2 Non-pecuniary cost of untruthful reporting

Another version of the model considered above, and with a result similar to that of Proposition 2, emerges if instead of costly auditing we assume that there is a non-pecuniary cost
to the borrower of not reporting truthfully. This model was proposed by Diamond [1984],
and the cost of untruthfulness may be explained by the reaction of other agents than the
bank (social degradation etc.), or even ethical considerations.

If the non-pecuniary cost of untruthful reporting is $\varphi(y)$, then the incentive compatibility
condition for the borrower becomes

$$R(y) + \varphi(y) = \overline{R}$$

for all y and some constant $\overline{R}$. Indeed, if there were y_1, y_2 with $R(y_1) + \varphi(y_1) > R(y_2) +
\varphi(y_2)$, then y_2 would not be reported if occurring, and we have a contradiction of incentive
compatibility.

The next step is to invoke efficiency considerations, and we get a counterpart of the previous result:

PROPOSITION 3: *Let R be an incentive-compatible repayment rule under non-pecuniary cost which is efficient in the sense that it minimizes expected non-pecuniary cost at the given expected repayment. Then R has the form*

$$R(y) = \min\{y, \overline{R}\},$$

and the auditing region is $A = \{y \mid y \le \overline{R}\}$, for some $\overline{R} > 0$.

PROOF: Let R^* be another incentive-compatible repayment rule with auditing region A^* such that $\mathsf{E}[R^*(\tilde{y})] = \mathsf{E}[R(\tilde{y})]$. Because R^* is a repayment rule, it satisfies $R^*(y) \le y$ for all y, and by incentive compatibility, it satisfies $R^*(y) + \varphi(y) = \overline{R}^*$ for some $\overline{R}^* > 0$. If $\overline{R}^* \ge \overline{R}$, we would have

$$\mathsf{E}[R^*(\tilde{y}) + \varphi(\tilde{y})] = \overline{R}^* > \overline{R} = \mathsf{E}[R(\tilde{y}) + \varphi(\tilde{y})],$$

from which we get that $\mathsf{E}[R^*(\tilde{y})] > \mathsf{E}[R(\tilde{y})]$, a contradiction. It follows that $\overline{R}^* = \overline{R}$, and because the standard contract obviously minimizes $\mathsf{E}[\overline{R} - R(\tilde{y})]$ over all repayment rules, we have the conclusion. □

5.3.3 Truth-telling in repeated contractual relationships

If no auditing is possible, the possibilities of having the borrower reporting true outcome of the investment are much smaller. However, if the lender-borrower relationship is not a once-and-for-all affair, but is repeated regularly, the loss of future business may influence the borrower, as illustrated in the simple two-period context, inspired by Bolton and Scharfstein [1990]. We assume that the borrower invests 1 unit of money and receives a random outcome $\tilde{y}$, which takes the value y_H with probability p and $y_L < y_H$ with probability $(1 - p)$, and pays back to the bank in accordance with the standard contract. This is repeated for two periods, the random choice of outcome at $t = 1$ being independent of that at $t = 0$. We assume that $y_L < 1$, so the borrower can pay at most y_L in the case of low outcome.

The repetition of the loan contract makes it possible for the bank to threaten the borrower with termination of the contract, not in the case of untruthful reporting, something which cannot be observed by the bank anyway, but in the case that reported outcome at the end of the first period is y_L. Clearly, this has as a consequence that the borrower is punished not so much for untruthful reporting as for bad results, but this is a cost of asymmetric information which has to be faced. On the other hand, if the borrower stands to gain more from another round of the contract than she loses by paying R when outcome is high, rather than opportunistically reporting low outcome, the threat of termination will result in truthful reporting.

Assuming discounting rates to be 0, the incentive compatibility condition for the borrower is then

$$-R + p(y_H - y_L) \geq -y_L,$$

where the left-hand side expresses the net gain from repeating the contract given that y_H was the outcome at $t = 0$ (namely the difference between y_H and y_L in the second period given that y_H is realized, minus the repayment of R on the first loan), and the right-hand side is the outcome from paying only y_L at period 0 and terminating the contract. Reorganising, we get that

$$R \leq py_H + (1 - p)y_L = \mathsf{E}\tilde{y}. \tag{4}$$

The present value to the bank of the contractual arrangement can be computed as

$$-1 + (1 - p)y_L + p(R - 1 + y_L) = p(R - 1) - 1 + y_L,$$

and it is non-negative if

$$R \geq 1 + \frac{1 - y_L}{p}. \tag{5}$$

We conclude that there is a possibility of a contractual relationship between lender and borrower if a repayment R can be found which satisfies both (4) and (5), which again means that we must have

$$1 - y_L \leq p\left(\mathsf{E}\tilde{y} - 1\right),$$

showing that the difference between investment value and low outcome, that is, the possible investment loss, should not be too big compared to the average gain of carrying out the investment.

5.3.4 Sovereign debt

In the previous subsection, we considered situations where the discontinuation of the relationship between the bank and its borrower was the only way of forcing the latter to repay the debt. A particular case is that of *sovereign debt*, where the borrower is a sovereign state. In this case the lender has no legal means of collecting debt which is not repaid, and this circumstance does indeed present a temptation for the borrower to repudiate the debt. Historically, sovereign lending goes back to the Middle Ages, and although history offers numerous examples of debt which was not paid – and lenders that were killed instead of being repaid – the borrowing business was nevertheless very lucrative in the long run, showing that, after all, the incentives to repay were generally strong.

The following very simple model of sovereign lending goes back to Allen [1983] and illustrates what is at stake; at this level, there are no banks involved, and the debt is assumed to be contracted in the market. We assume that the sovereign country borrows I, which is invested in a one-period production process giving output $f(I)$, where f is a concave production function; no risk is involved. The terms of the contract are such that the country must repay $(1 + r)I$ at the end of the year, where r is the riskless level of interest. The optimal amount of investment (and borrowing) I^* is found by maximizing

$$f(I) - (1 + r)I,$$

which gives us the standard condition

$$f'(I^*) = 1 + r. \tag{6}$$

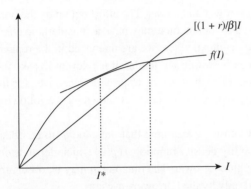

Figure 5.4 Sovereign debt. If optimal investment size I^* is in the region where the ray with slope $(1+r)/\beta$ is below the production function (as in the figure), then it is optimal to repay debt. Otherwise the debt is repudiated.

Now we add the possibility of repudiating debt. If the country keeps the amount which was designated for repayment, its payoff increases by the amount $(1 + r)I$, but then it loses the gains from future rounds of investment because no lending is possible in future years. With a discount factor $\beta > 1$, this loss amounts to

$$\sum_{t=1}^{\infty} \beta^t [f(I) - (1 + r)I] = \frac{\beta}{1 - \beta} [f(I) - (1 + r)I].$$

The debt will be repaid as long as this loss exceeds the gain from repudiating debt, which reduces to the condition

$$(1 + r)I \le \beta f(I). \tag{7}$$

We see that for the country to have the necessary incentives to repay, the optimal investment found in (6) should satisfy (7). Whether or not this is the case depends on the production function and the parameters, as illustrated in Fig. 5.4, where the ray through the origin with slope $(1 + r)/\beta$ must intersect the production function at a value I which exceeds I^* defined in (6).

Although intuitive, the simple model does not cover all relevant aspects of sovereign lending, and it neglects the uncertainty aspect which is involved and which has played a major role in recent examples of countries repudiating (or rather restructuring) sovereign debt, such as Argentina after 2001. Also, it may be noticed that so far the model deals only with borrowing in the market, typically by bond issues, which on the one hand is typical for contemporary sovereign debt, but on the other hand neglects the contractual aspects which was our principal interest in the matter.

5.3.5 Repayment under moral hazard

We have already seen (Chapter 1) that moral hazard may be an important factor in the relationship between borrower and lender. The effort put up by the borrower in the process of transforming the loan to an outcome may have a considerable effect on the size of this outcome. In our present context, where we are interested in the repayment function entering the contract between borrower and lender, it is relevant to ask whether the repayment function may be chosen in such a way as to provide incentives for the borrower towards greater effort. This may indeed be the case, as shown by the following model taken from Innes [1990].

As in many previous cases, we assume that outcome $\tilde{y}$ (to be obtained using the loan) is random, with probability density function $f(y, e)$ which depends on effort e, which is a real number chosen by the borrower. The outcome y may be observable to all parties, but the effort e is observed only by the borrower-investor.

Given the repayment function $R(\cdot)$, the borrower will choose so as to maximize expected profit

$$\pi(R, e) = \int (y - R(y)) f(y, e) \, dy - C(e),$$

where $C(e)$ is the money cost of effort e, assumed to be convex. The optimal effort level, which depends on the contract R, is denoted e^*. For the lender, we assume that the contract must yield a given expected return R_L^0, and we may now search for the best possible contract for the borrower, given these constraints,

$$\max \ \pi(R, e^*)$$

such that

$$0 \le R(y) \le y, \text{ all } y, \tag{8}$$

$$\pi(R, e) \le \pi(R, e^*), \text{ all } e,$$

$$\mathsf{E}[R(\tilde{y})|e^*] \ge R_L^0.$$

The resulting contract is efficient (because it maximizes the payoff of the borrower for a given payoff to the lender), and it has some remarkable properties, summarized in the following proposition:

PROPOSITION 4: *Suppose that for all pairs of effort levels e_1, e_2 with $e_1 > e_2$, the ratio $\dfrac{f(y, e_1)}{f(y, e_2)}$ is increasing in y. If $R^*(\cdot)$ solves the maximization problem (8), then there is some threshold value y^* of y such that*

$$R^*(y) = \begin{cases} 0 & \text{for } y \geq y^*, \\ y & \text{for } y < y^*. \end{cases}$$

The result obtained is sufficiently unexpected to merit some comment before embarking on its proof. The repayment function, shown in Fig. 5.5, prescribes that the borrower-investor should return *all* of the outcome to the bank as long as this outcome is below a certain threshold y^*. If it exceeds the threshold, the borrower is free to keep *everything*; the lender gets nothing.

PROOF OF PROPOSITION 4: We simplify the maximization problem by replacing the incentive compatibility constraint $\pi(R, e) \leq \pi(R, e^*)$ by its first-order condition (this can be done when the first-order conditions are both necessary and sufficient, as is the case when π is a concave function of e),

$$\pi'_e(R, y) = \int (y - R(y)) f'_e(y, e)\, dy - C'(e) = 0.$$

The optimal contract can now be found by maximizing the Lagrangian

$$(y - R(y))(f(y, e) + \mu f'_e(y, e)) + \lambda R(y) f(y, e)$$

over all $R(y)$ with $0 \leq R(y) \leq y$ for each y. Here μ and λ are multipliers belonging to the second and third constraint of the maximization problem.

Inspecting the form of this Lagrangian, we see that it can be written alternatively as

$$y(f(y, e) + \mu f'_e(y, e)) + (\lambda - 1) f(y, e) R(y) - \mu f'_e(y, e) R(y),$$

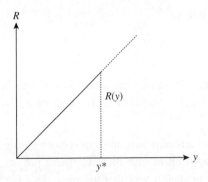

Figure 5.5 Repayment under moral hazard: If the probability of a good result of the investment depends on the effort of the borrower-investor, then the loan contract may contain incentives in the form of smaller or no repayment to the bank when y is sufficiently large.

where the first member is independent of the size $R(y)$ of the repayment at y, so the second and third member is decisive for the maximum. If the coefficient of the second member is numerically bigger than that of the third,

$$(\lambda - 1)f(y,e) \geq \mu f_e'(y,e), \tag{9}$$

then the whole expression is increasing in $R(y)$, which should therefore be chosen as big as possible, $R(y) = y$. In the other case,

$$(\lambda - 1)f(y,e) < \mu f_e'(y,e), \tag{10}$$

the expression is maximized by choosing the smallest possible value of $R(y)$, $R(y) = 0$.

We have, therefore, that the repayment is either everything or nothing, and it remains only to investigate conditions (9) and (10) a little more closely. We are interested in the function which takes any

$$y \mapsto \frac{f_e'(y,e)}{f(y,e)},$$

and we claim that it is increasing in e. Indeed, if $e_1 > e_2$ are arbitrary, then we have that

$$\frac{f(y,e_1)}{f(y,e_2)} = \frac{f(y,e_2 + (e_1 - e_2))}{f(y,e_2)}$$

is increasing in y, and the same holds when multiplied with the positive number $(e_1 - e_2)^{-1}$. Letting e_1 go to e_2, we get that

$$\lim_{e_1 \to e_2} \frac{\dfrac{f(y,e_2 + (e_1 - e_2))}{e_1 - e_2}}{f(y,e)} = \frac{f_e'(y,e_2)}{f(y,e_2)}$$

is increasing in y.

Because (9) can be written as

$$\frac{f_e'(y,e)}{f(y,e)} \leq \frac{\lambda - 1}{\mu}$$

(assuming $\lambda \neq 1$), we have that this inequality is satisfied below a certain threshold level y^*, and above this level, (10) holds. This gives us the repayment function stated in the proposition.   □

The possibility that the bank may refrain from collecting any repayment is a powerful incentive for putting enough effort into the investment project. The size of the threshold is, of course, chosen in such a way that the bank does not lose money (this is also guaranteed by the formulation of the problem). It goes without saying that a contract such as that derived here is rarely encountered in real life; indeed, the bank management would be reluctant to accept contracts specifying that no repayment should be made even if the borrower is able to repay. For increased realism, one may replace the constraint $0 \leq R(y) \leq y$ by

$$b(y) \leq R(y) \leq y, \ b(y) = \begin{cases} 0 & y < \underline{R}, \\ \underline{R} & y \geq \underline{R}. \end{cases}$$

The optimal contract will be of the same type, with everything repaid until a given threshold, after which repayment reduces to $\underline{R}$. Because $\underline{R}$ may be chosen well above zero, the present version would be a more realistic one.

5.4 The role of collateral in reducing moral hazard

If the borrower cannot or does not repay, the loss to the lender may be reduced if the borrower has pledged a *collateral*, an asset which becomes the property of the lender if the borrower does not fulfil her obligations. The collateral, its kind and size, is specified in the contract, and the presence of collateral clearly influences the other terms of the contract. We shall discuss collateral in several contexts; at this stage, we are interested in its role when setting up the loan contract and its possibilities in providing suitable incentives for the borrower to repay the debt.

It seems obvious that if the contract with no collateral specifies a repayment of R, and the borrower has an outcome $y > R$ so that repayment is possible, then the borrower will gain R from pretending inability to pay and defaulting on the loan. However, if the borrower has pledged a collateral of size C, then the gain is reduced to $R - C$, and there will be no gain at all if C exceeds R, which typically will be the case. This indicates that collateral may do away with the problems of asymmetric information in the lender-borrower relationship, and one would expect collateral to be a natural ingredient in any loan contract.

However, the matters are less simple for several reasons. As pointed out by Barro [1976], the value of collateral to the borrower may differ from its value to the lender. Suppose that the loan of size 1 specifies a repayment R and a collateral $\tilde{C}$. Collateral is an asset with a market value, but this market value may be subject to random changes. We assume that the value of the collateral is a random variable with density $f(C)$. In this situation, the probability of default is

$$p = \mathsf{P}\{\tilde{C} < R\} = \int_{-\infty}^{R} f(C) \, dC,$$

showing that the default probability is an increasing function of R with $\dfrac{dp}{dR} = f(R)$. Given that the borrower defaults, the expected value of the collateral is

$$\frac{1}{p} \int_{-\infty}^{R} C f(C) \, dC < R,$$

and the expected repayment with this collateral is

$$\int_{-\infty}^{R} C f(C) \, dC < pR.$$

Thus, the collateral itself induces (ex post) moral hazard in the borrower-lender relationship because the fluctuating values of the collateral give an incentive to strategic default. In practice, this has led to the practice of *over-collaterization*, which means that the value of collateral should be considerably greater than R, and to rules for supplementary collateral in the case where the value of the original collateral drops below a certain limit.

So far, no informational problems were involved. To understand the role of collateral under conditions of asymmetric information, we need to develop the model somewhat further, following the approach of Boot et al. [1991]. We have here a bank which offers a loan of size 1 to be used for investment. The investment project of the borrower succeeds with probability $p_\theta(e)$, giving an outcome y, and fails with probability $1 - p_\theta(e)$, in which case outcome is 0. Here θ is the type of investor, which is either B ('bad') or G ('good'), and e denotes the effort of the borrower-investor. We assume that e can be either e_L or e_H, with $p_\theta(e_L) < p_\theta(e_H)$ for all θ, and that $p_B(e) < p_G(e)$ for all e. Effort has a monetary cost to the borrower, denoted $V(e)$, with $V(e_L) < V(e_H)$.

We assume in the following that

$$p_B(e_H) - p_B(e_L) > p_G(e_H) - p_G(e_L),$$

so effort matters more for the bad than for the good borrower. In this situation, quality and effort are substitutes, and we should expect that in a first-best optimum, good investors choose e_L, while bad investors choose e_H. Indeed, the optimization problem of the borrower consists in choosing $e \in \{e_L, e_H\}$ so as to maximize

$$p_\theta(e)y - V(e) - \rho,$$

where ρ is the repayment rate at which society can borrow (and society has to pay back, no matter whether the investments succeed or fail). For the good investor ($\theta = G$), we have that e_L is optimal if

$$p_G(e_L)y - V(e_L) - \rho \geq p_G(e_H)y - V(e_H) - \rho$$

or

$$p_G(e_H) - p_G(e_L) \leq \frac{V(e_H) - V(e_L)}{y}, \tag{11}$$

and for the bad investor, we similarly obtain that e_H is chosen if

$$p_B(e_H) - p_B(e_L) \geq \frac{V(e_H) - V(e_L)}{y}. \tag{12}$$

Thus, the intuitive optimal choices are indeed obtained when we extend out assumptions on the probabilities above to the following inequalities:

$$p_B(e_H) - p_B(e_L) \geq \frac{V(e_H) - V(e_L)}{y} \geq p_G(e_H) - p_G(e_L).\tag{13}$$

The assumption states that the burden of choosing greater effort, normalized with respect to the outcome at stake, is smaller than the effect for the bad investors, but higher than that of the good investors.

In the full infomation situation leading to the first-best optimum, there is no specific reason for having a collateral in the contract. However, with less than full information, such a reason will be present, as we shall see. Indeed, it is intuitive that collateral may urge the bad investors to exert the necessary effort, but it is less clear whether this would not induce the good investors to oversupplying effort.

It is assumed that neither the quality of the investor nor effort provided can be observed by the bank. Expanding on the results obtained above, we say that *there is moral hazard* if the investor choosing e_H in the first-best optimum (that is, the bad investor) will choose e_L if offered an unsecured loan with repayment $\rho/p_B(e_H)$ in the case of success, and 0 otherwise (so that the expected repayment would allow society to pay back according to ρ). This happens when

$$p_B(e_L)\left(y - \frac{\rho}{p_B(e_H)}\right) - V(e_L) \geq p_B(e_H)\left(y - \frac{\rho}{p_B(e_H)}\right) - V(e_H),$$

or

$$[p_B(e_H) - p_B(e_L)]y - (V(e_H) - V(e_L)) \leq [p_B(e_H) - p_B(e_L)]\frac{\rho}{p_B(e_H)}.$$

To avoid moral hazard, we must look for a second-best equilibrium, where the bank proposes a contract $(R_\theta, C_\theta)_{\theta=B,G}$ specifying repayment and collateral for each type, and the investors choose the contracts which were designed for their type, meaning that it should result in maximal expected borrower payoff

$$p_\theta(e^*)[y - R_\theta] - (1 - p_\theta(e^*))C_\theta - V(e^*)$$

subject to the constraints

$$p_\theta(e^*)R_\theta + (1 - p_\theta(e^*))C_\theta \geq \rho,$$

$$e^* \in \mathrm{argmax}_{e \in \{e_L, e_H\}} p_\theta(e)[y - R_\theta] - (1 - p_\theta(e))C_\theta - V(e)$$

for each θ. Here the first inequality is the participation constraint, stating that the expected repayment should be at least that of the first-best optimum, and the second is the incentive compatibility constraint for type θ.

PROPOSITION 5: *In the second-best equilibrium (under moral hazard), good investors are offered an unsecured loan contract with repayment*

$$\rho(G) = \frac{\rho}{p_G(e_L)}, \quad C_G = 0$$

whereas for the bad investors, assuming that $(p_B(e_H) - p_B(e_L))y - (V(e_H) - V(e_L)) \geq 0$, *the equilibrium contract is a secured loan with*

$$R_B = \frac{\rho}{p_B(e_H)} - (1 - p_B(e_H))\frac{C_B}{p_B(e_H)},$$

$$C_B = -p_B(e_H)y + \rho + \frac{p_B(e_H)[[V(e_H) - V(e_L)]]}{p_B(e_H) - p_B(e_L)}.$$

PROOF: For the first part of the proposition, there is nothing to prove, because the good investors would choose e_L already in the first-best optimum. For the bad investors, observe that the optimal choice is a secured loan, with effort level e_H. Because we are maximizing expected payoff of borrowers under the given constraints, the repayment R_B and the collateral C_B should be chosen as small as possible while satisfying these constraints, and from the participation constraint we get

$$p_B(e_H)R_B + (1 - p_B(e_H))C_B = \rho$$

and the expression for R_B. From the incentive-compatibility constraint with equality,

$$p_B(e_H)(y - R_B) - V(e_H) - (1 - p_B(e_H))C_B = p_B(e_L)(y - R_B) - V(e_L) - (1 - p_B(e_L))C_B,$$

we get that

$$(p_B(e_H) - p_B(e_L))[y - R_B + C_B] = V(e_H) - V(e_L)$$

or

$$C_B = -y + R_B + \frac{V(e_H) - V(e_L)}{p_B(e_H) - p_B(e_L)}.$$

Inserting R_B and solving for C_B, we get the desired solution.

It remains to check that the bad investor will actually choose the secured loan instead of an unsecured loan with the higher repayment $\frac{\rho}{p_B(e_L)}$, and for this to hold, we must have that

$$p_B(e_H)(y - R_B) - V(e_H) - (1 - p_B(e_H))C_B \geq p_B(e_L)\left(y - \frac{\rho}{p_B(e_L)}\right) - V(e_L)$$

or

$$(p_B(e_H) - p_B(e_L))y - (V(e_H) - V(e_L)) \geq (1 - p_B(e_H))C_B + p_B(e_H)R_B - \rho.$$

Inserting the expression for R_B, this reduces to the condition $(p_B(e_H) - p_B(e_L))y - (V(e_H) - V(e_L)) \geq 0$, which was assumed in the proposition.   □

The message of the proposition is quite intuitive: Collateral serves other purposes than just reducing the loss of the lender in the case of borrower default. It may also act as an incentive for the (bad) investor to increase the effort necessary for securing an acceptable result of the investment. This method for preventing moral hazard may be seen as the stick (losing an asset) where that of the previous section was the carrot (high outcome leading to reduced repayments). What we have seen here are, however, only some of the many aspects of using collateral, a practice which is indeed so widespread as to be almost natural in a lender-borrower relationship. The possible negative effects of collateral indicated in the beginning of the section, which are connected with the possible changes of value of the assets used, will concern us at a later stage when dealing with troubled banks and financial crises.

5.5 Group lending and microfinance

In this and previous chapters, we have discussed problems of monitoring investment carried out by the borrower, and we have considered the moral hazard problems that can arise when monitoring is incomplete or absent: The borrower may be tempted to choose more risky investments than what is optimal for society, with detrimental results for the lenders and for society as a whole. The high interest rates prevailing in many countries, notably in developing countries, will make this problem even more acute, cf. our discussion in Section 1.3.2.

In this situation, arrangements which reduce the possibility of the moral hazard problem will improve social welfare. One such device is that of *peer monitoring*, where several borrowers monitor each other; an arrangement which has had some success in developing countries. We comment on the application to *microfinance* later in this section; at present, we are mainly concerned with showing that peer monitoring may be a useful way to deal with the moral hazard problem, following the approach of Stiglitz [1990].

5.5.1 A formal model of group lending
The set-up in our present model is similar, even if not identical, to that of the moral hazard model of Section 1.3.2. We assume that borrowers can undertake one of two projects, with outcome in the case of success either $y_G(L)$ or $y_B(L)$. The new feature of our present model is the presence of the variable L which denotes the amount borrowed and invested. The probabilities of success are π_G and π_B, where $\pi_G > \pi_B$ and

$$\pi_G y_G(L) > \pi_B y_B(L)$$

for all L, so the safer investment is better for society than the more risky investment. It is seen that project size is variable in this model, and we assume that the techniques differ between projects; for both there is an initial fixed cost $\bar{L}_j$ such that $y_j(L) = 0$ for $L \leq \bar{L}_j$, and we assume that

$$\bar{L}_G < \bar{L}_B \quad \text{but} \quad \frac{dy_G}{dL} < \frac{dy_B}{dL} \text{ for } L \geq \bar{L}_B.$$

Thus, the risky project has a higher fixed cost than the safe investment, but once it begins to deliver output, the marginal product is higher at any level of investment. The two production functions may look as in Fig. 5.6.

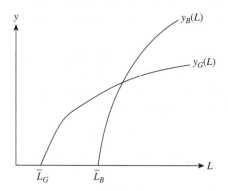

Figure 5.6 Production functions for safe and risky technologies. The safe technology begins to yield output at a lower level of input than the risky one, but marginal product is greater in the risky technology.

Borrowers are all identical, and in addition to capital, they must supply effort, the amount of which is determined uniquely by project size, so it can be formulated as a money cost $v(L)$ with $v' > 0$.

The expected utility of a borrower who has chosen project j is

$$U_j(L, R) = \pi_j u(y_j(L) - RL) - v(L), \quad j = G, B,$$

where R is the repayment rate (per unit of capital borrowed), which throughout the model is assumed to adjust so that expected profit of the bank is 0 and where $v(L)$ is the disutility of effort. The von Neumann-Morgenstern utility function u captures the attitude towards risk of the borrowers (with usual properties, $u' > 0$, $u'' < 0$).

To find the equilibrium choice of credit contracts in this model, specifying size of project L as well as repayment R, we first consider the contracts which are such that the borrower is indifferent between the two projects, that is

$$U_G(L, R) = U_B(L, R).$$

By our assumptions,

$$\frac{\partial U_G}{\partial L} = \pi_G u'(y_G(L) - RL)\left[\frac{dy_G}{dL} - R\right] - v'(L)$$

$$< \pi_B u'(y_B(L) - RL)\left[\frac{dy_B}{dL} - R\right] - v'(L) = \frac{\partial U_B}{\partial L},$$

at any such (L, R), so increasing loan and project size slightly with fixed repayment rate will make the borrowers prefer the risky technology B. For the lender, the zero-profit contracts are defined by

$$\pi_G R = r \text{ or } R = \frac{r}{\pi_G},$$

where r is the funding repayment rate, when the borrowers choose G, and similarly

$$R = \frac{r}{\pi_B}$$

when the borrowers choose B. Thus, the equilibrium contract maximizing expected utility of borrowers under a zero-profit constraint for the lender is a contract (L^*, R^*) at the boundary between the regions where borrowers choose G and B (see Fig. 5.7), and we may assume that G is chosen.

This contract is, however, not quite satisfactory; indeed it is a contract with *credit rationing*, in the sense that at the given interest rate, borrowers would prefer to borrow more than what is stipulated by the contract. However, lenders are not willing to offer more because that would lead to the choice of B by borrowers, and thereby to losses. We are not specifically interested in this rationing aspect, which shall concern us in the chapter to follow, but rather we shall see that there is an arrangement which may improve welfare by making borrowers monitor each other.

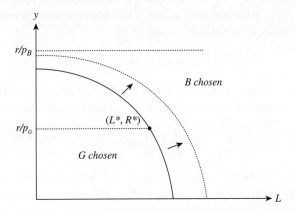

Figure 5.7 The region of contracts, for which investors choose the safe technology, is bounded, and this makes it difficult to engage in large-scale investments. The introduction of some joint liability decreases the zero-profit interest rate, but the increased liability is an increased burden on borrowers. However, the rationing of capital can be relaxed, thereby allowing for investment on a larger scale than before.

Formally, we assume now that contracts are signed with *two* borrowers rather than with a single borrower. The projects are independent, but each borrower is now committed to a repayment of a fraction q of the loan of the other borrower, in the case that the latter is unable to pay. We may assume that the borrowers act cooperatively, and either both choose G or both choose B. Expected utility of a borrower now becomes

$$p_j^2 u(y_j(L) - RL) + \pi_j(1 - \pi_j)u(y_j(L) - (R + q)L), \ \ j = G, B.$$

The obligation q on behalf of the other borrower is an increased burden on the borrower, but on the other hand, the repayment may be lower. The zero-profit condition for the bank now becomes

$$\pi_G R + \pi_G(1 - \pi_G)q = r,$$

which defines R as an implicit function $R(q)$ of q with derivative $\dfrac{dR}{dq} = -(1 - \pi_G)$, so the increased obligations are partially offset by a reduced interest rate.

As above, we consider the contracts (L, R) where the two borrowers are indifferent between G and B, and they must now satisfy

$$p_G^2 u(y_G(L) - RL) + \pi_G(1 - \pi_G)u(y_G(L) - (R + q)L)$$
$$= p_B^2 u(y_B(L) - RL) + \pi_B(1 - \pi_B)u(y_B(L) - (R + q)L).$$

Inserting $R = R(q)$, we get a locus of combinations (L, q), where L is an upper limit of the loan sizes offered by the zero-profit bank when the cosigning partners reimburse q.

To see what happens to the borrowers after the introduction of joint liability, one may choose a contract where the borrower is indifferent between the two projects and fix the level of expected utility obtained at this contract to

$$\overline{U} = \pi_j^2 u_j + \pi_j(1 - \pi_j)u_{jq} - v(L),$$

with $u_j = u(y_j(L) - R(q)L)$ and $u_{jq} = u(y_j(L) - R(q)L - qL)$, $j = G, B$. Using implicit function it can be found that without joint liability, when G is chosen and $q = 0$, one has

$$\left. \frac{\partial L}{\partial q} \right|_{U = \bar{U}} = 0,$$

so for small changes from 0 of q, these changes and those of the repayment rates offset each other from the point of view of expected utility of borrowers. However, this is not the full story, because the frontier between the regions of G and B will move as well.

As previously, the boundary between the regions where G and B are chosen is given by

$$U_G = \pi_G^2 u_G + \pi_G(1 - \pi_G)u_{G,q} = \pi_B^2 u_B + \pi_B(1 - \pi_B)u_{B,q} = U_B$$

and viewing this as a relationship connecting q and L, one may use implicit function theorem to find

$$\frac{\partial L}{\partial q} = -\frac{M_B - M_G}{\dfrac{\partial U_B}{\partial L} - \dfrac{\partial U_G}{\partial L}},$$

where

$$M_j = -\pi_j^2 u_j'(1 - \pi_G)L + \pi_j(1 - \pi_j)u_{jq}'\pi_G L, \ j = G, B.$$

If $q = 0$, we have $M_G = 0$ and $M_B < 0$, so

$$\frac{\partial L}{\partial q} > 0.$$

This tells us that starting from a case of no liability, if q is increased from 0, then the increase in L from the prevailing loan limit is bigger than the change in L needed to maintain constant expected utility, meaning that the borrowers will actually become better off by introducing a moderate liability. In addition, the larger scale of investment may presumably have beneficial effects on overall income and economic growth in the community.

5.5.2 Grameen bank and microfinance

In the previous subsection, we have considered a particular model of *group lending*, an institution which has been made famous by a particular financial institution, the Grameen Bank in Bangladesh, whose founder, Muhammad Yunus, was awarded the Nobel Peace Prize in 2006. The aim of Grameen is to alleviate poverty among the poorest families and to focus on women's income and empowerment. Initial loans are small, $100 or below, but can become larger. The main innovation was the creation of loan circles, usually of five women, in which the members used social pressure to ensure high rates of repayment and thereby to sustain the group's creditworthiness.

The high repayment rates of the banks following the ideas initiated by the Grameen Bank contrasted with the poor results obtained by financial institutions working according to standard financial practice, and indeed the traditional financial sector would have problems in servicing poor borrowers with no credit histories. The Grameen model of financial intermediation was therefore greeted with considerable enthusiasm, which to some extent has overshadowed the need for a rigorous analysis of the workings of financial intermediation in poor countries and among poor people in more developed countries. Not all the institutions set up according to the Grameen model have been equally successful, and theoretical analyses of group lending has uncovered the complicated nature of incentives rather than found a simple key to successful lending to the poor. Also, the initial impressive records of repayment, which secured that the banks could finance their activities by the interest paid in the microcredits, has changed to a situation where the institutions are heavily supported by donor countries.

The discussion of financial intermediation for the poor has moved beyond group lending and now involves other forms of financial intermediation, including insurance, so it has developed to a special discipline, *microfinance*, with its own textbooks, see e.g. Armendáriz and Morduch [2005]. By its nature, this discipline is closer to the economics of development than to the economics of banking, and we shall leave it at this point.

5.6 Exercises

1. A bank contemplates a new line of business, which it wants to propose to customers having large amounts in their deposit account with the bank. The bank offers credit which is earmarked for investment in security portfolios. The portfolios are registered and followed currently on the internet so that the bank can see the composition at any time.

How should the loan contract be set up for this particular segment of customers?

After some time, it is decided to restructure this particular service, allowing the customers to use a percentage of the loan for investment in other activities such as trading in antique furniture, paintings, etc. How should the contract be adapted to be useful in this new situation?

2. A bank wants to offer loans to entrepreneurs of a new type. Loans have the size €1.5 million, and the payoff obtained by the entrepreneur cannot be observed directly by the bank; however, it is known that it follows an exponential distribution with density $0.5e^{-0.5y}$, and its exact size can be verified at a cost of €100,000. The bank wants to use a standard contract, and to attract consumers of this type they have decided that no expected profits are to be obtained on this type of contract.

Find the repayment of this contract.

3. A bank plans to develop a new type of credit contract tailored for innovative new business. However, it has observed that many of the newly established firms get into problems because of the lack of the entrepreneurs' skills in handling the paperwork and accounting, even though this may be obtained through suitable training or assistance.

Suggest the type of credit contract needed for the bank to handle this problem.

After some time, a local business school sets up a cheap and easily accessible course for new entrepreneurs, and there are indications that it is widely used and has raised the general level of skills. Should the contract used hitherto be revised, and if so, how?

4. In a country there is a large number of small transportation firms, each having only a few vehicles. The industry is very competitive, so profits are small on average and subject to considerable variation over time.

The firms complain that they have problems in getting credit and that loan rates are high. Faced with such complaints, the banks point to a large number of cases where the borrowers default on their credit.

For purposes of income taxation, there is a system of registration installed which keeps track of the activity of each vehicle in the industry. The banks argue that if they were allowed access to this data, it would improve the credit situation of the firms.

Give a theoretical explanation of why the banks might be right. Could there be other ways of improving the situation?

5. Consider a borrower-lender situation where the lender knows only the probability distribution of the outcome of the borrower's investment but cannot observe the outcome actually realized. Explain that in this situation, the borrower may act in an opportunistic way and report low outcome when it is in fact high, so the lender cannot rely on a usual loan contract.

The lender decides that she will need collateral from the borrower in the form of an *option* to buy the assets of the firm at the price R (the repayment of the loan). Will this arrangement solve the problem?

6. A bank has had unsatisfactory results from credit offered for production of musical performances. Even though the shows tend to have a good attendance, the producers point to the need for giving away tickets for free, for offering rebates to selected groups and for arranging special events for the media, all circumstances which tend to reduce the revenue to such an extent that the bank in most cases has had to accept a renegotiation of the credit with a resulting reduction in repayments. Taken as a whole, the bank loses money on these loans.

The bank wants to consider alternative ways of administering the credit because it suspects that the results for the producers are often better than what they communicate to the bank. Give a suggestion for an alternative way of regulating the relationship between the bank and this type of customer.

5.7 Comments

As mentioned in the text, the results about risk sharing have their roots in the economic theory of insurance, which was developed in the 1950s and 1960s. Proposition 1 appeared in Arrow [1963], which dealt with optimal contracts in health insurance.

The theory of loan contracts under costly monitoring, leading to the standard contract, is taken from Townsend [1979] and Gale and Hellwig [1985]. The implication of costly monitoring for financial intermediation has been touched upon earlier and will also show up in subsequent chapters. For an approach to other aspects of the loan contract than repayment, see e.g. Chemmanur and Fulghieri [1994].

Collateral is an important aspect of the borrower-lender relationship, and we will return to it later. The message of the model by Besanko and Thakor [2004] is that collateral may be used to prevent moral hazard, but it may seem more intuitive to use collateral when there is adverse selection, and this situation will be considered in Chapter 6.

The microfinance literature was commented on in the text. The work by Stiglitz [1990], which considers microfinance as loans with joint liability, frees the treatment of the missionary approach which was otherwise characteristic of the microfinance literature of the early 2000s.

Chapter 6

Credit Rationing

6.1 Access to credit and supply of credit

One of the apparent puzzles of banking theory is that although lending in the financial sector is largely confined to private enterprise and guided by considerations of profit maximization, the market for credits is *not* balanced through the working of the price mechanism. Individuals may be denied credit even if they are willing to pay arbitrarily high interest rates. Thus, the market does not achieve equality of demand and supply; there is no value of the price charged in this market, that is, the interest rate – or in a simple two-period setting, the repayment per unit loan – for which the demand for loans equals the supply.

This puzzle is, however, no more complicated than for common sense to suggest a plausible solution: Those individuals who state their willingness to pay arbitrarily high interest rates may presumably cause problems when it comes to the repayment of credit, and such customers should rather be avoided by the bank. Rephrasing this argument in the language of economics textbooks, we expect the supply of credit to be *backward bended*, and if this is so, there may be no intersection of the demand and supply curves, such as illustrated in Fig. 6.1.

Even if this argument may be simplistic, in particular because the market for financial services, including credit, is far from being a purely competitive one where supply and demand make sense, it does point to something important, namely the considerations of lenders when assessing the creditworthiness of borrowers. We saw already in Chapter 1 that this situation is one where asymmetric information is present in one form or another, and therefore it certainly merits a closer study.

This closer scrutiny of the lender-borrower relationship *ex ante*, before it has materialized, has two aims. First of all, we want to complete the reasoning about backward-bended demand; this is done by showing that *expected* repayment in many situations may vary with *nominal* repayment in such a way that from a certain level, the expected repayment decreases when the nominal repayment increases, cf. Fig. 6.2.

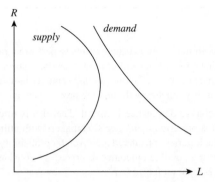

Figure 6.1 Backward-bending supply and (ordinary) demand: There may be no equilibrium at any repayment rate.

The relationship between nominal and expected repayment of debt is, however, important for other reasons than providing a theoretical underpinning for backward-bending supply, which, as mentioned, remains a somewhat unsatisfactory approach to the market for credit. The type of market failure which is at work may be expected to give rise to suboptimal allocation, and in this context it is important to investigate whether equilibrium occurs with too small a provision of credit, as suggested by the credit rationing approach, or whether on the contrary too many applications for credit are being granted in equilibrium, as compared to a social optimum.

6.2 Asymmetric information and credit rationing

6.2.1 A model of adverse selection with credit rationing

One of several possible explanations of the relationship pictured in Fig. 6.2 is delivered by the adverse selection model of Stiglitz and Weiss [1981], the basic ideas of which we describe here.

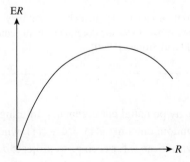

Figure 6.2 A possible relationship between nominal and expected repayment: Expected repayment is eventually decreasing.

Box 6.1

Stochastic dominance. In many contexts, one wants to perform a ranking of different random prospects according to some general criteria. Clearly, a specific decision maker can rank all prospects by expected utility, but this ranking is purely individual – another decision maker with a different utility function will rank the prospects in another way.

Here the notion of stochastic dominance is useful. The idea is to consider one lottery as better than another if it is preferred by *all* decision makers with utility functions belonging to a certain family. If the lotteries considered are given by probability distributions over real numbers, considered as the possible outcomes or prizes, we consider ways of defining the distribution (function) F to be preferred to F':

First-order stochastic dominance: F first order stochastically dominates F' if, for each decision maker with a monotonically increasing utility function, expected utility with F is better than expected utility with F',

$$\int u(x)\,dF(x) \geq \int u(x)\,dF'(x). \tag{1}$$

Thus, all individuals considering large outcomes to be better than small outcomes will prefer the lottery F to the lottery F'. It is easily shown that if F stochastically dominates F', then $F(x') \leq F(x)$ for each x (one may use (1) with the function which is 0 below x and 1 above x).

Second-order stochastic dominance: If the two lotteries have the same mean,

$$\int x\,dF(x) = \int x\,dF'(x),$$

so that they differ only in the way that the outcomes are spread around the mean, then F second order stochastically dominates F' if

$$\int u(x)\,dF(x) \geq \int u(x)\,dF'(x) \tag{2}$$

for all *concave* utility functions u. Thus, as long as the decision maker is risk averse, F will be preferred to F'. The degree of risk aversion will not matter for the mutual ranking of the two lotteries.

Higher order stochastic dominance can also be defined, but they are not important for our purposes. The use of second-order stochastic dominance in the context of economic models was initiated by Rothschild and Stiglitz [1970].

Assume that there are many potential entrepreneurs differing in type τ. The investor of type τ has a project with random outcome $\tilde{y}(\tau) = \mu + \tilde{z}(\tau)$, where $\mu > 0$ is a constant and $\tilde{z}(\tau)$ is a random variable with mean 0 for each τ, so projects do not differ in mean value, but only in their riskiness. We assume that $\tilde{z}(\tau)$ is distributed according to the distribution function $F(z|\tau)$, which is differentiable in both z at τ, with a density $f(z|\tau)$. The types τ, which characterize the entrepreneurs, are themselves distributed in the interval [0, 1] with a probability distribution G and density g. We shall assume in the sequel that for $\tau' > \tau$, the distribution $F(z|\tau)$ second order stochastically dominates $F(z|\tau')$. Thus, an investor of type τ' applying for a loan has a more risky project than an investor of type $\tau < \tau'$.

The bank offers loans according to a standard contract with repayment R, and the profit for the entrepreneur at the outcome z will be

$$\pi(z, R) = \max\{\mu + z - R, 0\}, \tag{3}$$

as depicted in Fig. 6.3. Define $\Pi(\tau, R) = \int_{-\infty}^{+\infty} \pi(z, R) f(z|\tau) \, dz$ as the expected outcome for an entrepreneur of type τ. For z such that $\mu + z - R < 0$, that is, for $z < R - \mu$, the contribution to integral is 0, so the integral can be written as a sum of the constant part $\mu - R$ multiplied by the probability of non-zero profit, which is $1 - F(R - \mu|\tau))$, plus the integral of z over the range of non-zero profit,

$$\Pi(\tau, R) = (\mu - R)(1 - F(R - \mu|\tau)) + \int_{R-\mu}^{\infty} z f(z|\tau) \, dz.$$

We rewrite the integral as

$$\int_{R-\mu}^{\infty} z f(z|\tau) \, dz = - \int_{-\infty}^{R-\mu} z f(z|\tau) \, dz = - \left[z \, F(z|\tau) \right]_{-\infty}^{R-\mu} + \int_{-\infty}^{R-\mu} F(z|\tau) \, dz,$$

where we use first that $\tilde{z}$ has expected value 0, and then perform integration by parts. Because the first member on the right-hand side yields $-(R - \mu)F(R - \mu|\tau)$, we obtain

$$\Pi(\tau, R) = \mu - R + \int_{-\infty}^{R-\mu} F(z|\tau) \, dz.$$

As $\pi(\cdot, R)$ is a convex function, and $-\pi(\cdot, R)$ is therefore concave, we know from stochastic dominance that expected profits for entrepreneurs increase with riskiness.

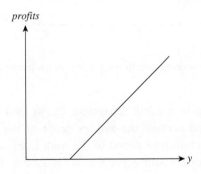

Figure 6.3 The profit function in a standard contract.

Let $\theta(R) = \min\{\tau \mid \Pi(t, R) \geq 0\}$ be the smallest type for which it is interesting to apply for a loan, so $\theta(R)$ is defined implicitly by $\Pi(\theta(R), R) = 0$. Using the implicit function theorem, we get that

$$\theta'(R) = -\frac{1 - F(R - \mu | \theta(R))}{\int_{-\infty}^{R-\mu} F_\tau'(z | \theta(R)) \, dz} > 0, \tag{4}$$

where the denominator is positive due to second-order stochastic domination.

The average expected profit of borrowers is

$$\overline{\Pi}(R) = \frac{1}{1 - G(\theta(R))} \int_{\theta(R)}^{1} \Pi(\tau, R) g(\tau) \, d\tau,$$

and *expected repayment* for the bank is

$$\rho(R) = \mu - \overline{\Pi}(R).$$

As outlined in the previous section, we are interested in the functional form of $\rho(\cdot)$. If R increased, then some types with relatively low risk drop out, leaving the bank with the more risky investors. Thus, we have an instance of adverse selection as also considered previously (in Chapter 1).

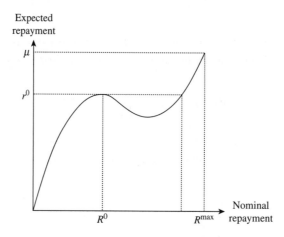

Figure 6.4 The expected repayment rate in the Stiglitz-Weiss model of credit applications under adverse selection.

Intuitively, the increase in nominal repayment results in a loan portfolio which on average is more risky, and because the average profit of the investors increases with riskiness, we would expect average payoff to the bank to be reduced, which is exactly the kind of relationship that would explain credit rationing. Summing up, if nominal repayment is increased, the market adapts, and as a consequence the loan portfolio gets more risky. Depending on the magnitude of the market response, the total effects on expected repayments may be positive or negative, with the latter effect more plausible the higher the level of nominal repayment. In other words, we have a situation as depicted by Fig. 6.2.

6.2.2 Rationing in a market with competition among lenders

As pointed out by Arnold and Riley [2009], the intuitive argument shows that there may be a certain level R_a of nominal repayment at which adverse selection sets in, so a higher R forces some less risky types out of the market, but there is more to it. Consider the situation where R has been increased to its maximal value $R^{\max}$ at which $\theta(R^{\max}) = 1$ so the type $\tau = 1$ is marginal, $\Pi(1, R^{\max}) = \overline{\Pi}(R^{\max}) = 0$. Then $\rho(R^{\max}) = \mu$, so the bank gets the entire average payoff and thus attains its maximum over the range of possible values of R.

EXAMPLE 6.2 Suppose that the projects which need to be financed have payoffs which are uniformly distributed in the interval $[0, 2\tau]$, where $0 \leq \tau \leq 2\tau$. The project of type τ has mean τ, and at the repayment rate R, the project owner will apply for a loan if expected payoff $\int_0^{2\tau} y \, dy$ exceeds R, or equivalently if

$$\tau \geq \sqrt{\frac{R}{2}}.$$

Expected repayment on the project of type τ is

$$\int_0^{\sqrt{R/2}} y \, dy + \int_{\sqrt{R/2}}^{2\tau} R \, dy = R - \frac{R^2}{4\tau}.$$

We now add an assumption on the distribution of types, namely that its density has the form $g(\tau) = \tau/2$ for $0 \leq \tau \leq 2$, and $g(\tau) = 0$ otherwise. Then overall expected repayment at the nominal rate R is

$$\rho(R) = \int_{\sqrt{R/2}}^2 \left[R - \frac{R^2}{4\tau} \right] \frac{\tau}{2} \, d\tau = R - \frac{3}{8}R^2 + \frac{1}{8}R^2 \sqrt{\frac{R}{2}}.$$

Inserting some possible values of R, we get

R	$\rho(R)$
1	0.7134
2	1
3	1.0028
4	0.8284

showing that expected payoff first increases and then decreases when R is increased.

Therefore, the graph of ρ must look as in Fig. 6.4; it may have a local maximum from which an increase in R entails a reduction in ρ, but eventually $\rho(R)$ will increase again so as to attain the maximum in $R^{\max}$.

If we add the funding of the competitive banks, assuming that the funding rate r is competed down to the level where average payoff to the bank is 0, then the expected payoff relationship ρ can be used to define a demand function in the market for loanable funds. Let ρ^* be defined as

$$\rho^*(r) = \min\{R \mid \rho(R) = r\},$$

so $\rho^*(r)$ gives the smallest nominal rate at which the average repayment is r. Then $1 - G(\theta(\rho^*(r)))$ is the largest set of active projects which is compatible with r. We then have the demand function

$$D(r) = 1 - G(\theta(\rho^*(r))),$$

as illustrated in Fig. 6.5. The demand curve has a jump at the level $r^0 = \rho^*(R^0)$ corresponding to repayment rate R^0, where ρ has the local maximum and begins to decrease.

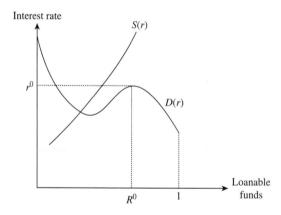

Figure 6.5 Rationing equilibrium in the adverse selection model with competition among banks for loanable funds.

Combining the demand for funds with a supply curve $S(r)$, we can get situations where there is no intersection, because $S(r)$ passes through the jump of $D(r)$ at r^0. In this case rationing is necessary, because there are not enough loanable funds available at r^0 to satisfy all applicants for credit with repayment rate R^0. On the other hand, if the bank sets the repayment rate to the other value $R > R^0$ at which $\rho(R) = \rho(R^0)$, then demand is too small, but now it is supply and not demand that is rationed.

The rationing equilibrium in the market happens only when the supply curve is suitably situated so as to pass through the jump. Intuitively, the likelihood of a rationing equilibrium therefore depends on the size of this jump, and closer consideration (as in Arnold and

Riley [2009]) shows that it will in most cases be of rather small size, so the explanation of credit rationing based on adverse selection seems to be one which applies only in a few situations.

6.2.3 Credit rationing with moral hazard

The linkage of the credit rationing phenomenon to the instances of asymmetric information, which, as we have seen, are central for the functioning of banks, can be developed further if we consider the simple model of moral hazard which we considered in Section 1.3.3. Here the investors all have the choice between two projects I_B and I_G, where I_j has outcome j with probability π_j and 0 with probability $1 - \pi_j$, $j = B, G$, whereby $B > G$, but $\pi_G G > 1 > \pi_B B$. The choice of project cannot be observed by the bank. The investor receives the outcome and repays R if $y_j > 0$ and 0 otherwise.

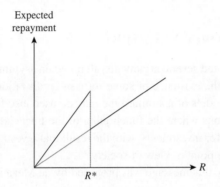

Figure 6.6 Expected repayment in the moral hazard model.

As was noticed, the investor will choose project I_G only if

$$R \leq R^* = \frac{\pi_G G - \pi_B B}{\pi_G - \pi_B}.$$

This means that expected repayment, which is $\pi_G R$ if $R \leq R^*$ and $\pi_B R$ if $R > R^*$, has a form as shown in Fig. 6.6. The shape of this curve does not quite fit with that of Fig. 6.2, but the main features, namely that it is increasing to some (local) maximum after which it falls down to lower values, remain intact, even if the curve consists of two linear segments with slope π_G (first part) and π_B (second part).

6.2.4 Costly monitoring and credit rationing

The need for monitoring the investment, and the cost of doing so, may also lead to the eventually decreasing relationship between nominal and expected repayment, as pointed out by Williamson [1986].

Assume that the standard contract is used, so monitoring at the cost c_m is initiated whenever outcome is below w. If the random outcome $\hat{y}$ has the probability distribution function $F(y)$ and density $f(y)$, then expected repayment given the repayment level R becomes

$$\rho(R) = \int_0^R (y - c_m)f(y)dy + \int_R^\infty Rf(y)dy.$$

To see how this changes with R, we find the derivative w.r.t. R,

$$\rho'(R) = (R - c_m)f(R) - Rf(R) + \int_R^\infty f(y)dy = [1 - F(R)] - c_m f(R).$$

When R becomes large enough, the first member of this expression gets close to 0, and unless the density goes as quickly to zero, which rarely happens, the derivative will become negative for large enough R, which once again gives us a relationship as illustrated in Fig. 6.2.

6.3 Under- or oversupply of credit?

Because we have presented several arguments, all based on asymmetric information in one version or another, for the existence of some form of credit rationing, it would be fair at this point to add that models of a similar type may be used also for the opposite point of view, displaying situations where the functioning of the financial intermediaries leads to an oversupply of credit for investments, with the result that investments are initiated which are suboptimal from the point of view of society.

A model with exactly this message was proposed by de Meza and Webb [1987]. As in other models we have considered, investment projects yield a high outcome y_H if successful and a low outcome $y_L < y_H$ otherwise. The investors are now assumed to possess an initial amount W of wealth, which, however, is insufficient for carrying out the investment, normalized to 1, so they have to borrow $B = 1 - W$. Borrowing follows a standard contract, so repayment for investor i is RB when outcome is y_H and y_L when outcome is low (where we have assumed that $y_L < BR$).

Investors differ among each other only in the probability π of success of their version of the investment project. Assuming that the risk-free rate of interest is r, then an investment project is beneficial for society as long as

$$\pi y_H + (1 - \pi)y_L \geq 1 + r, \tag{5}$$

and assuming that π_i has continuous variation in the population of investors, the marginal investment project is the one where (1) is satisfied with an equality sign.

If the quality of the investor, as measured by the probability π of success, was observable, then the decision of society would be to carry out investment whenever (5) is satisfied, meaning that credits should be forthcoming in exactly these cases. We assume now that π

is *not* observable, so credit has to be obtained without information about π. In the market, the investor with success probability π will accept loans with repayment rate R as long as

$$\pi(y_H - RB) \geq (1 + r)W, \tag{6}$$

where the left-hand side expresses the expected profit from the investment, and the right-hand side is the profit to be obtained by investing all wealth in a risk-free asset. The inequality (6) gives us the market constraint on the demand for credits: Only the projects satisfying this condition will appear in the market when the repayment rate is R, and the success probability of the marginal project is an increasing function $\pi(R)$ of R.

On the other side of the market, the bank will supply credit as long as expected profits are non-negative. Assume that the success probabilities are distributed in the population according to a distribution with density function $f(\pi)$, then the conditional density of the value π, given that $\pi \geq \pi(R)$, is written as $f_R(\pi) = \dfrac{f(p)}{1 - F(R)}$. Now the condition for non-negativity of profits becomes

$$RB \int_{\pi(R)}^{1} \pi f_R(\pi)\, d\pi + y_L \int_{\pi(R)}^{1} (1 - \pi) f_R(\pi)\, d\pi - (1 + r)B \geq 0. \tag{7}$$

We assume that financial intermediaries can enter at will, so equilibrium in the market is characterized by a zero-profit condition, meaning that (7) is satisfied with equality.

Writing the average success probability of projects in the market as

$$\bar{\pi}(R) = \int_{\pi(R)}^{1} \pi f_R(\pi)\, d\pi,$$

the zero-profit condition may be written as

$$\bar{\pi}(R)RB + (1 - \bar{\pi}(R))y_L = \bar{\pi}(R)(RB - y_L) + y_L = (1 + r)B,$$

and using that $\bar{\pi}(R) > \pi(R)$, because we have taken the average over all probabilities greater than $\pi(R)$, and $RB > y_L$, we get that

$$\pi(R)RB + (1 - \pi(R))y_L < \bar{\pi}(R)RB + (1 - \bar{\pi}(R))y_L = (1 + r)B.$$

Adding to this equation the version of (6) holding for the marginal investor,

$$\pi(R)(y_H - RB) = (1 + r)W,$$

we get that

$$\pi(R)y_H + (1 - \pi(R))y_L < 1 + r,$$

which compared with (5) shows that the marginal investor in the market has a project which, from the point of view of society, should not have been carried through. We have thus shown the following:

PROPOSITION 1: *Assume that the success probabilities have a continuous density with positive density function. Then some of the investment projects which obtain credit in a zero-profit equilibrium are suboptimal from the point of view of society.*

Because the presence of suboptimal investment projects can be seen as a result of competition among banks, it might be remedied by adding a tax on R; increased R leads to higher $\pi(R)$, and zero profit of banks is achieved before the competition has driven repayment rates too low.

It may, of course, come as a surprise that in the present model we have an oversupply of credit, whereas the very similar model of Stiglitz and Weiss considered in the previous section displayed an undersupply. The models are, however, not identical, although the differences may not be too visible at first sight. What matters is how the available set of projects to be financed are characterized. In the Stiglitz-Weiss model, we had a family of projects with very different returns – the expected outcome might be the same, but the variance would differ among projects. In the present model, there are only two possible outcomes, the high and the low one; what makes projects different is the probability of success. For applications of the models, one has to consider which of the two ways of modelling the demand for credits is the most relevant one.

6.4 Collateral as a sorting device

We have already, in the previous chapter, considered *collateral* as a means of improving the repayment behaviour of borrowers, thereby increasing expected repayment as compared with the situation without collateral. Obviously, any device which reduces the gap between nominal and expected repayment will also reduce a shortage of supply as compared with demand for credit. It therefore comes as no surprise that collateral also plays a crucial role in the present context.

There is, however, an additional aspect of collateral which makes it worthwhile to single it out for special treatment, namely the *signalling effect*. The willingness to pledge collateral signals a high probability of success for the investor, a signal which is important because it may entail reduced nominal repayment. In the present section, we look more closely at this signalling effect, following the seminal contribution of Bester [1985].

We consider a situation of the type that we have discussed repeatedly in the previous sections, namely one with two types of borrowers, one more risky than the other one. For simplicity, we may assume that the investment projects to be financed, all having the amount of 1 unit, arc such that the outcome in the case of success is $y > 0$ and in the case of failure 0, and that the probabilities of success are π_G and π_B with $\pi_G > \pi_B$. The investor is assumed to be risk averse with von Neumann-Morgenstern utility u, so expected utility of a loan contract with repayment R and collateral C is

$$U(R, C; \pi_j) = \pi_j u(W + y - R) + (1 - \pi_j) u(W - C), \quad j = B, G,$$

where W is initial wealth. The value of the collateral C is assumed to be $v(C)$, where v is a concave function expressing the additional cost incurred by its disposal, and expected profit of a contract with a borrower of type j is then a function of R and C,

$$V(R, C; \pi_j) = \pi_j R + (1 - \pi_j) v(C) - (1 + r), \tag{8}$$

where r is the risk-free rate of interest.

We assume that the market is such that competing financial intermediaries may enter whenever risk-adjusted profits are positive, so expected profits are zero in an equilibrium. In Fig. 6.7, we show the curves given by $V(R, C, \pi) = 0$, that is, zero expected profit as defined in (8), for fixed values $\pi = \pi_G, \pi_B$ of the success probability, as well as for $\pi = \bar{\pi}$, the average probability of success, determined by the proportions of good and bad borrowers in the population. These curves have slope

$$\frac{dR}{dC} = -\frac{\dfrac{\partial V}{\partial C}}{\dfrac{\partial V}{\partial R}} = -\frac{(1 - \pi) v'(C)}{\pi}$$

which is numerically decreasing in C, and they pass through the point A, where the repayment is $1 + r$ and the collateral such that $v(C) = 1 + r$, so the loan is fully collateralized, and the lender bears no risk at all. The three zero-profit curves in the figure correspond to π_G (the lowest one), π_B (the highest), and $\bar{\pi} = \lambda_G \pi_B + \lambda_B \pi_B$, the average probability of success given that the two types of borrower are represented in proportions λ_G, λ_B.

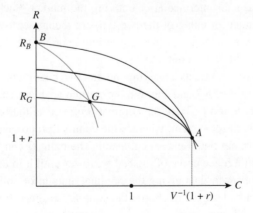

Figure 6.7 Separating equilibrium in the signalling model.

We now add asymmetric information; borrower type cannot be observed. We are looking at contracts $(R_j, C_j)_{j=B,G}$ specifying both repayment and collateral, where as previously we assume that there is a contract proposed for each type of borrower. For such a pair of contracts to be an equilibrium, we demand that

- the contracts are *incentive compatible* in the sense that each type is as well off with its contract as with that of the other type:

$$\pi_G u(W + y - R_G) + p(1 - \pi_G)u(W - C_G) \geq$$
$$\pi_G u(W + y - R_B) + (1 - \pi_G)u(W - C_B)$$
$$\pi_B u(W + y - R_B) + (1 - \pi_B)u(W - C_B) \geq$$
$$\pi_B u(W + y - R_G) + (1 - \pi_B)u(W - C_G);$$

- the bank earns zero expected profit on each contract,

$$\pi_G R_G + (1 - \pi_G)v(C_G) - (1 + r) = 0,$$
$$\pi_B R_B + (1 - \pi_B)v(C_B) - (1 + r) = 0;$$

and

- no bank can propose a new contract on which it can earn positive profit, i.e. there is no pair (C, R) such that either

    (a) $V(R', C', \pi_B) > 0, U(R', C', \pi_B) \geq U(R_B, C_B, \pi_B)$,

    (b) $V(R', C', \pi_G) > 0, U(R', C', \pi_G) \geq U(R_G, C_G, \pi_G), U(R', C', \pi_B) \leq U(R_B, C_B, \pi_B)$, or

    (c) $V(R', C', \bar{\pi}) > 0, U(R', C', \pi_G) \geq U(R_G, C_G, \pi_G), U(R', C', \pi_B) \geq U(R_B, C_B, \pi_B)$.

Here the first two equilibrium conditions are standard and have been commented upon already, but the last one is new. It states that the equilibrium should be stable against competition from financial intermediaries entering the market. Such a potential entrant might propose a contract for either of the two types or a contract to be used by both, but if the proposal is at least as good as the equilibrium contract for the borrower, then the entrant can earn no profit on the contracts.

It is rather easy to find contracts satisfying the first two conditions, using the geometric approach illustrated in Fig. 6.7 and Fig. 6.8. Of particular interest is the contract specified as the two points B and G. Here the contract proposed to the bad borrowers has no collateral but rather high repayment, whereas the contract proposed to the good borrowers has a lower repayment but non-zero collateral. The point G can be found from B by moving along the indifference curve of the bad borrower until it intersects the zero-profit curve of the good borrower, thus giving the minimal amount of collateral for which the bad borrower will not be tempted to choose the contract designed for the good borrower. The good borrowers will then prefer their own contract because their indifference curves have smaller (absolute) slope than those of the bad borrower.

The two contracts have been selected so as to minimize collateral given that the contracts yield zero expected profit. With a view to the third equilibrium condition, we see that other contracts would be open to competition from entrants offering lower collateral. But the no-entrance condition poses more restrictions, and we need to check that they are satisfied by our particular choice of contracts; as it turns out, this is not always the case!

First of all, we check that there is no potential entrant who can come up with a contract which lures away any of our types of borrowers and still gives positive expected profits. The bad borrowers are indeed quite safe because none of the contracts which are as good for them as B can yield positive profits (except for B itself they are all below the relevant zero-profit curve). One might propose a contract which is better for the good borrowers (below the relevant indifference curve through G but above the zero-profit curve, meaning that condition (a) may be violated). But all such contracts would be interesting for the bad borrowers as well, because they are below their indifference curve through B, and therefore it has to be treated as a (pooling) contract which is available for the market as a whole. This means that we must check condition (c) and see whether it can earn positive profits given that both types participate.

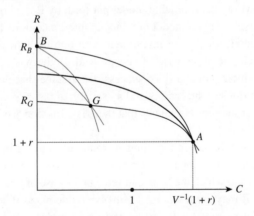

Figure 6.8 A case of no equilibrium: The candidate for separating equilibrium can be improved by a pooling contract.

This in turn depends on the position of the indifference curve of the good borrower through G. If this indifference curve remains below the zero-profit curve with respect to the average probability, then profits cannot be positive, so (c) is satisfied, and consequently the contracts in B and G define an equilibrium. If, however, the two curves do intersect, as illustrated in Fig. 6.8, then there are contracts (R', C') which are better for both types of borrower and leave the entrants with positive profits, meaning that G and B do not define an equilibrium.

The problems do not stop there: If B and G do not correspond to an equilibrium, then what does? Because this is the only possibility for a *separating* equilibrium (where the types get different contracts), the only remaining possibility would be a *pooling* contract of the type just considered. But pooling contracts also cannot satisfy the equilibrium conditions, because it will always be possible for an entrant to propose something better to the good borrowers alone, moving along their indifference curve through the actual contract to something which is below that of the bad borrowers. We conclude that in the case depicted in Fig. 6.8, *no equilibrium exists.*

This possible non-existence of equilibrium, which is a rather well-known feature of models of adverse selection built into a framework of markets and competition, is, of course, a somewhat unsatisfactory state of affairs because it shows that our model needs some improvement, either in the way that we define an equilibrium or perhaps in some other aspects of the construction. There is no immediate remedy for these shortcomings, and the illustration of signalling by collateral which is given by the model must be considered with this particular reservation.

6.5 Collateral and rationing

That the use of collateral as a remedy for credit rationing may depend crucially on market conditions is shown by the following model put forth by Besanko and Thakor [1987]. We consider an adverse selection model of financial intermediation. There are two investment possibilites, namely (a) a safe investment with non-random payoff b, and (b) an investment which yields R in the case of success and 0 otherwise. The investors – and borrowers – differ in their probability of success; we assume that there are two types of investor, with probabilities of success π_1 and π_2 satisfying $0 < \pi_1 < \pi_2 < 1$. The bank cannot observe the type of investor but knows that there is a fraction γ of investors which are type 1.

Because we shall allow for credit rationing, a credit policy of the bank will be described by three parameters, namely a repayment rate α for the loan, an amount of collateral C which must be posted and which the bank can seize in the case of failure, and a probability λ of granting a loan. It may seem strange to involve randomness in a contract – once the bank and the client have agreed, a lottery is performed to decide whether the client will actually receive the credit – but in the optimal solutions to be derived, λ is always either 0 (no credit) or 1 (credit is granted).

It will be assumed that the value to the bank of collateral C will be somewhat smaller than the nominal amount, discounted by a given factor $\beta < 1$, so as to account for the cost of selling the collateral in the market.

Assuming that the bank has chosen credit policies $(\alpha_i, C_i, \lambda_i)$, $i = 1, 2$, and that the borrowers take the credit contract offered to their type, expected profits to the bank are

$$\gamma\lambda_1(\pi_1\alpha_1 + (1 - \pi_1)\beta C_1 - r) + (1 - \gamma)\lambda_2(\pi_2\alpha_2 + (1 - \pi_2)\beta C_2 - r), \qquad (9)$$

where r is the repayment rate which the bank faces in its funding.

We shall restrict ourselves to the situation where the contracts are *incentive compatible* in the sense that the borrowers of type i prefer the contract $(\alpha_i, C_i, \lambda_i)$, $i = 1, 2$, so

$$\lambda_1(\pi_1(R - \alpha_1) - (1 - \pi_1)C_1 - b) \geq \lambda_2(\pi_1(R - \alpha_2) - (1 - \pi_1)C_2 - b) \qquad (10)$$

$$\lambda_2(\pi_2(R - \alpha_2) - (1 - \pi_2)C_2 - b) \geq \lambda_1(\pi_2(R - \alpha_1) - (1 - \pi_2)C_1 - b). \qquad (11)$$

That a contract with a value $\lambda_i = 0$, where the client gets no credit, does not invest and has expected outcome 0, is incentive compatible means that choosing the contract meant for the other type, where credit may be granted, will result in negative expected profits, so the client stays away from the loan market.

In addition to (10) or (11), we also demand that the expected gain from investing in the risky prospect should be non-negative,

$$\lambda_i(\pi_i(R - \alpha_i) - (1 - \pi_i)C_i - b) \geq 0, \ i = 1, 2, \qquad (12)$$

because otherwise the difference between the borrowers would not matter or would be obvious (one or both types choosing the safe investment).

Full information. Assume for the moment that the bank had full information about customer types so that the incentive compatibility conditions (10) and (11) are not needed, and the bank maximizes (9) subject to (12). Then the optimal contracts $(\alpha_i^0, C_i^0, \lambda_i^0)$, $i = 1, 2$ are such that

$$\alpha_i^0 = R - \frac{b}{\pi_i},$$

$$C_i^0 = 0,$$

$$\lambda_i^0 = \begin{cases} 1 & \pi_i R - b \geq r, \\ 0 & \text{otherwise.} \end{cases}$$

Indeed, the bank (which here acts as a monopolist) can extract all surplus from the borrowers, so expected payoff from investment $\pi_i R$ minus expected repayment to the bank (with no collateral) $\pi_i \alpha_i$ equals the repayment b from the safe investment. Collateral will indeed be 0 because $\beta < 1$ means that less surplus could be extracted from the borrower if it took the form of expected value of collateral. Credit is either granted to all investors of the type, namely as long as expected profits $\pi_i \alpha_i - r = \pi_i R - b - r$ are non-negative, or not granted at all.

Optimal choices under asymmetric information. Because we deal with a case of asymmetric information, the above result is interesting only as a benchmark, and we now turn to the relevant equilibrium, where the bank maximizes (9) under the constraints (10), (11) and (12).

PROPOSITION 2: *Under asymmetric information, the optimal credit policy* $(\alpha_i^*, C_i^*, \lambda_i^*)_{i=1}^2$ *of the monopoly bank satisfies*

$$\alpha_i^* = \lambda_1^* \left(R - \frac{b}{\pi_1} \right) + (1 - \lambda_1^*) \left(R - \frac{b}{\pi_2} \right), \; i = 1, 2,$$

$$C_i^* = 0$$

$$\lambda_1^* = \begin{cases} 1 & \pi_1 R - b - r \geq b \dfrac{\pi_2 - \pi_1}{\pi_1} \dfrac{1 - \gamma}{\gamma}, \\ 0 & \textit{otherwise.} \end{cases}$$

$$\lambda_2^* = 1.$$

It may be noticed that the repayment rates are the same for both types, as is the amount of collateral specified, which is 0, so the contracts differ only in the probabilities λ_i: The less risky borrowers get access to credit with probability 1, whereas the risky borrowers are rationed. Thus, the possibility of collateral has not done away with credit rationing in this model.

PROOF OF PROPOSITION 2: We write the Lagrangian for a modified maximization problem, where we have skipped condition (10) and use (12) only for $i = 1$,

$$L = \gamma \lambda_1 (\pi_1 \alpha_1 + (1 - \pi_1)\beta C_1 - r) + (1 - \gamma)\lambda_2(\pi_2 \alpha_2 + (1 - \pi_2)\beta C_2 - r)$$

$$+ \mu \left[\lambda_2(\pi_2(R - \alpha_2) - (1 - \pi_2)C_2 - b) - \lambda_1(\pi_2(R - \alpha_1) - (1 - \pi_2)C_1 - b) \right] \quad (13)$$

$$+ \nu \left[\lambda_1(\pi_1(R - \alpha_1) - (1 - \pi_1)C_1 - b) \right]$$

Because the constraints (10) together with (12) for type 1 puts a limit to the size of α_2, we search for the maximum among parameter values where $\dfrac{\partial L}{\partial \alpha_2} = 0$, and this implies that the Lagrange multiplier μ must equal $1 - \gamma$. But then L is linear as a function of C_2 with a coefficient which is negative, meaning that $C_2^* = 0$. Similarly, we get from $\dfrac{\partial L}{\partial \alpha_1} = 0$ that

$$\nu = \gamma + \mu \frac{\pi_2}{\pi_1}, \quad (14)$$

which again shows that $C_1^* = 0$.

Next, we use the complementary slackness condition: If in the optimum a Lagrange multiplier is non-zero, then the corresponding inequality must be fulfilled with equality. Therefore, (9) implies that

$$\lambda_1^*(\pi_1(R - \alpha_1^*) - b) = 0$$

so either $\lambda_1^* = 0$ or $\alpha_1^* = R - \dfrac{b}{\pi_1}$. If the incentive compatibility constraint (11) is satisfied with inequality so that

$$\lambda_2(\pi_2(R - \alpha_2) - b) > \lambda_1(\pi_2(R - \alpha_1) - b) = \lambda_1\left(\frac{\pi_2}{\pi_1}b - b\right),$$

then α_2 could be increased without violating the constraints, so we conclude that equality must hold, from which we get that

$$\alpha_2^* = R - \frac{b}{\pi_2} + \frac{\lambda_1}{\lambda_2}\left(\frac{b}{\pi_2} - \frac{b}{\pi_1}\right). \tag{15}$$

Inserting the values found in (9), we can write expected profit as

$$\Pi = \gamma\lambda_1\left[\pi_1 R - b - r - b\frac{\pi_2 - \pi_1}{\pi_1}\frac{1 - \gamma}{\gamma}\right] + (1 - \gamma)\lambda_2(\pi_2 R - b - r),$$

from which we get that

$$\frac{\partial\Pi}{\partial\lambda_2} = (1 - \gamma)(\pi_2 R - b - r) > 0,$$

so $\lambda_2^* = 1$. Similarly, we have that

$$\frac{\partial\Pi}{\partial\lambda_1} = \gamma\left[\pi_1 R - b - r - b\frac{\pi_2 - \pi_1}{\pi_1}\frac{1 - \gamma}{\gamma}\right],$$

so $\lambda_1^* = 1$ when the right-hand side is non-negative, and $\lambda_1^* = 0$ otherwise. Using this together with (15), we have obtained all the values stated in the proposition.

It remains only to check that the two constraints omitted in our analysis are actually also satisfied; this is left to the reader. □

It might come as a surprise that although collateral is possible, it is not used in the optimal contracts. We know from the full-information case that collateral is inefficient as an instrument of attracting surplus from the borrower; but one might still think that collateral would be useful as a sorting instrument, so why doesn't the bank offer lower loan rates to borrowers accepting a higher collateral? Starting with the full-information solution, the bank might lower the interest rate from α_1^0 and increase collateral from 0 so as to construct a contract that would attract low-risk borrowers. However, for each such contract, it would be better for the firm to convert collateral increase back to interest rate for the low-risk borrowers, and therefore collateral is also inefficient as a sorting device.

Equilibrium under competition. So far, the results obtained differ much from the model of the previous section, where competition and sorting by collateral would eliminate the rationing of credit. This is not so surprising given that we have considered a bank which had a monopoly in the market. Therefore, it makes sense to reconsider the above results in a situation more like the one treated previously, where there are many banks competing for borrowers and where ease of access to the market implies that expected profits are 0. Under full information, we would then have that

$$\alpha_i^0 = \frac{r}{\pi_i}, \quad C_i^0 = 0, \quad \lambda_i^0 = 1, \quad i = 1, 2,$$

reflecting that under competition the full surplus is left with the borrower. Under asymmetric information, an equilibrium is a pair of contracts $(\alpha_i, C_i, \lambda_i)$, $i = 1, 2$ which maximize expected profits (9) under the incentive compatibility constraints (10) and (11) together with the constraints

$$\pi_i \alpha_i + (1 - \pi_i)\beta C_i = r, \quad i = 1, 2, \tag{16}$$

which express the zero expected profits condition – the surplus is competed away for each of the two borrower types.

For the analysis of equilibria, we shall need to know something which was not so important before now, namely the *terminal wealth W* of the borrower, which poses an upper limit to the amount that can be posted as collateral.[1] To see why this matters, we find the equilibrium values of the two contracts, beginning with that of the high-risk borrower. Here we must have $\alpha_1^* = \frac{r}{\pi_1}$ and $C_1^* = 0$ because, as before, collateral is inefficient for type 1, and because of (16). Moving now to the low-risk borrower, and assuming first that W is large, we use (16) again to get that

$$\alpha_2^* = \frac{1}{\pi_2}(r - (1 - \pi_2)\beta C_2). \tag{17}$$

The equilibrium value C_2 can now be found using the incentive compatibility condition (10) with equality,

$$C_2^* = \frac{r(\pi_2 - \pi_1)}{\pi_2(1 - \pi_1) - (1 - \pi_2)\pi_1\beta},$$

where we have taken $\lambda_1^* = \lambda_2^* = 1$ (no credit rationing), because under competition all borrowers can obtain a loan as long as the above conditions are fulfilled.

However, for the above values to constitute a solution to the equilibrium problem, we need that the wealth W of type 2 borrowers is at least as great as C_r^*. So if

$$W < \frac{r(\pi_2 - \pi_1)}{\pi_2(1 - \pi_1) - (1 - \pi_2)\pi_1\beta},$$

then the contracts for low-risk borrowers must specify a collateral which is no bigger than W. Then (17) gives that

$$\alpha_2^* = \frac{1}{\pi_2}(r - (1 - \pi_2)\beta W),$$

---

[1] As in the model of the previous section, it is not obvious that an equilibrium exists, but this can be assured by suitable conditions on the parameter values.

but the incentive compatibility constraint (10) does not hold any more with $\lambda_2 = 1$, and to obtain an equality it should instead be

$$\lambda_2^* = \frac{\pi_1(R - \alpha_1^*) - b}{\pi_1(R - \alpha_2^*) - (1 - \pi_1)W - b},$$

which is < 1. Thus, in this case collateral works as a sorting mechanism but cannot function alone, because the amount of collateral which can possibly be posted is too small. Consequently, to distinguish between borrowers, an additional instrument is needed, which here is the possibility of obtaining credit. As a consequence, the rationing of borrowers, which was largely absent under conditions of monopoly and also in the equilibrium under perfect competition, as long as borrowers had sufficient wealth for collateral, has re-entered because it is needed in order to deter high-risk borrowers from taking the otherwise attractive low-risk contract.

6.6 Exercises

1. A newly opened bank has as its field of business the supply of credit to small restaurants in the area. There are two types of such restaurants, namely grill bars with a small but steady income, and gourmet restaurants whose earnings are subject to very great variations. Earlier attempts to service both types of restaurant have failed, as the interest rate demanded turned out to be too high for the establishment of grill bars with borrowed capital.

Discuss what the bank can do to attract both types of customers. What will be the effect when it turns out that competing banks also become interested in this line of business?

2. In a particular sector of the economy, there are two types of enterprise: Type 1 engages in export to emerging markets, whereas type 2 directs its activities towards the home market. Business credit has traditionally been given against collateral in the form of real estate mortgage deposited with the bank. The credit market has been at equilibrium for some time.

Give a short description of the equilibrium, and explain the differences in the contracts for the two types of borrower.

As a result of new legislation as well as increased uncertainty in the real estate market, the value of collateral to the bank decreases, and the cost to the borrower of pledging collateral increases. In this new situation, the enterprises ask for government support with two different lines of argumentation, namely (1) that the export industry of the country is particularly severely affected, and (2) that the traditionally stable credit market is in danger of a major breakdown.

Give an assessment of these two lines of argumentation.

3. A new export-oriented industry is characterized by many small entrepreneurs having only limited capital of their own, so they need credit from the banks. The business is very promising in the sense that the profits earned may be large, depending, however, on the skills of the entrepreneur, but each firm in the industry is subject to a general risk of losing its investment in the overseas market.

The sector is complaining that credit is too tight. Sketch a model of the situation which can be used to assess whether these complaints are justified, and give suggestions for regulation if the particular credit market is not functioning in an optimal way.

4. In a particular field of industry, several new firms have been set up to exploit recent technological developments. It turns out, however, that there are not only innovators experienced in the field but also complete newcomers among the entrepreneurs.

The government wants to support the new field and has set up an independent financial institution which offers credit to the entrepreneurs. The institution must be self-financing but is not intended to earn profits.

Give a suggestion, based on relevant theory, for the credit policy of the new financial institution.

After some time, the existing private banks realize that they may compete with the government institution in offering credit to the firms in this industry. Does this change the situation in the market, and if it does, how?

5. A bank has experienced some problems with their credit to a particular type of investment where investors are subject to some risk and where the way in which the investor conducts business cannot be monitored by the bank, whereas final outcomes are publicly observable. Give a theoretical explanation of the problems that the bank will have in such a situation.

It is now suggested to introduce a new type of contract, where the fixed repayment is supplemented by a percentage of each investor's gain. Will this solve the problems of the bank?

6.7 Comments

The approach to credit rationing which views it as a consequence of a backward-bending supply curve for loans is taken from Freixas and Rochet [2008]. In particular, the Stiglitz-Weiss model of adverse selection in credit markets has received much attention in the literature, as is also evidenced by the comments by Arnold and Riley [2009] and the model by de Meza and Webb [1987], which arrives at opposite conclusions, showing again that our reasoning is crucially dependent on the assumptions.

The model of collateral as a sorting device will be recognized as a version of the classical model of health insurance under adverse selection by Rothschild and Stiglitz [1976]. The existence problem has been considered by many authors, e.g. Wilson [1980], and there are no easy solutions.

Although the idea of introducing collateral in our discussion of credit market equilibria was that this may indeed be an instrument for overcoming the excess demand for credit, the final section shows that market conditions may be such that rationing reappears even when collateral can be pledged.

Chapter 7

Credit Risk

7.1 Introduction

As lending remains one of the basic fields of business of a bank, it is natural that credit risk should be one of the most important types of risk. Indeed, defaults of important debtors, which gave rise to subsequent failure of banks, started off much of the regulation of banks as we know it today. Keeping a reserve against losses on credit, or better, avoiding such losses by suitable action, is at the heart of bank management.

In order to assess the amount of loss which may derive from debtor obligations that are not fulfilled, one needs a model of debtor behaviour, or at least a model of when loans are not paid back. Starting with the second of these two ideas, we consider what are called *reduced form* models, giving the probability of default on loans depending on observable characteristics of the debtors. Although simple and easily adaptable to statistical analysis, the reduced models are often lacking a theoretical foundation; they may therefore work well in periods where no disturbing phenomena occur but may fail when such disturbances happen, as was the case when the financial crisis set in. The alternative leads to a more detailed consideration of the economic situation of the debtor, because defaults on obligations happen when the debtor experiences economic problems. This is what is done in the *structural models* where the asset values of the debtors are assessed in order to estimate how far they are from bankruptcy. Although more intuitively appealing as providing not only an assessment of losses but also an explanation of the losses, the structural models tend to perform less well statistically unless they are suitably adapted by adding some features which make them look more akin to the reduced form models.

We conclude the chapter with a brief discussion of the Basel II rules for credit risk, according to which the banks are allowed to use their own internal models, together with a description in rough outline of such internal models.

7.2 Reduced form models

The reduced form models work directly with the probability of default rather than deriving this probability from underlying events. Thus, in the context of reduced models the default is seen as an unpredictable event which can occur at any moment in the future; the task of the model builder is to find a reasonable explanation of the *hazard rate*, that is, the probability of a default in any small interval of time.

7.2.1 The simple Poisson model of default

In its simplest possible version, a reduced model takes the form of valuing a loan with maturity T, repaid to the sum F, where default may occur following a Poisson process with intensity λ, so the probability of default in a time interval Δt is independent of other time intervals and has the size $\lambda \Delta t$. Under these circumstances, the probability at time 0 that the borrowing firm has not defaulted before maturity is $e^{-\lambda T}$, and assuming that everything is lost at default, the expected present value of the loan is

$$e^{-\lambda T} F e^{-rT} = F e^{-(r+\lambda)T},$$

with r being the risk-free rate of interest.

It is seen that in the case considered, the riskiness of the loan may be assessed using the intensity as a *default spread*. This spread takes care of the risk involved in the loan, and in the Poisson model it is a fixed parameter which may be particular for this investment, but which does not depend on time or other variables (because so far there are no others). This simplicity is appealing, but quite insufficient if the model is to be used to assess real-world credit risk, and to allow for more variation, it is usually assumed that the intensity λ depends on other phenomena which are then introduced into the model. This leads to the general class of hazard processes, where the intensity itself is a stochastic process. We shall not develop this further in the present context, but we return briefly to more sophisticated versions of the Poisson model when we consider the commercial credit risk models.

7.3 Structural models

In the structural approach, the valuation of a loan extended to a certain borrower (who then becomes an *obligor* in the terminology of credit risk assessment) is derived from the assessment of the business situation of the borrower. Because default on credit happens when the obligor is unable to pay, one can trace the likelihood of this latter event and thereby obtain a probabilistic assessment of the value of the asset as a whole.

7.3.1 The options approach to assessment of the debtor

The key to this line of study, where the value of the loan is assessed through the value of the obligor, is the observation by Merton [1974] that extending a loan to a firm can be considered as the combination of two transactions, namely (1) a purchase of the assets of

Box 7.1

The Altman Z-score. A widely used method to determine whether a given firm is financially healthy is the Z-score proposed by Altman [1968]. The method generalizes the traditional approach of assessing firms according to suitable *accounting ratios*, such as Working Capital/Total Assets, Sales/Total Assets, etc. For each of these accounting ratios, one may find a suitable threshold, so firms with a ratio above the threshold are sound, whereas firms having ratios below tend to go bankrupt. The Z-score introduces a linear combination of accounting ratios, the original one proposed being

$$Z = 0.012T_1 + 0.014T_2 + 0.033T_3 + 0.006T_4 + 0.009T_5,$$

where

T_1 = Working Capital/Total Assets,

T_2 = Retained Earnings/Assets,

T_3 = Earnings Before Interest and Taxes (EBIT)/Total Assets,

T_4 = Market Value of Equity/Book Values of Total Liabilities,

T_5 = Sales/Total Assets.

The coefficients and the threshold were found from a sample of firms, half of which had filed for bankruptcy. The method used was *linear discriminant analysis*, a statistical technique, which may be explained briefly as follows: Given the observed values of $T_1, \ldots, T_5$ divided into two groups (succesful and unsuccesful firms), we look for a linear combination which maximizes the ratio

$$S = \frac{\sigma^2_{between}}{\sigma^2_{within}}$$

between difference in variance between the two groups (when variables are aggregated according to the given linear combination), and the sum of the variances inside each group. The threshold can then be found as the average of the aggregated means in each group.

The Altman Z-score is an easy and widely used tool. Its usefulness is, of course, limited by that of the accounting ratios on which it is based, and because some firms (such as financial firms) are only purely assessed using only their accounts, its limitations should be taken into account. Also, the method is still lacking a theoretical foundation (as are indeed many of the classical accounting techniques).

the firm by the lender, combined with (2) an option for the firm to buy back its assets at the maturity of the loan with the exercise price equal to the repayment. Indeed, if the loan has to be paid back at time T with the amount F, then the firm has the possibility of leaving its assets to the lender, which it will do if the value of its assets at time T, V_T is smaller than F, or repaying the loan (if $V_T \geq F$). Using the theoretical framework of continuous finance, the value of the option may be assessed using the Black-Scholes formula, so the value of the loan to the lender may be assessed.

In order to apply the theory to financial markets in continuous time, we have to make the standard assumptions of frictionless markets and continuous trading, and that there are no arbitrage possibilities. There is a riskless asset with known and constant interest rate r

(so the yield curve is flat). Also, it is assumed that the assets of the firm follow a geometric Brownian motion

$$\frac{dV_t}{V_t} = \mu dt + \sigma \, dZ_t$$

or

$$dV_t = \mu V_t \, dt + \sigma V_t \, dZ_t$$

with Z_t a standard Wiener process. For the Black-Scholes formula to hold, we need that this value process can be simulated by a suitable (dynamic) portfolio obtained in the financial market.

If the loan terminates at T and has to be repaid in the amount F, then using the Black-Scholes formula, the value at time t of the call option given to the firm is

$$E_t(V, T, \sigma, r, F) = V_t N(d_1) - F e^{-r(T-t)} N(d_2), \text{ where}$$

$$d_1 = \frac{\ln\left(\frac{V_t}{F}\right) + \left(r + \frac{\sigma^2}{2}\right)(T - t)}{\sigma \sqrt{T - t}}, \tag{1}$$

$$d_2 = d_1 - \sigma \sqrt{T - t},$$

and $N(\cdot)$ is the standard normal cumulative probability distribution. Using (1), we get a valuation of the loan at time t as

$$D_t(V_t, T) = V_t - E_t(V, T, \sigma, r, F) = V_t - V_t N(d_1) + F e^{-r(T-t)} N(d_2)$$

$$= V_t N(-d_1) + F e^{-r(T-t)} N(d_2) = V_t [N(-d_1) + \rho_t N(d_2)]. \tag{2}$$

Here we have introduced the notation

$$\rho_t = \frac{F e^{-r(T-t)}}{V_t}$$

for the ratio of nominal discounted debt to value of firm, known as the quasi-debt ratio. It may be noticed that the growth rate μ does not appear in the formula (as usual in option pricing).

7.3.2 Default spreads
If the loan has the form of a bond, it is costumary to express value in terms of yield-to-maturity $y_t(T)$, defined as

$$D_t(V, T) = F e^{-y_t(T)(T-t)};$$

taking logarithms and rearranging terms, we get the following expression

$$y_t(T) = -\frac{1}{T - t} \ln\left(\frac{D_t}{F}\right),$$

and the *default spread* $s_t(T) = y_t(T) - r$ can then be found as

$$s_t(T) = -\frac{1}{T-t} \ln\left(N(d_2) + \frac{V_t}{Fe^{-r(T-t)}} N(-d_1)\right).$$

The quantity $V_t/Fe^{-r(T-t)} = \rho_t^{-1}$, which is the inverse of the quasi-debt ratio, is known as the *expected relative distance to loss*. The formula for the credit spread shows that the addition to the risk-free rate of interest, which may be interpreted as the credit risk premium of this particular bond, depends on the volatility of the value of the assets of the firm (which is $\sigma \sqrt{T-t}$, occurring in the expressions for d_1 and d_2) and the quasi-debt ratio, which can be seen as a leverage ratio, expressing the value of the firm in relation to the promised payment of the loan.

We now use Itô's lemma on the function D_t of t and V_t,

$$dD_t = \left(\frac{\partial D}{\partial t} + \mu \frac{\partial D_t}{\partial V_t} + \frac{\sigma^2}{2} \frac{\partial^2 V_t}{\partial D_t^2}\right) dt + \sigma \frac{\partial D_t}{\partial V_t} dZ,$$

and from the expression (2) for D_t we get that

$$\frac{\partial D_t}{\partial V_t} = N(-d_1), \quad \frac{\partial^2 D_t}{\partial V_t^2} = 0,$$

so the value of the debt follows a geometric Brownian motion with volatility parameter

$$\sigma_D = \frac{V_t}{D_t} \frac{\partial D_t}{\partial V_t} \sigma = \frac{N(-d_1)}{N(-d_1) + \rho_t N(d_2)} \sigma.$$

Thus, the standard deviation of the debt can be found from that of the firm value by multiplying by the elasticity of the debt value with respect to the firm value. Practitioners use either default spread $s_t(T)$ or the standard deviation σ_D to assess the debt, even though the first measures the behaviour over the time interval from t to maturity, whereas the second gives the instantaneous volatility. Going back to the formulas, it is seen that they depend on the same basic variables (maturity, quasi-debt ratio, volatility).

7.3.3 Expected shortfall

In the following we take a closer look at the expression for the value of debt in the case $t = 0$. We may rewrite (2) in this case as

$$D_0(V, T) = Fe^{-rT} - N(-d_2)\left[Fe^{-rt} - \frac{N(-d_1)}{N(-d_2)} V_0\right], \tag{3}$$

where the second member on the right-hand side is the value of the European put option. We have

$$d_2 = \frac{1}{\sigma \sqrt{T}}\left(\ln\left(\frac{V_0}{F}\right) + \left(r - \frac{\sigma^2}{2}\right)T\right),$$

and this gives us an interpretation of $N(-d_2)$: When the value of the assets V satisfies (1), then the process $S = \ln V$ satisfies

$$dS_t = \left(\mu - \frac{\sigma^2}{2}\right) dt + \sigma \, dW_t$$

(as is easily seen using Itô's lemma), meaning that the logarithm of the asset value at T has expected value $\ln V_0 + \left(\mu - \frac{\sigma^2}{2}\right)T$, and default occurs when asset value is below or equal to the repayment value of the debt (or, taking logarithms, when $\ln V_T \leq \ln F$). Normalizing by subtracting the mean and dividing by the standard deviation $\sigma \sqrt{T}$, we get that default happens when the normalized random variable is below

$$\frac{1}{\sigma \sqrt{T}} \left[\ln F - \ln V_0 - \left(\mu - \frac{\sigma^2}{2}\right)T\right],$$

which is almost $-d_2$, with the only difference being the parameter μ appearing instead of r.

To obtain an interpretation of $N(-d_2)$ (which contains r rather than μ), we need to invoke the so-called *equivalent risk-neutral measure*. In the financial market, the absence of arbitrage possibilities means that for each choice of numeraire (an asset such that all prices are measured relative to the price of this asset) there is an equivalent (having the same null sets) underlying measure for which the process of all assets are martingales (have zero drift). Taking the risk-free asset B with

$$dB = rB \, dt$$

as numeraire, we get the so-called risk-neutral equivalent measure. We have that for any financial asset, for example V (which may not itself be traded, but which can be simulated by assets in the market), the asset $\frac{V}{B}$ is a martingale under the equivalent martingale measure, meaning that it has no drift relative to B. Therefore, we can write the process as

$$dV_t = rV_t \, dt + \sigma V_t \, dW_t$$

under the risk-neutral measure, and we have that $N(-d_2)$ is the probability of default relative to this measure.

The term 'risk-neutral' for this probability measure comes from the above property – that all securities have the same drift r – so neither risk lovers nor risk averse investors are remunerated by the market.

Having found an interpretation of $N(-d_2)$, we proceed to the quantity $\frac{N(-d_1)}{N(-d_2)}$ appearing in (3). Suppose that the value of the assets has reached the default level F at some date before T (the probability of this event has just been assessed). To recover, the assets have to reach their previous position, and given that values grow at the rate r, the value must be at least $V_0 e^{rT}$ at time T. Turning to logarithms, the normalized random variable must be above the level

$$\frac{1}{\sigma\sqrt{T}}\left[V_0 + rT - \left(F + \left(r - \frac{\sigma^2}{2}\right)T\right)\right],$$

which is recognized as d_1, and the probability that this happens is $N(-d_1)$ (where we have used the symmetry of the normal distribution). We can now conclude that $\frac{N(-d_1)}{N(-d_2)}$ is the probability of recovery given that default has occurred.

From this we may proceed to interpreting the quantity

$$\left[Fe^{-rt} - \frac{N(-d_1)}{N(-d_2)}V_0\right]$$

as the *expected shortfall* associated with default, namely the present value of the loan repayment which will not be made in the agreed way due to default, and the expected repayment, which again is found as the value of the assets (which become the property of the lender after default) times the probability of recovery after default.

Summing up, formula (3) shows that the value of the loan can be found as the nominal value of the repayment with deduction of a quantity which is the probability of default times expected shortfall at default.

7.4 Credit risk management and bank regulation

One of the reasons for the interest in methods of credit risk assessment is that credit risk plays an important role in the regulation of banks. It has been standard to demand that banks hold a certain amount of equity as a reserve against the losses that it may experience on its credit engagements, and this amount of equity has been specified precisely because of the emergence of the first Basel Accord (Basel I) in 1988. Subsequently elaborated and expanded, the rules of the Basel Accord specify the amount of equity that the bank must hold as a fraction (the so-called Cooke ratio, set at 8%) of the total amount of risk-weighted assets.

That assets should be weighted according to riskiness seems reasonable enough because some assets are more likely to cause losses than others, and the reserve held against losses should reflect the likelihood of losses. When it comes to the quantification of risk weights, there are several approaches available for the bank. It may choose fixed risk weights, specified in the Basel Accord, for each type of asset, which is called the *standardized approach*, or it may use what is called the *internal ratings method*, where the fixed risk weights are replaced by asset-specific calculations.

7.4.1 The standardized approach

This uses a simple system of risk weights depending on (i) type of asset and (ii) rating of the specific asset within each type. The risk weights are roughly as follows:

	AAA to AA-	A+ to A-	BBB+ to BBB-	BB+ to B-	Below B	Unrated
Claims on sovereigns	0%	20%	50%	100%	150%	100%
Claims on banks etc.	20%	50%	100%	100%	150%	100%

Claims on BIS, IMF and ECB have risk weight 0%. For claims on corporates, the risk weights are

AAA to AA-	A+ to A-	BBB+ to BB-	Below BB-	Unrated
20%	50%	100%	150%	100%

Claims on credit cards, personal finance, car loans, etc. should be given 75% weight; claims on residential property, 35%; whereas commercial real estate should be taken up at full weight, 100%. Some specific loans, such as overdue loans, have to be given 150% weight, that is, more than full weight.

Although easy to use, the standardized approach has the drawback of assigning the same risk weights to assets which may be very different, and many banks may find it preferable to use a more flexible, even if more costly, method. This means that they would choose an internal ratings method.

7.4.2 Internal ratings-based methods

Although the first steps here are similar to those of the standardized approach, namely categorizing the assets into different types (sovereign, bank, corporate, retail, equity), the internal ratings-based approach allows for individualized assessments rather than fixed percentages in each of these categories.

The basic approach to assessment is as follows: For each type of engagement (exposure), the bank should assess the following risk parameters,

> probability of default (PD),
> exposure at default (EAD),
> loss given default (LGD),
> maturity (M).

The internal ratings methods come in two versions, namely *Foundational IRB*, where the banks calculate the PDs, whereas the remaining risk parameters are given (by the national supervisor); and *Advanced IRB*, where the bank calculates all risk parameters.

Given the risk parameters, the size of risk-weighted assets can be calculated using risk weights, which are provided in the Basel II documents. The process of assessment should satisfy a number of minimum standards so that the credit risk assessment used for capital regulation purposes not only reflects reality but also complies with the methods used for risk assessment in the decision making of the bank.

7.5 Commercial credit risk models

The general approach to credit risk measurement outlined in Sections 7.1 and 7.2 above has found several practical applications, inspired by the possibilities opened up by Basel II. Here banks were allowed to calculate their capital requirements using internal models, as long as those models satisfied general principles and were accepted by the regulatory authorities. The four methods to be discussed are all developed by commercial consultancy firms, offering the banks the option of implementing the models adapted to the particular bank.

7.5.1 CreditMetrics™

The main goal of the method is to construct a probability distribution of the changes in the value of the credit portfolio over a year. The choice of a year as the basic unit of time is natural in the context of an assessment based on credit ratings, because the latter are usually revised once a year. Because returns on credit portfolios are typically *not* normally distributed, but are skewed and have fat tails, it is important that the method captures more than mean and variance.

The basic tool for the computations is a *transition matrix* between credit ratings. There are two basic steps, in the sense that the approach starts with treating bonds and assessing their loss probabilities. Once this is done, one may use the results to proceed first to loans which are given to firms, rather than those having the form of bonds, and secondly to portfolios (of loans and bonds).

Credit assessment of a bond. If we operate with k ranking levels and default, then the transition matrix M has the dimension $(k+1) \times (k+1)$, whereby the last row (corresponding to the default state) has zeros everywhere except in the last column (default is assumed to be an absorbing state, in which you can enter but from which you cannot depart). Elements m_{ij} of M specify the probability that the obligor (the term used in the context of risk assessment for a borrower or issuer of a corporate bond), which initially is rated at level i, changes rating to level j after one year. Clearly, using powers of M, we have matrices specifying the probability of moving from level i to level j over several years.

Suppose that the particular bond changes to level j after one year; we must then assess its value, given that the particular credit position may last longer. For this, we need a *forward risky discount rate structure* of the following type:

Ranking level	Year 1	Year 2	$\cdots$	Year T
1	r_1^1	r_1^2		r_1^T
$\vdots$	$\vdots$	$\vdots$		$\vdots$
k	r_k^1	r_k^2		r_k^T

Using this discount rate structure, one may find the value after one year of a credit position rated at level j next year, with yearly cash flows c_τ from next year, to its expiry at say, year t, as

$$c_1 + c_2\left(1 + r_j^1\right) + \cdots + c_t\left(1 + r_j^{t-1}\right).$$

(Here c_τ for $\tau < t$ corresponds to coupon payment, and c_t is coupon plus repayment of the nominal bond value.)

For the default state, one has to use a different approach. The assessment will be based on the probability of recovering the debt, typically depending on the details of the credit position (senior or subordinated debt, etc.). Again this is based on historical data and gives an average percentage of recovery together with a standard deviation.

Clearly, using M together with the discount rate table, given the observed time 0 rating of the bond, we get a probability distribution of values after one year, and this (discrete) distribution may then be used to calculate mean, variance and VaR.

Credit risk assessment of loans. The above approach, which basically consisted in computing net present values of future cash flows from bonds, taking the risk into consideration through the system of discount rates, very explicitly relies on the special features of bonds. A loan to a firm does not have this structure, and indeed its value depends much more directly on the specific features of the firm.

To proceed from here, CreditMetrics™ uses the Merton approach, linking default to the value of the firm. Assuming that the assets of the firm follow a geometric Brownian motion

$$\ln\left(\frac{V_t}{V_0}\right) = \left(\mu - \frac{\sigma^2}{2}\right)t + \sigma \sqrt{t}\tilde{z}_t,$$

we get that

$$\tilde{z}_t = \frac{\ln\left(\frac{V_t}{V_0}\right) - \left(\mu - \frac{\sigma^2}{2}\right)t}{\sigma \sqrt{t}},$$

and the probability that the asset value falls under some critical level v_t is

$$P\{V_t \le v_t\} = P\left\{\tilde{z}_t \le \frac{\ln\left(\frac{v_t}{V_0}\right) - \left(\mu - \frac{\sigma^2}{2}\right)t}{\sigma \sqrt{t}}\right\}.$$

Because $\tilde{z}_t$ has the distribution $N(0, 1)$, we get corresponding critical thresholds z_t for the normalized rate of change which has mean 0 and variance 1, which can then be converted back to critical rates of change by

$$r_t = z_t\sigma \sqrt{t} + \left(\mu - \frac{\sigma^2}{2}\right)t.$$

To find the critical values v_t, which should be considered as thresholds in asset values for different ratings, one may use the forward discount rates corresponding to the rating given to the firm considered. Given the critical values, we then have a probability distribution of the obligor in rating levels (inclusive defaults) at one year from now. This will differ from a similar bond due to the individual characteristics of the firm (the parameters μ and σ^2 which enter into the computation).

Correlations. Having come so far, we have a method for assessing single credit positions, but we still need to proceed from here to assessing the portfolio, which means introducing correlations. If all positions were uncorrelated, we could get a system of transition matrices (this time of a dimension corresponding to all assignments of levels to positions) simply by multiplying the transition probabilities, but typically they are correlated, and moreover the correlations will change over time because they are linked to events in the underlying economy.

In CreditMetrics™, correlations can be introduced when all the single positions have been treated as above, so for each bond or loan, there are normalized thresholds and associated probabilities of rate of change being within the intervals corresponding to rating levels. If the correlations are known, then the probability of any list of ratings for the components of the portfolio can be computed using the multivariate normal distribution. In particular, one can compute the probability distribution of the value of the portfolio, and from this the VaR of the credit portfolio, which can be considered as the final goal of the approach. For large portfolios, the calculation of multidimensional normal probability distributions may, however, be overwhelming, and instead one must rely on simpler assumptions and analysis of specific scenarios.

The data used in the computations are either general (such as the transition probabilities and discount rate structures) and provided or firm specific, pertaining to the individual loan (means and variances of the value process). The latter must be estimated specifically, and because the asset value process of a firm is not observable, it is suggested to use stock market returns rather than asset returns, and also to replace the specific firm by a class of similar firms in order to obtain a sufficient empirical background material for the estimates.

7.5.2 The KMV methodology
This is, instead, based directly on the Merton approach, using the asset value process to find a 'distance to default', which is then combined with an empirically established relationship to estimate a default frequency.

As above, we consider a loan to a firm whose asset values V follow a geometric Brownian motion with drift μ and variance σ^2. We assume that the liabilities of the firm consist of long-term debt and equity. In this case the value E of equity is the value of a call option on the assets of the firm, where the latter depends on V, σ, K_l, the nominal value of liabilities, its maturity T and the risk-free rate r. To find E, the KMV method solves the option value equation

$$E = f(V, \sigma, K_l, T, r) \tag{3}$$

for V, using market data for E and an initial guess for σ. This V is used together with an equation for σ_E, the volatility of the equity process, namely

$$\sigma_E = \eta\sigma, \ \eta = \frac{V}{E}\frac{\partial E}{\partial V},$$

where η is the elasticity of equity with respect to asset values, and $\partial E/\partial V$ is the delta of the call option. Here σ_E can be observed from market data, and the equation is then solved for σ, which is reinserted in (3) etc.

Having found usable values of σ, we may proceed as in the previous subsection and find that the firm defaults when the asset values reach a critical level K (in practice the value of long-term debt plus half the value of short-term debt). From this we define a *distance-to-default DD* as the difference between expected value of assets after one year, $\mathsf{E}[V_1]$, expressed in standardized form, i.e.

$$DD = \frac{\mathsf{E}[V_1] - K}{\sigma V_0}.$$

(We have divided by σV_0 because we need asset level volatility rather than asset return volatility.) The area below the default point K is then given by $\Phi(-DD)$ (where, as usual, Φ is the cumulative normal distribution function).

One may think of the distance to default as a first measure of the soundness of the firm considered, when considered today: On average, it will be DD away from the default point if left to itself in one period. Thus, the computation of DD can be considered as the counterpart of obtaining the rating of the firm in CreditMetrics™.

The next step is to link the DDs to historical default rates from the KMV database, giving the EDF (expected default frequency). For example, from all the firms with a DD of 3, about 1.5% defaulted. The EDFs give an expression of the quality of the obligor, and as such they can be compared to ratings given by other credit rating institutions (as used in CreditMetrics™).

So far we have sketched the approach towards finding EDFs for a given position at a given horizon. This may be used to evaluate a single cash flow $(C_1,\ldots,C_n)$ at dates $t_1,\ldots,t_n$, using a standard formula for expected net present value,

$$PV = (1 - LGD)\sum_{i=1}^{n}\frac{C_i}{(1 + r_i)^{t_i}} + LGD\sum_{i=1}^{n}\frac{(1 - Q_i)C_i}{(1 + r_i)^{t_i}}.$$

Here LGD is *loss given default*, the percentage of the original sum that cannot be recovered in case of default (something which can be extracted from the information already used), and Q_i is the probability of default related to t_i. The KMV methodology uses a modified version of the EDFs, taking the Q_is as so-called risk-neutral EDFs, making a correction so that they fit with the original options pricing model; we shall not go into details here.

The final result of the computations, the loss distribution of the portfolio, is obtained by assuming that it is sufficiently diversified, even if there are pairwise correlations between assets, because in this case the form of the loss distribution is known (the normal-inverse Gaussian), meaning that VaR can be computed as well as mean, variance, skewness, etc. The distribution is skewed and has heavy tails.

The basic step of the KMV approach, finding *EDF*s, can be seen as a way of sidestepping the need for external input in the form of ratings in the CreditMetrics™ approach. Indeed, translating *EDF*s to ratings and back again to *EDF*s allows KMV to produce a transition matrix which can be used in a credit migration approach. The KMV approach has the advantage of delivering the ratings when and as often as they are needed, whereas taking ratings from the rating agencies often means that they come rather late and may be incorrect. On the other hand, the reliance of the KMV approach on stock market data can lead to overreactions and departures from 'true' evaluations of the firms.

7.5.3 CreditRisk+™

It uses an actuarial approach seeing defaults as events following a Poisson process. This means that the model does not go into the origins of default (as in the previous models where it comes as a consequence of reduced ranking or unfavourable development over time of assets). Instead, it sees default as a random event happening with a certain probability. The basic assumption is that the Poisson distribution can be used to model defaults, so

(1) the probability of default in a given time interval depends only on the length of this interval, not on the date at which the interval starts; and

(2) for large portfolios, the individual probability of default of an obligor is relatively small, so the overall number of defaults in a period of time is independent of any other period.

Following the logic of this model, credit risk is a question of number of defaults (and the probability of this) in the period considered, as well as the size of the losses.

Thus, the first step in the model would be to find the number of defaults in a given time interval as

$$P(n \text{ defaults}) = \frac{\mu^n e^{-\mu}}{n!} \text{ for } n = 0, 1, 2, \ldots,$$

where μ is average number of defaults in the interval.

Using the Poisson distribution means that both the mean and the variance is equal to μ. However, it turns out by looking at historical default rates (corresponding to μ) that the standard deviation (volatility) usually differs quite a lot from $\sqrt{\mu}$. Therefore, CreditRisk+™ proposes to adjust the mean default rate by considering it as stochastic with mean μ and some volatility σ_μ.

Exploiting this idea, CreditRisk+™ proceeds as follows: Initially, the portfolio is divided into parts (or bands) with common exposure (which is done mainly to reduce the amount of data to be processed). For each obligor i, there is an exposure L_i (namely the loss given default), a probability P_i of default and an expected loss $\lambda_i = L_i P_i$. This is normalized by a unit amount L of exposure chosen, leading to parameters $v_i = L_i/L$ for relative exposure and $\epsilon_i = \lambda_i/L$ for relative expected loss. Then these values are rounded to the nearest integer, and all the obligors with the same rounded v, ϵ and μ value are put into the same band or category, giving a total of m bands. Each band j is now characterized by the three parameters v_j, ϵ_j and μ_j, and by our construction, we have $\epsilon_j = \frac{v_j}{\mu_j}$, so $\mu_j = \frac{v_j}{\epsilon_j}$, and μ_j is estimated as the sum of the $\frac{v_i}{\epsilon_i}$ over all i belonging to band j.

To proceed, one uses generating functions for probability distributions: For band j define

$$G_j(z) = \sum_{n=0}^{\infty} \mathsf{P}\{\text{loss} = nL\}\, z^n = \sum_{n=0}^{\infty} \mathsf{P}\{n \text{ defaults}\}\, z^{nv_j};$$

because the number of defaults follow a Poisson process, we have

$$G_j(z) = \sum_{n=0}^{\infty} \frac{\mu_j^n e^{-\mu_j}}{n!} z^{nv_j} = \exp\left(\mu_j(z^{v_j} - 1)\right).$$

The point of using probability-generating functions is that sums of independent random variables translate to products of their generating functions, so assuming independence between bands, we get the generating function for the whole portfolio as

$$G(z) = \prod_{j=1}^{m} e^{\mu_j(z^{v_j} - 1)} = \exp\left(\sum_{j=1}^{m} \mu_j\, (z^{v_j} - 1)\right).$$

The generating function itself is not our final goal; rather, we want the probability distribution for which it is a generator, and this we can find from

$$\mathsf{P}\{\text{loss} = nL\} = \frac{1}{n!} \frac{\partial^n G(z)}{\partial z^n}\bigg|_{z=0} \quad \text{for } n = 1, 2, \ldots$$

From this loss distribution one may now proceed to compute VaR, mean, variance, etc.

7.5.4 CreditPortfolioView™

It sees default as caused by underlying economic factors, and the basic idea of the approach is to determine a number of indicators for default and recovery, used to compute the relevant probabilities (which are thought of as changing over time). It is thought that this approach fits well with speculative obligors who are sensitive to credit cycles and macrovariables.

In CreditPortfolioView™, default probabilities for a debtor in industry or country j at time t are given by

$$P_{j,t} = \frac{1}{1 + e^{Y_{j,t}}},$$

with $Y_{j,t}$ a 'country speculative-grade specific index' defined as

$$Y_{j,t} = \beta^0 + \beta_j \cdot X_{j,t} + v_{j,t}$$

$$= \beta_j^0 + \left(\beta_j^1\ \beta_j^2\ \cdots\ \beta_j^m\right) \begin{pmatrix} X_{j,t}^1 \\ X_{j,t}^2 \\ \vdots \\ X_{j,t}^m \end{pmatrix} + v_{j,t},$$

where β_j is the vector of coefficients or sensitivities for group j, $X_{j,t}$ is a vector of macrovariables and $v_{j,t}$ an error term. One may think of the error terms as *innovations*, changing the impact of the macroenvironment and thereby the default probabilities. The relevant macrovariables are specified for each group, and under suitable assumptions, the sensitivities may be estimated.

One of the main advantages of this approach is that it allows for correlations among the groups, reflecting the impact of background factors on the different obligors and their creditworthiness. The computation is roughly as follows: One starts with a transition matrix obtained from historical data. Then the transition probabilities are changed according to the above computations: If the default probability computed at t is higher than the historical rate, then this points to a downturn in the business cycle, and all the transition probabilities are revised accordingly, because downwards migration is also more likely in that case. Conversely, if the simulated default probability is lower, then the downwards transition probabilities are decreased. The method allows for time-dependent transition matrices, so an asset can be followed over many future periods.

7.6 Consumer credit and scorecards

One of the fields where credit risk assessment is carried out routinely is the field of consumer credit. The field has some characteristic features of its own. Managing consumer credit largely boils down to the question of accepting a particular individual as future debtor, so it is a question of accepting or rejecting an applicant based on whatever information may be available at that moment.

The way in which this question of accepting or rejecting a potential customer is treated in practice is by *credit scoring*, classifying customers as good or bad according to some general observable characteristics. The underlying model states that a consumer i may turn out to be good (G) or bad (B) with probabilities p_G^i and $p_B^i = 1 - p_G^i$, which in their turn depend on a vector of characteristics of the individual $x^i = (x_1^i, \ldots, x_n^i)$ such as income, family status, gender, etc, with $x_j^i \in \{0, 1\}$, all j. Given a system of scoring weights $s = (s_1, \ldots, s_n)$, which may be positive or negative, one may compute the overall scoring of individual i as

$$s^i = s \cdot x^i = \sum_h s_h x_h^i,$$

and the decision whether to accept or reject the individual as a customer is then taken based on a *threshold K*: Individual i is accepted if

$$s^i \geq K$$

and rejected otherwise.

This procedure, known as the *scorecard* approach to consumer credit, is easy to apply, but obviously its merits will depend on the way in which the weights and the threshold are selected.

7.6.1 Reduced form approaches to scorecards

Here the primitive concept is the default, which is seen as a random event, the probability of which depends on several factors.

A natural way of modelling the defaults would be using a Poisson process or a generalization, the Cox process known from survival analysis, where the intensity (the probability of a default in an infinitesimal interval starting at t) is a function $\lambda(t, x^i)$ of the underlying variables,

$$\lambda(t, x^i) = \lambda(t, 0)e^{s^i \cdot x^i}, \tag{4}$$

with $\lambda(0)$ the basic hazard function for $x^i = 0$ (and where $s^i \cdot x^i = \sum_{j=1}^{n} s^i x_j^i$ is the inner product of the vector x^i and a vector s^i), so the probability of survival (no default before t) for an individual i is

$$S_i(t) = e^{-\int_0^t \lambda(u, x^i)\, du}.$$

The model is known as the *proportional hazards* model, because $\lambda(t, x^i)$ and $\lambda(t, 0)$ as functions of t differ only by the multiplicative constant $e^{s^i \cdot x^i}$. If hazards are independent of time, as it is assumed in the applications to consumer credit, this reduces to the simpler expression $S_i(t) = e^{-\lambda(x^i)t}$.

However, for the purpose of scorecard analysis, a slightly different version is more convenient, using the logistic rather than the exponential distribution, so the probability of no default before t is

$$S_i^*(t) = \frac{e^{h(x^i)t}}{1 + e^{h(x^i)t}},$$

where the intensity (or hazard) function satisfies

$$\frac{h(x^i)}{1 - h(x^i)} = \frac{h(0)}{1 - h(0)}e^{s^i \cdot x^i}. \tag{5}$$

Identifying the property of being a good customer with survival over a given time horizon from $t = 0$ to $t = 1$, we have that the probability of accepting customer i is $p_i^a = S_i^*(1)$, so

$$\log\left(\frac{p_i^a}{1 - p_i^a}\right) = \log h(x^i) = s^i \cdot x^i,$$

where we put $h(0) = 1$. We may think of the expression $s^i \cdot x^i$ as the *score* of consumer i, and to decide whether i is G or B, we need a cut-off value s^*, such that i is considered as G when above s^*.

7.6.2 A structural approach

In the following, we consider what may be called a *structural* approach to consumer credit risk and the scorecard method, following the work by de Andrade and Thomas [2007]. The point of departure is (as in the structural approach to general credit risk) the interpretation of the credit as an option. In this case, the underlying stochastic process cannot be a company value (as in Merton's approach), so we introduce an unobservable (at least for the present) stochastic process Q^i, for the consumer i, which contains all the information which is relevant for the creditworthiness of consumer i. The probability of a consumer being accepted as borrower, P^i, is assumed to be an increasing function of Q^i,

$$P^i = f(Q_i).$$

Access to credit has a value R^i to the consumer i, assumed to be an increasing function of P_i,

$$R^i = h(P^i).$$

In this situation, losing the access to credit, for example through failure to pay back a loan, entails a loss of R^i, so again we can use consideration of options: The consumer has an option on buying her creditworthiness, assessed to the value R^i, at the price D^i. For practical reasons, direct observation of creditworthiness must be replaced by indirect observation of the scorecard information. Letting S^i be the score of individual i, we assume that the option problem carries over to a similar problem, with the strike price D^i replaced by a default threshold K^i of the individual score.

In order to use this approach, we need to know something about the underlying stochastic process for S^i. We assume that

$$dS^i_t = \sigma dW_t + A^i_t dY^i_t,$$

where W_t is standard Brownian motion and where dY^i_t is a Poisson process with intensity λ^i, which describes the possible jumps in creditworthiness, where the random variable A_t gives the size of the jump taking place at t. This combination of Brownian motion and Poisson jumps (known as jump-diffusion) is often used for modelling a process which contains *both* a continuously evolving part and discrete displacements. One might also add a trend (deterministic function of t) to the equation, but because an independent non-stochastic evolution over time of credit-worthiness doesn't seem realistic, we omit it. Actually, we shall omit also the jumps, considering the very simple diffusion process

$$dS^i_t = \sigma^i dW_t. \tag{6}$$

In this case, one can find an expression for probability of default before T,

$$p^i(T) = 2\Phi\left(\frac{K^i - S^i_0}{\sigma \sqrt{T}}\right),$$

where Φ is the probability distribution function of the standard normal distribution.

Having found the default probability, we may get back to the original problem of deciding whether to accept or to reject a given customer, because this can now be decided using a threshold value of $p^i(T)$. For this, one might be guided by the same considerations as above, namely selecting the threshold in such a way that the discrimination between accepted and rejected becomes as great as possible.

The structural approach may be useful for finding the default distribution of a portfolio of consumers so as to estimate the loss distribution of the latter. We shall not pursue this matter any further, but refer to de Andrade and Thomas [2007].

7.7 Exercises

1. The binomial loss model: Consider a bank with a loan portfolio consisting of m identical loans, which in the case of a default gives rise to a loss of size ℓ. Each of the loans may default with a given probability p, and the defaults are supposed to be independent.

Find the loss distribution. Explain that average number of defaults tends to p as m becomes large.

Suppose now that the default probability depends on a random variable $\widetilde{z}$ in $[0, 1]$ with density f, so $p = p(z)$. Now the defaults are only *conditionally independent*, meaning that they are independent once the value of $\widetilde{z}$ is realised. Let $\overline{p} = \int_0^1 p(z)f(z)\,dz$ be the mean probability of default.

Let $\widetilde{x}_i$ be the random variable which is 1 if firm i defaults and 0 otherwise. Find an expression for $\widetilde{N}_m$, the number of defaults, and show that

$$\mathrm{Var}\left(\widetilde{N}_m\right) = m\mathrm{Var}(\widetilde{x}_i) + m(m-1)\mathrm{Cov}\left(\widetilde{x}_i, \widetilde{x}_j\right) = m\overline{p}\,(1-\overline{p}) + m(m-1)\left(\mathsf{E}\left[p\,(\widetilde{z}\,)^2\right] - \overline{p}^2\right).$$

Use this to conclude that the variance of $\dfrac{\widetilde{N}_m}{m}$ converges to $\mathsf{E}\left[p(\widetilde{z}\,)^2\right] - \overline{p}^2$ for $m \to \infty$. What does this mean for the losses of the bank?

2. Regulatory arbitrage: In some cases, a bank can choose to treat a given risk as either credit or market risk. Suppose, for example, that a loan with maturity T can be modelled as a simple Poisson risk with default intensity λ, and assume that the capital charge on the loan is 8% of its expected value. Alternatively, the loan can be transformed to a marketable security which the bank, however, chooses to keep in its own portfolio, and it induces a capital charge corresponding to $\mathrm{VaR}_{0.99}$. For which values of λ will the bank keep the loans on its books rather than transforming them to a security?

3. A bank has made a loan with a rate of 10%. It expects a probability of default of 5%. If the loan is defaulted, the bank expects to recover 50% of its money through the sale of its collateral. What is the expected return on this loan?

4. A bank has given an ordinary bank loan to company X, which also has issued bonds to finance its activities. The loan is serviced according to the contract, but after some time the bonds issued by X move from rating A to rating B. Will this have implications for the amount of capital that the bank has to hold?

5. [Cuthbertson and Nitzsche, 2005] A financial firm holds an initially A-rated bond with current value \$112 and an initially B-rated bond valued at \$108. Each bond can be in three possible states at the end of the year, namely, A-rated, B-rated or D-rated (i.e. in default). The value of both bonds in the default state is \$51. If the A-rated bond moves to B-rated, its value at the end of the year is \$109. If the B-rated bond moves to A-rated, its value rises to \$110. If either bond stays in its current rating, its value is unchanged at year end.

The transition probabilities for the A- and B-rated bonds are as follows:

$$P_A = (0.92, 0.07, 0.01), \quad P_B = (0.03, 0.90, 0.07),$$

where the three coordinates indicate the probability of moving to rating A, B and D, respectively.

Find

  (i) the mean value of the two bonds;

 (ii) the standard deviation in value for each of the bonds taken separately;

(iii) the value of the two-bond portfolio in each future state and the migration probability matrix, assuming independence between the movements of bonds A and B;

 (iv) the mean and standard deviation of the two-bond portfolio; and

  (v) the marginal risk of adding bond B to bond A.

7.8 Comments

There are may texts available dealing with credit risk at different levels, from introductory, as e.g. Baesens and Gestel [2009]; to intermediate, as Joseph [2013]; to more advanced, such as Duffie and Singleton [2003], Duffie [2011], Lando [2004]. The treatment in this chapter cannot do justice to this field, and our aim is to provide some background for the subsequent discussion of problems related to the regulation of banks, which comes in later chapters.

A comprehensive treatment of consumer credit can be found in Finlay [2010].

Chapter 8

Securitization and Shadow Banking

8.1 Introduction: What is securitization?

8.1.1 The rise of securitization

One of the characteristic features of modern banking is the increased use of *securitization*, the process of converting bank assets in the form of loans to marketable securities which can then be sold to the general public. Although the basic idea of securitization is by no means new, having been used for centuries in connection with mortgage credit, its development into a mass phenomenon is quite recent, beginning in the 1990s and growing rapidly in the years before the financial crisis of 2007–8.

As often happens, the securitization model was considered as mainly beneficial to the financial sector and to society in its initial stage. Indeed, the transfer of bank assets to marketable papers was considered as a way of attracting new investors who would not have been forthcoming otherwise, thereby extending the overall potential for investment. The negative aspects were largely overlooked or considered as less important. In the aftermath of the financial crisis, these shortcomings have been the object of more active studies, and several serious problems were identified, which in many cases were related to the way in which the securities were issued. Because the failure of very large amounts of these securities was a spectacular part of the financial downturn, more attention was to be expected, and the research of the years following the crisis have given a better, if still not a full, understanding of the pros and cons of securitization.

The chapter is organized as follows: We begin with an overview of the securitization process and the typical securities emerging from this process. Then we move to the theoretical considerations of securitization, why banks might like it and why it may give rise to problems; the first model considered here dates back to some years before the crisis, when securitization was considered in most respects a beneficial phenomenon, whereas the next one, appearing after the crisis, takes a more pessimistic view.

In Section 8.3, we consider securitization in the context of *shadow banking* (introduced in Chapter 2), where the focus is on the negative effects of neglecting some of the risks involved. That otherwise competent agents in financial markets may neglect risk takes us in Section 8.4 to the role of the professional *rating agencies*, which were notoriously wrong in their assessments. This may be caused by specific problems in the sector, but it may also be a result of the increasing complexity of the securities constructed.

In the final section, we consider a problem which is perhaps not directly related to the discussion of securitization, but it has to do with mortgage credit and its impact on the economy. It is shown that in a simple model of mortgage credit, the interaction of the financial sector with the property market can create cyclical movements in real estate prices, meaning that a financial crisis like the one in 2007–8 can be considered as a foreseeable event rather than a shock.

8.1.2 Types of securitization

All forms of securitization involve the setting up of a special entity, the so-called *special purpose vehicle* (SPV) in the form of a trust or a fund, which sells the securities to the public. This construction means that there is an additional layer between the bank originating the loans and the investors who are ultimately funding these loans, separating them from the other assets of the bank in case the lenders default on the loans. The SPVs may be set up for one particular portfolio, but there are also cases of SPVs that take care of many different securitization arrangements.

Pass-through. As the name indicates, the *ownership* of the assets is transferred to the investors. The portfolio is placed in a trust which sells certificates of ownership of this entire portfolio to the investors. The originator of the loan, which typically is a bank, services the portfolio and collects interest and principal on the loans, deducting a fee for these services and passing the rest on to the investors (hence the name, 'pass-through'). Ownership of the loans (and mortgages in the case where the loan is in fixed property) is with the holders of the certificate. As a consequence, the loans disappear from the balance of the originator.

The classical form of a pass-through, called a *static* pass-through for reasons to be explained below, is illustrated in Fig. 8.1. As can be seen from the figure, the construction usually contains a *credit enhancer*, which makes it easier to sell the debt certificates to investors. In principle the credit enhancement takes the form of an insurance against defaults, guaranteeing a certain payoff even if the lenders do not repay. A particular form of this insurance arrangement is the *credit default swap*, which is bought in the market rather than signed with an insurance company. The originator pays a fee to the credit enhancer.

Some prominent examples of pass-throughs are the US institutions for mortgage credit, Freddie Mac and Fannie Mae, which became notorious during the financial turmoil of 2008. The Federal Home Loan Mortgage Corporation (shorthand, Freddie Mac), originally an indirect agency of the US federal government, developed the first pass-through security in 1971, and the Federal National Mortgage Association (FNMA, or Fannie

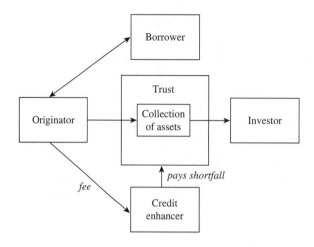

Figure 8.1 Schematic overview of the structure of a pass-through.

Mae) developed a similar construction in 1981. The securities are backed by portfolios of privately insured and uninsured mortgage loans. Monthly interest and full repayment of principal is guaranteed by Freddie Mac, although the timing of principal payments is not. The general public has considered the two institutions as federal agencies even though they were formally private (Fannie Mae was made a private corporation in 1968, and Freddie Mac was created in 1970 to break the monopoly of Fannie Mae).

A *dynamic pass-through* differs from a static one in the structure of the portfolio of loans against which the securities are sold. Here, the loans are usually short term, whereas the securities issued against the pool of assets have a much longer maturity, meaning that new loans have to enter the pool to replace those that have expired. Thus, the SPV reinvests the funds for a fixed period, the revolving period, during which only interest is paid to certificate holders. This design is most often used with credit card loans, where repayment periods can be very low, something which fits poorly with investors' desire for keeping the funds invested for some minimum period.

Asset-backed bonds. The second main type of securitization gives rise to the so-called *asset-backed bond* (ABB). In this case, the SPV is a subsidiary of the originator created only for this purpose. The consequence is that the assets remain on the balance sheet of the originator (at least when consolidated so as to include subsidiaries). The underlying assets are typically securities which give rise to a cash flow, but this is not passed on to investors. Instead, the subsidiary transfers the assets to a trustee who takes care of paying the investor, but the latter are payed according to a fixed schedule. The construction is illustrated in Fig. 8.2 (p. 150).

Normally, the ABBs are *overcollateralized*, in the sense that the value of the assets exceeds the amount of bonds issued against these assets. This means that funds are channeled into the subsidiary, in principle to be used as a reserve against defaults on the remaining assets, but some of it may be taken out in the form of dividend payments.

Pay-through. This is a mixture of the two previous forms, in the sense that the assets remain on the balance of the originator (ownership is not transferred to the investor), but the proceeds from the assets are earmarked for servicing the bonds.

The construction is used in the so-called *collateralized mortgage obligations* (CMOs) issued by Freddie Mac from 1983. The CMOs are issued so as to fit several different

---

Box 8.1

Securitization and regulatory capital arbitrage. One of the reasons that securitization became so widespread was that it made it possible to reduce capital charges. The following example (taken from Jones [2000]) illustrates the idea:

Suppose that a bank has the following balance sheet:

Bank			
Loans	200	Deposits	176
– Reserves	2	Equity	22
Total Assets	198		

Here the capital ratio is 22/200 = 11% if only tier 1 capital (equity) is included, and 24/200 = 12% if the reserves are also counted as capital. Arranging now a securitization to the amount of 40 means that an SPV is set up which acquires loans from the bank to this amount, financing them with asset-backed securities (ABS). Now there are two firms, the SPV (which is not a bank and to which capital regulation does not apply), and the bank, now with a reduced amount of loans:

SPV			
Loans	40	ABSs	40

Bank			
Loans	160	Deposits	136
– Reserves	2	Equity	22
Total Assets	158		

Here it is assumed that the bank can reduce deposits corresponding to the issue of ABSs. The capital ratio of the bank is now 24/160 = 15% which is clearly an improvement over the 12% above.

In practice, the transactions between the bank and the SPV are less simple. The bank may want to support the credit rating of the ABSs issued by the SPV, assuming some obligations towards the latter, and this may reduce the capital ratio.

The use of securitization for reducing capital charges is an example of *regulatory arbitrage*: Under any given system of regulation, banks will act so as to comply with the rules in the most advantageous way, and their choices are not always in accordance with the intentions of the regulators.

---

investors, so the issue is divided into several classes prioritized for receipt of principal (so class A gets principal payments until it is completely paid off, then class B is paid, etc.), with maturity from 5 to 20 years. The reason that investors may be interested in the different classes is that maturity as such is assessed differently by different investors, but also that the risk of lender prepayment in the case of a general lowering of interest rates varies with the maturity.

The complicated nature of the CMO, based as it is on different mortgages and separated into tranches with different ratings, has its roots in the desire to create a type of security which could be marketed broadly, satisfying different investor demands with respect to risk and return. The disadvantage of this structure is that it becomes increasingly difficult to assess such papers, and indeed these papers in particular turned out to be wildly overrated when the crisis struck in 2008. Some European countries have had specific rules governing mortgage credit, producing in some cases securities which were as safe as government debt, but with European integration the national systems are getting aligned.

As indicated above, not only mortgage loans but also other types of loan transactions can be the basis for a securitization. In the early phase, car loans, played a major role, and they are still quite important. *Certificates of Automobile Receivables* (CARS) were issued from 1985 and remained for some years the largest sector of the asset-backed securities market. CARS are pay-throughs and the underlying assets deteriorate much quicker than does the fixed property behind mortgage loans, but although individual depreciation is rather unpredictable, the overall rates are rather stable, and this is stated in the sales material for the particular certificates.

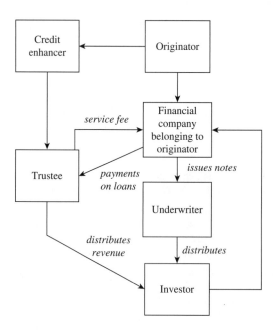

Figure 8.2 Schematic overview of an asset-based bond.

Credit card receivables have been subject to securitization since 1986, and up until the financial crisis they constituted the largest sector of asset-backed securities. But also other assets have entered the securitization process (including junk bonds, finance leases, unsold airline seats, song royalties and proceeds from tobacco litigation, as well as unsold old and natural gas). Even intellectual property (trade marks, brand names, product designs, etc.) has been made the subject of securitization.

8.2 Securitization and asymmetric information

As shown in the previous section, there are advantages in securitization derived from accounting rules and taxation, and indeed the idea of turning ordinary credit transactions into marketable papers would seem to be a way to enhance credit so as to make it more easily available and cheaper. It is therefore not surprising that securitization became extremely popular during the 1990s and then increasingly in the following years. After the very big losses experienced on these securities during the financial crisis of 2007–8, the attitude changed, and the wave of securitization was blamed as the main factor leading to this crisis. Even though this may be exaggerated, there are some inherent problems, and we shall have a closer look at these in this and the following section. In view of previous chapters, it comes as no surprise that the main theme here is asymmetric information.

8.2.1 A simple model of securitization

The securitization process is indeed open to many instances of asymmetric information, which may have as a consequence that the market functions in a suboptimal way. We consider here a simple model of securitization adapted from Gorton and Souleles [2005]. Here a bank faces the task of financing projects which last for one period, each project demanding an investment of 1 unit. The bank has an initial amount W of capital for this investment, and due to the rules for capital regulation, there is a limit kW to the number of projects that can be financed. For simplicity we assume that $kW = 1$, meaning that the bank will be able to engage in exactly one project.

The quality of a project will depend on the effort of the bank, and this effort $e \in [0, 1]$, is either e_L ('low') or e_H ('high'), with $e_H > e_L$. Effort matters in the sense that a project returns outcome y_H with probability e and y_L with probability $1 - e$, with $y_H > 1 > y_L$, but it has a cost $h(e)$, with $h(e_H) > h(e_L)$. The choice of effort determines the quality of both projects, but the random outcomes of the two projects are independent. Because y_H and y_L are project outcomes as seen from the point of view of the bank, we may think of y_H as the agreed repayment when the project is successful and of y_L as project outcome in the case of failure and default of the investor. We assume that effort is desirable, from the point of view of society, in the sense that

$$e_H y_H + (1 - e_H)y_L - (1 + r)h(e_H) > e_L y_H + (1 - e_L)y_L - (1 + r)h(e_L), \qquad (1)$$

where r is the risk-free rate of interest.

If the bank can fund the loans using deposits with an interest rate r_D in addition to its own capital, its expected profits as evaluated at $t = 0$ are

$$(1 + r)^{-1}[ey_H + (1 - e)y_L - (1 - W)(1 + r_D)] - h(e).$$

By (1), the bank will choose high effort, and in the absence of securitization, this is the outcome of the simple model.

We now add the possibility of selling the loan in a market. An investor will buy the loan if the expected profits are at least as large as could be obtained in the bonds market with interest rate r, and assuming competition, the price $p(e^*)$ of this particular security must satisfy

$$p(e^*) = (1 + r)^{-1}[e^* y_H + (1 - e^*)y_L],$$

where e^* is the effort level which the investor expects to be chosen by the bank. In this situation, high effort cannot be an equilibrium choice, because the bank will gain from choosing e_L while selling at the price $p(e_H)$. If $p(e_L) \geq 1$ so that the bank does not lose money on the sale of its loans, there is an equilibrium where the loans will be sold at price $p(e_L)$, and the bank chooses effort level e_L for preparing the loans which are to be sold through securitization.

If the bank is constrained by capital regulation, it will be advantageous to sell loans through securitization as long as this activity yields a non-negative profit. If not, then the profit from securitization must be compared with the profit from funding the project through ordinary banking. From $r_D \leq r$, we get that

$$(1 + r)^{-1}[e_H y_H + (1 - e_H)y_L - (1 + r_D)] - h(e_H)$$
$$\geq (1 + r)^{-1}[e_H y_H + (1 - e_H)y_L - (1 + r)] - h(e_H),$$

and using (1), we have

$$e_H y_H + (1 - e_H)y_L - (1 + r) - (1 + r)h(e_H) > e_L y_H + (1 - e_L)y_L - (1 + r) - (1 + r)h(e_L),$$

so

$$(1 + r)^{-1}[e_H y_H + (1 - e_H)y_L - (1 + r_D)] - h(e_H) > p(e_L) - 1 - h(e_L),$$

and it follows that banking is more profitable than loan sales. Consequently, the bank would prefer traditional loans, and it will turn to securitization only when it has reached the limit for traditional loans set by capital regulation.

This may, however, change if we assume that the bank is risk averse, maximizing expected utility of profits rather than expected profits. If the bank has a von Neumann-Morgenstern utility function u, then expected utility at date $t = 1$ if the banking contract is chosen takes the form

$$U_B = e_H u(y_H - (1 + r_D) - (1 + r)h(e_H)) + (1 - e_H)u(y_L - (1 + r_D) - (1 + r)h(e_H)). \quad (2)$$

By risk aversion, U_B is smaller than

$$u(e_H y_H + (1 - e_H)y_L - (1 + r_D) - (1 + r)h(e_H)), \tag{3}$$

which is the utility of getting the expected profit from the banking contract as a cash downpayment at $t = 1$. If the difference between (3) and (2) is big enough, and if r_D is sufficiently close to r, then the securitization alternative yielding a utility at $t = 1$ of

$$u((1 + r)(p(e_L) - h(e_L))) = u(e_L y_H + (1 - e_L)y_L - (1 + r) - (1 + r)h(e_H))$$

may exceed U_B, so the bank will prefer securitization.

Summing up, securitization may be a preferable alternative to traditional banking for the financial intermediary, because in this way the constraints from capital regulation can be loosened, and the immediate sale of the loan portfolio may be better than keeping it on the books. It may, however, have negative effects for welfare if the quality of the loans being securitized tends to be lower than those kept on the books.

8.2.2 Securitization and business cycles

The introduction and subsequent widespread use of securitization may change the role of banks from traditional originators of loans to holders of securities. This has some unexpected consequences because banks may become more vulnerable to business cycles and may destabilize the financial markets. This can be seen in the following model of securitization, which follows the work by Shleifer and Vishny [2010].

We consider an economy over three periods $t = 0, 1, 2$. Investment projects are decided upon at $t = 0$ and at $t = 1$; all of them cost 1 unit of money and have a payoff Y at $t = 2$ which is not subject to uncertainty. All investment projects must be financed by loans from the banks, and the banks demand a fee f when initiating the investment. We may think of the fee as the bank's share in the net outcome $Y - 1$ of the investment, the remaining share being left to the entrepreneur.

The bank has equity E_0 at $t = 0$, which is available as money. The bank may keep it or it may use it for initiating loans. Loans may be kept as such on the books of the banks, or they may be sold as securities which pay exactly 1 at $t = 2$.

When writing securities, the bank must keep a fraction d (this can be explained in many different ways, for example as a signal to the market about the quality of the loan backing up the security). Let P_0 and P_1 be the security price; we assume that $P_0 = 1$, so the bank does not gain from issuing securities at $t = 0$. In the following, we focus on the case where $P_1 < 1$, so the economy is at the beginning of a downturn. We assume these prices to be known at $t = 0$.

Securitization makes it possible for the bank to initiate more investments than if they had to be financed only by the equity, namely a total of E_0/d investment projects. Because $P_1 < P_0$, it is better to initiate all projects right away than to wait.

Box 8.2

Lehman Brothers and its bankruptcy in 2008. The failure of Lehman Brothers in September 2008 is generally considered as the most significant event of the 2007–8 financial crisis.

At the time of its bankruptcy, Lehman brothers was the fourth-largest investment bank in the United States, engaged in many different types of financial services. One of the main reasons that the bank became financially strained was its engagement in securitization; in particular, it had issued very large amounts of CMOs based on subprime mortgages of which it had kept large positions in lower-rated mortgages. With the increasing problems in the real estate market, these positions lost value very quickly, and because they were used as collateral in repo transactions, the consequence was a steadily growing need for additional funding. This development, which was followed by a large drop in share values, forced the bank into negotiations with potential buyers, which did not succeed, and the bank filed for bankruptcy on September 15, 2008.

In the years before its failure, Lehman Brothers had developed a practice of treating repo arrangements, where securities are used as collateral, as outright sales of securities in its financial reports, thereby hiding the true quality of its assets to the general public.

We now add another source of funding for the banks, taking the situation closer to that of shadow banking: We assume that the bank can borrow in financial markets against collateral in the form of securities. Because the payoff of the securities is safe, the bank does not pay interest. But as it receives outside funding, it is subject to capital regulation, specifying that equity must constitute a fraction h of total assets or, equivalently, of total liabilities, equity plus loans,

$$\frac{E_t}{E_t + L_t} \geq h, \ t = 0, 1, \tag{4}$$

which is taken to hold with = in the following. Thus, a bank may originate loans using all available funding at $t = 0$, which amounts to E_0/h, giving rise to $N_0 = E_0/dh$ investment projects.

Having initiated N_0 projects at $t = 0$, the bank will have a security portfolio to the size of $N_0 d = \dfrac{E_0}{h}$ at $t = 0$. This portfolio constitutes the assets of the bank, and in order to obtain it, the bank has borrowed to the amount of L_0, which by (4) has the size of $E_0(1 - h)/h$.

We assume that all profits earned by initiating loans are paid out as dividends, so the value E_1 of the equity at $t = 1$ moves in the same way as portfolio values, meaning that $E_1 = E_0 P_1$. But then (4) will be violated unless the bank reduces its loans, and in order to do so it has to sell securities and pay back the loans. Let S be the amount of securities sold by the bank. They sell at the price P_1, so the total assets after the sale must be $(N_0 d - S)P_1$, and to find E_1 we must subtract the value of the loans, which is $L_0 - P_1 S$. The capital ratio then takes the form

$$\frac{(N_0 d - S)P_1 - (L_0 - P_1 S)}{(N_0 d - S)P_1}.$$

Inserting $L_0 = E_0(1 - h)/h$ and $N_0 d = E_0/h$, we obtain the expression

$$S = \frac{E_0}{h} \cdot \frac{1 - P_1}{P_1} \cdot \frac{1 - h}{h}$$

for the amount of securities to be sold in the market at $t = 1$. Because each security sells for a price which is below the value at which it was issued, the bank realizes a *loss* in this period.

We need now to check whether this strategy, using all available capital for securitization at $t = 0$, is better than postponing securitization. Because investment and securitization may be initiated both at $t = 0$ and $t = 1$, the bank might keep some part of the equity liquid and either (a) initiate a loan at $t = 1$, or (b) buy securities, which are underpriced at $t = 1$.

Using 1 unit of money for securitization at $t = 0$, the profit at $t = 0$ is $\dfrac{f}{dh}$, followed in $t = 1$ by a loss on the sale of securities due to the capital constraint as found above. Because $1/dh$ securities can be issued, the gain is f/dh, but it is followed by a loss to the size of $1 - P_1$ on each of the securities that have to be sold at $t = 1$, so net profits are

$$\frac{f}{dh} - \left[\frac{1}{h} \cdot \frac{1 - P_1}{P_1} \cdot \frac{1 - h}{h} \right],$$

EXAMPLE 8.3 The following is a numerical example of the workings of the Shleifer-Vishny model. Suppose that the bank obtains a fee $f = 0.1$ from initializing projects and that security prices at $t = 1$ are $P_1 = 0.9$, so

$$\max \left\{ f, \frac{1 - P_1}{P_1} \right\} = 0.111,$$

which is the best result to be obtained from traditional financial activity, initializing projects against a fee or trading in securities.

If participation in securitized projects amounts to $d = 0.2$, then the upfront profit at $t = 0$ per investment contract is

$$\frac{f}{d} = 0.5,$$

and if the bank also uses external funding for securitization, with a value of capital ratio of $h = 0.2$, the profits per unit of capital invested are

$$\frac{f}{dh} - \left[\frac{1}{h} \cdot \frac{1 - P_1}{P_1} \cdot \frac{1 - h}{h} \right] = 0.28,$$

so (5) is satisfied, and profits from securitization exceed those of the alternative strategies.

Incidentally, it is seen that it is better for the bank to pursue non-leveraged securitization in this example. If, instead, the fall of prices had been smaller, then the leveraged version becomes more profitable and eventually will outperform the non-leveraged version.

which should be compared to (a) profit f at $t = 1$ from initiating a loan of 1 unit, or (b) profit $\dfrac{1 - P_1}{P_1}$ from buying securities for 1 unit of money at $t = 1$. Assuming that

$$\frac{f}{dh} - \left[\frac{1}{h} \cdot \frac{1 - P_1}{P_1} \cdot \frac{1 - h}{h}\right] > \max\left\{f, \frac{1 - P_1}{P_1}\right\}, \tag{5}$$

we get that the securitization approach is the most advantageous for the bank.

It is seen that in our simple model of securitization, banks are not only initiating loans but are also holding securities, and in a beginning – and even anticipated – downturn (with falling security prices), the banks will act in a way which aggravates the situation because (1) they prefer investing during the boom rather than postponing investment; and (2) they are selling securities in order to satisfy their capital constraint, once the downturn sets in.

8.3 A model of shadow banking

In the previous section, we saw that securitization may be advantageous for banks but causes financial fragility. This is also what emerges in the case where securitization has become an important part of financial intermediation rather than just another financial activity. Following the ideas of Gennaioli et al. [2013], we consider a model where financial investors use intermediators who profit from securitization.

There are m investors (considered here as agents who want to place certain amounts of money and receive a return) and n intermediators. Investors can choose deposits with intermediators or buy securities issued by them, but they have no immediate access to investment projects, which is why they need intermediators. The intermediators can invest in a safe project with payoff R, or they can choose a risky investment with a payoff $A > 0$ with probability π_s in the case of success and 0 otherwise. The success probability π_s depends on the state of nature $s \in \{1, 2, 3\}$, with $\pi_1 > \pi_2 > \pi_3$. The states may be thought of as corresponding to the upper part of a business cycle, a downturn and recession, respectively. Intermediators can issue securities in the projects, or they can accept deposits from the investors against a payment r.

It is assumed that $R > A$, the safe project also has the highest payoff, but it is in limited supply. Therefore, intermediator j invests I_j^s in the safe project but also invests I_j^r in the risky project. Part of this investment is sold to the market as securities to the amount S_j^r. The intermediator may also buy securities issued by the other banks, to the amount T_j^r. It is assumed that what is bought in the market is a complete mixture of the individual projects. Assuming independence of projects (and using the law of large numbers), the mixed security bought in the market gives a certain payoff of $\pi_s A$ in state s, $s = 1, 2, 3$. Investor i places deposits D_i and possibly buys securities in the risky project to the amount T_i^r.

The reason why intermediator j sells her own securities and buys those issued by other intermediators (in the same project) is that the amount of safe investment and the securities issued by *other* intermediators can be used as collateral for raising debt with investors (receiving deposits), whereas securities issued by the bank itself cannot. This assumption is important for the conclusions to be drawn from the model. We may justify it by assuming that each individual bank is subject to some independent risk of failure, which, however, can be diversified away when the bank buys securities in the market, which therefore can be used as collateral for the debt. Thus, S_j^r denotes the amount of securities issued by j *and* sent off to be mixed with securities issued by other intermediators, whereas T_i^r and T_j^r denote purchases of mixed securities by investors and intermediators. We assume that deposits are fully collateralized, so deposits with intermediator j satisfy

$$rD_j \leq RI_j^s + \pi_3 AT_j^r. \tag{6}$$

Because deposits are fully collateralized, there is no need for securitization of the safe project, as the securities would sell at a price q^s such that $rq^s = R$. We therefore assume that only the risky project is securitized.

Investors are assumed to be very risk averse in the sense that they are oriented towards the worst-case payoff of investments, which for investor i is

$$\min_h rD_i + \pi_h AT_i^r,$$

under a budget constraint saying that deposits and purchases cannot exceed initial wealth W_i,

$$D_i + T_i^r \leq W_i.$$

The extreme risk aversion of investors fits with rule (6) for pledging collateral – depositors are sure of getting their promised return even in the most adverse state of nature.

Intermediators are assumed to maximize expected profits. If the state probabilities are p_1, p_2, p_3, then average success probability of the risky project is $\bar{\pi} = p_1\pi_1 + p_2\pi_2 + p_3\pi_3$, and expected profits of intermediator j are

$$RI_j^s + \bar{\pi}AT_j^r + q\left(S_j^r - T_j^r\right) - rD_j.$$

Here q is the price at which risky securities are traded in the market. The budget constraint of the intermediator,

$$I_j^s + I_j^r - q\left(S_j^r - T_j^r\right) \leq W_j + D_j,$$

states that investments in the safe and risky project minus net income from securitization must be covered by initial wealth W_j and deposits D_j. Also, the amount of securities issued by intermediator j cannot exceed the amount of projects initiated,

$$S_j^r \leq I_j^r.$$

In equilibrium, the securities issued should also be those purchased, so

$$\sum_{j=1}^{n} S_i^r = \sum_{i=1}^{m} T_i^s + \sum_{j=1}^{n} T_j^s.$$

Furthermore, deposits placed should equal deposits received,

$$\sum_{i=1}^{m} D_i = \sum_{j=1}^{n} D_j.$$

For our study of properties of the equilibrium, it is convenient to add some assumptions on the payoffs of the projects. As already mentioned, we assume that $R > p_1 A$, so the safe project is the most profitable one; however, its supply I_0 is limited,

$$\sum_{j=1}^{n} I_j^s \leq I_0 < \sum_{i=1}^{m} W_i + \sum_{j=1}^{n} W_j,$$

so the safe investment cannot absorb all investment demand. In addition, we assume that $\bar{\pi} A > 1$, so on average, risky projects are better than storing liquidity. However, storing is better than the risky project in the worst state of nature, $\pi_3 A < 1$.

Because investors are extremely risk averse, they will never hold risky securities, $T_i^r = 0$ for all i. The securities must be held by the intermediaries, and the amount of projects initiated and securities issued is $I^r = \sum_{i=1}^{m} w_i + \sum_{j=1}^{n} w_j - I_0$. As all intermediaries are risk neutral, they are indifferent between holding their investments in projects or holding securities bought in the market; hence security prices satisfy $q = 1$. Total deposits must satisfy

$$\sum_{i=1}^{m} D_i \leq R I_0 + \pi_3 A I^r.$$

If the intermediators compete for depositors, then the equilibrium interest rate must equal the payoff that an additional unit of deposit gives rise to, so

$$r = \bar{\pi} A$$

as long as the payoff of the safe investment is large enough to cover the need for collateral. If this is not the case, then the cost of receiving 1 additional unit of deposits must also take into account the cost of maintaining sufficient collateral, so (6) is satisfied. The equilibrium deposit rate will therefore decrease with the amount of deposit placed. If investor wealth is very large, then it may be too costly to pledge collateral; the equilibrium deposit rate falls to 1 and investors choose to hold some of their wealth as cash rather than as deposits or securities.

It is seen that securitization has an important role in this model because without it the investors, being risk averse, would accept to invest through intermediators only to the extent that their deposits can be covered by the safe investments and the worst case payoff of risky investment. Securitization allows for an extension of investment in projects above this limit.

Securitization with myopic agents. Things may, however, change if we assume that agents *neglect* the possibility of a recession, assuming that $p_3 = 0$. Because the worst case is now $s = 2$, the rule determining the size of deposits that a intermediator j may accept is

$$r D_j \leq R I_j^s + \pi_2 A T_j^r, \tag{7}$$

and this limit is less restrictive than that of (6), because $\pi_2 > \pi_3$. Investors still prefer deposits to risky securities which may default, so the equilibrium will be as above, although at different values of the deposit rate. Because the ability of intermediators to take on deposits is larger when the worst case contemplated is less damaging, the equilibrium interest rate will be higher in this situation.

However, the improved conditions for the intermediators come at a cost: The bad case $s = 3$ has been neglected, but not eliminated, and when it occurs, the payoff obtained from the risky investment is insufficient to cover the deposits claimed by investors. Intermediators default and investors experience losses.

This is not qualitatively different from what would happen in traditional banking when banks neglect risks, and a specific role played by securitization has not been identified. However, adding an extra feature to the model will make this easier.

Partial revelation of information. In order to obtain a situation where securitization gives rise to financial fragility, we extend the model so as to capture three rather than two periods of time. As before, investment, securitization and deposit decisions are made at $t = 0$, and at this stage, agents ignore the state $s = 3$. Then at $t = 1$, some information is revealed about the future state to materialize; we assume that some of the investment projects turn out to be *early*, giving payoff A at $t = 1$, whereas other projects are *late*, so their payoff (either A or 0) comes only at $t = 2$. The fraction q of early projects can take two values, q_h and q_l, with $q_h > q_l$. The value of q, assumed to be public, is also a signal about the state at $t = 2$. If $q = q_h$, then s is either 1 or 2, whereas if $q = q_l$, it will be either 2 or 3. Thus, a low fraction of early projects signals a possible downturn of the economy.

For the decisions at $t = 0$, things are as in the previously considered case (with agents neglecting the possibility of $s = 3$). Here intermediators will use securitization in order to attract deposits, which they can do up to the limit given by (7). If intermediators have wealth w_j, they may invest without securitizing (being risk averse they are indifferent between the risky payoff and its mean value), and we assume that intermediators hold such investment projects.

If at $t = 1$ the share of early projects is q_h, then nothing upsets the decisions made because the expectations of the agents were correct and $s = 3$ cannot occur. Otherwise, if $q = q_l$, then the state $s = 3$ at $t = 2$ enters as a possible outcome, so investors must reconsider their situation, given that intermediators do not any longer hold sufficient reserves to cover payback in the worst possible state. Indeed, the deposits taken exceed what is now possible by the amount

$$(\pi_2 - \pi_3)AS_j^{r*},$$

where S_j^{r*} is the amount of risky projects (neglecting the worst case) that was securitized.

Given this state of affairs, investors may want to reconsider their deposits, which now have become risky and therefore have lost value to the risk-averse investors. They are therefore willing to sell the excess deposits to possible buyers, and fortunately there are such buyers, namely the intermediators who received the payoff of early projects (a fraction q_l of all the intermediaries). These intermediaries need to keep some of this payoff as a guarantee to their own depositors, but whatever remains, that is

$$A\left(I_j^{r*} - S_j^{r*}\right) - (\pi_2 - \pi_3)AS_j^{r*},$$

can be used for buying up excess deposits of the other intermediaries at a discount.

For this transfer of deposits between intermediaries to be successful, the liquidity of intermediaries with early projects should be large enough to absorb the excess deposits. The value at which these deposits are transferred is

$$V_1 = q_l\left[A\left(I_j^{r*} - S_j^{r*}\right) - (\pi_2 - \pi_3)AS_j^{r*}\right],$$

which must be at least equal to the value to investors, which is $V_1^{\min} = (1 - p_l)\pi_3 AS_j^{r*}$ (assuming symmetric equilibria at $t = 0$ so all intermediators have made the same choices), and cannot exceed

$$V_1^{\max} = (1 - q_l)\mathsf{E}\left[\pi \,|\, q = q_l\right]AS_j^{r*},$$

which is the expected gain to the liquid intermediators from the deposits absorbed.

If the unsecuritized investments of intermediators are insufficient to absorb the excess of deposits, then the value ends at $V_1^{\min}$ and depositors must accept the risk of losses if $s = 3$ obtains. Thus, widespread securitization has the effect that even a relatively mild downturn can result in a considerable drop in the value of debt as the economy adapts to the new and less optimistic outlook. At the same time, the liquidity of intermediators created at $t = 1$ by projects paying off early has been used up in buying claims for deposits.

We still need an explanation of *why* agents would neglect the risk of a serious recession when the initial decisions were made, and for the moment this is left as an assumption. We shall encounter other such instances of shortsightedness in models in later chapters, and a discussion of this phenomenon is postponed for the moment.

8.4 Rating agencies

The rise of securitization has brought with it a need for public information about quality of securities. Assessing the future returns of a security the origin of which may be obscure is not easy, and the size of the market makes it difficult for any single investor to acquire the necessary background knowledge. It is therefore not surprising that a *credit rating agency* (CRA) has a role to fulfil, and these agencies have played a considerable role, both when new securities are to be sold in the market and when existing portfolios need to be assessed. We have seen already (in Chapter 7) that the ratings produced by such agencies enter into the internal models for credit risk assessment of the banks.

The credit ratings agencies were criticized for the role which they allegedly played in misinforming the public about debt which eventually proved valueless. There are indeed weak spots in the way they produce ratings; in particular, it is unfortunate that it is the seller of the security who pays for the ratings produced by the CRA, and it would seem obvious that the CRA has incentives to inflate the ratings, producing a result looking much like that observed before the crisis of 2007–8. As always, things may be less simple, as CRAs may be less biased than they appear, as we shall see below.

8.4.1 Reputation effects

Because there are many credit rating agencies and they compete with each other for customers, it can be argued that the success of a CRA depends on its performance, or rather on the way that the public assesses its performance. If therefore a CRA is systematically overvaluing the securities that are sent to the market, it will eventually be considered as less trustworthy and it will lose customers. The CRA has to worry about its reputation, and this, it is argued, will keep it on the right track. The argument carries some weight, but it also has some limitations, as illustrated in the following simple model inspired by the work of Mathis et al. [2009].

Assume that we need to assess an investment project of size 1 which may give a return $R > 1$ with probability μ, and otherwise fails completely. The investment takes the form of securities which are sold in the market. We assume that $\mu R < 1$ so without additional information, the investment is not profitable. However, there is a CRA which can observe whether the project succeeds or fails and which subsequently states a rating, which is either G (good) or B (bad). If the rating is B, then the project is not initiated. The CRA is paid a fee f if investment takes place.

The CRA may either be sincere, so it reports the quality of the project, or it may be opportunistic, stating that a project is good when it is actually bad, because fees are paid only when securities are issued. We allow for mixed strategies and let π denote the probability of stating G when the investment is not profitable, that is, the probability of declaring that a bad project is good. If the CRA assesses a large number of projects, then π can be seen as the fraction of bad projects which are characterized as good. The income of the CRA is $[\mu + (1 - \mu)\pi]f$, where f is the fee to be described below.

The choice of π by the CRA is unknown to the market, but security issuers and buyers assign a subjective probability $q = P\{T\}$ to the truthfulness of the CRA (where T is the event that the CRA reports its observation correctly), based on past performance. We may think of this probability as the quality or the reputation of the CRA as perceived by issuers and investors; the actual quality is decided by the CRA itself through its choice of π.

The quality of information q matters because it determines the probability $p(q)$ of success as perceived by investors through the equation

$$\mu = p(q)[\mu + (1 - q)(1 - \mu)\pi], \tag{8}$$

and the market buys the securities only if

$$p(q)y(q) \geq 1, \tag{9}$$

where $y(q) \leq R$ is the nominal return promised to investors (and paid only in the case of success).

If the CRA misrepresents at the rate π, then the probability that a bad project gets the rating B is then

$$a(q,\pi) = q + (1 - q)(1 - \pi(q)) = 1 - (1 - q)\pi(q),$$

which we may interpret as the *accuracy* of the CRA given its quality and its strategy. Using (8), we can write

$$p(q) = \frac{\mu}{1 - (1 - \mu)a(q,\pi)}, \tag{10}$$

so there is a lower bound a^* for the accuracy, which by (9) is such that $p(q) < \frac{1}{R}$ when $a < a^*$.

We consider the working of the CRA over many periods, with $t = 1, 2, \ldots$ At the beginning of period t, the quality parameter for the CRA is q_t. When the CRA uses its strategy π_t, some projects are financed, and others are not. At the end of the period considered, investors observe the actual outcome of the project; there are three possible outcomes, namely success (S), failure (F) and project not financed (N).

Investors and issuers may now update their beliefs with regard to the quality of the CRA, using Bayes' rule.

$$P\{T|S\} = \frac{P\{S|T\}P\{T\}}{P\{S\}} = \frac{\mu q_t}{\mu} = q_t, \quad P\{T|F\} = \frac{P\{F|T\}P\{T\}}{P\{F\}} = \frac{0 \cdot q_t}{1 - \mu} = 0, \tag{11}$$

and

$$P\{T|N\} = \frac{P\{N|T\}P\{T\}}{P\{N\}} = \frac{q_t}{a(q_t,\pi_t)} \tag{12}$$

when $a(q_t,\pi) \neq 0$.

The updating in (11)–(12) pertains to each investment project, and we assume that the overall updating is done by averaging the posterior probabilities over all the projects. If at date t the quality parameter is q_t and the strategy of the CRA is π_t, then the quality parameter at $t + 1$ is

$$q_{t+1} = \mu q_t + (1 - \mu)(1 - \pi_t)\frac{q_t}{a(q_t,\pi_t)}. \tag{13}$$

The payoff of the CRA is taken as the discounted sum of period t payoffs, with a discount factor $\delta < 1$. The payoff in any period is obtained from collecting fees for each project which is initiated. Whether a project is initiated depends on the CRA itself, which should give it the assessment G, but also on the issuers and investors, who will engage with projects only if $pR \geq 1$, where p is the subjective probability of success, which can be found from equation (10).

At the moment of decision, the strategy π of the CRA is, however, not revealed to the issuers and investors, so that they must act according to their expectations; we shall assume for simplicity that they expect it to be equal to that chosen in the previous period. It follows that there is a lower bound $\underline{q}$ for the parameter, so projects are only initiated when $q \geq \underline{q}(\pi)$. If q drops below this value, then the CRA will do no business, and we shall assume that it will be closed down.

Now we consider the choices of the opportunistic CRA, starting at $t = 1$ and taking as given the value π_0. Suppose that the initial values are $q_1 < 1$ and $\pi_0 = 0$. Because the period payoff $[\mu + (1 - \mu)(1 - q_t)\pi_t]f$ is an increasing function of π_t, the CRA has the option of choosing $\pi_1 = 1$ and obtaining a period 1 payoff of f at the cost of being closed down from period 2 onwards. To prevent this possibility, we shall assume that

$$(1 - \mu)f < \frac{\delta}{1 - \delta}\mu f, \tag{14}$$

so the gain obtaining by a switch from true reporting to maximal misreporting is smaller than what could be obtained by truthful reporting in each future period. Given that (14) holds, the CRA will be interested in a sequence $(\pi_t)_{t=1}^{\infty}$ of strategy choices with associated sequences of the quality parameter determined by (13), giving rise to payoff

$$\sum_{t=1}^{\infty} \delta^{t-1}[\mu + (1 - \mu)(1 - q_t)\pi_t]f$$

and subject to the constraint

$$q_t \geq \underline{q}(\pi_{t-1}), t = 1, \ldots,$$

so the CRA avoids being closed down.

Although the short-sighted maximization of current period fee is not optimal behaviour, it may still be the case that $\pi_t > 0$ is preferred to truth telling. A deviation from truth telling will entail a decrease in the quality parameter according to (13), because $(1 - \pi) < a(q, \pi)$ for $\pi \neq 0$. However, the fall in quality may be chosen arbitrarily small by suitable choice of (small) $\pi > 0$, meaning that there is a sequence $(\pi_t)_{t=1}^{\infty}$ such that the associated sequence $(q_t)_{t=1}^{\infty}$ converges to some q^* and $q_t > \underline{q}(\pi_t)$ for all t. The payoff derived from this sequence is clearly larger than what could be obtained by truthfulness. We conclude that although the threat of closure forces the CRA away from absolute untrustworthiness, there is still a limit to the effects of reputation in this model.

8.4.2 Asset complexity and ratings inflation

Although the consideration of reputation may prevent a CRA from inflating its ratings too much, other factors, some of them beyond the control of the CRA, may also influence the result. The following model, adapted from Skreta and Veldkamp [2009], considers the problem from a slightly different angle.

We consider here a model of savers-investors who are potential buyers of a particular security in the market. The initial wealth is 1, and the return of the risky and riskless assets are $\tilde{r}$ and r. For simplicity, we specify the utility function as

$$u(w) = -e^{-\rho w},$$

where w is the wealth of the investor (cf. Chapter 1, Section 1.4), and we assume that the risky asset is normally distributed with mean $\bar{r}$ and variance σ^2. In this case risky projects can be assessed by their certainty equivalents, namely as

$$W(\sigma) = \mathsf{E}u(m\tilde{r} + (1-m)r)) = (1-m)r + m\bar{r} - \frac{1}{2}\rho m^2 \sigma^2,$$

where $\bar{r}$ and σ^2 are mean and variance of the normal distribution.

In the optimal portfolio, the price of the security (measured relative to that of the risk-free asset) must equal the marginal rate of substitution between the two assets, so

$$p = \frac{(\bar{r} - r) - m\rho\sigma^2}{r}.$$

which depends positively on expected payoff $\bar{r}$ and negatively on the standard deviation σ. The amount m of securities purchased is assumed fixed, so investors do not shift to other securities when prices change. Therefore, issuer profit is determined by the price alone.

We shall assume that investors know the mean $\bar{r}$, but not the variance. It is possible to obtain information about σ through a ratings agency at a cost c, but this cost is too high for the individual investor. The issuer also has the option of purchasing ratings of the asset, one or several, but she will disclose only one of them to the investors, and only the most favourable one.

In our present model, we assume that only σ is subject to uncertainty, and that it can take either of the two values σ_{max} and σ_{min}, with $\sigma_{max} > \sigma_{min}$, each with probability $1/2$. The ratings agency observes the true value with some error but passes the observation on without distortion; we denote by α the probability that the observed value of σ is the true one.

For the investor, expected utility without information will be

$$\frac{1}{2}W(\sigma_{max}) + \frac{1}{2}W(\sigma_{min}) = (1-m)r + m\bar{r} - \frac{1}{2}\rho m^2 \left[\frac{1}{2}\sigma^2_{max} + \frac{1}{2}\sigma^2_{min}\right],$$

and the security price is

$$p_0 = \frac{(\bar{r}_0 - r) - m\rho\sigma^2_0}{r}, \text{ with } \sigma^2_0 = \frac{1}{2}\sigma^2_{max} + \frac{1}{2}\sigma^2_{min}.$$

If the issuer uses the CRA, then the resulting rating will be used only if it is σ_{min}. With the information as outlined above, the investor will then assign a posterior probability

$$\alpha^* = \frac{\alpha + (1-\alpha)\alpha}{2\alpha - 2\alpha^2 + 1}$$

to the event that the true value is σ_{min}, and the expected utility of the portfolio is therefore

$$\alpha^* \mathsf{E}u(W(\sigma_{min})) + (1 - \alpha^*)\mathsf{E}u(W(\sigma_{max})) = (1 - m)r + m\bar{r} - \frac{1}{2}\rho m^2 \sigma_1^2,$$

where $\sigma_1^2 = \alpha^* \sigma_{max}^2 + (1 - \alpha^*)\sigma_{min}^2$. As a consequence, the asset will be sold at price

$$p_1 = \frac{(\bar{r} - r) - m\rho\sigma_1^2}{r}.$$

As long as the cost of rating is not too high, this is better for the issuer than the case of no information. Because the results of the rating are published only when they result in σ_{max}, we have that the published ratings are systematically biased *above* the true mean, even though the CRA itself delivers unbiased ratings, making errors with the same probability whether σ is high or low.

The probability α of making correct ratings has an influence on the outcome. When α is reduced towards $1/2$, which could be thought of as a result of successively increased complexity of securitization products, the difference between the security prices with and without published ratings is reduced, but the cases where projects rated as good turn out to be bad will increase, and seen in this perspective the ratings inflation will persist.

8.5 Mortgages

The question of whether business cycles are accentuated by the financial sector has been debated for years. Because many of the more spectacular events connected with a downturn are related to bank runs or defaults of banks, it seems reasonable to expect that there is a connection, but some distance remains to establishing the financial sector as the main cause. It would seem that something more than just financial speculation is called for, and an obvious candidate would be real estate prices: When property prices increase, the expectation of capital gain will increase demand for real estate, and if this demand can be based on borrowed money, then a bubble seems well under way. It should, however, be brought to mind that a consistent theory of cycles should also explain why the prices started their upward movement and why banks may be willing to finance the bubble.

A model taking these aspects into consideration, proposed by Kiyotaki and Moore [1997], will be outlined below in a simplified version, following Freixas and Rochet [2008]. We consider an economy over time, $t = 0, 1, \ldots$, with one consumption good in each period; consumers maximize the expected value of discounted future consumption. There is also a capital good ('land'), which can be used as collateral in loan contracts as well as for other purposes as indicated below.

There are two types of agents, namely entrepreneurs, who have access to technology and own the land but have no endowment of the consumption good, and lenders, who have endowments of the consumption good. The entrepreneurs need to borrow the consumption good, which they invest in production. There are constant returns to scale in production, and 1 unit of the consumption good combines with k units of land to yield y units of the consumption good in the next period.

In order to produce, the entrepreneur must borrow the consumption good needed for input in the production. We assume that the lender demands full collateral, something which may look strange in our context of no uncertainty in output, but this is important for the workings of the model. At time t, the entrepreneur can obtain at most $q_{t+1}(1 + r)^{-1}$ as a loan, corresponding to the present value of the collateral, one piece of land, at the time when the loan must be paid back, which therefore is the amount that can be borrowed.

With $q_{t+1}(1 + r)^{-1}$ units of the consumption good, the entrepreneur needs to use $kq_{t+1}(1 + r)^{-1}$ units of land in production. Assuming that this is ≤ 1, there is a remainder which can be used for other purposes. If this remainder can be rented out at a rate h_t, there is an additional income to the amount of $h_t(1 - kq_{t+1}(1 + r)^{-1})$.

To close the model, we need two additional pieces of information concerning the determination of (a) the rate h_t and (b) the price of land, q_t. For the rent to be paid when hiring land, we assume a linear relationship between price and quantity, formulated as

$$h_t(l_t) = b - al_t, \tag{15}$$

where $a, b > 0$ are constants, and l_t is the amount of land available for renting out (which means that it is not used in production). The price of land is assumed to be determined by market conditions, so

$$q_{t+1} + (y - (1 + r))\frac{q_{t+1}}{1 + r} + h_t\left(1 - \frac{kq_{t+1}}{1 + r}\right) = q_t(1 + r). \tag{16}$$

Here the right-hand side is what is obtained at date $t + 1$ if the land was sold at t. The left-hand side of (16) shows what can be obtained by keeping the land for one period and then selling it: The sale will bring in its price, q_{t+1}, and to this must be added the income earned from using the land from t to $t + 1$, which is the profit (after paying interest on the loan) from production and the rent from hiring out remaining land.

Inserting (15) with $l_t = 1 - kq_{t+1}(1 + r)^{-1}$ into (16), we get (after multiplying by $(1 + r)^{-1}$ on both sides) that q_t can be found as a second degree polynomial ϕ in q_{t+1},

$$q_t = \phi(q_{t+1}). \tag{17}$$

The graph of this polynomial will have a form as illustrated in Fig. 8.3. This graph intersects the diagonal twice; in each of these we have an equilibrium where the price will remain unchanged from one period to the next one. But there are also periodic equilibria defined by points $q^1 < q^2$ such that

$$q^1 = \phi(q^2), \quad q^2 = \phi(q^1). \tag{18}$$

To get some intuition for what happens in such a cycle, we notice that (17) and (18) is a *backwards* dynamical relationship: The price q_t is an equilibrium price compatible with

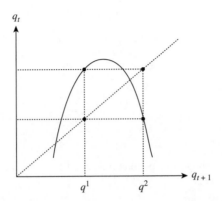

Figure 8.3 Dynamics in the simple Kiyotaki-Moore model. In the case shown, there is a two-period cycle in the price of land: The curve is a graphical representation of the backwards dynamics in (18) and shows the value of q_t which will give equilibrium at date t when the expected price of land in the next period is q_{t+1}.

an expected next period price q_2, and this price is again an equilibrium given that agents expect q_1 in the next period etc. What happens in such a two-period cycle is the following: High prices of land in the future mean that its value as collateral is high, but then rental income decreases, and this is consistent with the current price of land only if the latter is low. If prices are low in the future, the same argument produces that the current price must be low.

The connection between home prices and other economic activities is an old theme in economic theory, and the relevance of research on this interconnection was emphasized by the financial crisis of 2007–8, which was closely connected with conditions in the American housing market for real estate.

8.6 Leverage cycles

When discussing loans and loan contracts, we have seen that collateral plays an important role. And perhaps this role has not yet been fully appreciated, so in this section we take another look at loan contracts with collateral, based on the work of Geanakoplos [2010]. We consider a very simple world with two periods, 0 and 1; there is only one good, which may be consumed or stored from one period to the next. There is an infinity of individuals, indexed by $i \in [0, 1]$. All individuals are endowed with 1 unit of the good, and in addition they are endowed with an asset yielding a random payoff in the next period, namely either 1 unit of the good in the case of success or $1/4$ unit in the case of failure, as shown in Fig. 8.4. The individuals are risk neutral, so what matters to them is expected amount of the good available for consumption.

The individuals, who are otherwise all alike, differ in their subjective assessment of the probability π of success, and assuming that π is uniformly distributed in $[0, 1]$, we may identify this probability with the index i of the individual.

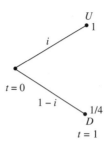

Figure 8.4 Event tree in the simple two-period version of the model. The asset pays 1 unit of goods in state U and 1/4 unit in state D.

8.6.1 Trade in the asset, no loans

Because the individuals have different assessments of the expected payoff of the asset, they may trade the asset at date 0. Individuals with small values of i may therefore sell their asset to individuals with larger i, and equilibrium in this trade will occur at a price p of the asset for which

$$p = i \cdot 1 + (1 - i)\frac{1}{4} \tag{19}$$

for a particular individual i, so the price p paid for an asset exactly equals its average payoff. Because individuals are patient, there is no discounting of future payoffs. At the equilibrium price p, all individuals $i' < i$ will want to sell their asset, giving a supply of i. The demand for the asset comes from agents $i'' > i$, and its size is $\dfrac{1 - i}{p}$, so market clearing gives rise to the equation

$$p \cdot i = 1 - i. \tag{20}$$

Solving (19) and (20) gives that $i = 0.59$, and the equilibrium price of the asset is $p = 0.69$.

8.6.2 Trade in assets, with loans

In the situation considered above, optimistic individuals (assigning a probability greater than 0.59 to the successful outcome) would like to buy more assets, but they are restricted by their wealth constraint, because they can use at most 1 unit of the good for buying assets. Assume now that we add the possibility of contracting debt; optimistic individuals can borrow goods (to be used for buying additional assets) from less optimistic individuals against a promise of delivering back the good in the next period. The loans must be fully collateralized, so the lender will carry no risk, and the interest rate is therefore 0, the risk-free interest rate in our economy.

The risky asset is the only one which can be used as collateral, and because it will pay only 1/4 in the case of a failure, this amount is what can be borrowed against 1 unit of the asset posted as collateral. If an optimistic individual borrows as much of the asset as possible, the resulting amount y must satisfy

$$y - 1 = \frac{1 + \frac{1}{4}y}{p}$$

because the amount of assets acquired must be paid by the endowment plus the loan, which cannot exceed $1/4$ times the collateral.

As before, the equilibrium can be found using (19) together with the condition that the amount of goods received by individuals selling the asset should equal the amount used for buying the asset,

$$p \cdot i = (1 - i) \cdot 1 + \frac{1}{4} \tag{21}$$

(buyers use their endowment plus the amount borrowed). Solving the system consisting of (19) and (21) gives that the individual indifferent between selling or buying is $i = 0.7$, and the price of the asset is $p = 0.78$. The introduction of loans has had the effect of increasing demand for the asset, and as a consequence asset prices have increased, and with the higher price of acquiring the asset, the latter has ceased to be an attractive investment for the not very optimistic individuals.

In the equilibrium, the loan to value ratio is $0.25/0.78 = 32\%$, and the haircut, which is the percentage subtracted from the market value of the asset, is $0.53/0.78 = 70\%$. Its inverse, the *leverage*, is computed as the value of assets divided by own capital invested, which is

$$\frac{0.78}{0.78 - 0.25} = 1.47.$$

This leverage is determined by the condition that the borrower promises to pay back $1/4$ in all cases, but it depends also on the market price of the asset, which in turn is determined by demand and supply; if the distribution of individuals along the scale of optimism changes, so does the equilibrium leverage.

So far, all loan contracts promise a repayment of $1/4$ independent of state. We might open up for other loan contracts, allowing the borrower to promise a higher payment in all cases. With such a contract, the borrower would default in the bad case, delivering only $1/4$, so the lender must treat this contract as a risky investment, to be assessed according to the subjective probabilities of the good and the bad outcomes. In equilibrium, only the loan contract with $1/4$ borrowed against 1 unit of the asset will be traded in the equilibrium. In this sense, the leverage is endogenous, determined by the equilibrium behaviour of the individuals.

8.6.3 Leverage in a model with three periods

We now add another period to the model, so in each state attained at $t = 1$, there is a similar possibility of moving up or down. The asset now pays off only at $t = 2$, with repayment 1 unless there were two consecutive downward movements, in which case the repayment is $1/4$, see Fig. 8.5. Keeping our identification of individual i with the probability of an upward movement, we get that individual i assessed the probability of failure as only $(1 - i)^2$.

The new feature of the extended model is that loans can be contracted only for one period, after which they are repaid and the collateral is returned to the borrower.

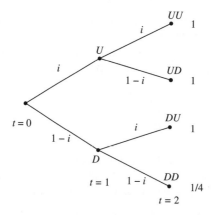

Figure 8.5 Event tree for three-period version of the model. The asset pays 1 in all states except *DD*, where it pays 1/4.

This means that loans have the form of a *repo* contract, where the lender buys the asset from the borrower under the obligation to buy it back after one period.

We now take a closer look at the asset market in the different states. If at $t = 1$ the state is U, then the asset pays 1 with certainty in the next period; its price is 1; and there is no reason for trade in the asset. If, however, the state is D, then things are very different: The probability of failure is now greater than at $t = 0$, consequently the market price p_D of the asset will be smaller than its initial price p_0. At $t = 0$, the borrowers used their endowment of the good plus all they could borrow in order to buy the asset, and the loan contract would specify that at most p_D units of the good could be borrowed against 1 unit of the asset posted as collateral. Now the borrowers cannot deliver back the goods borrowed; the collateral is seized by the lenders; and the individuals who borrowed at $t = 0$ are out of the market.

To see in detail what will happen, we consider as before a marginal individual, who is indifferent between buying or selling the asset. At $t = 1$ and in state D (as mentioned above, we are not interested in state U, where nothing happens), we denote this marginal individual by i_1; the marginal individual at $t = 0$ is denoted i_0. The counterpart of (19) is

$$p_D = i_1 1 + (1 - i_1)\frac{1}{4}, \tag{22}$$

and the condition for market clearing at state D is

$$\frac{i_1}{i_0}p_D = \frac{1}{i_0}(i_0 - i_1) + \frac{1}{4}.$$

The left-hand side is the amount of goods transferred to sellers of the asset: Only the individuals $i \leq i_0$ are in the market, and they now have all the consumption goods and all assets, so each of them holds $\frac{1}{i_0}$ of both, so if all in the segment $[0, i_1]$ sell their assets, then $\dfrac{i_1}{i_0}$ assets will be on sale. On the right-hand side, we have the amount of goods that can be put forward by individuals in $[i_1, i_0]$, plus the amount that can be borrowed using all the assets as collateral. The expression can also be rewritten as

$$i_0 = \frac{4}{5} i_1 (1 + p_D).$$ (23)

Moving now to the equations determining i_0 and p_0, we have that

$$i_0 p_0 = (1 - i_0) + p_D,$$ (24)

because the amount of goods transferred to sellers of the asset at $t = 0$ must equal the amount of goods that the buyers own plus what they can borrow on all assets acquired, which is p_D (the largest amount of goods which can be delivered in all cases at $t = 1$, using 1 unit of the asset as collateral). The final condition to be considered is that determining the marginal individual i_0: Using 1 unit of either for a leveraged purchase of the asset, the individual will get a payoff of $1 - p_D$ at state U and nothing at state D, against a downpayment of $p_0 - p_D$, giving an expected payoff of

$$i_0 \frac{1 - p_D}{p_0 - p_D}.$$

Alternatively, individual i_0 may keep the good, which with probability i_0 keeps its value at U and with probability $(1 - i_0)$ can be used for a leveraged purchase of the asset at $t = 2$, which will give a gain of

$$i_0 \frac{1 - \dfrac{1}{4}}{p_D - \dfrac{1}{4}} = \frac{i_0}{i_1},$$

giving the expression

$$i_0 \frac{1 - p_D}{p_0 - p_D} = i_0 + (1 - i_0)\frac{i_0}{i_1}.$$ (25)

Solving the system (22) – (25) gives

$$i_1 = 0.638, \ p_D = 0.729, \ i_0 = 0.882, \ p_0 = 0.959.$$

The price of the asset has gone down by a third from period 0 to period 1; even though the probability of the good outcome at $t = 2$ has not decreased drastically, for the marginal individual i_0 it has changed from $1 - (1 - i_0)^2 = 0.986$ to 0.882, which is only about 10%. This fall in prices is caused not only by reduced chance of success but also by the defaults and the disappearance from the market of optimistic individuals who might otherwise demand the asset. As a result, what occurs is already a downturn at $t = 1$, not caused by any change in the fundaments.

It may be noticed that leverage was

$$\frac{0.959}{0.959 - 0.729} = 4.16$$

in $t = 0$ and changed to

$$\frac{0.729}{0.729 - 0.25} = 1.522$$

in $t = 1$, showing that the possibility of using borrowed money to buy assets has been reduced drastically. This was not due to external disturbances but was, so to speak, a consequence of ordinary market behaviour. The possibility of leverage combined with the organization of the credit market as a short-term repo market has – by itself, so to speak – led to a situation where the small random movements of the market transform into a major economic crisis.

The insights obtained using this model shed new light on the financial crisis and in particular on the developments leading up to the crisis. Instead of seeing the crisis as a result of an exaggerated optimism in the real estate market, we may see the boom in house prices as a logical consequence of what happens in financial markets, and the downturn which came in 2007–8 was just the natural consequence of the initial bad news which had the effects that we have considered above. The problem was not so much the real estate market or the use of houses as collateral, but rather the short-term financing of long-term engagements and the way that collateral enters into these arrangements.

8.7 Exercises

1. [Greenbaum and Thakor, 2007] A bank A has two loans, both to be repaid after one period. The repayments are independent and identically distributed random variables, yielding \$500 with probability 0.8 and \$250 with probability 0.2. However, the bank knows that investors cannot distinguish its loan portfolio from another bank B that has the same number of loans, which, however, will repay \$500 with probability 0.5 and \$250 with probability 0.5. According to the belief of the public, there is a probability of 0.6 that A has the good loans.

Bank A wants to securitize the portfolio. The cost of communicating the true value of its loans to potential investors amounts to 8% of its true value.

Can A find another arrangement given that the cost of disclosing the true state to a single agent is very small?

2. A company is set up for a specific business activity which lasts exactly one year. It can invest €1 million of its own but must borrow another €2 million. The business activity is risky, with an estimated mean profit of €4 million, and an estimated standard deviation of €3 million. In order to obtain the loan through sale of securities, the company buys a credit default swap (CDS) which promises full payment to bondholders in the case that the company defaults.

What is the probability that the CDS will be exercised?

3. Explain how it is possible to speculate by buying up credit default swaps when an economic downturn is imminent. What is the inherent weakness of such a speculative strategy, even when the expectations turn out to be true?

4. Show that, in the reputation model for credit rating agencies considered in Section 8.4.1, there is no simple stationary equilibrium (q^0, σ^0) (where q^0 is confirmed period after period by the updating and where $\sigma^0 \in [0, 1]$ is probability of false reporting).

5. In many models of securitization, instability arises when a bank sells out of its portfolio of securities created in previous periods either by itself or by similar financial intermediaries. Discuss whether this instability could be reduced by separating institutions creating new securities from institutions holding portfolios of these securities.

8.8 Comments

There are several texts on securitization, e.g. Davidson et al. [2003], most of them from the years before the financial crisis, after which some scepticism set in. For further details on the technical part of the securitization process, and for credit enhancers, in particular credit default swaps, the specialized literature on financial markets should be consulted.

The models of securitization and the possible instability to which it may give rise are rather recent, and we return to this topic in Chapter 14 when we consider bank runs and bank crises, also including runs on shadow banks.

The role of the credit ratings agency in the financial crisis, and in particular in creating the bubble that burst, is described in White [2009]. There are several other explanations of the ratings inflation of this period than those given in the text.

The Kiyotaki-Moore model of business cycles caused by the financial sector has been developed further by several authors; see e.g. the survey article by Gertler and Kiyotaki [2010].

Chapter 9

Investment Banking and Corporate Finance

9.1 Introduction: Investment banking

In this chapter, we discuss the particular field of activity of a financial intermediary known as *investment banking*. As mentioned in Chapter 2, investment banks are concerned with setting up and changing the capital structure of private corporations, dealing with matters of arranging loans, issue of securities and buying or selling of firms. There is a tradition in the United States that investment banking should be separated from ordinary ('commercial') banking, going back to the Glass-Seagall Act from 1933, which was eventually abandoned in 1999. In Europe, investment and commercial banking have traditionally coexisted in financial enterprises.

The traditional business of an investment bank is to assist its customers in raising funds in capital markets and advise them in cases of mergers and acquisitions. Also, the investment bank takes an active part in attracting investors in connection with issuance of securities and possibly negotiating with other firms which may have been singled out for future mergers. Investment banks often contact potential clients for mergers and acquisitions, and if their proposals are well received, they carry out the deal for the clients.

Other important activities of the investment bank are *trading* securities and *asset management*, and in recent years, issue and sale of new securities created on the basis of other financial assets (see Chapter 8). Also, the investment bank offers consultancy services for customers who want to invest either directly or in securities, and in connection with this activity, they maintain a department doing financial analysis. Because most of these activities have been or will be commented upon in other contexts, we concentrate on those aspects of investment banking that involve direct contact with customers in connection with capital structure of the firm.

In the present chapter, we take a closer look at *corporate finance*, which is the environment in which the investment bank has to do business. The subject of this study is capital structure of the firm, ways of attracting capital and types of contracts needed to regulate the behaviour of entrepreneurs and investors, and the role of the investment bank in this context. In the following section, we outline the celebrated Modigliani-Miller theorem about the irrelevance of capital structure; then we turn in Section 9.3 to a discussion of financial contracting. We then proceed in Section 9.4 with a treatment of the decision about going public and the much debated underpricing issue. Section 9.5 deals with mergers and acquisitions, and finally, we deal with a topic which is only slightly related to the other issues of the chapter, namely *Islamic banking*, where the financial intermediary should avoid loan contracts with interest payments and instead enter into a partnership agreement with the entrepreneur, thereby arranging a relationship akin to what is considered in Section 9.3.

9.2 Capital structure

The capital structure of an investment project, or of a firm, describes the sources of financing for the project of the firm. In most cases, a project will need external capital, and this external capital may take the form of either shares or debt. In the first case, the suppliers of capital become owners of the firm or project, participating in the risk in the sense that they share in the profits and losses which may occur. In the second case, the lenders are entitled to a fixed payment or an agreed part of the outcome, depending on the loan contract (cf. Chapter 5). Many of the important financial decisions in corporate finance are related to finding an optimal capital structure, which in simple versions boils down to determining an optimal ratio of debt to equity.

9.2.1 The Modigliani-Miller theorem

In the present section, we present the Modigliani-Miller theorem about the irrelevance of capital structure for the value of the firm. Consider a firm which is engaged in only one project starting at time $t = 0$ and yielding a random payoff $\tilde{y}$ at $t = 1$. For simplicity, we assume that there is only a finite number S of states of nature. The firm (which is initiated at $t = 0$ and terminates at $t = 1$) can be financed either by equity or by bonds; in the latter case, one says that the firm is *levered*, and otherwise it is *unlevered*.

If the firm issues bonds, the bondholders will have a claim at $t = 1$ of a certain value D. For states of nature s such that $y_s < D$, the firm is *bankrupt* and the bondholders will receive y_s as long as the latter is ≥ 0, so the payoff for the bond (or any other type of debt with face value D) is

$$\tilde{d} = (d_s)_{s \in S} \, , \ d_s = \min\{D, \max\{y_s, 0\}\}, \ s \in S.$$

This can also be written as

$$\tilde{d} = \min\{D, \tilde{y}^+\},$$

where for any random variable $\tilde{a}$, $\tilde{a}^+$ is defined by $a_s^+ = \max\{a_s, 0\}$, $s \in S$.

The present value of the debt (at $t = 0$), denoted D_0, can be assessed as the value of any uncertain prospect: In the absence of arbitrage probabilities, there are (risk-neutral) probabilities $(\pi_s)_{s \in S}$ such that the value of the firm can be written as

$$D_0 = \frac{1}{R} \sum_{s \in S} \pi_s d_s,$$

with R the risk-free repayment rate. In the case where there are no bankruptcy states, $y_s \geq D$ or $d_s = D$ for all s, then

$$D_0 = \frac{D}{R} \sum_{s \in S} \pi_s = \frac{D}{R},$$

meaning that debt is contracted at the risk-free rate of interest. If bankruptcy can occur, we have that $D_0 < \frac{D}{R}$.

The holders of equity, which are the owners of the firm, are entitled to receive what is left from the payoff when the creditors are paid off. Their payoff in state s is

$$\tilde{e}_s = \max\left\{0, \tilde{y}_s - \tilde{d}_s\right\}$$

due to limited liability; the shareholders are responsible only to the amount of their invested capital and are not supposed to cover negative payoffs at $t = 1$. Because

$$\max\{0, y_s - d_s\} = \max\{0, y_s\} - \min\{D, y_s\} = \max\{0, \max\{0, y_s\} - D\},$$

we get that

$$\max\{0, y_s\} = e_s + d_s$$

for each state $s \in S$. The present value of equity is

$$E_0 = \frac{1}{R} \sum_{s \in S} \pi_s e_s,$$

and writing the value of the levered firm as

$$V_0^l = E_0 + D_0 = \frac{1}{R} \sum_{s \in S} \pi_s(e_s + d_s) = \frac{1}{R} \sum_{s \in S} \pi_s y_s^+ = V_0^u,$$

where V_0^u is the value of the unlevered firm (where all capital is equity), we have thus proved:

PROPOSITION 1: (Modigliani-Miller) *The market value of a firm is independent of its capital structure.*

The Modigliani-Miller theorem states that debt can be contracted without affecting the value of the firm, so owners may replace equity by debt without affecting their consumption possibilities.

In view of the theorem, we can write the repayment rate of the unlevered firm as

$$R^u = \frac{\mathsf{E}[\tilde{y}^+]}{V_0}$$

with $V_0 = V_0^u = V_0^l$. In the levered firm, we have also to consider the expected repayment of the debt,

$$R_d = \frac{\mathsf{E}[\tilde{d}]}{D_0},$$

and writing the cost of equity to the firm in a similar way,

$$R^l = \frac{\mathsf{E}[\tilde{e}]}{E_0},$$

we obtain that

$$R^l = \frac{\mathsf{E}[\tilde{y}^+ - \tilde{d}]}{E_0} = \frac{R^u V_0}{E_0} - \frac{R_d D_0}{E_0} = R^u + (R^u - R_d)\frac{D_0}{E_0}.$$

Thus, we have shown that the expected return on equity equals expected return for a pure equity stream minus a premium, which is related to the financial risk because it is found as the debt-equity ratio times spread between repayment in the firm and repayment rate on debt.

9.2.2 The Modigliani-Miller theorem with taxes

It is customary, although of marginal importance in our context, to also discuss the case where the profit of the firm is subject to taxation at a rate $\tau \in [0, 1]$. The levered firm then pays taxes in state s to the amount $t_s = \tau(e_s - D)$ unless s is a bankruptcy state, in which case it pays nothing. Thus, the tax payment is the random variable $\tilde{t}$ defined as

$$\tilde{t} = \tau(\tilde{y}^+ - D)^+,$$

and its present value is $T_0 = \tau \frac{1}{R} \sum_{s \in S} \pi_s \max\{y_s^+ - D, 0\}$. The debtholders now receive

$$d_s = \min\{D, \max\{y_s^+ - t_s, 0\}\} = \min\{D, y_s^+\},$$

which is exactly as without taxes, and the shareholders get

$$e_s^t = y_s^+ - d_s - t_s$$

in state s. We have that the value of the firm V_0 satisfies

$$V_0 = E_0^t + D_0 + T_0$$

with $E_0^t = \tau \frac{1}{R} \sum_{s \in S} \pi_s e_s^t$. In our new set-up, the value of the unlevered firm is

$$V_0^{u,t} = (1 - \tau)\frac{1}{R} \sum_{s \in S} \pi_s y_s^+,$$

and the value of the levered firm is

$$V_0^{l,t} = \frac{1}{R} \sum_{s \in S} \pi_s \left(e_s^t + d_s\right) = \frac{1}{R} \sum_{s \in S} \pi_s[(1 - \tau)y_s^+ + \tau \min\{y_s^+, D\}]$$

$$= (1 - \tau)\frac{1}{R} \sum_{s \in S} \pi_s y_s^+ + \tau \frac{1}{R} \sum_{s \in S} \pi_s d_s = V_0^{u,t} + \tau D_0.$$

We see that in the presence of taxation, capital structure matters: The value of the firm increases linearly with the level of debt.

9.3 Financial contracting

9.3.1 Venture capital

One of the ways in which a firm can extend its capital is to invite a venture capitalist, who will supply capital in exchange for some influence on the way in which the firm is managed. As with all other sources of finance for the enterprise, there is a cost, namely the possibility that the venture capitalist will take over control of the firm, but seen from the other angle, such a possibility will often be necessary to persuade an outsider to invest in a firm with an uncertain future.

Due to the nature of the uncertainty facing a firm in its initial states of growth, the relationship between entrepreneur and venture capitalist cannot be written into a contract which specifies the rights of both in all the eventualities that may occur. Therefore, the contract must take the form of specifying who is *in control* of management, contingent on future observable events. In other words, we are dealing with an *incomplete contract* which specifies the decision maker rather than the decisions to be made.

In the following, we give a brief discussion of this type of incomplete financial contract, following the work by Aghion and Bolton [1992]. We consider a contract between an entrepreneur and an investor who has K units of capital to invest at time $t = 0$. There are three dates in the model, namely $t = 0$, where investment decisions are made; an intermediate date $t = 1$; and the final date $t = 2$, where the outcome of the investment is obtained. The project is subject to uncertainty, and for simplicity we assume that there are only two states of nature, namely s_g, which occurs with probability q, and s_b, which has probability $1 - q$. The state of nature is determined at $t = 1$; also, at $t = 1$, an action a is chosen, and the payoff $R(a, s)$ is then determined as a function of a and s. To make things as easy as possible, we assume that $R(a, s)$ is always either 0 or 1. Also, there are only two possible actions, which for reasons to be explained below are denoted a_g and a_b.

To allow for incomplete information, we assume that s is privately observable *but cannot be used in contracts*, so a contract between entrepreneur and investor cannot use s as a condition for some of its provisions. However, the parties can observe a *signal* $\tilde{v}$, taking values 0 or 1, which is random but gives information about s in the sense that the conditional probabilities satisfy

$$\beta^g = \mathsf{P}\{v = 1 \mid s = s_g\} > \frac{1}{2}, \ \beta^b = \mathsf{P}\{v = 1 \mid s = s_b\} < \frac{1}{2}.$$

We are concerned in this model with finding out who should decide upon the choice of a, or, as it is usually formulated, with the *allocation of control rights*. If for both entrepreneur and investor only payoff matters, then there would be no conflict of interest, and the decision could be taken by either of them. Therefore, we assume that the entrepreneur has a utility function of the form

$$u_e(r, a) = l(a, s) + r,$$

where $l(a, s)$ is a non-monetary benefit derived from taking action a in state s, and r is the monetary outcome. The investor is concerned only with monetary outcomes, and if there were no information problems, her optimal action would be the one maximizing $R(a, s)$ for the given s. We define the first-best action (without informational constraints) as

$$a^*(s_i) = \arg \max_{j \in \{g, b\}} R(a_j, s_i) + l(a_j, s_i)$$

and assume that $a^*(s_i) = a_i$ for $i = g, b$.

Next, we define the quantities $y^i_j = R(a_j, s_i)$ and $l^i_j = l(a_j, s_i)$ for $i, j = g, b$. The optimality of the decisions a_g and a_b can be formulated as

$$y^g_g + l^g_g > y^g_b + l^g_b,$$

$$y^b_b + l^b_b > y^b_g + l^b_g,$$

and the investment must satisfy a feasibility constraint

$$q y^g_g + (1 - q) y^b_b \geq K,$$

which says that under full information, its net present value should be better than the investment K.

We assume that the entrepreneur is compensated by the investor in accordance with a monetary transfer, which may depend on the signal at $t = 1$ as well as on the final payoff R. Because all the relevant variables take values in $\{0, 1\}$, the money transfer may be written as

$$t_v R + T_v,$$

where T_v is a payment which depends only on the signal, whereas t_v is an additional payment, also depending on v, paid only in the case that $R = 1$. The residual, $R - T(v, R)$, is the money payoff to the investor.

Entrepreneur control. We may now consider the problem of control rights, and we do this by finding the parameter values for which the entrepreneur chooses the optimal decisions so that control may be exerted by the entrepreneur. With the compensation rule given above, we have that the entrepreneur will select action as

$$a^E(s_i, v) = \arg\max_{j \in \{g,b\}} \{t_v y^i_j + T_v + l^i_j\}, \ i = g, b,$$

and the action found using this choice function may in general differ from $a^*(s_i)$.

Suppose that t_v and T_v are such that the entrepreneur would choose a_g when $v = 1$ and a_b when $v = 0$ independently of the realization of s. In this case, there would be a basis for renegotiation in cases where $v = 1$ and $s = s_b$ or $v = 0$, $s = s_g$. Let us consider the first of these cases: Without renegotiation, the investor gets $y^b_g(1 - t_1) - T_1$; therefore, the entrepreneur may propose a renegotiation of the contract, leaving the investor with exactly this payment but now changing the decision to a_g. This will give the entrepreneur an outcome of

$$\left(y^b_b + l^b_b\right) - y^b_g(1 - t_1) + T_1 > \left(y^b_g + l^b_g\right) - y^b_g(1 - t_1) + T_1 = y^b_g t_1 + T_1 + l^b_g,$$

where we have used the conditions on a_g and a_b stated above. Because the expression on the right-hand side is the outcome before renegotiation, it is clear that the entrepreneur may propose this renegotiation, which will re-establish the first-best decision rule.

The second case (where $v = 1$, $s = s_g$) may be treated in the same way. It seems therefore that by allocating the control rights to the entrepreneur and allowing for a renegotiation of the contract at $t = 1$, one may always achieve the first-best result. However, we have not considered the feasibility constraint; there are no efficiency losses, but because all efficiency gains go to the entrepreneur, the payoff to the investor may be too low, and the investment will not be taken on.

There are, however, cases where entrepreneur control gives the first-best choice rule even without renegotiation.

PROPOSITION 2: *If private benefits l are comonotonic with total revenues $y + l$, so that $l^g_g > l^g_b$ and $l^b_b > l^b_g$, then entrepreneur control is feasible for achieving the first-best decision.*

PROOF: We choose a constant remuneration scheme with $t(v, R) = t$ for all v and R. Then the first-best actions are chosen by the entrepreneur when

$$t + l^g_g > t + l^g_b$$

$$t + l^b_b > t + l^b_g,$$

which are satisfied for all $t \geq 0$ by our assumptions. To obtain individual rationality for investor, we fix t such that $qy^g_g + (1 - q)y^b_b - t = K$; this is possible by our assumptions above. $\square$

Though positive, the result is not quite satisfactory, because we have assumed that the entrepreneur has a utility which is representative of society as a whole. The interesting cases arise when there is a conflict between the entrepreneur interests and those of the collective.

To see when entrepreneur control is feasible, we introduce some notation. Let

$$\Delta^b = \left(y_b^b + l_b^b\right) - \left(y_g^b + l_g^b\right), \quad \Delta_y^b = y_b^b - y_g^b$$

be the gain to society as a whole and for the monetary payoff only by choosing a_b instead of a_g given state s_b; both of these quantities are positive by our assumptions. We then introduce the following quantities:

$$\pi_1 = \left[qy_g^g + (1-q)y_b^b\right]\frac{\Delta^b}{\Delta_y^b}$$

$$\pi_2 = qy_g^g + (1-q)y_g^b$$

$$\pi_3 = q\left[\beta^g y_g^g + (1-\beta^g)y_g^g\frac{\Delta^b}{\Delta_y^b}\right] + (1-q)\left[\beta^b y_g^b + \left(1-\beta^b\right)y_b^b\frac{\Delta^b}{\Delta_y^b}\right].$$

We then have the following characterization of the case for entrepreneur control.

PROPOSITION 3: *Entrepreneur control is feasible and achieves the first-best decision if and only if* $\max\{\pi_1, \pi_2, \pi_3\} \geq K$.

PROOF: We need to consider three types of contracts, namely (1) those which are renegotiation-proof, (2) those that involve full renegotiation in state s_b (where $l_b^b < l_g^b$), and (3) those contracts that involve renegotiation in state s_b only when $v = 1$.

(1) For a contract to be renegotiation proof, it must induce the entrepreneur to choose a_b in state s_b so that

$$t_v y_b^b + l_b^b \geq t_v y_g^b + l_v^b,$$

or

$$t_v \geq \frac{l_g^b - l_b^b}{y_b^b - y_g^b}.$$

Denoting the quantity on the right-hand side by $\hat{t}$, we have that for feasibility we need that

$$q(1-\hat{t})y_g^g + (1-q)(1-\hat{t})y_b^b \geq K,$$

which is seen to be equivalent to

$$\pi_1 \geq K.$$

(2) The investor's expected payoff is maximized in this class of contracts when $t_1 = t_0 = 0$. In this case, the entrepreneur chooses action a_g in both states of nature. The corresponding payoff to the investor is π_2. Therefore, contracts with full renegotiation in state s_b will be feasible if and only if $\pi_2 \geq K$.

(3) The investor's expected payoff is maximized in this class of contracts when $t_1 = 0$ and $t_0 = \hat{t}$. This induces renegotiation in state s_b only when $v = 1$, and in this case, the investor's payoff is π_3. So, this type of contract will be feasible if and only if $\pi_3 \geq K$. $\quad\square$

Investor control. As was the case for the entrepreneur, we may find specific situations where investor control gives the first-best decision, in particular when the monetary benefits are comonotonic with total payoff. If we use the remuneration schedule $t(v, R) = \hat{t}R$, by which the payment to the entrepreneur is proportional to payoff, then investor chooses a_i in state s_i, $i = g, b$. Indeed, the profit to the investor from choosing a_j in state s_i is $(1 - \hat{t})y_j^i$, and because by comonotonicity we have that $y_g^g > y_b^g$ and $y_b^b > y_g^b$, we get that the profit in state i from choosing a_j is maximized when $i = j$. Consequently, we have the following counterpart of Proposition 1:

PROPOSITION 4: *If monetary benefits y are comonotonic with total revenues $y + l$, so that $y_g^g > y_b^g$ and $y_b^b > y_g^b$, then investor control is feasible and achieves the first-best decision.*

If the conditions of the proposition are not satisfied, we may look at contracts with renegotiation at $t = 1$. Assume that $y_g^g < y_b^g$, and consider a remuneration scheme with $t_v \leq 1$ and $T_v = 0$. Then the investor will not choose a_g in state s_g, because

$$(1 - t_v)y_g^g < (1 - t_v)y_b^g.$$

In order for the investor to choose another action at $t = 1$, we need a renegotiation which redefines t_v; if $\hat{t}_v$ is the new value, then it must satisfy

$$(1 - \hat{t}_v)y_g^g \geq (1 - t_v)y_b^g$$

or

$$\hat{t}_v \leq 1 - (1 - t_v)\frac{y_b^g}{y_g^g}. \tag{1}$$

Thus, investor control will result in the first-best decision after a renegotiation in state s_g if and only if the initial remuneration scheme t_v in the contract is such that there is $\hat{t}_v \geq 0$ which satisfies (1), or, equivalently, if and only if $1 - t_v \leq \frac{y_g^g}{y_b^g}$. Assuming that the investor proposes t_v, we may take $1 - t_v = \frac{y_g^g}{y_b^g}$.

PROPOSITION 5: *When monetary returns are not comonotonic with total payoff, then investor control is feasible and achieves the first-best solution if and only if*

$$\left[qy_b^g + (1 - q)y_b^b\right]\frac{y_g^g}{y_b^g} \geq K.$$

PROOF: After renegotiation, the investor gets $(1 - t_v)y_b^g$ if $s = s_g$, and she gets $(1 - t_v)y_b^b$ in accordance with the initial remuneration scheme if $s = s_b$. Expected payoff to the investor is therefore

$$\left[qy_b^g + (1 - q)y_b^b\right](1 - t_v) = \left[qy_b^g + (1 - q)y_b^b\right]\frac{y_g^g}{y_b^g},$$

which should be $\geq K$ for feasibility.   □

Contingent control. We have now considered the cases where the decision about the action a is controlled by either the entrepreneur or by the investor. However, there may well be cases where the control should depend on the state. For this, we assume that neither monetary nor private benefits are comonotonic with total payoff. Below we consider the latter case and assume that $y_g^g < y_b^g$ and $l_b^b < l_g^b$.

For these values of the variables, the first-best action will be selected under investor control only in state s_b (independent of the value of v), and under entrepreneur control only in state s_g (again independent of v). So if control could be made to depend on s, we should give control to the entrepreneur at $s = s_g$ and to the investor at $s = s_b$. However, only the signal can be used in the contract, but if the signal is sufficiently well correlated with s, one might expect that a contract where control rights are given to the entrepreneur when $v = 1$ and to investor when $v = 0$ might approximate the first-best decision. If, in addition, the conditions in Propositions 2 and 4 are violated so that entrepreneur control is not feasible and investor control does not achieve the first-best, then the contingent control allocation described here may dominate both unilateral control allocations, at least for sufficiently correlated signals. We formulate this as

PROPOSITION 6: *If neither monetary nor private returns are comonotonic with total benefits, then there are values of K such that*

> (i) *entrepreneur control is not feasible,*
>
> (ii) *investor control is not first-best efficient,*
>
> (iii) *both unilateral control allocations are dominated by the contingent control allocation such that the entrepreneur chooses at $v = 1$ and the investor chooses at $v = 0$ when (β^g, β^b) tends to $(1, 0)$.*

The contracts with contingent control are clearly the more interesting ones. Unilateral control corresponds to classical cases of financing, where either investors buy the right to decide or investors earn more as passive shareholders. But the more elaborate contract, where the control right may shift depending on future conditions corresponds to financing by debt where entrepreneurs may retain control depending on their ability to meet certain conditions specified in the contract. In the model considered, we have discussed the shift of control rights, but we did not go into the question of optimal contracts. We turn to this now.

9.4 Initial public offering

One of the ways in which a firm may get access to additional financing is by raising equity capital in the public equity market. The first attempt of a firm to get capital is called an *initial public offering* (IPO). This may be a way in which the original entrepreneurs may get some of their investment back, and it may also be used to obtain additional liquidity in an ongoing concern.

An IPO involves four types of agents, as shown in Fig. 9.1. The first of these is the issuing firm, which is going public. In order to sell its shares, it needs the assistance of some institutions in the financial market. The first of these is the *investment bank*, which is assumed to have a superior knowledge of the market and its demand so as to achieve a reasonable pricing of the issue, and it becomes responsible for the credibility of the final offering price. With the price given, the firm needs to find intermediaries, called *underwriters*, to introduce the shares in the market; usually the investment bank is also one of the underwriters. The final type of agent consists of investors who may consider buying the new issue.

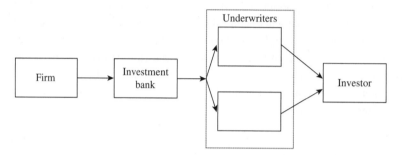

Figure 9.1 Initial public offering: Once the decision to go public has been taken, the shares of the firm must be initiated into the market, and this involves financial intermediaries.

9.4.1 The decision to go public

Because the firm seeking additional financing which does not take the form of standard bank credit has several options, namely private financing through venture capitalists or public financing through an IPO, the question arises as to whether some systematic differences can be expected between firms choosing one or the other. The following simple model, adapted from Chemmanur and Fulghieri [1994], may point to some structural differences.

We consider a firm which has a project to be developed. We let τ be a variable taking two possible values τ_g and τ_b, which measures the quality of the project in the sense that outcome at $t = 1$ is given by

$$y_\tau = \tau K + \tilde{\varepsilon}, \tag{2}$$

where K is the amount invested. The last member on the right-hand side is random displacement, assumed to be normally distributed with mean 0 and variance σ^2. We assume that $\tau_g > \tau_b$.

The quality of this project is known to the entrepreneur, but not to investors, but the latter may receive a signal about quality at a cost c; this signal (which corresponds to an evaluation by an outsider) takes values e_g and e_b, and we assume that

$$P\{e_g | \tau = \tau_g\} = 1, \; P\{e_g | \tau = \tau_b\} = q \in (0, 1).$$

Thus, the signal will never report bad quality when quality is actually good, but there is a probability strictly between 0 and 1 that it reports good when it is actually bad.

We assume that the entrepreneur holds m shares and contemplates issuing n more shares. If the shares are sold to a venture capitalist, then the latter will take on some of the risk of the project. We assume that expected utility of an uncertain wealth $\widetilde{W}$ satisfies

$$E\left[u\left(\widetilde{W}\right)\right] = u\left(E\left[\widetilde{W}\right] - \rho \text{Var}\left(\widetilde{W}\right)\right),$$

where $\rho > 0$ is a constant which depends on the degree of risk aversion, so the entrepreneur maximizes expected payoff minus a risk premium.[1] In the case where the shares are sold to the market, we shall assume that the investor is risk neutral.

Private financing. We consider first the case where a single venture capitalist buys the shares; this will be compared later to the case of public financing. Because there is a possibility of getting further information about the project at a cost, the private investor is offered two types of contract, namely (a) an unconditional price contract, or (b) a conditional contract with information production, where price per share depends on the outcome of the costly evaluation.

Let p_0 be the investor's prior probability of τ_g. Then performing an evaluation will result in a posterior probability

$$p_1 = E[\tau_g | e = e_g] = \frac{p_0}{p_0 + q(1 - p_0)} > p_0.$$

Thus, after receiving the signal e_g, the payoff becomes a random variable where the first member on the right-hand side in (2) takes the value $\tau_g K$ with probability p_1 and $\tau_b K$ with probability $1 - p_1$; let V_g be its mean value,

$$V_g = p_1 \tau_g + (1 - p_1)\tau_b + E[\tilde{\varepsilon}],$$

and σ_g^2 its variance. If s_g is the minimal share of the firm's equity to be offered for an investment of K, the break-even point for an investor, where investment is just merely acceptable after receiving e_g, must satisfy

$$K + c = s_g V_g - \rho s_g^2 \left(\sigma_g^2 + \sigma^2\right).$$

If the evaluation results in e_b, the quality is τ_b with certainty, and the mean value of the first term in (2) is $V_b = \tau_b K$. Again, the minimal share s_b under which an investment K will be forthcoming must satisfy

$$K + c = s_b V_b - \rho s_b^2 \sigma^2.$$

---

[1] This is the case if the entrepreneur has a utility function of the form

$$u(w) = -e^{-2\rho w}$$

and $\tilde{w}$ is normally distributed, cf. Box 1.4; however, some of the random variables considered below are not normally distributed, so we cannot make this rationalization here.

For the unconditional contract, the smallest acceptable share s_u must be such that

$$K = s_u V_u - \rho s_u^2 (\sigma_u^2 + \sigma^2),$$

where V_u is the expected value of the random payoff which yields $\tau_g K$ with probability p_0 and $\tau_b K$ with probability $(1 - p_0)$, and σ_u^2 is its variance.

For the entrepreneur, the choice of contract to be proposed will depend on the quality of the project. If $\tau = \tau_g$, then the entrepreneur offers the contract which involves evaluation if $s_g < s_u$, and offers the unconditional contract otherwise. Because the use of the first type of contract involves the payment of evaluation cost, which is reflected in the contract through a lower price, this first type will be chosen when c is small, whereas the second type is chosen for large values of c, and consequently, there is a critical value c^* such that type one is optimal for $c \leq c^*$ and type two for $c > c^*$. For the investor, an evaluation does not change the ex ante expected payoff, but reduces risk. If the investor is very risk averse, this reduction may not be large enough, so there is an upper limit ρ^* for the coefficient of risk aversion ρ of investors who will accept the evaluation contract with the conditions described above.

If $\tau = \tau_b$, then the entrepreneur may offer an evaluation contract, and the evaluation will be e_g in some cases, so the expected share to be offered is $p_1 s_g + (1 - p_1) s_b$. Assume now that the parameter values are such that the entrepreneurs with $\tau = \tau_g$ offer evaluation contracts. If the entrepreneur offered an unconditional contract, then τ_b would be revealed; denoting the lowest share which can be offered in this situation by s_B, we have that the evaluation contract is proposed when

$$p_1 s_g + (1 - p_1) s_b < s_B.$$

We may summarize the findings as follows.

PROPOSITION 7: *For $\rho < \rho^*$ and $c < c^*$, there is an equilibrium in which the entrepreneur proposes an evaluation contract and the investor accepts it.*

Public offering. Here the entrepreneur is facing a number N of investors simultaneously, and both a number of shares to be sold and a price for each share have to be chosen. The investors may choose to buy or to refrain from buying, or they may choose to carry out an evaluation before deciding. We denote by α the probability that an investor carries out an investigation.

If $\tau = \tau_g$, the required capital K may be obtained by the entrepreneur selling n_g shares at a price P_g such that $P_g n_g = K$. If investors evaluate, they will get the message e_g, so the entrepreneur will be rather sure of selling this number of shares.

If $\tau = \tau_b$ but the entrepreneur still tries to sell it as a good project, only a fraction μ of the informed investors will believe that the project is good and buy the shares. The fraction θ of the n_g shares actually sold will then be

$$\theta n_g = N[(1 - \alpha) + \alpha \mu],$$

where α is the probability that an investor will seek information about the project. If the probability that an entrepreneur with $\tau = \tau_b$ occurs among the projects selling n_g at price P_g is β, then the probability that an uninformed investor considers the project to be a good one is

$$p_2 = \mathsf{P}\{\tau_g \,|\, n_g, P_g\} = \frac{p_0}{p_0 + \beta(1 - p_0)}.$$

For a pooling contract of this type (where all projects are sold as good) to be an equilibrium contract, the uninformed investor should not pay more for a share than its expected vaue, so

$$P_g \le p_2 \frac{V_g}{m + n_g} + (1 - p_2) \frac{\theta V_b}{m + \theta n_g}. \tag{3}$$

In addition, investors seeking information should expect this to be profitable in the sense that the cost of collecting information is no greater than the expected loss from buying shares in a bad project,

$$c \le (1 - \pi)(1 - q)\left[P_g - \frac{\theta V_g}{m + \theta n_g}\right]. \tag{4}$$

It remains only to find equilibrium values of α and β. The probability α of collecting information should be such that the entrepreneur with $\tau = \tau_b$ is indifferent betwen issuing $\theta n_g = N[(1 - \alpha) + \alpha q]$ shares at price P_g or selling the bad project as bad, which amounts to issuing $n_b > n_g$ shares at price $P_b < P_g$, so

$$\frac{m}{m + n_b} V_b = \frac{m}{m + \theta n_g} \theta V_b,$$

where n_b and p_b are such that $n_b p_b = K$ and $p_b = \dfrac{V_b}{m + n_b}$.

Finally, the probability β that an entrepreneur with $\tau = \tau_b$ sets price P_g is determined by the condition that investors should be indifferent between seeking information or not seeking it, which means that the inequalities (3) and (4) should hold with an equality sign. Intuitively, an equilibrium exists if the cost c of acquiring information and the probability q of getting a wrong signal are both small enough.

We summarize this reasoning in the following:

PROPOSITION 8: *An equilibrium in the public financing market exists for small enough values of c. In equilibrium, entrepreneur choice is as follows:*

(i) *If $\tau = \tau_g$, n_g shares at the price P_g are issued, raising an amount K.*

(ii) *If $\theta = \theta_b$, a mixed strategy is used: With probability $\beta > 0$, the entrepreneur pools with the good projects, selling θn_g shares and raising θK for investment, and with probability $1 - \beta$, n_b shares are issued at price P_b, raising the whole amount K.*

The investors choose to seek information with probability α and buy only upon the signal e_g; with probability $1 - \alpha$ they do uninformed bidding.

Choosing between public and private financing. The main reason for setting up this model is that it allows for a comparison of the two different ways of financing the firm. Because the venture capitalist was risk averse while the market was risk neutral, it should not come as a surprise that public financing is the obvious – indeed the only – choice for ρ large enough. Therefore, we shall be more interested in the case where ρ is rather small. In this case, the venture capitalist may be interested in buying shares, provided that information cost is not too high, and in addition, the number of shares kept by the entrepreneur, is not too small, a circumstance which assures the venture capitalist that the project is not too bad. Indeed, it can be shown [Chemmanur and Fulghieri, 1994] that the following holds:

PROPOSITION 9: *If $\rho_M < \rho^*$ and m is not too small, then there is a threshold value c^* of c such that for $c < c^*$, the firm finances its project by going public, and for $c \geq c^*$ it chooses private financing.*

The intuition behind the role of c in determining the choice of public versus private financing is that in public financing, the cost of information retrieval is eventually to be paid by the entrepreneur (in the form of reduced price of shares), so there are cost savings connected with private financing, which, however, have to be counterweighted by the risk premium, which depends on the degree of risk aversion of the venture capitalist.

If evaluation cost is related to degree of innovativeness of the project – it may be more costly to assess a fundamentally new project than a project which is closely related to other existing enterprises – then again the cost of going public may be too high, so we should expect young and innovative enterprises to rely more on private financing. On the other hand, if K is large, then the price at which shares can be sold to a venture capitalist will be low, whereas the same restriction does not apply to public financing. Also the project uncertainty as given by the variance σ^2 matters because it influences the risk premium of the venture capitalist; with high project uncertainty, public financing becomes the preferred method.

9.4.2 The IPO underpricing issue

Once the decision to go public has been taken, the next step is the introduction of the firm into the market. This IPO can take the form of a sale at a fixed price, or it can be arranged as an auction, but the most common method is *bookbuilding*: The underwriter receives confidential bids (price and quantity of shares) from invited brokers, and based on these bids a price is set by the underwriter, and the shares are sold to the bidders.

Ideally, the price at which shares are sold at the IPO should reflect the value of the firm, and assuming that the eventual stock market pricing of shares corresponds to this value, the IPO prices should be close to the prices obtained after one day or one week. It turns out, however, that IPO prices are systematically lower, to the size of around 15%, than the closing prices after one day of trade. This phenomenon of *IPO underpricing* has been observed in many countries and seems to be independent of the method used in the IPO.

Several explanations of the phenomenon have been proposed, most of them being elaborations of the adverse selection argument put forward by Rock [1986]. The basic idea is that the market has an informational advantage over the firm and the underwriter. This may seem strange at first sight, because the firm ought to know very well what is up for sale, but on the other hand, much of what is relevant here has been communicated to the market in the prospects preceding the sale, and the expertise of the buyers with regard to the future performance on the stock exchange may well exceed that of a single agent, the underwriter.

It is assumed that there are *two kinds of agents* in the market: There are *informed investors* having perfect knowledge of the value of the new issue; they can use this knowledge for their own investments only (so, in particular, they cannot work as consultants for other investors). All other agents (including the underwriter) are *uninformed*. The method of offering is a simplified version of bookbuilding: The issuer selects an offer price p and an offer quantity Z (of shares). Then subscriptions are received from investors, specifying a number of shares to be bought at this price. If oversubsciption occurs, then the orders are satisfied only partially.

Let $\tilde{v}$ be the (random) value of the firm which is offered for sale, and let $\bar{v}$ be its expected value. We assume in the following that there are rather few informed investors, so the demand of the informed investors is no greater than $\bar{v}Z$, the mean value of the shares offered. All investors are assumed to have the same initial wealth 1.

Because the informed investors observe the value, their demand is I (the number of informed investors) if $\tilde{v} < p$, and 0 otherwise. The uninformed investors, of which there are N, have decided to use a fraction t of their wealth for buying the share, so total demand is

$$\widetilde{D}(p) = \begin{cases} Nt + I & p < \tilde{v}, \\ Nt & p \geq \tilde{v}. \end{cases}$$

If oversubscription occurs, a method of rationing is called for. We assume that the underwriter selects the investors whose orders are filled by a lottery, where the probability of obtaining the ordered shares is π given by

$$\pi Nt + \pi I = pZ, \text{ so } \pi = \min\left\{\frac{pZ}{Nt + I}, 1\right\}$$

if excess demand occurs when $\tilde{v} > p$, and similarly, the probability of getting the shares ordered is

$$\pi' = \min\left\{\frac{pZ}{Nt}, 1\right\}$$

when $\tilde{v} \leq p$.

Having described the allocation mechanism, we turn to the behaviour of agents, in particular to the choice of t, the fraction of wealth used for purchase of the stock, by the uninformed investors. Being uninformed, they must base their choice on expectations π_e

of π and π'_e of π'. After the allocation, the expected utility of an uninformed investor with von Neumann-Morgenstern utility function u on wealth is

$$\pi_e P\{\tilde{v} > p\} E\left[u\left(1 - t + \frac{t}{p}\tilde{v}\right) \middle| \tilde{v} > p\right]$$

$$+ \pi'_e P\{\tilde{v} \le p\} E\left[u\left(1 - t + \frac{t}{p}\tilde{v}\right) \middle| \tilde{v} \le p\right] + (1 - \pi_e P\{\tilde{v} > p\} - \pi'_e P\{\tilde{v} \le p\}) u(1),$$

and the first-order condition for a maximum w.r.t. t is

$$\pi_e P\{\tilde{v} > p\} E\left[u'\left(1 - t + \frac{t}{p}\tilde{v}\right)\left(\frac{\tilde{v}}{p} - 1\right) \middle| \tilde{v} > p\right]$$

$$+ \pi'_e P\{\tilde{v} \le p\} E\left[u'\left(1 - t + \frac{t}{p}\tilde{v}\right)\left(\frac{\tilde{v}}{p} - 1\right) \middle| \tilde{v} \le p\right] = 0. \tag{5}$$

In an equilibrium, the expectations must not be contradicted by what happens in the market, so (5) must be satisfied for $\pi_e = \pi$, $\pi'_e = \pi'$.

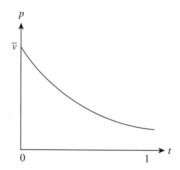

Figure 9.2 Uninformed investors' demand for shares in the adverse selection model of IPO underpricing. At a price which equals the expected value of the share, risk-averse investors are not interested in buying shares. For lower prices, the investment becomes increasingly interesting, even in view of the rationing of investment demand which must be expected.

To facilitate the analysis, we assume that (a) the utility functions of uninformed investors satisfy

$$u'(x) = b - ax$$

for some $a, b > 0$, and (b) the distribution of $\tilde{v}$ is symmetric with support in the interval $[0, b/a]$ (so $u'(x) \ne 0$ for all relevant values of x). Inserting into (5), we get that the first member in the right-hand side of (5) becomes

$$\pi P\{\tilde{v} > p\} E\left[(b - 1)\left(\frac{\tilde{v}}{p} - 1\right) \middle| \tilde{v} > p\right] - t\pi P\{\tilde{v} > p\} E\left[a\left(\frac{\tilde{v}}{p} - 1\right)^2 \middle| \tilde{v} > p\right], \tag{6}$$

and the second takes the form

$$\pi' P\{\tilde{v} \le p\} E\left[(b-1)\left(\frac{\tilde{v}}{p}-1\right)\Big|\tilde{v} \le p\right] - t\pi' P\{\tilde{v} \le p\} E\left[a\left(\frac{\tilde{v}}{p}-1\right)^2\Big|\tilde{v} \le p\right]; \qquad (7)$$

connecting the two expressions and using that $P\{\tilde{v} > p\} = 1 - P\{\tilde{v} \le p\}$, we get the first-order condition

$$\pi E\left[(b-1)\left(\frac{\tilde{v}}{p}-1\right)\right] - \pi t E\left[a\left(\frac{\tilde{v}}{p}-1\right)^2\right]$$

$$+ (\pi' - \pi) P\{\tilde{v} \le p\} E\left[(b-1)\left(\frac{\tilde{v}}{p}-1\right)\Big|\tilde{v} \le p\right] \qquad (8)$$

$$- t(\pi' - \pi) P\{\tilde{v} \le p\} E\left[a\left(\frac{\tilde{v}}{p}-1\right)^2\Big|\tilde{v} \le p\right] = 0.$$

Consider first the case $p = \bar{v}$, where the price of the shares is set at the mean of their value. By our symmetry assumption, the first member of (8) vanishes, and the remaining members are negative, showing that the first-order condition cannot be satisfied for any $t > 0$. This corresponds to our intuition about risk-averse investors, because they prefer the safe investment yielding 1 to a risky one with the same mean payoff. We therefore have that the demand for shares from the uninformed investors is zero at $p \ge \bar{v}$.

Let $p < \bar{v}$ and suppose that the price is lowered slightly from p. If t is kept fixed at the value which defines the demand at p, then the first two members of the left-hand side in (8) become numerically larger, but the increase caused by the first will dominate the decrease caused by the second, and assuming that $(\pi' - \pi)$ is small, the overall effect will be an increase in the right-hand side of (8), which must be counteracted by an increase in t in order to satisfy the first-order condition. We therefore have that the demand for shares from the uninformed investors has the usual downward-sloping form starting from $p = \bar{v}$, cf. Figure 9.2.

Now we can get back to the underpricing issue: When the initial price is set, it must necessarily be at some value $p < \bar{v}$ if all the shares must be sold, because otherwise only the informed investors will be in the market, and their demand is insufficient to cover the supply. Consequently, underwriters are not making errors or incorrect forecasts. What happens is that they must sell to risk-averse investors who want a compensation for the risk in order to buy the shares. Note that the uninformed investors are hit by the randomness in two ways – value may be lower than price, in which case their investment gives rise to a loss, but when value is higher than price and they stand to gain, they will have to share the gains with the informed investors, so they are getting rationed in their demand.

Although the theory of IPO underpricing is dealing with the very short run (from the day of introduction to the next day or a week after), there is some evidence pointing towards *long-run underperformance* of IPOs (see e.g. Ritter [1991]). There may be several rather straightforward explanations of this phenomenon, such as investor over-optimism and firms' exploitation of 'windows of opportunities', situations where the outlook is unusually bright, when deciding to go public.

9.5 Mergers and acquisitions

9.5.1 The simple tender offer and the free-rider effect

Suppose that a takeover is contemplated in a form where the shareholders of the target are approached with a bid for their shares. The purpose of the takeover is to increase the value of the firm; let v be the value of the target if the takeover occurs; to simplify notation we shall assume that the value is 0 otherwise. Let b be the bid.

In this situation, there is a *free-rider problem*, as pointed out by Grossman and Hart [1980]. The target shareholder will accept if

$$b \geq P\{\text{success} \mid \text{retain share}\}v. \tag{9}$$

Suppose that the individual shareholder is small and considers the probability of takeover as independent of her decision of whether to sell the share. Because they are all in the same position (and know this), a bid that would appear as advantageous for a shareholder would remain so even if some individual shareholder retains the share, meaning that the probability in (9) is close to 1 if the tender offer is advantageous. Consequently, the bid must be close to the full value of the improvement expected from the takeover so that the whole gain is absorbed by the target shareholders.

This situation may be avoided by the bidder if she can reduce the value of the post-takeover shares for target shareholders; if the value can be reduced by a fraction δ, then the bid will be succesful if $b > (1 - \delta)v$. If the bidder already holds a fraction α of the share, then the profit obtained by the bidder is

$$\alpha v + (1 - \alpha)\delta v,$$

which is non-zero, so the bidder can retain a positive profit from the takeover.

Adding incomplete information will not change the initial result in a fundamental way. In the typical takeover situation, the bidder knows more about the future earning possibilities of the firm than do the target shareholders. However, even with this asymmetry, the free-rider problem remains, at least when we look at an equilibrium: If a bid is succesful, then the offer should be at least

$$b^* = E[v \mid \text{offer}],$$

where the expression on the right-hand side is the expected value as perceived by target shareholders given that the offer is made. Thus, if $b < b^*$, the target shareholders would prefer to retain the shares, making the probability of success equal to 0, whereas they will prefer to sell when $b > b^*$. Consequently, the probability of succes given the offer is 1, and the equilibrium off b^* must be equal to the expected value of the future earnings. The target shareholders get the *average* gain from the takeover.

9.5.2 Several bidders

In the case where there are several firms bidding for the same target, the target shareholders seem to have an even stronger position. However, the case of competitive bidding for a firm usually arises in a context where target shareholders will accept to sell at highest bid, so the free-rider effect discussed above does not occur.

A simple framework for the study of competitive bidding would be the *English auction*: bidders leave the contest when current bid exceeds their valuation. This would leave the winning bidder with a profit corresponding to the difference between the highest and the second-highest valuation, and the latter would be the takeover bid. However, this outcome seems to fit badly with observed takeover auctions, where the initial bid is usually very high and no futher bidding takes place.

To model such situations, we assume that the first bidder is aware that the bid may give rise to secondary bids by others and that she wants to deter such bids. Let us consider a situation with only two bidders, 1 and 2. Bidder 1 sends an initial bid, after which Bidder 2 determines whether to enter; if not, Bidder 1 wins with the intial bid, and if Bidder 2 enters, the bidding process then follows that of an Engish auction.

We consider a set-up where bidders use threshold strategies: Bidder 1 has a critical threshold v^*; if her valuation is below v^*, she offers a minimum reservation price; then Bidder 2 enters, and the target is sold in an English auction. If the valuation is above v^*, then Bidder 1 makes a high bid b^D in order to deter Bidder 2 from entering.

If the first bidder wants to bid below b^D, then she should bid 0, because the second bidder infers that the valuation is below v^*, so an English auction will follow, and the shares will be bid up to v_2 anyway. Bidding higher than b^D also makes no sense, because b^D is chosen so as to deter Bidder 2 from entering. The deterrence occurs if the expected profit of the second bidder is non-positive,

$$\mathsf{E}[\pi_2(v_1, v_2) \mid v_1 > v^*] \leq 0, \tag{10}$$

so the profit of the second bidder does not depend directly on the level of the initial bid, but on the minimum valuation v_1^* communicated through this bid.

Assuming that valuations are distributed independently and uniformly in the interval $[0, 1]$, we can reformulate (10) as

$$c^I \geq \int_{v^*}^1 \int_{v_1}^1 \left(\frac{v_2 - v_1}{1 - v^*}\right) dv_1 dv_2. \tag{11}$$

Here the inner integral is the expected payoff to the second bidder given the value v_2 in the English auction (which follows only if the yet unknown v_2 exceeds v^*); this is followed by expectation taken over all possible values of v_2. Computing the integral and solving (11) with an equality sign, we get the threshold value

$$v^* = 1 - \sqrt{6c^I}.$$

The bid b^D, which makes the first bidder with $v_1 = v^*$ indifferent between deterring and accepting entrance, can now be found: If entrance is prevented, then payoff is $v_1 - b^D = 1 - \sqrt{6c^I} - b^D$. If Bidder 2 enters, average payoff in the English auction, given their valuation v_1, is

$$\int_0^{v_1} (v_1 - v_2)dv_2 = \frac{1}{2}(v_1)^2.$$

Inserting $v_1 = v^*$ and equating to the expression for payoff without entrance, we get

$$b^D = \frac{1}{2} - 3c^I.$$

It is seen that we have a situation where in many cases there will be only an initial high bid. The size of the deterring bid will depend on the cost of investigation for the competing bidder; the smaller this cost, the higher the bid needed to deter the competitor.

9.5.3 Means of payment

In the models treated above, it was assumed throughout that the acquiring firm had to pay the target shares in cash. However, in practice it is customary that payment takes the form of shares in the acquiring firm. This practice may also be explained in the context of our approach, following Hansen [1987], if we assume that the actual value w of the target is known to the target only, whereas the acquirer has a subjective probability distribution F (with density f) over w. For simplicity, we assume that $w \in [0, 1]$. Given the value of the target w, the acquirer can obtain a value $h(w)$ after a takeover.

We start by visiting the already well-known case of a single bidder making an offer b to the target. The latter will accept the offer in the case that $w \leq b$. The optimal bid must maximize the expected payoff of the bidder,

$$E\Pi(b) = \int_0^b [h(w) - b]f(w)dw = F(b)[E[h(\tilde{w}) \mid b] - b], \tag{12}$$

where

$$E[h(\tilde{w}) \mid b] = \frac{1}{F(b)} \int_0^b h(w)dw$$

is the expected after-takeover value given the bid b. The first-order condition for an interior maximum is

$$h(b) - b = \frac{F(b)}{f(b)},$$

and at such a maximum, the probability of trade is $F(b)$.

So far we have discussed cash payment; we now introduce the possibility of payment in the form of shares, in which the acquirer may propose a fraction p of the shares instead of a cash payment. Instead of proposing a cash payment b, which would give rise to an expected wealth (initial value of shares plus expected value from acqusition) of

$$F(b)[E[h(\tilde{w}) \mid b] - b] + v, \tag{13}$$

the acquirer might propose a stock offer

$$p^* = \frac{b}{v + h(b)}.$$

Then the expected wealth of the acquirer would be

$$F(b)(1 - p^*)[E[h(\tilde{w}) \mid b] + v] + (1 - F(b))v$$

$$= v + F(b)\left[E[h(\tilde{w}) \mid b] - \frac{b}{h(b) + v}[E[h(\tilde{w}) \mid b] + v]\right],$$

$$> v + F(b)[E[h(\tilde{w}) \mid b] - b],$$

where the last inequality follows because

$$\frac{v + E[h(\tilde{w}) \mid b]}{v + h(b)} < 1. \tag{14}$$

Comparing with (13) we get that expected wealth after proposing the fraction p^* of shares is at least as large as what could be obtained by proposing cash.

To find the optimal fraction of shares proposed, we notice that p will be accepted by the target as long as

$$p[v + h(w)] \geq w; \tag{15}$$

let w^* be the threshold value at which (15) is satisfied with equality. As before, we have that expected wealth of the acquirer given p is

$$v + F(w^*)[E[h(\tilde{w}) \mid p] - p(v + E[h(\tilde{w}) \mid p])], \tag{16}$$

where

$$E[h(\tilde{w}) \mid p] = \frac{1}{F(w^*)} \int_0^{w^*} h(w) f(w) dw$$

is the conditional expectation of the value of the target to the acquirer, given that the offer is accepted. Assuming that

$$h'(w) < \frac{v}{w} + \frac{h(w)}{w}, \tag{17}$$

we get from (15), using implicit function theorem, that

$$\frac{dw^*}{dp} = \frac{1 - ph'(w)}{v + h(w)} > 0,$$

so the threshold value w^* is an increasing function of p. Maximizing (16) with respect to p is then equivalent to maximizing with respect to w^*, and optimal expected wealth can be written as

$$v + F(w^*)\left[\mathsf{E}[h(\tilde{w}) \mid w^*] - \frac{w^*}{h(w^*) + v}\left(\mathsf{E}[h(\tilde{w}) \mid w^*] + v\right)\right]$$

with $\mathsf{E}[h(\tilde{w}) \mid w^*] = \mathsf{E}[h(\tilde{w}) \mid p]$.

We notice that the advantage of shares over cash is due to (14). Consequently, the larger v is, the closer the left-hand side in (14) will be to 1, and the smaller is the advantage of shares over cash. We may exploit this to explain that payment in shares is not the generally used method in takeover bidding. Indeed, for large v the difference between cash and shares as payment will be small, and any additional feature, such as, for example, tax advantages in cash payment, may cause the preferences to shift, so cash will appear as the preferred means of payment.

9.6 Islamic banking

Because we have been treating alternatives to classical bank credit in this chapter, it seems appropriate at this point to mention a special form of banking business which has emerged over the last few decades, namely *Islamic banking*. As might be expected, Islamic banks are mainly situated in countries where Islam is predominant, and although their share of financial activities is in most countries not very large, the principles of Islamic banking are slowly filtering into the financial markets.

The background for Islamic banking is the ban on lending with interest payment laid down in the Qu'ran and in the Muslim tradition. Traditional loan and deposit business is not compatible with orthodox Islam, and if financial intermediation is to be performed, other methods must be employed. Basically the loan or deposit contracts should be replaced by *participation*.

The basic principles of acceptable banking activity can be outlined as

(1) *risk sharing:* the contracts should reflect a symmetric distribution of risk and return between the participants,

(2) *materiality:* the financial transactions should be linked to some underlying real activity,

(3) *no exploitation:* neither party to the contract must be exploited, and

(4) *no financing of prohibited activities.*

Transforming the principles to practice may not be quite so straightforward, even though exclusion of some types of business (such as contracts involving futures, options or credit default swaps) is obvious. There are two main forms of financing [Khan, 2010]:

Participatory forms: Here the bank enters as a partner in the business planned by the borrower. This can happen either in the form called *midaraba*, where it supplies capital and some expertise but otherwise is a sleeping partner, and *musharaka*, where the bank takes a direct stake in the business.

Non-participatory forms: Here the contract is trade based, which means that instead of lending for the investment, e.g. equipment, the bank buys the equipment and allows the investor to buy it out over a period of time and at a higher price. In this way the contract is 'trade based' rather than being a standard loan contract. This so-called mark-up contract, or *murabaha*, is the typical non-participatory contract, but other forms exist as well, such as leasing contracts.

The participatory forms are considered as the most genuine types of Islamic banking business and prevail in the Islamic banks, but the other forms are also widely used.

The idea of participatory banking rather than traditional deposit and loan business has some interest in a completely different context [García et al., 2004], namely that of 'narrow banking', which will be commented on in a later chapter (Chapter 14 on bank runs). Because the contract between bank and depositor is not one where the latter is promised a fixed return, but one of participation in a given business with its profits or losses, there is no reason to fear that the bank might default on its obligations, which means that the threat of bank runs is largely done away with, and with it the cost of the traditional arrangements for avoiding bank runs. Because these costs are not easily assessed, the advantage of participatory rather than deposit-and-loan banking remains a theoretical issue, but it points to some future development of financial intermediation which could be useful in several respects.

9.7 Exercises

1. The value of an unlevered company is €720 million. Its marginal tax rate is 25%. Find the value of equity, of debt and of the whole company if it borrows €165 million at 8% annually as a perpetual debt, using this amount to repurchase equity.

2. Consider two firms A and B with the same cash flow of €5 million. The companies both have 5 million shares.

Company A has a debt of €10 million, and its shares are sold at a price of €8 and give a return of 10%. Company B has debt in the amount of €40 million. The debt is considered as risk-free, and the interest rate is 5%. There are no corporate taxes.

Find the value of firm A's assets, and also find the price and return of the shares of firm B.

A person owns 1 million shares of firm A, but dislikes the company and contemplates a change to investment in firm B, possibly combined with risk-free borrowing. Find the portfolio of shares in B and risk-free borrowing/lending that will give exactly the same return as the current investment.

3. Consider a risk-neutral wealth-constrained firm which must raise funds from investors in a competitive market. The manager can steal a part of the outcome y and leave only

$x(y) \leq y$ to share with the investors, and it pays $R(y) \leq x(y)$ to investors. Stealing involves a loss which is set to $\frac{1}{4}(y - x)^2$.

The return y is random, taking the value y_L with probability p, y_H with probability $1 - p$.

(1) Draw indifference curves of the firm in (x, R)-space (depending on whether the firm has high or low returns). Check whether they are convex or concave. Which firm type has the steeper indifference curves?

(2) What are the incentive compatibility constraints?

(3) Find the firm's ex post wealth constraint, assuming that the firm can always steal everything.

(4) Find the income which the firm can credibly pledge to investors as a function of $(x(y_L), x(y_H))$.

(5) How much of the cash flow can the firm credibly pledge to investors while maintaining efficiency?

4. [Tirole, 2006] An entrepreneur has some initial wealth W and wants to invest $I > W$ in a project which gives R with probability π and 0 otherwise. The probability π can take two different values π_H and π_L with $\pi_H > \pi_L$. In the case where $\pi = \pi_L$, the entrepreneur receives a private benefit B. There is limited liability, so an investor will lose money in the case of a failure of the investment.

Find the conditions for the entrepreneur to be able to attract investment to the project.

Now we add some structure to the model: It is possible to change the probability π_L to $\pi'_L > \pi_L$. The change will inflict a cost C on the entrepreneur. Show that if the right to change π_L is given to the entrepreneur, then the conditions for obtaining external finance are unchanged as long as $(\pi_H - \pi_L)B \geq (\pi'_L - \pi_L)C$. If the right is given to the investor, assume that the investor chooses to exercise this right whenever it is as good as not using it. Show that the condition for attracting finance is

$$\pi_H\left[R - \frac{B}{\pi_H - \pi'_L}\right] \geq I - W.$$

Comment on this result. What is the overall result of giving the investor this right?

5. Firm A is currently investigating the possible acquisition of firm B. The following basic data is available:

	Firm A	Firm B
Profit per share	€6	€1.80
Dividend per share	€4	€1
Number of shares	1,000,000	500,000
Stock price	€100	€25

You estimate that investors currently expect a steady growth of about 6% in B's profits and dividends. Under new management the growth rate is assumed to be increased to 8% per year, even without new investment.

What is the gain from the acquisition? What will be the cost of the acquisition if A pays €28 in cash for each share in B? And what is the cost if instead A pays one share in A for each three shares in B?

How do these results depend on the expected growth under new management?

9.8 Comments

Corporate finance is a field which is connected to banking mainly due to the fact that banks act as intermediaries in the financial processes and traditionally obtain considerable gains from this. There are several well-established textbooks in the field, e.g. de Matos [2001], Tirole [2006].

The Modigliani-Miller theorems appeared in Modigliani and Miller [1958, 1963], and they have obtained almost classical status in the economics of the corporate firm. It has many applications in fields which have little in common with ours, but they are also relevant to banks and have been invoked in the discussion of capital regulation of banks.

There is a considerable literature on control rights. For a survey, see e.g. Shleifer and Vishny [1997]. A survey of venture capital can be found in Rin et al. [2013]. The decision to go public has also attracted much theoretical attention; for a recent contribution, cf. e.g. Chemmanur and He [2011]. The IPO under- and overpricing issues have been dealt with at length in the literature; see the survey in Ritter and Welch [2002].

The debate about the short- and long-term gains from mergers and acquisitions has been going on for many years. See e.g. Bruner [2004].

There is a large literature on Islamic banking, but it is mainly of a descriptive character, and the attempts to integrate Islamic banking into the microeconomic theory of banking have been few. For an early contribution, see Khan [1986].

Chapter 10

Payments

10.1 Introduction

In this chapter, we consider an activity of banks which we have largely neglected in the previous discussion, namely transmission of payments. Here the focus is on transactions which take place during a very short period of time, typically a day. As a by-product of economic activity, there is a need for both large-sum payments as settlements in big business and small day-to-day payments in daily trade. We shall have a look at the specific problems arising in connection with both large and small payments.

A payment, big or small, involves the transfer of money (bank deposits) from one person to another, and in many cases this also involves transfer from one bank to another. It seems obvious that it would be too costly to deal with this on the basis of each individual transfer. Rather, the banks should wait to the end of the day and then carry out only the *net* transfers, which typically are much smaller than the total number of transactions that have taken place over the day.

This is where a central bank comes in: Traditionally, the daily clearing of interbank payments has been done by the central bank; each bank may have a positive or negative balance with the central bank, and they are settled only at the end of the day. But even though the time span (one day) is short, this method of *net settlement* gives rise to a counterparty credit risk because a bank may default at a time when its net position is negative.

In view of this, large-value payments operated by the central bank are nowadays RTGS (real-time gross settlement) systems, which means that the banks must obtain liquidity to transfer money each time this occurs, typically in the form of a loan from the central bank. Such loans come with a cost, which may take the form of an interest payment to the central bank, or the bank may have to offer collateral, again giving rise to an opportunity cost. We shall have a closer look below on RTGS systems and their consequences for efficiency and behaviour of banks.

When turning from large payments to the small payments which constitute the bulk of the payment transactions, an interesting feature is the recent development of *payment cards*. Payment card systems have become the object of economic research only in recent years; what has been analysed is, in particular, the cost of transfer using cards and the ways in which their distribution between purchasers and sellers influence the efficiency properties of the system.

We conclude the chapter with a brief treatment of bitcoin, which gives rise to new forms of payment not involving financial intermediaries.

10.2 RTGS systems

Before we consider payment systems, we take a short detour into basic economics, recalling the classical argument for use of money, by Samuelson [1958]. Because the model and its subsequent refinements can be found in many textbooks, our treatment here has only the purpose of setting up the basic structure of the model.

We consider a simple overlapping generations model, where at each date $t \geq 1$, there are two individuals alive, an old and a young individual. There is only one good, and each individual is endowed with 1 unit when young and with nothing when old. The good cannot be stored, so the old individual cannot consume anything (trading with the young individual makes no sense because the old individual has nothing to trade with). For completion of the model, we have an initial (old) generation which lives only at $t = 0$ and has no endowment.

A steady-state allocation, that is, an allocation where all generations get the same consumption bundle, is therefore one where each individual consumes 1 unit when young and nothing when old, a so-called no-trade allocation. With utility functions such that something of the good in both life years is better than 1 unit in only one of the years, this allocation is clearly not Pareto optimal. Indeed, by allocating a proportion δ of the endowment of the young individual in $t = 0$ to the old individual, the latter becomes better off, and the young individual may be compensated in her second year by receiving δ from the new young individual, and so on. As a result, everyone becomes better off.

Simple as it may look, this Pareto improvement involves a central authority which initially collects goods belonging to the young individual and redistributes them to the old individual. A simple way of achieving similar effects without coercion would be to introduce debt certificates or IOUs which are given to the old at $t = 0$; they subsequently exchange them for the good with the young, and the young do the same next year when they have become old, etc. In this way, the Pareto improvement may be sustained as an ordinary competitive equilibrium.

For our purpose, we notice that the introduction of debt certificates has a crucial role; the presence of money in the economy makes it perform better than it did without money. As we shall see, this holds even in more complicated settings and also when the problem is that some individuals get their endowment later than wanted rather than, as here, too early – only the model then becomes slightly more involved.

10.2.1 An overlapping generations model of RTGS

The model to be described here was proposed by Mills [2006], elaborating on Freeman [1996]. We need to capture the phenomenon that some payments are needed early in the day, whereas others may be postponed. This is done by looking at an overlapping generations model where the period corresponds to one day; it may seem strange that consumers live only two days, and this could be remedied easily, but the only effect would be complicating the essential features to be studied. The reason for the overlapping-generations context comes from the same source as in the classical model: We want a set-up where individuals must have recourse to money rather than solve their economic problems by simple barter. Because we need impatient consumers wanting credit, the model is slightly more complex than the previous one.

In each period t, there is a young consumer of type C (for 'creditor') living for two consecutive periods, as well as an old consumer of type C. In addition, there is a consumer of type D ('debtor') living only in this period. There are two goods; the consumer of type C has 1 unit of good 1 when young and nothing when old, and she has a utility function of the form

$$u(x_{1,t}, x_{2,t+1}),$$

where the first index refers to good and the second index to date; thus, consumer C uses only good 1 in her first year and only good 2 in the second life year. Consumer D has an endowment of good 2 and wants to consume both goods with a utility function of the form

$$v(x_{1,t}, x_{2,t}).$$

The reason that consumer D eventually becomes a debtor is that she has access to a technology which transforms input I of good 2 delivered early in the day to RI units later in the day, with $R > 1$.

Within each day, there are four stages:

> Stage 1: The consumers of type D may choose to obtain liquidity from the central bank.
>
> Stage 2: Young consumers C and consumers D trade good 1 for money, and investment is performed.
>
> Stage 3: Output is received; now consumers D trade good 2 for money with old consumers C.
>
> Stage 4: Money is repaid to the central bank.

As usual, we are interested in Pareto optimal allocations; we restrict attention to steady-state allocations, so consumers of the same type get the same bundle over time. Then the Pareto optimal allocations can be found by maximizing

$$u(c_1, c_2) + v(d_1, d_2)$$

(with c_1, c_2 the consumption of the consumer C and d_1, d_2 that of consumer D) over all I, c_1, c_2, d_1, d_2, satisfying the constraints

$$I \leq 1,$$

$$d_1 + c_1 \leq 1,$$

$$d_2 + c_2 \leq RI + (1 - I),$$

which state that investment cannot exceed total endowment of good 2 and that consumption of each good must be less than or equal to what is available. First-order conditions for a maximum under these constraints give us the necessary condition on marginal utilities

$$\frac{u_1'}{u_2'} = \frac{v_1'}{v_2'},$$

which under standard assumptions on utilities are also sufficient.

Assume that the central bank charges an intraday interest rate r for liquidity. We say that an allocation is *implementable* if it can be obtained using money and trading goods for money in stages 1–4 described above.

PROPOSITION 1: *Assume that the steady-state allocation given by* $(c_1, c_2), (d_1, d_2)$ *satisfies*

$$v(1 - c_1, R - (1 + r)c_2) \geq v(0, R),$$

$$u(c_1, c_2) \geq u(1, 0).$$

Then the allocation is implementable.

PROOF: We need to check that there are prices supporting this allocation such that it can be achieved using stages 1–4. We normalize the amount of money supplied at stage 1 to 1; if consumer D borrows 1 unit of money and buys the amount of good 1 that the young consumer C doesn't want, then the price p_1 of good 1 in money terms should satisfy

$$p_1(1 - c_1) = 1.$$

The consumer of type D may be assumed to invest the whole endowment 1 in production, giving an output R. This is used partly for consumption, partly for sale to the old consumer C, who has a saving in money terms which amounts to the value of what was not consumed last year, that is, $p_1(1 - c_1)$. The money price p_2 at which this saving is used for buying commodity c_2 must be such that

$$p_2 c_2 = p_1(1 - c_1),$$

so consumer D gets back exactly $p_1(1 - c_1) = 1$, that is, the amount of the original loan, in money at this sale. But in addition, she has to pay the interest on the loan, amounting to $r = r p_1(1 - c_1) = r p_2 c_2$, and the remaining amount $R - (1 + r)c_2$ is what is available for consumption. The result of the trading process is at least as good for D as staying away, and also for consumer C, trading goods against money is better than staying away. Thus, the steady state considered is supported by the trading mechanism. □

Although trading according to this mechanism represents a distinct improvement over autarky (where no money is provided), it does not achieve the first-best optimum outlined above, because there is a loss of real resources to the central bank furnishing credit. This might be remedied if the interest payment was somehow ploughed back into the economy, for example by distributing it among consumers. The main point is that from the point of view of resources made available, the mechanism sustains optimal allocations.

This is not a trivial point, because the alternative way of securing that credits are not misused, namely by demanding a *collateral*, does interfere with the production processes; indeed, if consumer D can obtain loans only by setting aside an amount ξ of good 2 to guarantee payment, then at most $1 - \xi$ can be invested, and therefore final consumption of consumer D reduces to

$$\xi + R(1 - \xi) - c_2 < R - c_2.$$

Comparing with the case where the interest paid to the central bank is ploughed back into the economy, we see that using collateral is inferior to paying interest; the demand for collateral implies foregone investment opportunities for society.

The policy conclusions to be obtained from this point to an advantage of RTGS systems (the system used in the United States) with interest payment over those using collateral (Europe). This conclusion should, however, be taken with some reservation because the model is quite simplistic and, in particular, does not deal directly with payments between banks, which are the main object of the study.

10.2.2 The intraday liquidity game

Following Bech and Garratt [2003], we describe here a simplified case of two banks A and B receiving payment requests either in the morning or in the afternoon. These requests are assumed to have fixed size normalized to 1, and there is a probability p of having a request in the morning and q in the evening (the two are independent and identical for both A and B).

A bank can choose between two actions m and a, namely paying a morning request in the morning or in the afternoon. There is a central bank which takes care of settlements, and it has a choice between three different payment regimes, namely

  (1) free intraday liquidity,

  (2) collateralized credit, and

  (3) credit with interest payment.

In each of these regimes, the bank incurs a cost depending on its situation, its own action, morning or afternoon payment, and the action of the other bank.

A strategy of a bank is a rule which prescribes the action to be taken by the bank. We assume that a bank can observe whether it has a morning request; it cannot, however, observe whether the other bank has a request. If the bank has no request, then there is no need for choosing between morning and afternoon payment, so in the following, we consider only the choice problem of a bank which has a morning request. With only two actions open to each bank, the strategic interactions can be described as a two-person game where each player has two strategies.

1. Free intraday liquidity: The payoff matrix of the game becomes:

	morning	afternoon
morning	$0, 0$	$0, -D$
afternoon	$-D, 0$	$-D, -D$

Here we have assumed that there is a cost D for the bank in delaying a payment (corresponding to the social cost of delay, so banks must compensate the parties for the damage caused by delay). Clearly, (morning, morning) is a Nash equilibrium, corresponding to intuition: When it costs nothing to have a negative balance in the morning, and delaying payment is costly, then payments should be made right away.

2. Collateralized credit: Here the payoffs are somewhat more complicated. We assume that pledging collateral involves a cost of C for the bank. If bank A pays in the morning, it has the cost C of posting the collateral in the morning, and if it gets no other payments in the morning, collateral must be posted once more in the evening. If also bank B has chosen morning payment, then the cost induced by the morning payment is $C + (1 - p)C$, and to this should be added the cost of posting additional collateral for an afternoon request, in case such one arrives. In total, the cost for bank A of the morning payment strategy is

$$C + (1 - p)C + qC;$$

the second term is the expected cost of collateral in the afternoon, which will be needed with probability q. Reasoning similarly for the other strategy combinations, we get the payoff matrix

	morning	afternoon
morning	$-(1 - p)C, -(1 - p)C$	$-C, -D + pC$
afternoon	$-D + pC, -C$	$-D, -D$

(where we have subtracted the cost $C + qC$ which is common for all the strategy combinations). If $D < C$, then afternoon payment is a Nash equilibrium, whereas morning payment will be a Nash equilibrium in the case of $C > D$.

This points to a possible inefficiency of the collateralized credit regime, at least if $C > D$, because both players are better off if both choose morning payment, which, however, is not a Nash equilibrium.

3. Interest payment on credit: Finally, we take a look at the case where banks incur a cost F if they have a negative balance at the end of the morning or afternoon. To find the costs, we must again separate into three terms: The first term expresses the cost of the morning request in the morning period; if both choose m, then this is $(1 - p)F$ for the bank considered (which knows that it has a morning request). The next term gives the expected cost of the morning request during the afternoon, and it is $(1-p)(1-q(1-q))F$ (probability that the other bank had no morning request times the probability that it is not extinguished in the afternoon, and the third term is the probability of a new request not balanced by a request of the other bank.

Working through the other combinations and cancelling terms which are common for all combinations, we finally get a payoff matrix of the following form:

	morning	afternoon
morning	$-(1 - p)F, -(1 - p)F$	$-F, -D$
afternoon	$-D, -F$	$-D, -D$

Here the selection of equilibria is slightly more complicated, depending on the parameters. If $D < (1 - p)F$, both will select afternoon payment. If $D > F$, morning payment is in equilibrium. But in the case where $(1 - p)F < D < F$ both morning and afternoon payment may be in equilibrium. Again, equilibria may not be efficient, something which may happen in the last case.

Although simple, this model does give some formal underpinning of the intuitive feeling that banks may choose to postpone payment in an RTGS system when the price of credit is high, thereby giving rise to an efficiency loss (in the model we have only considered inefficiency in terms of the payoffs of the banks, although we assumed that delayment cost reflected cost to society).

10.2.3 Efficiency considerations in RTGS systems with collateral

As illustrated in the previous section, the choice of payment regime has an impact on the behaviour of the participating banks, which will choose a timing of their payments which minimizes cost given what the other banks do. In the model considered above, payments requested in each part of the day had a fixed size but could be postponed. Following Buckle and Campbell [2003], we take another look at the situation, now assuming that the total payments of the day are fixed but that the timing is subject to the choice of the bank.

As before, we consider the intraday payments in a very simple framework, where the day consists of only two periods, morning and afternoon, and there are only two banks. At the beginning of the day, both banks post collateral with the central bank and obtain liquidity B_i^0, $i = 1, 2$. At the end of the day, banks have to settle their accounts with the central bank and then get their collateral back.

Assume that the total amount of payments to the other bank over the day is non-random and has the size M. However, each bank may decide upon the fraction α_i of its balance to be used for payments in the morning, giving rise to a total payment $M_i^m = \alpha_i B_i^0$ to the other bank. Given the choices α_i, $i = 1, 2$, the afternoon payments of the banks are

$$M_i^a = \min\left\{M - \alpha_i B_i^0, (1 - \alpha_i)B_i^0 + \alpha_j B_j^0\right\}, \; i, j = 1, 2, i \neq j.$$

At the end of the day, the balance of the bank will be what remains after the afternoon payments plus what has arrived from the other bank,

$$B_i^1 = \max\left\{B_i^0 + \alpha_j B_j^0\right\} + \min\left\{M - \alpha_j B_j^0, (1 - \alpha_j)B_j^0 + \alpha_i B_i^0\right\},$$

and the amount of payments that have been cancelled due to lack of liquidity balances is

$$L_i = \max\left\{M - B_i^0 - \alpha_j B_j^0, 0\right\},$$

for $i, j = 1, 2, i \neq j$.

Moving to the payoff of the two settlement banks, it seems reasonable to assume that they derive income from carrying out payments; if the fee to bank i per payment is f_i (and we assume that all payments have equal size 1), then bank i collects $f_i \min\left\{M, B_i^0 + \alpha_j B_j^0\right\}$. On the cost side, there is an opportunity cost c_i per unit of collateral posted with the central bank, and in addition we assume that there is a cost of having a payment cancelled due to lack of liquidity. This cost is presumably non-linear in L_i; we may take it as a quadratic function of the form $b_i L_i^2 = b_i\left(\max\left\{M - B_i^0 - \alpha_j B_j^0, 0\right\}\right)^2$, so the payoff function becomes

$$\Pi_i(\alpha_i, \alpha_j, B_i^0, B_j^0) = f_i \min\left\{M, B_i^0 + \alpha_j B_j^0\right\} - c_i B_i^0 - b_i\left(\max\left\{M - B_i^0 - \alpha_j B_j^0, 0\right\}\right)^2. \quad (1)$$

Each bank has two decision variables, α_i and B_i^0. However, it is seen from (1) that i's payoff is independent of α_i, whereas it depends positively on α_j for $j \neq i$. Consequently, there can be equilibria with $\alpha_1 = \alpha_2 = 0$, where $B_1^0 = B_2^0 = M$ (provided that $f_i > c_i$), but also equilibria with lower values of B_1^0 and B_2^0, sustaining the same equilibrium payments with lower cost.

Thus, in the symmetric case where f_i, c_i, b_i are all independent of i, we could have an equilibrium with

$$B_i^0 = \frac{1}{2}M, \; \alpha_i = 1, i = 1, 2,$$

and the same payments can be achieved with only half the collateral. Indeed, although the bank uses all of its liquidity balance to carry through half of the payments in the morning, both banks will have restored their liquidity balance at noon and can carry out the remaining payments in the afternoon.

This equilibrium is clearly efficient in the sense that there is no other outcome which gives a higher total payoff to the participants. However, it may be upset by even slight changes in the players' strategy choices, and it will therefore be difficult to sustain in practice. But coming to practical applications, we should also bear in mind that we have represented the continuum of payment times over the day by just two points in time, and that the total amount of payments over the day is far from constant. Actually, the size and dimension of the problem is such that banks may prefer rules of thumb to strategic behaviour. This means that the determination of liquidity balances should rather be a task of the central bank on behalf of the settlement banks. For a model of settlement along this line, see Peñaloza [2009].

10.3 Payment card systems

At the other end of the spectrum of payments, we find those carried out when consumers buy commodities, which may be done using cash (in which case we shall have nothing particular to say) or by using payment cards.

Since its emergence (the first payment card introduced was Diners in 1949) payment cards have developed into a very widespread means of payment. Payment cards come in several different versions, most commonly as either *debit cards* (where the customer draws on an existing account of hers in the issuing bank) and *credit cards* (where the bank offers a credit in connection with the payment). For the analysis to follow, the distinction is unimportant.

What matters for the economic theory of payment cards is the structure of fees which are charged to the participants. Below we consider a simple model of this fee structure, taken from Rochet and Tirole [2002]. When a payment to the amount of p is initiated by a purchase from a merchant, the card holder may be charged a fee f by her bank, known in this context as the *issuer*, which also sets a fee a, the *interchange fee*, to be paid by the merchant's bank, called the *acquirer*. This latter bank then delivers the money to the merchant, reducing it by a fee m. The situation is illustrated in Fig. 10.1.

There might be still another fee, namely one charged by the merchant and paid by the customer using cards. However, this is often ruled out by the firm or institution in charge of the credit card (or perhaps directly by law); one says that a *no-surcharge rule* is adhered to, and we shall assume this in what follows.

To find the effects of using or not using cards, we need a more detailed formulation of the situation than the figure. We therefore add suitable assumptions to the four main parties: Customer, issuer, acquirer and merchant.

(a) Customers. We assume that a customer has a benefit b_B (in money terms) of using card; the benefits are distributed between a lower bound $\underline{b}_B$ and an upper bound $\overline{b}_B$ according to a distribution with density $h(b_B)$. If the customer fee is f, then all consumers with

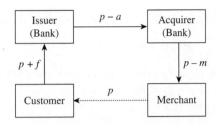

Figure 10.1 Simplified payment card system: When the customer uses the card to buy commodities of value p, then the customer pays $p + f$, her bank pays $p - a$ to the merchant's bank, and this bank pays $p - m$ to the merchant.

$b_B \geq f$ will use a card. The proportion of customers using cards and the average benefit given the fee f are $D(f) = \int_f^{\bar{b}_B} h(b_B) \, db_B$ and

$$\beta(f) = \frac{\int_f^{\bar{b}_B} b_B h(b_B) \, db_B}{D(f)},$$

respectively. Note that when f goes down, then new customers with lower benefit will switch to using the card, so β is an increasing function of f.

(b) Issuers. Because much of the discussion in the following will be related to the interchange fee, we shall assume that the issuers determine the customer fee when knowing a according to a functional dependence

$$f = f^*(c_I - a).$$

Here c_I is the real cost of making the transfer, so the function f^* depends on the net cost to the issuer (which may be negative). We shall not explain how this function arises, but it could be the result of some form of oligopolistic behaviour. We assume that f^* is increasing, so a greater interchange fee (resulting in smaller net costs) leads to a smaller customer fee.

(c) Acquirers. This sector is assumed to be perfectly competitive, so fees are passed directly to merchants, meaning that $m = a + c_A$, where c_A is the cost of transferring money to the merchant.

(d) Merchants. The only decision (related to card payment) left to merchants is to accept or not accept cards. We want to formulate the model so that this decision is important for obtaining customers and for the price at which the commodity can be sold (so merchants accepting cards can get away with higher prices). We assume therefore that there are two identical merchants with marginal cost d and that the buyers are spread out in the interval $[0, 1]$ (all buying 1 unit) with the firms at each end and transportation cost t (that is, a classical Hotelling model of monopolistic competition; distance may be taken literally but may as well refer to perceived quality differences between the firms).

Now we are almost ready for the first result. We introduce the notation

$$m''(a) = m - b_S = c_A + a - b_S,$$

where b_S is the merchant's benefit from receiving card payment (rather than cash). This is a linearly increasing function in a. Because $\beta(f^*(c_I - a))$ is decreasing in a, there is a specific value $\bar{a}$ of a such that

$$\beta(f^*(c_I - \bar{a})) = m''(\bar{a}).$$

For $a < \bar{a}$, the average buyer satisfaction of card payment exceeds the net cost to the merchant.

PROPOSITION 2: *There exists an equilibrium where both merchants accept cards if and only if $a \leq \bar{a}$.*

PROOF: Assume that both merchants take cards. Then we have a symmetric Hotelling model, and it is well known that in such models, the optimal price equals cost to the firm plus the transportation cost,

$$p^* = [d + D(f^*(c_I - a)) m''(a)] + t,$$

so total profit from serving all customers is t, and the profit of each is $\frac{t}{2}$.

Now we let one of the merchants, say 1, contemplate changing policy so as not to accept cards. In the new situation, we get that if all customers had benefit b_B, then this merchant would get all customers with a position smaller than x_1 given by

$$p_1 + tx_1 = p_2 + t(1 - x_1) - b_B,$$

which may be solved for x_1 to give

$$x_1 = \frac{1}{2} + \frac{p_2 - p_1 - b_B}{2t}.$$

Because customers have different benefits, we sum over all customers (all card users) to obtain the demand of merchant 1 as

$$\frac{1}{2} + \frac{p_2 - p_1 - D(f)\beta(f)}{2t}.$$

Because demand is linear and there are constant marginal costs, the optimal price of merchant 1 can be found by the 'half-overprice' rule as

$$p_1 = \frac{1}{2}[t + p_2 - D(f)\beta(f)] + \frac{1}{2}d,$$

where the first bracket is the price at which demand is zero. Similarly, we find the demand of merchant 2 as

$$\frac{1}{2} + \frac{p_1 - p_2 + D(f)\beta(f)}{2t}$$

and optimal price as

$$p_2 = \frac{1}{2}[t + p_2 + D(f)\beta(f)] + \frac{1}{2}[d + D(f)m''(a)], \tag{2}$$

where the second bracket expresses the fact that merchant 2 still has the cost of taking cards. Solving the two equations in p_1 and p_2, we get

$$p_1 = t + d - \frac{1}{3}D(f)[\beta(f) - m''(a)],$$

$$p_2 = t + d + \frac{1}{3}D(f)[\beta(f) + 2m''(a)].$$

We may now evaluate the profit π_1 of merchant 1 in the new situation: The mark-up (price minus cost) is $t - \frac{1}{3}D(f)[\beta(f) - m''(a)]$, which has to be multiplied by the demand; the latter was found above as a function of p_1 and p_2, so we need to insert them, after which we get the demand as

$$\frac{1}{2} - \frac{D(f)[\beta(f) - m''(a)]}{6t}.$$

We then have that

$$2t\pi_1 = \left(t - \frac{1}{3}D(f)[\beta(f) - m''(a)]\right)^2,$$

which is $\leq 2t\left(\frac{t}{2}\right)$ exactly when $\beta(f) \geq m''(a)$. $\qquad\square$

The result gives us a precise condition under which cards will be generally accepted. If it is not satisfied, there may be equilibria where one but not both accept cards. From the point of view of the issuer, it would seem preferable that cards are accepted by all merchants (there are more payments on which to earn a fee), so if issuers choose a, we would expect them to set it at $\bar{a}$.

We shall be interested also in the welfare properties of equilibrium. Assume that the customer fee is chosen by a social planner maximizing social surplus

$$W(f) = [\beta(f) + b_S - c_I - c_A]D(f) = \int_f^{\bar{b}_B} [b_B + b_S - c_I - c_A]h(b_B)\,db_B$$

under the constraint that both merchants should be willing to take cards, that is, $a \leq \bar{a}$. Neglecting for a while the latter constraint, we have first-order condition

$$W'(f) = -[f + b_S - c_I - c_A]h(f) = 0,$$

or assuming that $h(f) > 0$ (which holds if all consumer types are represented),

$$f = c_I + c_A - b_S.$$

Remembering now the constraint, we get that there are two cases to consider:

(i) $f(c_I - \overline{a}) \leq c_I + c_A - b_S$. Starting with $\overline{a}$, the planner may reduce a, thereby increasing the customer fee, until the latter becomes equal to the right-hand side. Then cards are accepted and social surplus is maximized, so the use of cards is socially optimal.

(ii) $f(c_I - \overline{a}) > c_I + c_A - b_S$. To achieve the optimum, we need to reduce fees, but this can be done only by increasing a from $\overline{a}$, and then the merchants do not accept cards any more.

Thus, regulation of card payment systems through the interchange fee f is only feasible to a certain extent, at least as long as merchants have the option of refusing cards. In the case (ii) above, this is clearly insufficient, and regulation cannot achieve efficiency unless supported by additional means.

10.4 Payments without intermediaries

In the previous sections, we have considered methods of payment involving banks, where the role of the bank was to provide trustworthiness of the transaction. As soon as payments are transacted in forms other than cash, and in particular when transactions are many and have a large size, there is a need for an institution which provides the necessary guarantees both to the sender and the receiver of the payment. Even when dealing with payments between banks, the role of the intermediary is crucial.

In view of this, it is particularly interesting that totally new methods of payment have established themselves – even if yet at a very small level – in recent years. The most important of these is payment with *bitcoins*, a fully electronic currency, which was developed following Nakamoto [2008]. In the debate, attention has been given to the fact that bitcoins constitute a new type of money, not issued and not controlled by any authority. These aspects of bitcoins, however interesting, are somewhat marginal to our theme, and we shall be more concerned with the possibility that bitcoin (or other so-called cryptocurrencies, currencies based on encryption and shared information about transactions) offer a method of payment that does not involve intermediaries.

Since its start in 2009, the number of bitcoins circulating has increased rapidly, as illustrated in Fig. 10.2, but there is still a way to go before the maximum of 21,000,000 is reached.

The need for an intermediary in the transmission of money from a payer to a payee is connected with the risk that the payer may use the same money for several payments. When the payment is done by transferring cash, this risk is absent or very low, but in electronic transfers it is quite considerable because the payer may transfer more than she possesses, and here a third party comes in, guaranteeing to the receiver of the transfer that it is genuine. This means, however, that the transaction of the payment is duplicated – the payer transfers the sum to the bank which transfers it to the receiver, with the resulting increase in transaction cost. There is also a problem with the inherent reversibility of the payment – the receiver cannot be absolutely sure of having received the payment because

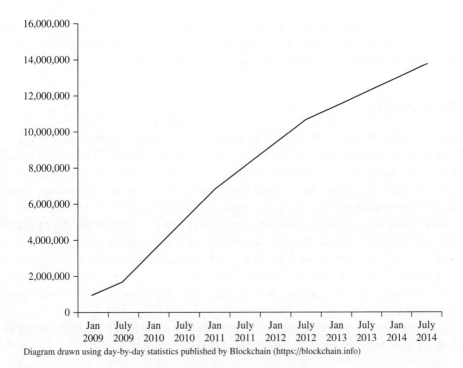

Diagram drawn using day-by-day statistics published by Blockchain (https://blockchain.info)

Figure 10.2 Bitcoins in circulation.

it may be called back in some cases. This is particularly troublesome for a small business obtaining card payment, which may be reversed if the consumer has complaints over the goods received.

The bitcoin system, while being a fully electronic method of payment, returns to the irreversibility of cash payment – an owner of a bitcoin is the only one having access to this bitcoin, and this access is what is transferred during the payment. On the other hand, the transfer itself is electronic and carries only a very low cost.

This is achieved using a network which is decentralized and where all transactions can be observed by anyone. Whenever a transaction, that is, a payment from a payer to a payee, is carried out, it is registered in the system, which may be thought of as a gigantic ledger with the date of transaction as well as the electronic identities of the two parties. Technically, transactions are registered as blocks in the computers (nodes) of the network. Each of the nodes can verify blocks, checking that the information registered conforms with the way in which it should be encoded. This process, known as *mining*, is very time-consuming and becomes increasingly so as the number of transactions increases. The system remunerates the successful verifiers (miners) by giving them a number of bitcoins. The total number of bitcoins is prefixed, but because mining becomes increasingly difficult as the number of transactions carried out increases, the limit is not expected to be reached in this century. When the possibilities of getting new bitcoins are all exploited, the miners will be remunerated by transaction fees collected from the users, but the fees are set at a very low level, so the system remains cheaper than using an intermediary.

10.5 Exercises

1. [Kiyotaki and Moore, 2002] Consider a model of exchange over three dates $t = 1, 2, 3$. There are three types of agent (I, II and III), with, say, one of each. The agent of type I wants consumption at $t = 1$ but has goods only at $t = 3$. The agent of type II has goods at date 1 but wants to consume at $t = 2$, and finally, the agent of type III wants to consume at $t = 3$ but has endowment at $t = 2$. Goods are perishable and cannot be stored.

Show that if agents can make commitments to deliver to owners of their IOUs (not only bilaterally but also after resale), then efficient allocation can be achieved.

Suppose that an agent of type I can make full bilateral commitment to deliver goods at $t = 3$ to anyone to whom the agent has sold an IOU at $t = 1$, but that agents of type III default on any agreement to deliver goods at date $t = 2$. What happens to the allocation in this economy?

Suggest a way in which efficiency may be restored, involving only the IOUs issued by agents of type III. Comment on the implications for the theory of money.

2. Construct and analyse a model which extends the intraday liquidity game model in the sense that there are three rather than two banks; as before, banks knowing that they have morning requests can choose to pay in the morning and in the afternoon. The central bank demands collateral, and posting collateral involves a cost of C.

What will happen if two of the banks merge into a single one?

3. Liquidity saving mechanisms: Suppose that a (small) number m of agents have to carry out a (large) number of payments. The kth payment is a number x_{ij}^k describing the amount transferred from i to j in the course of payment k. The sum of all payments is assumed to be zero.

Find the liquidity reserve necessary for individual i if her payments come before she receives any payments from other agents.

Discuss methods which can be used to reduce this liquidity reserve for the participants.

4. Suppose that in the payment card model of Section 10.3, the number of merchants in the market is increased from two to some large number n. What will happen to the equilibrium conditions in the market – will it still be an optimum for all merchants to accept credit cards, or can any merchant improve by refusing to take credit cards, given that all other merchants accept?

5. In a developing country, payments have traditionally been performed using cash, but it is desired that payment cards should be used more frequently. There are already some systems which are at work, and they are financed by fees paid by buyers and sellers to their banks as well as interchange fees between banks, but there is no surcharge to the seller for using a card, and this is also not wanted in the future.

A questionnaire among card users has shown that on the one hand they are very satisfied with the system, which they see as convenient and advantageous, but on the other hand they complain that there are only few sellers that accept cards.

Give suggestions for a regulation that could solve the problems indicated.

10.6 Comments

A discussion of payments almost necessarily takes as its point of departure the theory of money, and the discussion in this chapter is no exception. For theories of money based on transactions, see Ostroy and Starr [1990], Kiyotaki and Moore [2002]. The literature on RTGS systems has been extended to include liquidity saving mechanisms; see Martin and McAndrews [2008].

A recent direction of research which is not considered in the chapter is that of network topology of payments, in particular interbank payments; see e.g. Soramäki et al. [2007].

The theory of payment cards is of relatively recent date, and its emphasis is not so much the activity of banks as the influence on competition in the markets for the goods transacted using payment cards. As such it is a subfield of the theory of *two-sided markets*; see the survey in Rochet and Tirole [2006].

Bitcoins, or more generally, cryptocurrencies, provide a fascinating new field of research, but contributions are as yet rather few. For a discussion of the transaction fee, see Houy [2004].

Chapter 11

Competition and Risk Taking

11.1 Introduction

Banks are carrying out business under mutual competition. This is in itself not something which is peculiar to banks, but the way in which the competition between banks unfolds may give rise to some considerations which are specific to this field. The main reason for this is that the decisions of the financial intermediaries have an impact on the whole economy; banks are engaged in risk taking, and excessive risk taking may give rise to failures in the banking sector or even systemic crises, which profoundly influence the economy. The connection between competition and risk taking is important enough to merit attention, and in addition it is not obvious what the relation between these two phenomena is, whether increased competition forces banks into more and more risky business or, alternatively, whether such behaviour is due to lack of competition so that bankers can force their attitudes towards risk upon depositors.

In this chapter, we shall review both the traditional aspects of competition, that is, the choice of interest rates by banks so as to attract as much profitable business as possible, and the other aspects which pertain to the role of banks in the economy as a whole. We begin with the textbook case of perfect competition, where banks take the interest rates as given and beyond their influence. Although totally unrealistic as a model of real financial intermediation, this model serves a good purpose in setting the stage for the subsequent discussions of less than perfect competition in one way or the other. Among the models of imperfect competition, we shall use the model of spatial competition in a circular city repeatedly, because this model is useful in allowing us to trace the effects of the individual decisions in a particularly simple way. Within this framework, we can get some insights into the relationship between competition and risk taking.

11.2 Banks in perfect competition

A perfectly competitive bank considers the loan rate r_L, the deposit rate r_D, and the interbank rate r as given and beyond its influence, and it then chooses the levels of loans L and deposits D so as to maximize profit

$$\pi(D, L) = r_L L + rC - r_D D - c(D, L), \tag{1}$$

where C is the net position of the bank in the interbank market, and $c(D, L)$ is the cost function of the bank (for managing D and L). The net position in the interbank market is found as the difference between available funds and funds used for loans; we assume that a fraction $0 < \alpha < 1$ of deposits must be kept as a liquid reserve, so

$$C = (1 - \alpha)D - L. \tag{2}$$

Inserting (2) into the profit function (1), the latter becomes

$$\pi(D, L) = (r_L - r)L + ((1 - \alpha)r - r_D)D - c(D, L),$$

where the two different lines of business of the bank have been separated in the expression of the profit. First-order conditions for a maximum are

$$\frac{\partial \pi}{\partial L} = r_L - r - c'_L = 0, \quad \frac{\partial \pi}{\partial D} = (1 - \alpha)r - r_D - c'_D = 0,$$

Box 11.1

A digression into monetary macroeconomics. We may apply this simple equilibrium model to a classical problem of macroeconomics, namely monetary policy and the so-called money multiplier. In its simplest version, the money multiplier describes the impact of a government bond issue on the amount of deposits held by the public. If bond issue is changed by $\triangle B$, then this leads to an immediate change in deposit of the same amount. However, this change in deposits allows the banks to expand credit by $(1 - \alpha)\triangle B$, giving once more a corresponding change in deposits, and so forth. Summing all the changes in D, we get

$$\triangle D = \triangle B\left(1 + (1 - \alpha) + (1 - \alpha)^2 + \cdots\right) = \frac{1}{\alpha}\triangle B.$$

The quantity $1/\alpha$, known as the money multiplier, thus expresses the magnifying effect of the private banking sector on government monetary policy; for reasonable values of α, it is considerably larger than 1.

Returning to our model, we may begin by investigating how the interbank rate r reacts to a change in B. Inserting from (4) and (5) (see p. 218) into (5), and also inserting the expressions derived for r_L and r_D, we get

$$S(r(1 - \alpha) - c'_D) - \frac{I(r + c'_L)}{1 - \alpha} - B = 0,$$

Box 11.1 CONTINUED

which determines r as an implicit function of B. By the implicit function theorem, we have

$$\frac{dr}{dB} = \frac{1}{(1-\alpha)S' - \dfrac{I'}{1-\alpha}}.$$

Using (5), we then get that

$$\frac{\partial D}{\partial B} = (1-\alpha)S'\frac{dr}{dB} - 1 = \frac{(1-\alpha)S'}{(1-\alpha)S' - \dfrac{I'}{1-\alpha}} - 1 = \frac{1}{\dfrac{(1-\alpha)^2 S'}{I'} - 1}. \tag{3}$$

It is seen that under the standard assumptions that $S' > 0$, $I' < 0$, we get that $\frac{\partial D}{\partial B} < 0$, which is what should be expected. However, the numerical value of this partial derivative, which is the version of the money multiplier at force in the present model, differs much from that of the simple derivation above: Indeed, we have that

$$\left|\frac{\partial D}{\partial B}\right| < 1$$

because the numerical value of the denominator in the last expression in (3) is > 1. Thus, the magnifying effects have disappeared, having been soaked up by changes in the interest rates in the market.

---

which are recognized as the well-known conditions that price should equal marginal cost (funding cost plus management). The optimal values of L and D are denoted $L(r_L, r_D, r)$ and $D(r_L, r_D, r)$ to emphasize their dependence on the market rates r_L, r_D, r.

To proceed further, we also need to consider the other side of the market, that is, the demand for loans and for offering deposits to banks. Assume that there are n banks, indexed by $j = 1, \ldots, n$, and that the demand for loans facing the banking sector is derived from firms' investment behaviour, given by an investment function $I(r_L)$, so in equilibrium we have

$$I(r_L) = \sum_{j=1}^{n} L_j(r_L, r_D, r). \tag{4}$$

Similarly, we have that the savings of households, assumed to depend on the deposit rate r_D, is met in equilibrium by the choices of deposit by banks *and* the bond issuance B of the government,

$$S(r_D) = B + \sum_{j=1}^{n} D_j(r_L, r_D, r). \tag{5}$$

Finally, the interbank market of our small economy must be balanced,

$$\sum_{j=1}^{n} L_j(r_L, r_D, r) = (1 - \alpha) \sum_{j=1}^{n} D_j(r_L, r_D, r). \tag{6}$$

The three equations together give us the equilibrium values of r_L, r_D and r (provided that an equilibrium exists, which it does under standard assumptions).

11.3 The Monti-Klein model of a monopolistic bank

The model of the banking industry as working under conditions of perfect competition, such as presented in the previous section, lacks realism given that in most countries there are only a few banks, and moreover there are rather large costs connected with establishing new ones. Consequently, another approach is called for, and it would seem natural to begin at the opposite extreme with the case of a single bank, which can act as a monopolist, and then to allow for competitors, transforming the monopoly into an oligopoly of banks.

The basic model of the monopolistic bank was introduced by Monti [1972] and Klein [1971]. The model, together with its extension to oligopolistic banking considered later in this section, is known as the Monti-Klein model.

When the bank enjoys a monopoly in the market, the loan and deposit rates that will prevail depend only on the choices L and D by this bank, and the bank takes this dependency into account when maximizing profit

$$\pi(D, L) = (r_L(L) - r)L + ((1 - \alpha)r - r_D(D))D - c(D, L). \tag{7}$$

The first-order conditions for a maximum now become

$$\frac{\partial \pi}{\partial L} = r'_L L + r_L - r - c'_L = 0,$$

$$\frac{\partial \pi}{\partial D} = -r'_D D + (1 - \alpha)r - r_D - c'_D = 0,$$

which again are well known as the conditions that marginal revenue should equal marginal cost. The first-order conditions may also be expressed in terms of *Lerner indices*: We have

$$\frac{r_L - (r + c'_L)}{r_L} = -\frac{r'_L L}{r_L} = \frac{1}{-\dfrac{r_L}{r'_L L}} = \frac{1}{\varepsilon_L}, \tag{8}$$

where we have introduced the loan elasticity ε_L defined by

$$\varepsilon_L = -\frac{L'}{\dfrac{L}{r_L}}$$

and used that the derivative L' of L considered as a function of r_L equals $1/r'_L$. Alternatively, we may also express the first-order condition in the loan business using the Amoroso-Robinson formula

$$r_L = \frac{r + c'_L}{1 - \dfrac{1}{\varepsilon_L}}.$$

Similarly, we have the Lerner index expression for the deposit rate

$$\frac{r(1 - \alpha) - r_D - c'_D}{r_D} = \frac{1}{\varepsilon_D}, \tag{9}$$

with $\varepsilon_D = r_D D'/D$ the elasticity of deposits with respect to the deposit rate, or alternatively,

$$r_D = \frac{(1 - \alpha)r - c'_D}{1 + \dfrac{1}{\varepsilon_D}}.$$

The Monti-Klein model may be used for many purposes, and we shall see several applications of the model in the chapters to follow. At this point, we restrict ourselves to a rather simple case, namely that of a *bank levy*. In the wake of the government interventions to restore the financial markets after the crisis in 2007–8, several countries (among them Germany, the United Kingdom, France, Sweden and Hungary) introduced new ways of taxing banks. The taxes are argued to discourage too much risk taking, and they may be levied on short-term funding (as in the United Kingdom and Germany) or on risk-weighted assets (France). In Hungary, the tax is levied on assets and is higher for large than for small banks.

For our purposes, we shall assume that the tax is collected as a fixed percentage t of the loans L. This changes expression (7) for the profit of the bank to

$$\pi(D, L) = (r_L(L) - (r + t))L + ((1 - \alpha)r - r_D(D))D - c(D, L), \tag{10}$$

and the first-order condition with respect to L reduces to

$$\frac{r_L - \left(r + t + c'_L\right)}{r_L} = \frac{1}{\varepsilon_L}, \tag{11}$$

whereas the second equation in (9) remains unchanged (but the derivatives are taken in the new maximum). Assuming that the loan elasticity is approximately constant, it is seen that the Lerner index remains unchanged, so the tax is shifted to the borrowers. The depositors are only indirectly affected, at least as long as marginal cost c'_D is independent of L. This is the case when the cost function $c(D, L)$ is *separable*, having the form $c(D, L) = c_D(D) + c_L(L)$. Assuming constant marginal costs $c'_D = \gamma_D$, $c'_L = \gamma_L$, it is seen that the profit maximization in the Monti-Klein model separates into two separate problems, determined with loan and deposit rates, respectively, and an interference with one of these has no effect on the rates determined in the other one.

The model is easily extended to the case of a few banks, constituting an *oligopoly*, at least if we assume that banks choose quantities. If there are N banks, all having the same cost function $c(D, L)$, then the profit of the ith bank is

$$\pi_i(D, L) = (r_L(L) - r)L_i + ((1 - \alpha)r - r_D(D))D_i - c(D_i, L_i), \qquad (12)$$

with $L = \sum_{i=1}^{N} L_i$, $D = \sum_{i=1}^{N} D_i$, and the first-order conditions become

$$\frac{\partial \pi}{\partial L} = r'_L L_i + r_L - r - c'_L = 0,$$

$$\frac{\partial \pi}{\partial D} = -r'_D D_i + (1 - \alpha)r - r_D - c'_D = 0.$$

If $L_1 = \cdots = L_N$ and $D_1 = \cdots = D_N$, we get the expressions

$$\frac{r_L - \left(r + c'_L\right)}{r_L} = \frac{1}{N\varepsilon_L},$$
$$\frac{r(1 - \alpha) - r_D - c'_D}{r_D} = \frac{1}{N\varepsilon_D}, \qquad (13)$$

for the Lerner indices, showing that the loan and deposit rates move towards marginal cost as the number of competitors increases.

The assumption that banks choose the amounts of loans and deposits rather than the loan and demand rates is not a very realistic one, but modelling the case where banks choose rates and compete for loans and deposits is much less tractable because in this case the competition for deposits and loans are interconnected: Deposits are needed in order to fund the loans, and if a competitor is forced out of the deposit market, it must leave the loan market as well. This creates complications which make it difficult to use this approach in applications.

11.4 Monopolistic competition in the loan market

11.4.1 A circular city model of banking

In the preceding chapters, we have repeatedly considered situations where zero expected profits were among the conditions for equilibrium. The most natural market structure for this would be that of *monopolistic competition*, where each unit enjoys some degree of local monopoly but where the free entry of new competitors precludes that profits can grow to any significant level.

In order to rationalize the local monopoly power enjoyed by each of the firms in monopolistic competition, one has to introduce some exogenous condition by which the firms may be differentiated, and a standard one is *location*, which may be taken not in the strict sense of geographical distance but can also be interpreted as having to do with an underlying quality variable which will not be further specified. The following model is an adaptation of the much used model of Salop [1979], cf. also Freixas and Rochet [2008].

In the Salop circular city model, we assume that n firms, and in our case banks, are situated on a circle of total length 1, such that the distance between each of them is the same, namely $1/n$. The banks are taking deposits from the public who is evenly spread over the circle, and each bank customer incurs transportation cost of t per unit of distance travelled to the bank. This transportation cost should not be considered literally as a cost of carrying banknotes; rather, it should be seen as an abstract expression of customer preferences for the individual banks. There is a fixed cost of keeping a bank to the amount of f.

We begin the analysis by deriving society's optimum. The cost of providing deposit services to the public has two parts, namely (a) travel cost for the individual, which depends on the distance to the nearest bank, and (b) the fixed cost of the bank, depending linearly on the number n of banks.

For the travel cost, we have that the maximal distance to any bank will be $1/2n$, and the total cost of serving the customers of any given bank is therefore

$$2 \int_0^{\frac{1}{2n}} tx\,dx = \frac{t}{4n^2}.$$

The total cost to society must then be n times this quantity plus the fixed cost nf, resulting in a cost of

$$C = \frac{t}{4n} + nf.$$

We can now find first-order conditions for a minimum by differentiating with respect to n (conveniently ignoring that n is a discrete variable), and we get

$$\frac{dC}{dn} = -\frac{t}{4n^2} + f = 0$$

with solution

$$n^* = \frac{1}{2}\sqrt{\frac{t}{f}},$$

showing – as was to be expected – that the optimal number of banks varies positively with travel cost and negatively with the fixed cost of running a bank.

We now compare this social optimum to the solution found in a market with monopolistic competition and free entry. Due to the travel cost, each bank has a local monopoly, because customers close to the bank will have to pay for longer travel if they are served by a competitor. More specifically, if the loan rate of a bank is r_D and that of all competitors r_D' (we shall see later that we may restrict our attention to the case where all other banks choose the same rate), then the marginal customer who is indifferent between the given bank and the closest competitor is situated at x defined by

$$r_D - tx = r'_D - t\left(\frac{1}{n} - x\right), \tag{14}$$

with solution

$$x = \frac{1}{2n} + \frac{r_D - r'_D}{2t}. \tag{15}$$

By symmetry, the bank has all customers between $-x$ and x, so its demand is given by

$$D = \frac{1}{n} + \frac{\left(r - r'_D\right) - (r - r_D)}{t}.$$

Here we have added and subtracted the interbank rate r in the numerator of the second fraction. In this version, it looks like an ordinary demand function for a monopolist, selling a good (namely the service of holding deposits) and a price (the difference between what is paid to the depositor and what can be obtained in the interbank market). Because this demand function is linear, we can find the optimal price as one half of the price which deters demand, so

$$r - r_D = \frac{1}{2}\left[\frac{t}{n} + \left(r - r'_D\right)\right]. \tag{16}$$

Now, in a symmetric equilibrium the interest rates of all banks must be equal. Setting $r'_D = r_D$ in the equation above and solving, we finally get that

$$r_D = r - \frac{t}{n}. \tag{17}$$

The result is not surprising, given that in models of monopolistic competition based on distance to competitors, the mark-up which can be obtained by any firm is determined by the travel cost.

We may now add the condition that new banks enter as long as the profit earned by any bank, which is

$$\frac{1}{n}\frac{t}{n} - f = \frac{t}{n^2} - f,$$

is positive. Setting the above expression equal to 0 and solving for n finally gives that

$$n^0 = \sqrt{\frac{t}{f}}.$$

We thus have that the number of banks sustained by the market equilibrium is bigger than what is socially optimal, again a well-known conclusion of the Salop model (of which the present one is just a special case).

The suboptimality of the market solution may be remedied in various ways, the classical one being the imposition of a tax on the banks, thereby increasing the fixed cost f. We shall not pursue this matter further because it is a classical issue in industrial organization, but of secondary importance in our case; the problems of having too many banks would rather be considered as related to excessive risk taking than to fixed cost, and it would therefore be better to include this aspect explicitly.

We now move from the somewhat artificial situation of a bank with the only business of taking deposits to the more normal case where the bank has both deposits and loans. For this we assume that each individual in the society considered not only wants to deposit 1 unit of money but also wants to borrow the amount L, which is assumed to be < 1. It may seem strange at first glance that the individual wants to deposit 1 and then borrow L, presumably at a higher interest rate, but we have already encountered cases where this may be a rational behaviour, and therefore we shall not be detained by this detail.

If each individual can choose the bank for deposits and for loans independently, then we are dealing with two independent markets, namely the deposit market already considered and the loans market. In the latter, the limit between a bank with loan rate r_L and a neighbouring one with loan rate r'_L will be given, as before, by

$$r_L L + t_L x = r'_L L + t_L \left(\frac{1}{n} - x \right),$$

(where we have used t_L for transport cost in the loan business, which may differ from that of deposit business, to be denoted t_D from now on) with solution

$$x = \frac{1}{2n} + \frac{\left(r'_L - r_L \right) L}{2 t_L},$$

and total demand for loans is then

$$L \left(\frac{1}{n} + \frac{\left(r'_L - r_L \right) L}{t_L} \right).$$

Using the formula for monopoly pricing with linear demand and constant unit costs (which in the loan business is r, the funding rate of interest), we get the profit maximizing loan rate

$$r_L = \frac{1}{2} \left(r + \frac{t_L}{nL} + r'_L \right),$$

and the symmetric equilibrium price then becomes

$$r_L = r + \frac{t_L}{nL}. \tag{18}$$

We notice that profits are $\frac{t_D}{n^2}$ in the deposit business and $\frac{t_L}{n^2}$ in loan business.

Suppose now that a policy of *deposit rate regulation* is to be implemented, keeping deposit rates low with the purpose of keeping the cost of funding the loans as low as possible. We check the simple case, where r_D is set to 0, so no interest can be paid on deposits. What happens follows rather easily from the above analysis: Because loan and deposit businesses are independent, the loan business remains unchanged, with the same loan rate as before. The deposit business becomes more profitable for the banks, receiving now the deposits without paying interest. Each bank therefore earns $\frac{r}{n}$ on deposits and (as before) $\frac{t_L}{n^2}$ on loans. Thus, the policy has been a failure in the sense that it did not lead to a lowering of loan rates; it did result in higher profits for the banks, but this was not a declared purpose of the policy.

Things change, however, if we allow contracts whereby banks refuse to offer loans to individuals who do not place their deposits in this bank. In this case, the two types of business reduce to a single one. The method of pricing the loans is unchanged, but now we must take into account that the transportation cost is $t_D + t_L$ (because the customer must 'carry' both deposits and loans) and that the basic funding cost of the bank has to be reduced by the income derived from receiving deposits for free. In total, this means that the symmetric equilibrium loan rate will be

$$r_L^* = \left(r - \frac{r}{L}\right) + \frac{t_D + t_L}{nL},$$

which can be reformulated as

$$r_L^* = \left(r + \frac{t_L}{nL}\right) - \frac{1}{L}\left(r - \frac{t_D}{n}\right).$$

The second version has the advantage that it can be compared immediately with the solution obtained with no deposit rate regulation – the first bracket is the standard equilibrium loan rate r_L, and because r_L^* is obtained after subtracting something which is non-negative, we have that $r_L^* < r_L$.

The result – that one has to allow contracts where the banks tying deposit and loan activities of the individual together are useful if deposit rate regulation is to have any impact – is remarkable, in particular because this type of contract is usually frowned upon by competition authorities as an unacceptable restriction of free competition.

11.4.2 A circular city model with endogenous fixed costs

Although the introduction of fixed costs solves the problem of determining the equilibrium number of competing banks, it poses some new questions. In particular, the usual explanation of fixed cost, based on the need for machinery, buildings, etc., seems somewhat far-fetched when dealing with financial intermediation. In particular, it does not seem obvious that setting up a bank would necessarily be connected with large costs. It would be preferable to have an explanation of the fixed costs which comes from the nature of the business considered. We outline such an explanation, inspired by Dell'Ariccia [2001].

There are two periods in our model, $t = 0, 1$, and no discounting. In each period, a large number, normalized to 1, of new borrowers enters the loan market, wanting a loan L. At $t = 1$, there are both new borrowers and borrowers who were also present at $t = 0$.

All borrowers are either of type G (good), paying back at the end of the period with probability 1, or B (bad), paying back with probability 0. The bank cannot observe the type of a new borrower, but at $t = 1$ it can identify the borrowers revealed to be G or B in the first period. The bank will reject credit at $t = 1$ to borrowers whom they identify as old borrowers of type B. As before, borrowers and n banks are evenly distributed on the circle.

At $t = 0$, the loan contracts to be made by each of the n banks are such that the loan is renewed automatically if the borrower is G and terminated otherwise. The price paid for this contract will be r^0, paid both at the end of period 0 and period 1 by the good borrowers, and it is determined as

$$r^0 = r + \frac{(1 - \pi)}{2\pi}(1 + r)L + \frac{t_L}{nL}. \tag{19}$$

Here the middle term on the right-hand side is new: We assume that banks maximize expected profits, which for each customer served is $2\pi(r^0 - r) - (1 - \pi)(1 + r)L$, so that $\frac{(1-\pi)}{2\pi}(1 + r)L$ can be considered as a cost connected with the possibility that the borrower turns out to be B.

For the loan rate r^1, the equilibrium value is similarly found to be

$$r^1 = r + \frac{(1 - \pi)}{\pi}(1 + r)L + \frac{t_L}{nL}. \tag{20}$$

The profit obtained over two periods by each bank consist of profit from period 0, which by (19) amounts to

$$\frac{L}{n}\left\{\pi\left[\frac{1 - \pi}{\pi}L(1 + r) + \frac{2t_L}{nL}\right] - (1 - \pi)L(1 + r)\right\} = \frac{2\pi t_L}{n^2},$$

and profit from the market for new borrowers in period 1, with the loan rate given in (20) is

$$\frac{L}{n}\left\{\pi\left[\frac{1 - \pi}{\pi}L(1 + r) + \frac{t_L}{nL}\right] - (1 - \pi)L(1 + r)\right\} = \frac{\pi t_L}{n^2};$$

from this must be deducted the loss at $t = 1$ arising from old borrowers of type B, who turn to banks other than those close to them, amounting to $\frac{L}{n}(1 - \pi)L(1 + r)$. Summing, we get that a profit of

$$\frac{3\pi t_L}{n^2} - (1 - \pi)(1 + r)\frac{L^2}{n}.$$

At this point we may invoke a zero-profit condition which gives us a solution for n, namely

$$n = 3\frac{\pi}{1 - \pi}\frac{t_L}{1 + r}.$$

Thus the zero-profit condition determines the number of banks in the market without a need for a fixed cost. Alternatively, the result may be seen as an explanation of the presence of fixed costs in the banking sector. The economic explanation of the result is that each bank induces an externality on the other banks by sending the bad period 0 borrowers to the competitors, and the loss incurred by this externality depends on the number of banks in another way than the usual earnings. The model might be made more realistic by putting it into an overlapping generations framework, but the basic working of the economic mechanisms will be the same.

11.5 Risk taking and competition

The relationship between competition and risk taking in the banking sector is a recurrent theme in the public debate, yet a systematical theoretical investigation of this relationship has begun only relatively recently. The following model is based on that of Matutes and Vives [1996], which was constructed for the study of deposit insurance, but competition for depositors enters into its basic structure.

11.5.1 Risk taking and franchise value

We assume that banks can choose the level of riskiness of their loan portfolios, in the sense that the expected value of the return on loans has a constant value μ, whereas their dispersion on this mean value increases with a parameter σ, so that $\mathsf{E}[h(\tilde{r}_L)|\sigma]$ increases with σ for any convex function h (this means that loans are ordered in accordance with second-order stochastic dominance, cf. our discussion in Chapter 6). The bank has a loan portfolio L, and it has obligations D which should be paid an interest rate $r_D(\sigma)$, so the funding rate depends on the riskiness of the bank's loan portfolio. For simplicity, we assume that there is no equity, so $L = D$, and the bank fails when $r_L < r_D(\sigma)$. Let $p(\sigma)$ be the probability of success. In the simplest possible setting, this probability would be given by $p(\sigma) = \mathsf{P}\{\tilde{r}_L > r_D(\sigma)\}$, but in the computations below we do not need to specify how this probability is derived, and this will turn out to be an advantage when we turn to applications.

In the case of perfect information (of depositors), the deposit rate $r_D(\sigma)$ must ensure that depositors on average get at least as much as they would obtain on alternative investments. In the case of a failure, it is assumed that depositors take over the bank and get r_L, so the funding condition is

$$\mathsf{E}[\min\{\tilde{r}_L, r_D(\sigma)|\sigma] \geq 1$$

(where we have assumed no discounting). The expected profit of the bank given σ is

$$\Pi(\sigma) = D\,\mathsf{E}[\max\{0, \tilde{r}_L - r_D(\sigma)\}\,|\sigma],$$

and it will choose the riskiness parameter σ so as to maximize $\Pi(\sigma) + p(\sigma)V$, where V is the present value of future profits. These profits can be obtained only if the bank survives, known in the literature as the *franchise* or *charter value* of the bank, an asset which is lost if the bank must close down due to insolvency.

Using that $\max\{0, r_L - r_D\} + \min\{r_L, r_D\} = r_L$, we get that

$$\Pi(\sigma) + D = \mathsf{E}[\tilde{r}_L|\sigma]D = \mu D,$$

so $\Pi(\sigma) = (\mu - 1)D$ and consequently is independent of σ. It tells us that for $V > 0$, the risk of losing future profits will make the bank choose the minimal riskiness for its loans.

This situation changes, however, once we allow for incomplete information, so r_D is set by depositors not knowing σ. In this case, the depositors will expect the banks to choose profit-maximizing levels of riskiness, say $\hat{\sigma}$, so they demand a deposit rate $r_D(\hat{\sigma})$, giving them zero expected return. The banks choose a riskiness level σ^* which solves

$$\max_{\sigma}\{\Pi(\sigma) + p(\sigma)V\}, \tag{21}$$

and in equilibrium we demand that depositor expectations are confirmed by the actual choices, so $\hat{\sigma} = \sigma^*$.

In this new situation, the profit of the bank takes the form

$$\Pi(\sigma) = D\,\mathsf{E}[\max\{0, \tilde{r}_L - r_D(\hat{\sigma})\}|\sigma],$$

whereby $\max\{0, \tilde{r}_L - r_D(\hat{\sigma})\}$ is a convex function of r_L. By (second-order) stochastic dominance, $\Pi(\sigma)$ becomes an increasing function of σ. Therefore, there is now a trade-off between short-term and long-term profits, and the equilibrium level of riskiness will reflect this balancing of short- and long-term effects of risk taking.

Although the above model obviously exhibits some of the problems contained with risk taking in banks, the competition aspects are less clear. The level of competitiveness in the banking industry enters the model indirectly through the variable V. If the competition among banks is active, we should expect V to be relatively small because large profits in the banking sector would be eroded either by more aggressive pricing policies or by entry. On the other hand, lack of competition might be considered as a precondition for maintaining a high franchise value.

11.5.2 Risk taking, franchise value and regulation

It might be argued against the Matutes-Vives model that competition enters in a rather rudimentary way, and also we miss a method of regulating the risk-taking behaviour. The following model, adapted from Repullo [2002], takes account of these features while still retaining the general approach.

We assume that there are two periods of time and a number n of banks taking deposits from the general public and investing them in particular assets. There are only two such assets, namely a *safe* one, yielding the payoff α, and a risky investment giving payoff γ in the case of success, which occurs with probability π, and 0 otherwise. Shareholders demand a payoff $\rho > \alpha$, so the banks must use deposits for which they pay a deposit rate smaller than α. In addition, there is a regulation of banks according to which banks must use a fraction k of deposits as equity, which will be lost in the case of a bank failure.

It is assumed that the competitive situation of the banks can be described as in the circular city model with transportation cost t, cf. Section 11.4 above. In this model, there is a fixed number of depositors, normalized to 1.

Safe asset only. Suppose first that *only the safe asset* is available. Because the cost of taking 1 unit of deposits is $(\rho - \alpha)k$ (k units of equity must be set aside, and because equity costs ρ and earns only α, this gives rise to a cost of $\delta_S = \rho - \alpha$ per unit of equity), the symmetric equilibrium deposit rate can be found using (17) as

$$r_S(k) = \alpha - \delta_S k - \frac{t}{n}. \tag{22}$$

With this equilibrium rate, the profit earned per unit of deposits is

$$-k + \frac{1}{\rho}\left(\frac{t}{n} + \delta_S k + \alpha k\right) = -k + \frac{1}{\rho}\left(\frac{t}{n} + \rho k\right) = \frac{1}{\rho}\frac{t}{n}.$$

The bank also has the option of choosing a fraction of equity $< k$, but given the high rates on equity, this is not optimal. We can now find the franchise value V_S of the bank when only the safe asset is available. Because each bank earns $1/n$ of the total profit, we have that the franchise value must satisfy the equation

$$V_S = \frac{1}{\rho}\left(\frac{t}{n^2} + V_S\right),$$

from which we get that

$$V_S = \frac{t}{(\rho - 1)n^2}.$$

In particular, the franchise value does not depend on k (because a change in k will be offset by a change in the equilibrium deposit rate $r_S(k)$).

Risky asset only. Now we may repeat this analysis, assuming that all banks use *only the risky asset*. To find the cost to the bank of capital regulation, we notice that because equity is risky, the payoff ρ will be demanded only in the case of success, so the cost to the bank of 1 unit of equity is

$$\delta_R = \frac{1}{\pi}(\rho - \pi\gamma) = \frac{\rho}{\pi} - \gamma.$$

We now get a symmetric equilibrium deposit rate

$$r_R(k) = \gamma - \frac{t}{n} - \delta_R k. \tag{23}$$

Proceeding as before, we find the franchise value in this new situation from

$$V_R = \frac{\pi}{\rho}\left(\frac{t}{n^2} + V_R\right),$$

giving

$$V_R = \frac{\pi t}{(\rho - \pi)n^2}.$$

Both risky and safe assets. Having considered now the cases where only safe or only risky investments were possible, we consider the full model with both investments available, where, however, we restrict ourselves (as previously) to symmetric equilibria, where either all banks choose the safe investment or all the risky investment. We then get a safe or a risky equilibrium, but each must satisfy the additional condition that no bank would have an incentive to change investment, possibly accompanied with a change in the deposit rate. In the *safe equilibrium*, this means that the present value of a deviation should not exceed the franchise value in the safe equilibrium,

$$\max_r \left\{ -kD(r, r_S(k)) + \frac{\pi}{\rho}\left(\gamma - r_j + \gamma k\right) D\left(r, r_S(k)\right) + \frac{\pi}{\rho} V_S \right\} \le V_S, \qquad (24)$$

where the notation $D(r, r')$ is used for the fraction of the depositors using the bank with deposit rate r, given that the other banks have rate r'. Similarly, the risky equilibrium should also satisfy the condition

$$\max_r \left\{ -kD(r, r_R(k)) + \frac{1}{\rho}\left(\alpha - r_j + \alpha k\right) D\left(r, r_R(k)\right) + \frac{1}{\rho} V_R \right\} \le V_R, \qquad (25)$$

To find conditions for such equilibria to exist, we introduce the quantity

$$m(k) = \frac{1}{2}[\gamma - \alpha - (\delta_R - \delta_S)k]. \qquad (26)$$

We can then state the following proposition.

PROPOSITION 1: *If $\frac{t}{n} \ge m(k)$, then there is a safe equilibrium, and if $\frac{t}{n} \le m(k)$, there is a risky equilibrium.*

PROOF: Suppose that all banks except one has chosen the deposit rate $r_S(k)$ and the safe investment, and assume that one bank contemplates a change to the risky investment. To find the optimal value of r in (24), we repeat steps (14), (15) and (16) (where the interbank rate has been replaced by the repayment rate $\gamma - \delta_R k$ of the risky investment) to get the expression

$$\gamma - \delta_R k - r = \frac{1}{2}\left(\gamma - \delta_R k - r_S(k) + \frac{t}{n}\right), \qquad (27)$$

from which we get, after inserting (22), that the mark-up at the optimal deposit rate is

$$\gamma - \delta_R k - r = \frac{(\gamma - \delta_R k) - (\alpha - \delta_S k)}{2} = m(k). \qquad (28)$$

In the symmetric situation where all choose $r_S(k)$, the mark-up is t/n, and if this mark-up is at least as large as $m(k)$, then for a deviation to be advantageous we need that the market share of the deviating bank must increase. However, rearranging (28), we get that the optimal deposit rate is

$$r = \frac{1}{2}(\alpha - \delta_S k) + \frac{1}{2}(\gamma - \delta_R k) \leq \alpha - \delta_R k - \frac{t}{n} = r_S(k),$$

so the deposit rate is no smaller than that of the competitors, and therefore the market share is at best unchanged. We conclude that a deviation is not advantageous.

Suppose next that t/n is smaller than $m(k)$ and all banks have chosen the risky deposit rate $r_R(k)$, but one bank deviates, choosing the safe investment and the optimal deposit rate r' corresponding to this choice. Reasoning as above, we obtain that mark-up at this deposit rate is

$$\alpha - \delta_S k - r' = \frac{1}{2}\left(\alpha - \delta_S k - r_R(k) + \frac{t}{n}\right) = \frac{1}{2}(\alpha - \gamma - (\delta_S - \delta_R)) + \frac{t}{n} = \frac{t}{n} - m(k) \leq 0, \quad (29)$$

so at best the bank is losing money after the deviation. □

The result of Proposition 1 can be used by a regulator wanting the banks to choose the safe rather than the risky investment. Indeed, because $m(k)$ is linearly decreasing in k, we get that if the number of banks is large and the mark-up t/n small, then a risky equilibrium might be expected, but increasing k sufficiently will produce that the mark-up exceeds $m(k)$, thereby making possible a safe equilibrium. Thus, capital regulation can be used to counteract the tendency of increased competition towards greater riskiness in the banking sector.

11.5.3 A model with one big and many small banks

Before being able to conclude something about riskiness of big versus small banks, we have to specify in which sense we are speaking of 'risk'. When discussing the possible failure of a bank – as we shall do at length in chapters to follow – the usual interpretation of risk is as probability of failure. However, the standard way in which economic theory treats risk is *not* this one. Indeed, risk matters here only not in connection with probability of failure, and through this for expected payoff, but rather as a general phenomenon connected with dispersion of future uncertain incomes. In this case, if we return to the classical way of looking at risk – as connected with variance rather than with means, then a slightly different picture emerges.

We shall once again use a version of the circular city model to consider this problem in more detail. We assume now that there are $N/2$ small banks and a single large one. However, the large one has $N/2$ branches so that each branch has a small bank as nearest neighbor both to the right and to the left. The customers are, as usual, evenly spread over the circle, and they prefer the closest bank, measured by the transport cost t.

We assume that the customers have another perceived cost related to the risk of placing their deposits with the bank, namely a monetary equivalent of risk $y(\sigma)$, depending on the standard deviation of the repayment to the depositor.

We are interested in symmetric equilibria, where all the small banks have chosen the same deposit rate r_s. As previously, the deposit rates r_s, r_b of the small and the large banks can be found by looking at a customer at distance x from a small bank (and $\frac{1}{n} - x$ from a branch of the large bank). Assuming that risk aversion of depositors is expressed by a fixed deduction f_s, f_b from the payoff obtained when depositing in a small or a large bank, respectively, we can determine x by

$$r_s - tx - f_s = r_b^* - t(1 - x) - f_b,$$

where r_b^* is the given deposit rate in the large bank, from which we get that

$$x = \frac{r_s - r_b^* - (f_s - f_b) + t}{2t},$$

and demand for deposits with the small bank is

$$D_s = 2x = \frac{r_s - r_b^* - (f_s - f_b) + t}{t}.$$

We can then find the profit maximizing value of r_s (given r_b^*, f_s, f_b). Here it is assumed that (small as well as big) banks are risk neutral and that deposits are invested in a number of investment projects whose yields are identically and independently distributed with mean payoff y. Reasoning as in previous sections, we find the profit maximizing price from

$$y - r_s^* = \frac{1}{2}\left(r - r_b^* - (f_s - f_b) + t\right). \tag{30}$$

For the large bank, we can similarly derive optimal deposit rate given that of the small banks. The demand is

$$D_b = \frac{N}{2t}\left(r_b - r_s^* - (f_b - f_s) + t\right),$$

and optimal deposit rate can be found from

$$y - r_b^* = \frac{1}{2}\left(r - r_s^* - (f_b - f_s) + t\right). \tag{31}$$

Thus, for given f_s and f_b, and for given y, the yield of the investment, (30) and (31) give the interest rates and indirectly the market shares of the two types of bank. Clearly, the equilibrium is no longer symmetric when f_s and f_b differ.

We now assume that the risk deductions f_s and f_b are not fixed, but depend on the investment policy of the bank. More specifically, we assume that banks can choose different investments, thereby achieving larger y, but that the trade-off between payoff and risk is specified by an increasing function h, so

$$f_s = h(y_s), \quad f_b = h(y_b)$$

when banks choose payoff rates y_s and y_b. The derivative of h is assumed to be increasing in y, expressing the fact that greater payoff can only be achieved by a considerable increase in riskiness.

Given that payoffs can be chosen by the bank, the profits of the bank will be a function of y, the investment payoff. First-order conditions for a maximum for the small bank, given the payoff and interest rate of the small bank, and taking into account that f_s and r_s^* are functions of y, can be reduced to

$$D_s = h'(y_s)\left[\frac{D_s}{2} + \frac{y_s - r_s^*}{2t}\right]. \tag{32}$$

The increase in revenue due to an increase in investment payoff is to the left, whereas on the right-hand side, we have the decrease in revenue coming from change in the risk parameter and the adjustment to this change of the deposit rate.

For the large bank, we get the corresponding expression

$$D_b = h'(y_b)\left[\frac{D_b}{2} + \frac{y_b - r_b^*}{2t}\right]. \tag{33}$$

Comparing the expressions (32) and (33) and assuming that the equilibrium interest rent margin is not too different between banks, because D_b is roughly $N/2$ times D_s, we expect $h'(y_b)$ to be greater than $h'(y_s)$. Thus, we have a case where small banks are less risky than large banks, being hurt more than the large bank by the increase in deposit rates which is triggered by a rise in payoff.

11.5.4 Risk and competition with insured depositors

If the depositors are insured against losses due to bank failures, then the attitudes towards risk of the depositors will be irrelevant for their choice of bank, so competition among banks will be related to other aspects of their loan portfolios, as illustrated in the model by Allen and Gale [2000]. We have here n banks which are each choosing among investment prospects, characterized by a risk parameter s defined in an interval $[0, \bar{s}]$. The investment prospect with risk parameter s yields a profit s with probability $p(s)$ and 0 with probability $1 - p(s)$, where $p : \mathbb{R} \to [0, 1]$ satisfies $p(0) = 1$ (so the store-of-value investment has no risk but yields no profit), $p(\bar{s}) = 0$ and $p(\cdot)$ is a decreasing and concave function of s. The investment of type s can be carried out at arbitrary scale.

On the funding side, we assume that banks face an increasing supply curve, so that the deposit rate (which is the same for all banks) r_D is an increasing function of total deposits $\sum_{i=1}^{n} D_i$. We assume that $r_D(0) \geq 0$ and that $r_D(\cdot)$ is increasing and convex. Deposits are insured, and banks pay for the insurance at a fixed rate α.

In a Nash equilibrium, the ith bank chooses a pair (s_i, D_i), consisting of a risk parameter s_i and a level of deposits D_i, so as to maximize expected profit

$$p(s_i)\left(s_i - r_D\left(D_i + \sum_{j \neq i} D_j\right) - \alpha\right)D_i.$$

Assuming symmetric and interior equilibrium with $s_i = s$, $D_i = D$, $i = 1, \ldots, n$, the first-order conditions for a maximum are

$$p'(s)(s - r_D(nD) - \alpha) + p(s) = 0,$$

$$s - r_D(nD) - r_D'(nD)D - \alpha = 0.$$

Let $Z = nD$ be the total amount of deposits. We may consider the first-order conditions as a two-dimensional function

$$F(s, Z, n) = \begin{pmatrix} F_1(s, Z, n) \\ F_2(s, Z, n) \end{pmatrix} = \begin{pmatrix} p'(s)(s - r_D(Z) - \alpha) + p(s) \\ s - r_D(Z) - r_D'(Z)\dfrac{Z}{n} - \alpha \end{pmatrix} = \begin{pmatrix} 0 \\ 0 \end{pmatrix},$$

from which s (and Z) are determined as functions of n. Let DF denote the Jacobian of F,

$$DF = \begin{pmatrix} \dfrac{\partial F_1}{\partial s} & \dfrac{\partial F_1}{\partial Z} \\ \dfrac{\partial F_2}{\partial s} & \dfrac{\partial F_2}{\partial Z} \end{pmatrix} = \begin{pmatrix} p''(s - r_D(Z) - \alpha) + 2p' & -p'r_D' \\ 1 & -r_D'\dfrac{n+1}{n} - r_D''\dfrac{Z}{n} \end{pmatrix}, \tag{34}$$

Because the determinant $|DF|$ of DF is > 0 under our assumptions, we can find $\dfrac{ds}{dn}$ using implicit function theorem (and Cramer's rule for inverting matrices) as

$$\frac{ds}{dn} = -\frac{1}{|DF|}\left(\frac{\partial F_2}{\partial Z}, -\frac{\partial F_1}{\partial Z}\right)\begin{pmatrix} \dfrac{\partial F_1}{\partial n} \\ \dfrac{\partial F_2}{\partial n} \end{pmatrix} = -\frac{1}{|DF|}\left(\frac{\partial F_2}{\partial Z}, -\frac{\partial F_1}{\partial Z}\right)\begin{pmatrix} 0 \\ \dfrac{r_D'Z}{n^2} \end{pmatrix} = -\frac{p'\left(r_D'\right)^2 Z}{|DF|n^2} > 0.$$

We have shown that the level of risk increases when the number n of banks gets large. However, as pointed out by Boyd and de Nicoló [2005], the model lacks symmetry in the sense that there is competition for deposits but the portfolio selection side is unaffected, because all banks choose their risk level directly. Suppose instead that the bank grants loans at a loan rate r_L to entrepreneurs choosing projects with risk level $s \in [0, \bar{s}]$. Entrepreneurs maximize expected profits $p(s)(s - r_L)$, giving first-order conditions

$$s + \frac{p(s)}{p'(s)} = r_L. \tag{35}$$

It is seen from (35) that s is an increasing function of r_L: Higher loan rates cause the entrepreneurs to select projects with higher risk.

We assume that the demand for loans can be described by a demand relationship of the form $r_L(L)$ with $r_L' < 0$, $r_L'' \leq 0$ (and $r_L(0) > r_D(0)$ so that the market has equilibrium).

A bank i offering loans at r_L to entrepreneurs choosing risk level s and selecting the amount D_i of deposits will have expected profits

$$p(s)\left[r_L\left(\sum_{j=1}^n L_j\right) - r_D\left(\sum_{j=1}^n D_j\right) - \alpha\right]D_i.$$

If banks are funded through deposits, we must have $\sum_{j=1}^n L_j = \sum_{j=1}^n D_j$, so (35) takes the form

$$s + \frac{p(s)}{p'(s)} = r_L\left(\sum_{j=1}^n L_i\right), \tag{36}$$

which defines $s\left(\sum_{j=1}^N D_j\right)$ as a function of total deposits. Because s is an increasing function of r_L which is decreasing in $\sum_{j=1}^n D_j = \sum_{j=1}^n L_j$, we get that s is decreasing as a function of $\sum_{j=1}^n D_j$.

Thus, the bank i selects D_i so as to maximize

$$p\left(s\left(\sum_{j=1}^n D_j\right)\right)\left[r_L\left(\sum_{j=1}^n D_j\right) - r_D\left(\sum_{j=1}^n D_j\right) - \alpha\right]D_i \tag{37}$$

subject to

$$s\left(\sum_{j=1}^n D_j\right) < \bar{s}.$$

Write $Z = \sum_{j=1}^n D_j$. The first-order conditions for maximizing (11) are

$$(r_L(Z) - r_D(Z) - \alpha)[p'(s(Z))s'(Z)D_i + p(s(Z))] + (r'_L(Z) - r'_D(Z))p(s(Z))D_i = 0. \tag{38}$$

In a symmetric equilibrium, these first-order conditions are the same for all banks, and adding them we get

$$r_L(Z) - r_D(Z) - \alpha = \frac{(r'_D(Z) - r'_L(Z))p(s(Z))Z}{p'(s(Z))s'(Z)Z + p(s(Z))n}. \tag{39}$$

Let $\Phi(Z, n)$ be the quantity on the right-hand side. Then $\Phi(Z, n) > 0$ and $\frac{\partial \Phi}{\partial n}(Z, n) < 0$.

The second-order conditions for profit maximization in the symmetric equilibrium can be found by differentiating (39) with respect to Z, and we get that

$$r'_L(Z) - r'_D(Z) - \frac{\partial \Phi}{\partial Z}(Z, n) < 0.$$

Now the implicit function theorem applied to (39) gives

$$\frac{\partial Z}{\partial n} = -\frac{\dfrac{\partial \Phi}{\partial n}(Z, n)}{r'_L(Z) - r'_D(Z) - \dfrac{\partial \Phi}{\partial n}(Z, n)} > 0.$$

We have now shown that total equilibrium deposits increase with the number of banks in the market. It remains only to connect this to what has already been derived about the riskiness of investments in (36). We then get that

$$\frac{ds}{dn} = \frac{\partial s}{\partial Z}\frac{\partial Z}{\partial n} < 0.$$

We conclude that risk taking, as measured by s, decreases when the number of banks in business gets larger, which is quite the opposite conclusion to what we saw in the first version of the model.

It may be argued that this second version of the model is more in line with the basic ideas behind its construction: Since riskiness is chosen in a way which does not directly depend on the number of banks (either because each bank faces the same choice or because it is chosen by entrepreneurs different from the banks) we should think of it as systemic risk which cannot be diversified away, possibly together with some individual idiosyncratic risk. Because the latter can be diversified away, total risk will be reduced to the systemic component when there are enough banks.

What can be inferred from this and previous models is that there is no obvious connection between the competitiveness of the banking sector and its attitudes towards risk. The impact of the market structure on the risks taken by the banks will depend on the finer details of the market, so the number of banks and their market size is not by itself a factor which will point in the direction of either more or less safety of the deposits of the bank.

11.6 Exercises

1. In a country with a highly concentrated bank sector, it has been customary that banks hold rather small liquid reserves and meet the ordinary daily withdrawals of their depositors by short-term credit with other banks or the central bank.

To make banks hold a larger cash reserve, the government introduces a tax on these short-term loans. It is argued that this tax will be paid only by banks that fail to hold reasonable reserves, and therefore it will not result in changed loan rates.

Give an assessment of this argument by sketching a model for loan and deposit interest rate determination in the market described above.

2. Suppose that there are N banks of equal size, each engaging in one project, lending 1 unit of money at $t = 0$ against a repayment $\tilde{R}$ at $t = 1$, which is normally distributed with mean $\rho > 1$ and variance σ^2. All projects are assumed to be independent. The bank funds its loans by deposits with an interest rate of 0, and bank regulation requires that equity should be $1/10$ of the balance at any date.

Find an expression for (a) the probability that the bank is solvent in the sense that it is able to repay its debt of 0.9 at $t = 1$, and (b) the probability that the bank satisfies the capital requirements at $t = 1$.

Suppose that the N banks are merged into a single bank which is now engaged in N independent projects. Find the probabilities (a) and (b) for this bank.

Assume that the regulatory authorities close and liquidate a bank which does not satisfy the capital requirement. Find expected profit per unit of invested capital in the small and the large bank. Comment upon the result.

3. The financial sector of a country is characterized by the presence of a large number of rather small banks. This has traditionally been considered as beneficial for the general public, but recently there has been growing concern among policy makers that the banking sector is working inefficiently and that consequently loan rates are too high. On the other hand, there is no evidence that the banks are earning high profits. Describe a theoretical model for a banking sector with many banks, where the sector works inefficiently even though there is intensive competition.

In order to facilitate credit conditions for the general business environment in the country, the banks are encouraged to negotiate a temporary freeze on their competition for depositors through the deposit interest rate. Will this improve the situation for potential borrowers, and if not, what should be done?

4. Consider a banking sector with a few large banks and several small banks. The large banks have a capital of about 50 times that of a small bank. To improve competition in the market, it has been made easy to set up new banks.

The banks are funded at a stable interest rate, and they are not competing for funding. There are two types of credit engagement for the banks: Type 1 has very low risk, but also its payoff is only slightly above what could be obtained in the interbank market, whereas Type 2 has high payoff, but also a considerable risk of default, with an expected payoff lower than that of the first type. A bank can make several independent engagements of each type; however, all engagements have a fixed size, and a small bank can engage in at most around four of the type.

What will happen in this market? Are the small banks more or less risky than the big banks?

Suppose now that each of the engagements of Type 2 can have arbitrary size, except that the prevailing regulation prevents a bank from having more than 25% of its balance in any single engagement. Will this change the situation and the riskiness of small and large banks?

5. In a country where the banking sector is almost monopolized, a new government enforces an upper limit on loan rates. The banks argue that this will lead to a lowering of deposit rates, causing a reduction in savings and scarcity of credit to businesses. Discuss this argument. What are the crucial assumptions behind it?

11.7 Comments

The first sections on price competition in the banking sector mainly draw on material from the early stages of development of the theory of banking, cf. e.g. Klein [1971], Baltensperger [1980], where the notions of uncertainty and asymmetric information do not yet play an important role. The exposition in the first part of the chapter largely follows that in Freixas and Rochet [2008].

The later sections of the chapter, dealing with the interplay of competition and risk taking, are based on more recent contributions, such as Boyd and de Nicoló [2005]; see also Martinez-Miera and Repullo [2010].

Chapter 12

Irregularities in the Banking Sector

12.1 Introduction

Banking is a field of business where the failure of a firm has repercussions in many areas of economic activity, and the default of a bank may seriously affect the everyday life of ordinary people, not only the shareholders but also the depositors. For that reason, a bank failure is typically an event which is commented upon in the media, and in this context it may happen that the management of the bank is suspected not only of incompetent but also sometimes even illegal behaviour. As will be discussed in the next chapter on operational risk, cases of fraud do occur, some of them of a magnitude which brings the bank down. On the other hand, if banking is more susceptible to fraudulent behaviour than other forms of business, this should be traceable to some particular features of financial intermediation.

In the present chapter, we investigate whether there are some aspects of financial intermediation where fraudulent behaviour can occur without being detected, at least for sufficient time so that the people engaged in fraud can obtain sizeable gains and inflict considerable losses on third parties. There are indeed circumstances where suitably placed persons may exploit the bank to illegitimate purposes. Thus, in Section 12.2, we consider the mechanism of bankruptcy for profit, cases where an entrepreneur may find it advantageous to obtain credit, take out dividends, and then default on the obligation to pay back the loans.

In Section 12.3 we consider what can be seen as the opposite case, where the bank performs activities which may be unwanted or unhealthy for society. These cases cover a broad spectrum: We look at one where credit is dependent on information about creditworthiness, which, however, can be misspecified as a result of corruption, and another one with special relevance to real estate credit, occurring when the value of the implicit option of leaving the property to the bank is undervalued by the credit officers of the bank. Finally,

239

we consider the phenomenon of systematic renewal of non-performing loans, something which may be advantageous to banks in particular circumstances.

The final section of the chapter deals with a somewhat different but closely related problem, namely that of money laundering. The basic task of a money launderer is to transform money obtained by some kind of illegal activity into a legitimate sum of money, usable in exactly the same way as money acquired by lawful means. The techniques of money laundering, which by their very nature are complicated and difficult to discover, are reviewed briefly, and we consider the need for anti-money laundering measures by the authorities. Such measures will in most cases involve the monitoring of transactions by banks, and this gives rise to an incentive problem, because such monitoring is costly to the bank. Therefore, the government has to use a system of fines for unreported money laundering; however, the fines must be determined carefully in order to avoid excessive reporting by banks, because this will reduce the informational value of the bank reports and thereby the overall effects of the fight against money laundering.

12.2 The economics of looting

12.2.1 A simple model of bankruptcy for profit

In this section, we consider a model proposed by Akerlof and Romer [1993] for the analysis of deliberate bankruptcy, conducting business with the purpose of taking out of the enterprise more than its value minus the liabilities. The basic functioning of such a mechanism is that a firm with a net value V has a possibility of withdrawing to its owner a sum of money bigger than V, typically after having obtained a loan. Going bankrupt and taking advantage of limited liability, the lender may then get away with a profit. Following the authors, we think of the firm in question as a financial intermediary receiving deposits and purchasing assets, that is, as a bank, or, what may be the more typical case, a thrift.

The model has three periods 0, 1 and 2. The market rate of interest is r_1 from 0 to 1 and r_2 from 1 to 2. The firm begins its life at $t = 0$ with an initial capital W_0. It then acquires deposit liabilities L_0 and purchases assets A with initial value $A_0 = W_0 + L_0$. Being a financial intermediary, it is subject to capital regulation specified as $W_0 \geq cA_0$. The thrift receives a payment $\rho_1(A)$ at $t = 1$ and $\rho_2(A)$ at $t = 2$.

In period 1, the thrift pays a dividend Δ_1, and as the assets are assumed to be illiquid, it adjusts its liabilities so that after the payment of dividends, the liabilities are

$$L_1 = (1 + r_1)L_0 - \rho_1(A) + \Delta_1.$$

In period 2, the thrift can be liquidated after having received $\rho_2(A)$. The liabilities are

$$(1 + r_2)L_1 = (1 + r_2)[(1 + r_1)L_0 - \rho_1(A) + \Delta_1],$$

and the terminal net worth is the difference between the value of assets and liabilities.

Without limited liability, the decision problem of the owners (or managers; there is no difference in this model) of the thrift would be to maximize present value of the payments from the thrift by suitable choice of A. For technical reasons, this present value is computed at $t = 1$, so the problem is finding

$$V^* = \max_{A,\Delta_1} \frac{\rho_2(A) - (1 + r_2)[(1 + r_1)L_0 - \rho_1(A) + \Delta_1]}{1 + r_2} + \Delta_1$$

$$= \max_A \frac{\rho_2(A)}{1 + r_2} + \rho_1(A) - (1 + r_1)L_0$$

subject to the constraint

$$0 \leq cA_0 \leq W_0.$$

Notice that the quantity Δ_1 disappears from the expression to be maximized.

Now we turn to the limited liability case. We assume that the government guarantees the liabilities of the thrift and imposes an upper bound $M(A)$ on the dividend to be paid out to owners in period 1. Now the decision problem of the owners changes to that of finding

$$E = \max_{A,\Delta_1,\Delta_2} \left[\frac{\Delta_2}{1 + r_2} + \Delta_1 \right]$$

under the constraints

$$0 \leq cA_0 \leq W_0, \Delta_1 \leq M(A),$$

$$\Delta_2 \leq \max\{0, \rho_2(A) - (1 + r_2)[(1 + r_1)L_0 - \rho_1(A) + \Delta_1]\},$$

Here E is the value of the equity, which may well differ from the true economic value of the thrift, V^*.

For the statement of the following theorem, we introduce the notation M^* for the maximum of $M(A)$ over all A such that $0 \leq cA_0 \leq W_0$.

PROPOSITION 1: *(1) If $M^* \leq V^*$, then the thrift chooses A so as to maximize the true value.*

(2) If $M^* > V^*$, then the thrift chooses A so as to maximize $M(A)$; it pays dividends M^* in period 1 and defaults in period 2.

PROOF: (1) In this case, the net worth of the firm is non-negative after period 1, and nothing is gained by defaulting in period 2, or, equivalently, by setting $\Delta_2 = 0$. But in this case the second maximizaton problem above reduces to the first one, and the firm will maximize true value.

(2) Here the owners choose $\Delta_1 > V^*$, which results in a default at $t = 2$. This means that the choice of assets matters only insofar as they influence $M(A)$, and we have the result.

□

12.2.2 Examples of looting

The description given above seems quite abstract, and it might not be obvious that it describes real-world phenomena. Some examples will show that this is the case.

Yield curve speculation. Suppose that the firm acquires a bond with maturity at $t = 2$. The yearly interest r_L paid on this bond is determined by the equation

$$(1 + r_L) + (1 + r_L)r_L = (1 + r_1)(1 + r_2),$$

or, if we neglect product terms, approximately $r_L = (r_1 + r_2)/2$. We consider the case where $r_2 > r_L > r_1$.

EXAMPLE 12.1 Suppose that $r_1 = 2\%$, $r_2 = 10\%$; then $r_L = 0.0592$. If the capital invested is of size 1,000, the nominal or accounting gain in the first year is 59.20.

If the debt contracted is 990 (assuming that $c = 1\%$), then the accounting cost is $990 \times 2\% = 19.80$, giving a net accounting profit of 39.40, which is added to the own capital, giving a total of 49.40.

In principle, all of this could be paid out as dividends, but because all the funds are tied in the portfolio, the firm must contract an additional loan if it wants to pay dividends to its owner. If it chooses to pay out 30, it must borrow this amount, so the debt changes to

$$990 + 19.80 + 30 = 1039.80.$$

Own capital is, of course, diminished by the amount paid out, so it becomes 19.40, which still constitutes more than 1% of the total assets (which are $1,000 + 59.20 = 1059.20$). This payment constitues a one-year payoff of $19.40/10 = 194\%$ to the owners, which must be considered as quite satisfactory.

In the next year, there is not sufficient value in the firm to pay the debt, and it goes bankrupt.

The possibility of speculating in bankruptcy comes from current accounting practices: A bond held at $t = 1$ may be valued at par even though its market value would be smaller because interest rates are increasing over time. Therefore, the accounting return on the bond is r_L, which is greater than the real return r_1. If

$$r_L - r_1 > c$$

(where c is the fraction of the assets to be kept as equity), then the conditions for speculating in bankruptcy are satisfied because the thrift may obtain credit to the amount of $r_L - r_1 - c$ per unit of bonds invested and pay it out as dividends. Even when $r_L - r_1 = c$, the owners may exploit the situation to withdraw their original investment cA without violating the capital requirements. Needless to say, at $t = 2$ there will not be asset value enough in the thrift to pay the depositors, and the thrift goes bankrupt.

Development loans. The same formalism as in the yield curve example can be used to illustrate the possibilities of bankruptcy speculation in the context of construction and development loans. Such loans will typically be big enough to allow the developer to buy the initial property, start the building, and even pay the interest on the loan for the first periods. If the thrift sets a very high accounting loan rate for the first years, we are back in the previous situation with the possibility of stating an accounting income higher than the real one. If the loan is arranged as a non-recourse loan, so the borrower can walk away from the debt in the case of bankruptcy, it is even possible to select a phony developer as the contracting party.

Expected currency devaluation. Something largely similar to what happens in the previous examples can occur in a very different context, namely when a bank expects the home currency to depreciate. This can happen if the assets of the bank are denominated in local currency, say pesos, whereas the liabilities are denominated in foreign currency, say dollars. An expected devaluation of the peso will then give rise to peso interest rates which are higher than dollar interest rates.

Clearly, the banks may in this case use the situation to take out dividends due to incomes accounted for in pesos which do not correspond to dollar incomes. If the interest rate difference is bigger than the country risk, that is, the premium on the dollar interest rate which accounts for possible bankruptcies, then there is money to gain. This may happen if foreign lenders to the bank are confident that the government will assume responsibility for dollar-denominated loans taken by the banks in the country.

As pointed out by Akerlof and Romer [1993], this may very well be what happened in the Chilean financial crisis in 1979, where the peso had been stabilized at a given exchange rate relative to the dollar, followed by liberalization of international borrowing and lending. The exchange rate turned out to be unrealistic, and because it had been installed in order to curb inflation, and the latter proceeded largely unaffected, the result was that the peso became overvalued, so there was widespread expectation of a devaluation. The bank regulators were aware of the exchange rate risk and demanded that banks match dollar assets with dollar liabilities. However, this shifted the exchange rate risk to credit risk, because the bank would grant a dollar credit to a Chilean firm which, not being a bank, could engage in looting without interference from bank regulators.

Bubbles from looting. In some cases, the looting behaviour by even a small number of banks may have far-reaching effects on a sector of the economy or even economy-wide repercussions. The case of the US savings banks in the 1980s may be an example. These banks got into problems in the course of the decade, and a large number of thrifts had to be liquidated. The following gives a simple view of the mechanisms behind these events.

We begin by considering a model of land development (which was the activity behind the financial scandals). There are two types of developers, namely type 1, occurring with probability $1 - \beta$, with a demand for land

$$D_1 = (1 - \beta)(A - bp),$$

where the parameter A reflects some basic characteristics of the market, such as number of people moving to the particular region and their incomes; the value of A is known by type 1 developers.

Type 2 developers (having probability β) do not know A, but apart from this, their demand is similar,

$$D_2 = \beta(A^e - bp).$$

Here A^e is the value of A which type 2 developers expect, and we assume that they infer it from observing the current price of land according to a rule

$$A^e = \delta + \gamma p,$$

where $\delta, \gamma > 0$ are given parameters. The supply of land to developers is assumed linear of the form

$$S = d + ep$$

with $d, e > 0$ given parameters.

For a (rational expectation) equilibrium in the market, we must have that $S = D_1 + D_2$, and furthermore, the expectations of the uninformed agents should not be contradicted by the actual facts, so $A^e = A$. This means that the parameters have to satisfy

$$\delta = d, \ \gamma = b + e,$$

and inserting in type 2 demand, we get that

$$D_2 = \beta(d + ep).$$

We now add a third type of parasitical developers who are not in the market for profit, but are backed by looters among the banks. Banks will offer loans N to type 3 developers, and if building on one parcel of land costs B, and type 3 takes loans only for building, then such developers will have a demand

$$D_3 = \frac{N}{B}.$$

Because the real purpose is as yet concealed, the other developers will act as if they were type 1 or 2. The informed developers still observe A, but the uninformed but honest developers can use only land price, which is inflated due to the demand from the dishonest developers, in their estimate of A, and as a consequence, their demand will increase as well, and we get a bubble in the market. Indeed, it will appear to the type 2 developers that A has increased by the amount

$$\frac{1}{1 - \beta} \frac{N}{B},$$

and consequently the land price increases by

$$\frac{1}{1 - \beta} \frac{N}{B} \frac{1}{e + b}.$$

In this first phase, prices have increased considerably, and the looting banks, which may have charged high initial interest rates from the dishonest developers for their loans, can take out cash profits. Subsequently, as the true value of A is revealed (by vacancies and unsold property), prices fall; type 3 developers go bankrupt and their banks go bankrupt, but now also the type 2 developers are in trouble, having bought at unrealistically high prices. The result is that the whole sector is hit by the downturn; it is easily seen that if β is big enough, then the price movements may be very big, and the resulting crisis similarly widespread.

12.3 Malfunctioning of banks

Whereas the techniques of looting are related to the time structure of funds, there has been no explicit mentioning of uncertainty. It goes almost without saying that once uncertainty and, in particular, asymmetric information are taken into account, several new possibilities for fraudulent behaviour are opened up. We consider some of these in the present section.

12.3.1 A model of credit decisions with corruption

In the model, we have three participants, namely a firm (the 'chaebol' in Hwang et al. [2007]), a financial institution and the political system. Each of the participants is described as simply as possible: For the firm, we assume that its manager is endowed with either high (h) or low (l) level of efficiency (or competence), and the probability of h is π. The efficient firms have a higher cost (but also get a higher payoff) than the inefficient firms, the difference being $c > 0$. The state of the business environment may be either good (g) or bad (b), and g occurs with probability p. The outcome of production depends on both the effort and the state of nature in the following way:

	State of nature	
Efficiency	g	b
h	$1 + H$	$1 + L$
l	$1 + L$	1

It is assumed that outcome can be observed but that financial institutions are unable to distinguish between the two cases, which both give rise to the same outcome $1 + L$. Politicians may be able to distinguish, but on the other hand they may be accepting bribes (assumed to have the fixed size s) so as to persuade financial institutions to offer credit to firms with low competence. Politicians are honest with probability α, thus taking bribes with probability $1 - \alpha$, and they maximize expected utility.

The financial institutions have funds of size 1 which may be used to finance the firm's activities or alternatively may be invested in the interbank market at the fixed rate r of interest. The financial institution may set the loan rate R and the payoff t to politicians for correct (or rather, not demonstratively wrong) information about the firm's efficiency being high. If outcome is 1, then politicians did not report high effort correctly, and t is not paid out. We restrict attention to equilibria where the loan rate satisfies $R < L$, so low-effort firms are not excluded from the credit market. To get such equilibria we make the following assumption.

ASSUMPTION 1: $c > p(H - L)$.

The assumption says that the extra cost of an efficient firm is bigger than the expected difference in outcome. It follows from this assumption that charging a loan rate $\geq L$ will result in losses to the efficient firm, so the bank will not set such a high rate.

The next assumption has to do with the concept of 'overlending'.

ASSUMPTION 2: $pH + (1 - p)L - c > r > pL$.

Under Assumption 2, the expected payoff of an inefficient firm is smaller than the interbank rate, so society should extend credits only to efficient firms, for which expected payoff minus cost exceeds the interbank rate. For later use, we introduce the shorthand notation $\bar{R} = pH + (1 - p)L - c$.

We now turn to the optimization problems of each participant. For the firm of type h, expected profit is

$$E[\Pi_h] = pH + (1 - p)L - R - c,$$

and for type l it is

$$E[\Pi_l] = (1 - \alpha)(p(L - R) - s),$$

because it may bribe the politician with probability $1 - \alpha$ to communicate h to the bank, which then gives credit at rate R. The efficient firm will participate in the credit game if the loan rate is smaller than the expected payoff, that is, if

$$R < pH + (1 - p)L - c,$$

and the inefficient firm will participate if the bribe does not exceed the gain from participating, that is, if

$$s \leq p(L - R).$$

If efficient firms participate, then we must have

$$E[\Pi_h] = p(H - L) + L - R - c \geq 0,$$

and from Assumption 1 we get that in this case $L > R$, so $p(L - R) > 0$, meaning that there is room for a bribe of some positive size. The maximal bribe that the inefficient firm can afford is, of course, $s^{max} = p(L - R)$.

Turning to the politician, we have that corrupt politicians have expected payoff t if they signal an inefficient firm truthfully, and $p(t+s)+(1-p)s = s+pt$ if they signal untruthfully, so the difference $s + pt - t = s - (1 - p)t$ must be positive if she is to accept the bribe, and this gives a minimal acceptable bribe of the size $s^{min} = (1 - p)t$.

For given choices R and t of the financial institution, we now get incentive compatibility conditions for an equilibrium without corruption (in the terminology of Hwang et al. [2007], a no-collusion equilibrium), as $s^{min} \geq s^{max}$ or

$$t \geq \frac{p}{1 - p}(L - R). \tag{1}$$

If this condition is not satisfied in an equilibrium, it is an equilibrium with corruption (a collusion equilibrium). Consequently, the set of feasible pairs (R, t) is divided by the condition into two sets allowing for no-collusion and collusion equilibria, respectively.

Given that efficient firms participate, and (R, t) belongs to the no-bribery region, the bank has expected profit

$$\mathsf{E}[\Pi_N] = \pi R + (1 - \pi)r - t$$

because in the case where the firm is inefficient (occurring with probability $1 - \pi$), the bank will receive a correct signal from the politician and decline credit to the firm. The condition for participating in the credit market rather than concentrating on the interbank market is $\mathsf{E}[\Pi_N] \geq r$, and inserting, we get

$$t \leq \pi(R - r). \tag{2}$$

If (R, t) is in the bribery region, the dishonest politicians will signal h when true type is l, and expected profit is

$$\mathsf{E}[\pi_C] = [\pi + (1 - \pi)(1 - \alpha)p]R + [(1 - \pi)\alpha]r - [1 - (1 - \pi)(1 - \alpha)(1 - p)]t.$$

Here, $\pi + (1 - \pi)(1 - \alpha)p$ is the probability of getting R, which happens when the firm is efficient or when it is inefficient and the report is false but the state is good; $(1 - \pi)\alpha$ is the probability of getting r, happening when the firm is inefficient and the politician is honest; and finally $1 - (1 - \pi)(1 - \alpha)(1 - p)$ is the probability of having to pay t (in all cases except when the politician is caught telling a lie: Inefficient firm, dishonest politician and bad state). As before, the participation constraint $\mathsf{E}[\Pi_C] \geq r$ can now be reformulated as

$$t \leq \frac{\pi + (1 - \pi)(1 - \alpha)p}{1 - (1 - \pi)(1 - \alpha)(1 - p)}R - \frac{1 - (1 - \pi)\alpha}{1 - (1 - \pi)(1 - \alpha)(1 - p)}r. \tag{3}$$

Figure 12.2 shows the two feasible regions of pairs (R, t), as bounded by the participation constraints of the bank. The upper one, denoted $N(v)$ is the set of (R, t) which for the given array of parameters $v = (H, L, c, r, \pi, \alpha, p)$ is such that no corruption occurs, and similarly $C(v)$ is the set of all (R, t) which support corruption.

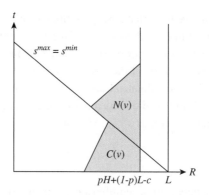

Figure 12.1 The scope for corruption in signalling creditworthiness: Different combinations of t, the value of truthful reports, and R, the loan rate, may give rise to corruption ($C(v)$) or honesty ($N(v)$).

We may now investigate conditions on v such that corruption cannot be prevented (so $N(v) = \emptyset$).

PROPOSITION 2: *Assume that the parameters satisfy the condition*

$$\frac{[1 - (1 - \pi)\alpha]r}{\pi + (1 - \pi)(1 - \alpha)p} \leq \bar{R} \leq \frac{pL + \pi(1 - p)B}{\pi + (1 - \pi)p}. \tag{4}$$

Then the financial institution cannot prevent corruption.

PROOF: It is easily seen that the rightmost expression in (4) is the value of R at which the boundary of $N(v)$ intersects the line $s^{max} = s^{min}$, so no combination (R, t) in $N(v)$ can satisfy the participation constraint of the firm. The leftmost inequality secures that there is an equilibrium.   □

Clearly, there may be cases where no-bribery equilibria are possible, but where the bank may choose not to deter it, namely if its expected profit is larger with bribery than without it. The next proposition gives conditions for this to happen.

PROPOSITION 3: *Assume that the parameters satisfy the condition*

$$\frac{pL + (1 - \pi)r}{\pi + (1 - \pi)p} \leq \bar{R} < \frac{pL - (1 - \pi)(1 - \alpha)(1 - p)r}{p[1 - (1 - \pi)(1 - \alpha)(1 - p)]}. \tag{5}$$

Then the equilibrium values of (R, t) will belong to $C(v)$.

PROOF: Suppose on the contrary that $(R, t) \in N(v)$. Then, because the isoprofit curve (that is, (R, t)-combinations where expected profits take the same value) in the no-collusion case are straight lines parallel to the boundary defined by a zero-profit condition, the optimum must be in $(\bar{R}, t^*)$, where t^* is the value at which the line $s^{max} = s^{min}$ intersects the vertical line at $R = \bar{R}$; we have

$$t^* = \frac{p}{1-p}\left(L - \bar{R}\right).$$

The point $(\bar{R}, t^*)$ belongs also to $C(v)$ by the leftmost inequality in (5), so we may compute the difference in expected profit at this point as

$$E[\Pi_N] - E[\Pi_N] = (1-\pi)(1-\alpha)\left(r - p\bar{R}\right) - \frac{p}{1-p}\left(L - \bar{R}\right),$$

which is negative because

$$\bar{R} < \frac{pL - (1-\pi)(1-\alpha)(1-p)r}{p[1 - (1-\pi)(1-\alpha)(1-p)]},$$

contradicting that maximal expected profit is attained in $N(v)$. $\square$

One may combine the results of the above two propositions to get a general statement about parameter values giving rise to collusion equilibria.

PROPOSITION 4: *Assume that the parameters satisfy the condition*

$$\frac{[1 - (1-\pi)\alpha]r}{\pi + (1-\pi)(1-\alpha)p} \leq \bar{R} < \frac{pL - (1-\pi)(1-\alpha)(1-p)r}{p[1 - (1-\pi)(1-\alpha)(1-p)]}.$$

Then the equilibrium will be such that dishonest politicians take bribes.

PROOF: The inequalities in the theorem are the least restrictive of those occurring in Propositions 2 and 3, showing that a collusion equilibrium will be established because either there are no (R, t) in the region $N(v)$, or those (R, t) which belong to $N(v)$ do not realize the maximum expected payoff. $\square$

So far the model explains that the banks take on bad loans, namely when corrupt politicians signal high efficiency for inefficient firms. This behaviour may be supported in equilibrium, namely when the cost of remunerating honesty is too high for the banks, and as a result, the banks have to accept that a proportion of the loans will not give the desired surplus (notice, however, that the original amount 1 which the banks lent to the firm can always be recuperated). From the point of view of society, however, allowing inefficient firms to receive credits involves a loss, because the money could be used better elsewhere.

The model and its results are applied by Hwang et al. [2007] to explain the 1997 crisis in South Korea as a result of increasing indebtedness of big companies. In distinction from other countries of Southeast Asia, the South Korean crisis hit the manufacturing sector more heavily than the real estate sector, and the excessive indebtedness of the big companies made them more vulnerable to the deteriorating business conditions.

12.3.2 Undervaluing the implicit option in non-recourse lending

One of the side effects of the subprime crisis has been an increased interest in the workings of real estate markets and their financial aspects. The relationship between market interest rates and house prices is, of course, well known, but also the workings of the financial intermediaries have a considerable impact on what happens in this market and thereby on the situation of the economy as a whole. In the following, we consider a particular way in which the credit policy of banks may influence financial stability, inspired by the work of Pavlov and Wachter [2004].

Consider an investor who acquires an asset at $t = 0$ using a bank loan of the size 1 with repayment rate R_L. The asset has two possible outcomes at $t = 1$, namely a high outcome $y_H > 1$ per unit invested, occurring with probability p, and a low one $y_L < 1$. We assume that the loans are *non-recourse*, so the investor can walk away from the debt at $t = 1$ by leaving the asset to the bank. This is standard practice in some countries, even if not in all.

The expected profit at $t = 1$ of the bank, which is funded at the fixed repayment rate R, is

$$pR_L + (1 - p)y_L - R = pR_L - (1 - p)(R - y_L) - pR,$$

which is non-negative if

$$R_L \geq \frac{v}{p} + R. \tag{6}$$

Here we have used the notation $v = (1 - p)(R - y_L)$, and the quantity v can be interpreted using the terminology of options: The non-recourse provision corresponds to giving the borrower a put option on the debt to be exercised at $t = 1$ with strike price y_L (settling the debt of R by leaving y_L with the bank). The expected loss to the bank connected with this option at $t = 1$ is $v = (1 - p)(R - y_L)$.

If for some reason the bank undervalues the put option offered to borrowers, then the result will be a loan rate which is too low, possibly violating (6), or alternatively an inflated fundamental value of the asset due to undervaluing of the funding cost. But the logical next question is then: Why should the bank undervalue the put option? To answer this question, we have to move a little further, describing the bank market and the management of banks.

The expected profit of the bank which aims at survival is

$$\Pi_1\left(L^1, R_L^1\right) = pL^1R_L^1 + (1 - p)y_lL^1 - RL^1$$

$$= pL^1R_L^1 - (pR + (1 - p)(R - y_l))L^1 = pL^1R_L^1 - (pR + v)L^1$$

when charging the repayment rate R_L^1 and contracting loans to the amount L^1, where v is the value of the implicit option. For a bank which aims at reaping profit in good years and defaulting in bad years the expected profit at R_L^0 and L^0 is

$$\Pi_0\left(L^0, R_L^0\right) = p\left(L^0R_L^0 - L^0R\right),$$

so the latter bank may be considered as solving the same maximization problem as the other one but neglecting the cost of delivering the option to the borrower. Indeed maximizing Π_0 is equivalent to maximizing $LR_L - LR$, that is, without concern for bad years.

Suppose that banks face a demand for loans of the form $L(R_L)$, and the market structure is that of a Cournot oligopoly (choosing the amount of loans and letting the market loan rate adapt). If all banks are far-sighted, then profit maximizing loan rates satisfy

$$\frac{R_L^1 - \left(R + \dfrac{v}{p}\right)}{R_L^1} = \frac{1}{n\varepsilon_L}$$

where ε_L is the elasticity of the demand for loans (cf. Section 11.3), whereas the rates of the short-sighted bank will be given by

$$\frac{R_L^0 - R}{R_L^0} = \frac{1}{n\varepsilon_L},$$

and not surprisingly, we have that $R_L^0 > R_L^1$, $\Pi_0 > \Pi_1$, because the short-sighted bank had lower perceived cost.

The difference between short- and long-sighted banks may become relevant if we assume that decisions are made by managers who receive a bonus B which depends on the profits obtained by the bank, say

$$B = c\Pi$$

for some constant $c > 0$. In bad years where banks experience losses, the managers will be discharged, so their payoff is zero. The objective function for the manager therefore becomes

$$pc(L(R_L - R)) = c\Pi_0(L, R_L),$$

so the banks choose the short-sighted behaviour.

The model may seem somewhat unrealistic, assuming as it does that the free entry equilibrium establishes itself before the uncertainty about the state of nature is revealed; the model applies to real estate investments where valuation crises happen with long intervals. The possible undervaluing of the option, in practice amounting to overstating the value to the bank of the property if the borrower defaults on the loan, is also a phenomenon with real-world counterparts. But the model as presented here would need to be elaborated upon so as to give an realistic explanation of the behaviour of bank managers.

12.3.3 Evergreening: Rolling over non-performing loans

In many contexts, banks have chosen to renew loans in cases where the borrowers have failed to comply with the stipulations of the loan contract. In any specific case, there may be individual reasons for this, but when the phenomenon becomes sufficiently widespread, the presence of non-performing loans on the books of the bank will eventually cause problems for the financial sector as a whole. It is therefore important to assess the reasons why banks keep the bad loans on their books. The following discussion is based on a simplified version of a model proposed by Niinimäki [2007].

We consider a model with a banking sector subject to perfect competition. Banks are all identical. Each bank has an initial capital normalized to 1, and this capital is financed by equity E and deposits $1 - E$. There are three periods of time in the model: At $t = 0$, the bank makes its credit decisions, lending to particular borrowers investing in assets. There are three types of assets in the model, namely (i) short-term ('fast') assets which terminate at $t = 1$, (ii) long-term assets which give an outcome at $t = 1$ and again in $t = 2$ (to be called slow assets), and finally (iii) long-term ('very slow') assets with an outcome only at $t = 2$. In each period the bank may choose to monitor the investment projects of the borrowers, in which case they will all succeed, or alternatively not to monitor projects, and then projects will succeed with probability $p < 1$.

If succeeding, a short-term investment has outcome Y at $t = 1$. A long-term investment has outcome $Y - 1$ at $t = 1$ and Y at $t = 2$, and a very long-term investment has outcome Y_2 at $t = 2$. Projects that fail have value 0.

When setting up loan contracts at $t = 0$, the bank can observe whether investment is fast or slow, but it cannot observe the type of slow investment project that the borrower has access to; this is revealed to the bank after the loan contracts have been signed. The general public, in our particular case the regulator, does not know the types of investment.

We begin with the case where the bank chooses only to contract with borrowers investing in slow projects. The bank has to pay a deposit interest rate r. If it chooses to monitor the contract, this gives rise to the additional cost of m. We shall assume that all assets have positive net present value when they are monitored. More specifically, we assume that

$$Y - 1 > r + m. \tag{7}$$

Furthermore, we assume that monitoring makes sense,

$$pY + b < 1 + r,$$

$$p(Y - 1) + b + \delta p(pY + b) < 1 + r,$$

where δ is the rate of discount, and b is the value to the borrower of not being monitored by the lender, so the short- and long-term investments are unprofitable if not monitored; for the very long investment, we assume similarly that

$$pY_2 + b < Y(1 + r).$$

Suppose that a bank chooses not to monitor the loans in period 1. Then a fraction $1 - p$ of them will default in this period. The bank receives pr_L as interest payment on the remaining loans used for slow investments, and if the losses $(1 - p)(1 + r)$ exceed this income, then the bank is insolvent, and the regulator will close the bank if the losses are observed.

We shall assume that regulators will observe losses if they figure on the balances of the bank, so a way to avoid being closed down is to roll over the non-performing loans. Technically, this means that the interest payment due at $t = 1$ is added to the principal, so the bank lends the amount $(1 - p)(1 + r)$ to borrowers with non-performing loans. Because there is no investment behind these loans, they will be non-performing also in period 2, and when the bank is liquidated at $t = 2$, the losses have to be taken into account.

Why, then, would a bank ever want to roll over a non-performing loan? The non-monitoring bank has a fraction p of the loans which are still performing at $t = 1$. Therefore, given the assumption on these assets, the bank obtains a net gain on the performing loans which is

$$p(1 + r_L)^2 - (1 + r)^2$$

at $t = 2$, and if the discounted value of this gain exceeds the losses from the first period,

$$\delta\left(p(1 + r_L)^2 - (1 + r)^2\right) > (1 - p)(1 + r) - pr_L, \tag{8}$$

then rolling over of non-performing loans is better for the bank than liquidation right away. This reflects our assumption of liquidation cost 0 for the slow and very slow assets, which means that the bank incurs a large loss by liquidation at $t = 1$. It may be noticed that the composition of the loan portfolio on slow and very slow assets has played no role in our simplified version of the model; this feature is important, however, because the unobservable character of this composition makes it possible for the bank to present the lack of income at $t = 1$ as a legitimate result of a high fraction of very slow assets.

In the ex ante perspective, the choice not to monitor the borrowers is advantageous to the bank if the monitoring cost m exceeds the gain from monitoring the loans,

$$m > (1 - p)(1 + r_L)^2. \tag{9}$$

It is easily seen that if p is not too close to 1 and if $1 + r_L$ is smaller than Y, then (9) is compatible with (7) and (8), so not monitoring loans may be rational for the banks also when it is disadvantageous for society. As mentioned already, this is mainly a consequence of the high cost of early liquidation.

So far the evergreening or rolling over of bad loans has been explained only as a consequence of rational behaviour in the case of high costs of monitoring. Adding the possibility of contracting for fast investments gives, however, a new dimension to the discussion, because evergreening may now be profitable also in the case where the bank ends up being insolvent at $t = 2$. Assuming that the regulators cannot observe the composition of loans with different purposes, a bank which does not monitor its assets and consequently loses can now choose to act as if a high proportion of loans were used for fast assets, the outcome of which is not reinvested. If all the defaulted loans are treated as fully performing short assets, then the bank may pretend to have reduced the assets by this amount, and if subject to capital regulation, according to which the equity must constitute a fixed share of assets, it may take out some of its equity at $t = 1$ in a situation where the bank has actually experienced a loss, while still rolling over all the non-performing loans.

12.4 Money laundering

In recent years, the preoccupation with criminal activities on a global level has led to a growing concern about possible ways of transforming money earned by illegal activities into legal sources of income, which can be used for legal purposes, but also for the financing of new illegal activity. This process by which income derived from illegal activities is transformed into legal income is known as *money laundering*, and most countries have introduced some form of supervision and control of the channels by which illegal money filters into the legal economy.

The basic principle of money laundering is simple: If it is possible to engage in some form of legal activity where the sources of the money invested are never controlled, then the outcome of this activity will appear as perfectly legal. This will be worthwhile even if the activity in itself is not profitable, the loss being considered as the cost of cleaning the money. The classical example is buying up a large number of lottery tickets – the purchase is anonymous, and by the law of large numbers, some of the lottery tickets will come out with gain, even if there is an overall loss. The system is, however, not easily practicable, because there are few lotteries of this absolutely anonymous character. Therefore, money laundering must take more sophisticated forms, and as a consequence it must involve some financial intermediaries (banks, real estate finance institutions, etc.), so banks become a natural place at which to survey possible money launderers.

12.4.1 The techniques of money laundering
Although there may in practice be an almost unlimited variety of methods for transforming illegally acquired money into legal sources of income, there is an established way of analysing such methods, dividing the process of money laundering into three stages:

(1) Placement: Here the illegal money is filtered into legitimate financial institutions for subsequent operations. Obviously, the placement operation is precarious, and it must be carried out using many financial institutions and possibly many agents so as to avoid the suspiciously large amounts of money that attract attention.

(2) Layering: At this stage, the illegal money is sent from the initial financial institutions to a large number of other institutions, involving several countries and transactions, so as to give the impression of small legal transactions, payment for deliveries of goods and services, etc. Also, money may be used for buying high-value items for which prices move considerably up and down (boats, houses, cars, diamonds), so as to change the form in which the money appears. This is the most complex stage of money laundering, often involving many other persons.

(3) Integration: In the final stage, the money gets back in (almost) legitimate form, for example by sales of assets acquired during the layering stage to companies set up and

controlled by the launderer. At this stage, it is very difficult to spot illegitimate money because many of the preceding transactions have been poorly documented. The money may now re-enter the economy for either legal or illegal activities.

In the three stages, the money launderer uses particular tools to achieve her goals. At the outset, there is a need for *structuring deposits* (also known as 'smurfing') because the launderer needs to split the total amount into many small and inconspicuous transactions (in the United States, transactions below $10,000 are not routinely reported to authorities), which may involve several persons (the 'smurfs') controlled by the launderer, or alternatively over a lengthy period of time. At the layering phase, the use of *overseas banks* is widespread, with a preference for banks in countries with bank secrecy laws (such as the Bahamas, Bahrain, Singapore). Also some countries in Asia have a traditional banking sector where deposits and withdrawals are not documented. Further, the setting up of *shell companies* facilitates the appearance of transactions as purchases or sales (with no commodities behind). But also legitimate companies may be useful, either large businesses with many cash transactions such as brokerage firms or casinos, where the dirty money can filter in together with legitimate money, or even small businesses with a high cash turnover (bars, strip clubs). The technique is then either to report higher sales, thereby making the money look legitimate, or alternatively to hide the money in the firms' accounts, assuming that the authorities will not compare the balances with the firms' financial reports.

12.4.2 The money laundering multiplier

One of the specific aspects of money laundering is its involvement with illegal activity, not only in the sense that the money to be processed has illegal origins but also in the forward sense: Some of the laundered money may be reinvested in criminal activities. This means that any new injection of money into this process will give rise to a final amount of laundered money which may be several times larger. The reason that this new investment in illegal activities should be included in the consideration is that in many cases clean money is necessary to start up any activity, legal as well as illegal.

The workings of this process can be illustrated as in Fig. 12.2 (taken from Masciandaro [1999]).

The initial inflow of money from illegal markets has the size L, as it is assumed that a fraction y of this needs to be laundered. The laundering has a cost, so of the amount yL put into laundering, only cyL is recovered as clean money. But then comes the second round: A fraction q of the newly obtained clean money is reinserted into criminal activity, where it has the return R; now the whole process can start over once more.

As can be seen from the figure, the original amount L obtained from illegal activity is multiplied by $qR(1-c)y$ in each round. Assuming that $qR(1-c) < 1$, the total amount of money which is laundered is

$$M = yL + (qR(1-c)y)yL + (qR(1-c)y)^2 yL + \cdots = \frac{y}{1 - qR(1-c)y}L. \qquad (10)$$

The fraction on the right-hand side of (10) may be considered as a *multiplier* related to the money laundering process.

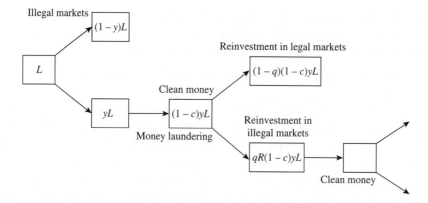

Figure 12.2 The multiplier process in illegal economic activity and money laundering: Initial illegal money is either reinvested in illegal activities or laundered, and the clean money may now be used both for illegal and for perfectly legal activities.

The simple model considered here may also be used to shed some light on the importance of anti-money laundering policies. We assume that such policies have as their result that the fraction c of clean money to be obtained per unit of money inserted will decrease. The amount of money laundered as a function of c can be illustrated as in Fig. 12.3; for given L we have that M is a convex function of c because

$$\frac{\partial M}{\partial c} = -\frac{yL}{(1 - qR(1 - c)y)^2}, \quad \frac{\partial^2 M}{\partial c^2} = \frac{2yL}{(1 - qR(1 - c)y)^3} > 0.$$

Adding a system of policy-maker indifference curves showing social cost connected with the flow of criminal money and regulatory activity, here taken as linear in M and c, we can find the optimal level c^* of anti-money laundering regulation.

The optimal policy choice reflects the social marginal rate of substitution between criminal activity and public regulation. In Masciandaro [1999], the model is used to illustrate the different situations in the regions of Italy, where the correlation between overall crime rate and total deposits in the banking system is particularly high in the South.

12.4.3 Detecting money laundering: The crying wolf problem

Most anti-money laundering policies rely on bank reporting of transactions to the relevant authorities. Such reports may either be rule based (all transactions above $10,000) or discretionary, the latter having been introduced because rule-based reporting can be prevented (by smurfing). Discretionary reporting should occur whenever transactions appear as 'suspicious', a term which cannot be clearly defined, but the meaning of this is continuously being sharpened to include more and more transactions. Both types of reporting put an additional cost on the bank, and in due course the question must arise as to whether this cost is duly offset by its consequences. A first treatment of this problem was given by Takáts [2011], which we follow in rough outline below.

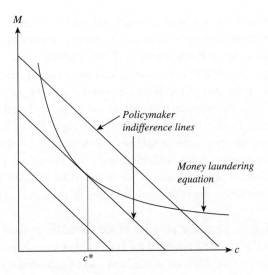

Figure 12.3 The money laundering curve shows how the amount M of money laundered depends on the cost c of laundering. If policy makers have preferences as shown by the linear indifference curves, an optimal level c^* of laundering cost can be determined.

The model has two agents, a bank and the government. The bank observed a transaction (there is only this one transaction), which has a prior probability α with $0 < \alpha < \frac{1}{2}$ of being money laundering. Money laundering is assumed to involve a cost $h > 0$ to society (in terms of facilitating future criminal activity).

If the bank reports money laundering, it can be prosecuted, and it is assumed that this increases social welfare (or reduces social cost) by ρh, where $\rho > 0$ is the proportion of h which is prevented by prosecuting the money launderer.

In order to be informed on the character of the transaction, the bank must monitor the transaction. In this case, the bank receives a signal σ taking values in $\{0, 1\}$ with probabilities as shown in the table below:

	Money Laundering	Legal Transaction
$\sigma = 0$	$1 - \delta$	δ
$\sigma = 1$	δ	$1 - \delta$

Here δ can be interpreted as the precision of the signal, with $\frac{1}{2} < \delta < 1$. The bank can compute the posterior probability of money laundering using Bayes' formula:

$$\beta_0 = \mathrm{P}[ML|\sigma = 0] = \frac{\alpha(1 - \delta)}{\alpha + \delta - 2\alpha\delta}$$

$$\beta_1 = \mathrm{P}[ML|\sigma = 1] = \frac{\alpha\delta}{1 - \alpha - \delta + 2\alpha\delta},$$

from which it is seen that $\beta_1 > \beta_0$.

The bank reports if it has received a signal and sends no report if it has no signal. Government also exerts an investigation effort I to discover money laundering. This effort has a cost, assumed to be of the magnitude kI^2 (in particular, marginal cost increases with I). The investigation effort may be conditioned on receipt of a report, choosing level I_0 if no report and I_1 in the case of receiving a report. Finally, the government can impose a fine F on the bank if it discovers an unreported case of money laundering.

We assume that bank monitoring effort M takes either high ($M = 1$) or low ($M = 0$) value. With high effort, the bank observes a signal, and with low effort no signal is observed. The monitoring cost is set to $m > 0$ for high effort and 0 for low effort. If the bank received a signal, it may choose to report ($R = 1$) or not to report ($R = 0$). We let R_0 and R_1, with values in $\{0, 1\}$, be the report depending on the value of the signal. There is a fixed cost $c > 0$ of reporting.

Before considering the incentive problem of the bank, let us have a look at the situation as it would be if it could be arranged by a social planner maximizing social welfare. First of all, we notice that the decision of the bank can be considered as choosing the pair (M, T), where $T \in \{0, 1\}$ is a reporting threshold, meaning that signals $\geq T$ are reported. Although in this formulation, we exclude the reporting strategy ($R_0 = 1, R_1 = 0$), we are not changing the optimization problem, because the reporting strategy ($R_0 = 0, R_1 = 1$) gives the same information to the government and is cheaper in monitoring cost as long as the low signal is the more likely one (when considering first-best optimum, we need not consider the fine which is a transfer payment between agents). Actually, the formulation can also be used when we take the incentive problem into account and consider second-best optima. If reporting when a signal is low (and money laundering less likely) is part of the optimal strategy for the bank, then it should also report when a signal is high.

Now we may reformulate the model using notation p_T for probability of reporting (= probability that the signal is $\geq T$), and q_{1T} (q_{0T}) for probability of money laundering given reporting (no reporting). It is easily seen that $q_{11} = \beta_1$ and $q_{01} = \beta_0$. The choice $T = 0$ means that reporting is uninformative, so $q_{10} = q_{00} = \alpha$.

We have the following:

PROPOSITION 5: *Under suitable parameter values, the first-best optimum is attained where the bank chooses the strategy $(M, T) = (1, 1)$ (monitoring and reporting only when a signal is high). The government's best responses I_0^* and I_1^* are < 1 and are given by*

$$I_0^* = \frac{q_{01}\rho h}{2k},$$

$$I_1^* = \frac{q_{11}\rho h}{2k},$$

so $I_0^* < I_1^*$, and the government does not levy any fines.

Proof: Given the reports of the bank, in an optimum the government will choose I so that marginal cost equals marginal social benefit, that is, where $2kI_i^* = \beta_i \rho h$, so

$$I_i^* = \frac{\beta_i \rho h}{2k}$$

for $i = 0, 1$. Similarly, if the government gets no informative signals, then optimal investigation level is determined by $2kI^* = \alpha \rho h$, giving

$$I^* = \frac{\alpha \rho h}{2k}.$$

Now

$$\alpha \delta \rho h I_1^* + \alpha(1 - \delta)\rho h I_0^* - \alpha \rho h I^*$$

is the difference in gains from prosecuting money laundering when the bank changes no monitoring and reporting to monitoring and informative reporting. The additional cost associated with this change consists of m, the cost of monitoring, and expected cost of reporting, in total

$$m + (\alpha + \delta - 2\alpha\delta)c,$$

and if the parameters are such that

$$\frac{\alpha \delta \beta_1 (\rho h)^2}{2k} + \frac{\alpha(1 - \delta)\beta_0 (\rho h)^2}{2k} - \frac{(\alpha \rho h)^2}{2k} > m + (\alpha + \delta - 2\alpha\delta)c,$$

then the social welfare is higher with bank monitoring and reporting than without.

Also, we have that if

$$\beta_1 \rho h < 2k$$

then the marginal expected gain from government investigation given the reporting policy $(1, 1)$ of the bank,

$$\beta_0 \rho h + \beta_1 \rho h < 2\beta_1 \rho h,$$

is smaller than the marginal cost of investigating at $I = 1$, which is $2k$, so in the social optimum, government investment is less than 1. □

The fines levied by the government are irrelevant for the social optimum, but they play a significant role once we consider the incentive problem for the bank. Indeed, although it is optimal for society that the bank is monitoring and reporting, in the absence of fines this might not be rational for the bank. However, under certain conditions there is a level of F for which the social optimum can be implemented.

PROPOSITION 6: *Let $\underline{F}, \overline{F}$ be defined by*

$$\alpha I_0^* \underline{F} = (1 - p_1)q_{01}I_0^* \underline{F} + p_1 c + m$$

$$c + m = (1 - p_1)q_{01}I_0^* \overline{F} + p_1 c + m,$$

respectively. If $\underline{F} \leq \overline{F}$, then the social optimum can be implemented with fines in the interval $[\underline{F}, \overline{F}]$.

PROOF: To achieve the social optimum, we need that the bank chooses $(M, T) = (1, 1)$, and the government's optimal responses are I_0^* and I_1^*. For the choice of the bank to be optimal, it must satisfy two incentive compatibility constraints: (a) the expected cost to the bank should not be smaller if it chooses $M = 0$, that is,

$$\alpha I_0^* F \geq (1 - p_1)q_{01}I_0^* F - p_1 c - m,$$

and $\underline{F}$ is the smallest value of F such that this constraint is satisfied; and (b) the expected cost should not be smaller if the bank monitors but reports at all signals,

$$c + m \geq (1 - p_1)q_{01}I_0^* F - p_1 c - m,$$

with $\overline{F}$ the largest value for which this inequality holds. The conclusions of the proposition follow easily.   □

The result obtained shows that for the social optimum to be implementable (using fines), the cost c of reporting should not be too small; indeed,

$$\underline{F} = \frac{p_1 c + m}{(\alpha - (1 - p_1)q_{01})I_0^*} \leq \frac{c}{q_{01}I_0^*} = \overline{F}$$

will be violated if c is sufficiently small. The reason is that low cost of reporting will lead to excessive reporting, with the result that the information is reduced so that society must use resources on investigation in excess of what is optimal.

Even when there exists a fine F which implements the social optimum, the actual level may differ and indeed may not belong to the interval $[\underline{F}, \overline{F}]$. Too big F will again induce the bank to report in all cases, thus reducing information content. These cases of excessive reporting may be considered as 'crying wolf', denouncing money launderers also in cases where money laundering is unlikely. Too small and too big fines will produce this situation – the case of too big fines being socially inferior to that of too small fines because in the latter case, although government has excessive investigation cost, the bank at least saves the cost of monitoring and reporting.

12.5 Exercises

1. A group of small banks contemplates signing a contract with a new company. The business plan consists in buying mortgage-based securities and holding them for three years, and it is generally expected that property values and security prices will rise in this period. To protect the banks, it is agreed that the firm should keep 10% of the value of its assets as equity.

Are there reasons for special concern for the participating banks, and if so, what should they do to protect themselves against losses?

2. A bank has a large customer with a business plan which is quite satisfactory: The enterprise has bought up empty industrial building sites which are situated close to the city centre, and a plan for building luxury apartments has been prepared and has received all the necessary government permits. Part of the property has been sold to other enterprises at this stage, and large profits have been realized already.

The customer asks for credit to finish the plans for the remaining part. Give an assessment of this engagement.

3. Consider a type of loan contract where collateral is used. The value of the collateral is assumed to be rather volatile, so periods of increasing value are followed by cases where the value is drastically reduced.

Assume that there are many banks competing for the borrowers. Explain how the value of the collateral influences the loan rates. Under which conditions may the banks neglect the implicit option of ending the contract by giving up the collateral.

4. A bank has had a rather aggressive credit policy, so its loan portfolio has reached the maximal size given the capital regulation. Explain that if a borrower defaults on a loan, then the capital ratio is violated. Discuss what the bank can do if it does not want to increase its capital in the short term; in particular, explain that extending the loan even if the bank does not expect to get anything back from the borrower could be a possibility.

What are the implications of this for the behaviour of banks in situations where capital ratios are increased?

5. A small country has recently been pointed out as one where criminal organizations from other countries use the banks for money laundering purposes. The government has therefore decided to introduce new policies, including large fines on the banks which have been used for money laundering.

Because the banks' own reporting cannot fully be relied upon, it is decided that each bank should have an obligation to report suspected money laundering, not only in their own banks but also in the other banks of the country. Because the payment network of the banks is rather dense, it is hoped that this will reveal so many cases that the country will cease being of interest for money laundering.

Comment on this policy and its possible side effects.

12.6 Comments

The simple model of the 'economics of looting', taking a loan with the deliberate intention of not repaying, has been elaborated upon in other contexts, such as e.g. Sarr et al. [2011], but with less direct implications for financial intermediation.

The role of corruption and its impact on the financial sector has not yet been given much attention from a theoretical point of view, but there are contributions dealing with the empirical aspects; see Beck et al. [2006], Barth et al. [2009]. The role of real estate prices and credit conditions in the financial crisis has been amply commented upon; the emphasis on the implicit option is, however, specific for the contribution of Pavlov and Wachter [2004]. For another exposition of their ideas, see Pavlov and Wachter [2011].

In Watanabe [2010], a case of evergreening is reported and discussed, pointing to the connection with capital regulation.

The extent to which money laundering is carried out is by its very nature not very well known. For a recent discussion, see Schneider [2010]. Taking on the role of detecting and preventing money laundering also has implications for financial institutions, Favarel-Garrigues et al. [2011].

Chapter 13

Operational Risk

13.1 Introduction: What is operational risk?

The methods for assessing and controlling the different types of risk in a bank could so far, with few if any exceptions, be seen as applications of the same fundamental approach (identifying risk factors, quantifying them, deriving probabilities of loss, collecting results, using correlations, and finally presenting results in terms of VaR or other measures). There is, however, one of the risk types for which it makes little sense to use the standard approach, namely operational risk, and the treatment of this type of risk falls outside the general program me.

Operational risk has to do with the internal processes in the bank but also with its relations with the external world. The following is its description in Basel II, where operational risk is defined as the risk of loss resulting from inadequate or failed internal processes, people and systems or from external events (Basel Committee on Banking Supervision [2001b], p. 94). This definition includes legal risk but excludes strategic and reputational risk.

Losses arising in this way can occasionally be very large – the over 200-year-old Barings Bank was actually brought to bankruptcy due to a loss of this type – and banks as well as regulatory authorities are very keen on keeping operational risk as low as possible. On the other hand, it can be seen from its very definition that operational risk is much less easy to assess than the other types of risk (interest rate risk, market risk, credit risk) because fraud or errors may arise at unexpected places in the organization. As is seen, operational risk also includes litigation risk, which, in particular in the US, is of rising importance, causing very considerable losses to the banks.

In the context of Basel regulations, the events that give rise to operational losses are divided into seven types. The event types are shown in Table 13.1.

Because the risk factors are so diffuse, and future losses are so difficult to assess, it might seem safer to start at the aggregate level rather than by considering the details (in contrast with our approach to the other risk types, where we have started with

263

Table 13.1 Event Types According to Basel II

Even Type	Name
1	Internal fraud
2	External fraud
3	Employment practices and workplace safety
4	Clients, products and business practices
5	Damage to physical assets
6	Business disruption and system failures
7	Execution, delivery and process management

Source: Basel Committee on Banking Supervision [2003].

the individual asset or liability and then moved to portfolio risk on the aggregate level). We may feel reasonably sure about the overall level of losses caused by operational risk (at least when disregarding spectacular events such as the Barings Bank failure, which, after all, happen with very small probability) and the best we can do is to set aside a capital reserve for the average operational loss. This leads to the rules to be discussed in the next section.

13.2 Reduced form approaches to operational risk

13.2.1 Probability of loss events

Large operational losses occur not very frequently, but the frequency of their occurrence varies much over time; this points to some common features with other types of losses such as traffic accidents, fires, earthquakes, etc., topics of what is called non-life insurance.

The basic building block in the actuarial theory of insurance is the Poisson distribution. Insurance companies want to find the distribution of the claims which their customers can get due to insurance contracts that the company has written. The Poisson distribution will give us the probability of k incidences of loss during the time interval from t_0 to t_1 as

$$P(k) = \frac{\lambda^k}{k!} e^{-\lambda(t_1 - t_0)};$$

the background assumptions here are that the probability of an event in each small time interval is independent of what happened in any other time interval and equal to $\lambda \Delta t$. The parameter λ is called the intensity of the process.

The Poisson process is fundamental to insurance theory, but it is not used in the above pure form because it fits badly with observed data, where among other things one has systematical changes in the frequency of losses over time. Such phenomena can be incorporated into the model if one allows for intensities that change over time, possibly even in a stochastic way. Such phenomena can, however, be incorporated into the process by letting the intensity change over time, leading to more complex models.

Box 13.1

Rogue traders and bank losses. One of the potential sources of losses to banks is the trading desk. Traders handle securities amounting to very large sums, and losses due to errors or fraud may be so serious that they threaten the survival of the bank. To prevent this from happening, traders have very strict limits within which to operate. A *rogue trader* is a trader who is employed by a bank and carries out unauthorized operations; this may be done in order to increase the profits of the bank, often fuelled by a system of large bonuses.

A spectacular example is the downfall of Barings Bank in 1995, brought about by speculative trading in futures on a Japanese stock index, carried out by Nicholas Leeson, the chief derivative trader of Barings Bank in Singapore. The trader was able to transfer unhedged positions to a special account so that only the hedged positions appeared in the daily reports. The speculation itself was initiated to recover a loss which had appeared previously, and this was actually achieved in the early stages. Later, several events (among them the Kobe earthquake) made the stock index volatile, and the particular trading method, which had been reasonably successful at the outset, resulted in steadily growing short positions in the unhedged account (for the trading strategy, cf. Brown and Steenbeek [2001]). This accumulated debt finally brought the bank down in February 1995. The losses accumulated amounted to $1.4 billion.

That a loss of this size could accumulate was, of course, partially due to deficient risk management in the bank, but at this time the Basel rules covered only credit risk, with no specific rules for marketable assets. The event contributed to the formulation of the amendments to Basel I, which included explicit rules for dealing with market risk.

The impressive loss from rogue trading, which actually brought down a more than 200-year-old bank, has been surpassed by even larger losses, such as the loss of around €5 billion in Société Générale in 2008, caused by trading in European stock index futures. The trader to whom the loss was attributed has argued that the methods were approved by the bank and also used by other traders in the bank. In general, trade in derivatives is not only a source of large profits but also of large losses, not all of which can be attributed to rogue trading.

13.2.2 Loss distributions

For a model of operational loss to be useful, it must describe not only the likelihood of the event (a major operational loss) but also the distribution of such losses. At this point there is very little guidance to be found in theory, because operational losses may arise from a very large number of causes. Relying on empirical distributions may be a possibility, but often parametric models, using loss distributions from a specific family of distributions given by parameters estimated from data, are preferred. It remains, however, to select the relevant family of distributions. There are many possibilities, such as the following:

Exponential distributions have density and distribution functions

$$f(x) = \lambda e^{-\lambda x}, \quad F(x) = 1 - e^{-\lambda x}, \ x > 0,$$

and one parameter $\lambda > 0$. It should be noticed that the probability of losses above x, which is $e^{-\lambda x}$, goes very quickly to zero, something which may be unfortunate in the context of operational losses.

The *Weibull* distribution is a generalization of the exponential distribution with density and distribution functions

$$f(x) = \alpha \beta x^{\alpha-1} e^{-\beta x^{\alpha}}, \quad F(x) = 1 - e^{-\beta x^{\alpha}}, \; x > 0,$$

for $\alpha > 0, \beta > 0$ parameters.

The *Gamma* distribution has density function

$$f(x) = \frac{\beta^{\alpha}}{\Gamma(\alpha)} x^{\alpha-1} e^{-\beta x}, \; x \geq 0$$

for parameters $\alpha > 0, \beta > 0$.

The *Pareto distribution* has

$$f(x) = \frac{\alpha \beta^{\alpha}}{x^{\alpha+1}}, \quad F(x) = 1 - \left(\frac{\beta}{x}\right)^{\alpha}, \; \beta < x < \infty,$$

where $\beta > 0$ determines the scale and $\alpha > 0$ the shape.

As noticed, some of these distributions have the property that very large losses can occur with a non-negligible probability, something which also emerges from empirical loss distributions. This property, known as *heavy tails*, is sufficiently important to merit some additional attention.

13.2.3 Heavy tails and the tail index

A probability distribution function F is said to have a heavy tail if

$$1 - F(x) \sim x^{-\alpha} \quad \text{for } x \to \infty,$$

where $\alpha > 0$ is some number; here notation $\sim$ means that the functions on both sides have the identical asymptotic behaviour (their ratio goes to 1 for $x \to \infty$). Alternatively, the property may be stated in terms of the density function f of F as

$$f(x) \sim x^{-(1+\alpha)} \quad \text{for } x \to \infty. \tag{1}$$

It is seen that the property of having a heavy tail is satisfied only for some distributions, the (standard) normal distribution with density

$$\frac{1}{\sqrt{2\pi}} e^{-\frac{x^2}{2}}$$

goes faster to zero than any power function, so (1) cannot be satisfied for any α. On the other hand, the (standard) *Cauchy* distribution with density

$$\frac{1}{\pi(1 + x^2)}$$

has a heavy tail according to (1). The lognormal distribution which satisfies

$$F(x) = \Phi\left(\frac{\log x - \mu}{\sigma}\right)$$

with Φ the distribution function of the standard normal distribution, has moderately heavy tails, because

$$F(x) \sim x^{-1} e^{-\log^2 x}.$$

The constant α used in the definition of heavy tails may be used to characterize the tail. Formally, for a heavy-tailed distribution function F, we have that

$$1 - F(x) = x^{-1/\gamma} L(x) \quad \text{for } x > 0, \tag{2}$$

where $\gamma > 0$ and L is a slowly varying function satisfying

$$\lim_{t \to \infty} \frac{L(tx)}{L(t)} = 1.$$

The quantity $1/\gamma$ is called the *tail index* of a distribution function F. Thus, the tail index specifies the power function of x whose behaviour in the tail comes closest to $1 - F$, and the greater the index, the heavier the tail of the distribution. If F satisfies (2), then the density function f of F satisfies

$$f(x) \sim x^{-\left(1 + \frac{1}{\gamma}\right)},$$

EXAMPLE 13.2 For some of the heavy-tailed distributions, the tail index can be found directly from the probability distribution of density functions. Here are a few examples.

Pareto distribution. Here we have directly that

$$P[|X| > x] = \left(\frac{\kappa}{\kappa + x}\right)^{\alpha},$$

so the tail index is α.

The t-distribution with α degrees of freedom has density function

$$\frac{\Gamma\left(\dfrac{\alpha + 1}{2}\right)}{\sqrt{\pi \alpha}\,\Gamma\left(\dfrac{\alpha}{2}\right)} \left(1 + \frac{x^2}{\alpha}\right)^{-(\alpha+1)/2},$$

so tail index can be found as the degrees of freedom.

The log-gamma distribution has density

$$\frac{\alpha^{\beta}}{\Gamma(\beta)} (\log x)^{\beta} x^{-(\alpha+1)},$$

and because $(\log x)^{\beta}$ is a slowly-varying function, we get that the tail index is α.

For estimation of the tail index, the most well-known estimator is the Hill estimator for γ. Let $\widetilde{X}_1, \ldots, \widetilde{X}_n$ be independent and identically distributed according to F, and let $\widetilde{X}_{n,1} \geq \cdots \geq \widetilde{X}_{n,n}$ be the order statistics based on $\widetilde{X}_1, \ldots, \widetilde{X}_n$. Then the Hill estimator $\hat{\gamma}_H$ (of order k_n) is defined as

$$\hat{\gamma}_H = \frac{1}{k_n} \sum_{i=1}^{k_n} \log \widetilde{X}_{n,i} - \log \widetilde{X}_{n,k_n+1},$$

where $k_n < n$ is such that $k_n \to \infty$ but $\dfrac{k_n}{n} \to 0$ for $n \to \infty$. Thus, typically only a few of the largest order statistics are used.

13.2.4 Stable distributions

Because losses add up from many events, it may seem preferable to use families of distributions such that sums of independent variables with this distribution again have distributions from the family, although presumably with other parameter values. The standard example is provided by normally distributed random variables, sums of which are again normal. However, the search for distributions with suitably heavy tails means that we must look for other families of distributions with this property.

The distribution of a random variable $\widetilde{X}$ is *stable* if for all n there are constants $c_n > 0$ and $d_n \in \mathbb{R}$ such that

$$\widetilde{X}_1 + \cdots + \widetilde{X}_n \overset{d}{=} c_n \widetilde{X} + d_n$$

for $\widetilde{X}_1, \ldots, \widetilde{X}_n$ independent, identical copies of $\widetilde{X}$ (here the notation $\overset{d}{=}$ means that the two random variables have the same distribution).

It can be shown that the only possible choice for c_n is

$$c_n = n^{1/\alpha}$$

for some $\alpha \in [0, 2]$. For $\alpha = 2$ we have the family of normally distributed variables. Here are some other stable families.

The Cauchy(γ, δ) distribution has density

$$f(x) = \frac{1}{\pi} \frac{\gamma}{\gamma^2 + (x - \delta)^2}, \quad -\infty < x < \infty$$

(we have seen a Cauchy$(1, 0)$ distribution above). This distribution is stable with parameter $\alpha = 1$. The Lévy(γ, δ) distribution has density

$$f(x) = \sqrt{\frac{\gamma}{2\pi}} \frac{1}{(x - \delta)^{3/2}} e^{-\frac{\gamma}{2(x-\delta)}}, \quad \delta < x < \infty,$$

and it is stable with parameter $\alpha = 1/2$. Both the Cauchy and the Lévy distributions are heavy tailed.

For all stable distributions with $\alpha < 2$, one has

$$P\left[\widetilde{X} > x\right] \sim \gamma^{\alpha} c_{\alpha}(1 + \beta)x^{-\alpha},$$

where γ and β are constants characterizing the distribution (the family of all stable distributions can be characterized by four parameters, one of them being α), and $c_{\alpha} = \sin\left(\dfrac{\pi\alpha}{2}\right)\Gamma(\alpha)\pi^{-1}$. This shows that these stable distributions all have heavy tails and as such are eligible for the modelling of operational losses.

13.2.5 Extreme value theory

Since the operational losses that we are dealing with are those that are unusually large, we are interested in what happens in the tail of the distribution. The relevant theoretical basis for this is the *extreme value* theory (EVT), cf. e.g. Embrechts et al. [1997], which deals with either maxima or values above a certain threshold and of sequences of random variables (many of which will represent ordinary everyday outlays and therefore will not show up as operational losses). There are two possible approaches to such large losses.

In the *block maxima* models, we think of operational losses as subdivided into blocks (corresponding to periods, one month or one year) and find the distribution of the maxima of these blocks. For large losses x, the distribution of these maxima can be found as

$$F(x) = \begin{cases} \exp\left(-\left(1 + \xi\dfrac{x - \mu}{\beta}\right)^{-1/\xi}\right) & \xi \neq 0, \\[2mm] \exp\left(-e^{-(x-\mu)/\beta}\right) & \xi = 0, \end{cases}$$

where $1 + \xi\frac{x-\mu}{\beta} < 0$, and x is defined in the intervals $(\mu - \frac{\beta}{\xi}, \infty)$ if $\xi < 0$, $(-\infty, \mu - \frac{\beta}{\xi})$ if $\xi < 0$ and everywhere if $\xi = 0$. Here μ is a location parameter (usually set to 0), β a scale parameter and ξ defines the shape of the distribution. This exact distribution may, however, not be easy to work with, and somewhat simpler approximations may be used in practice.

Peaks over thresholds: Even if we are interested in the tail events, the large losses, we may not be satisfied with choosing only the maximal losses in a given period, because we will then miss the information about several large losses happening in the same period. Thus, it may be more useful to look at losses which are very large in the sense that they are above a certain level, leading to the study of *excesses* over a threshold level: Given an independent and identically distributed sequence of random variables $\widetilde{X}_1, \ldots, \widetilde{X}_n$ with common distribution F, we are interested in the variable $\widetilde{Y} = \widetilde{X} - u$ in cases where it is non-negative. A large loss occurs in the event that $\widetilde{X} > u$, and the distribution of excesses is the conditional distribution

$$F_u(y) = P\{\widetilde{X} - u \leq y \mid \widetilde{X} > u\} = \dfrac{F(x + y) - F(u)}{1 - F(u)}.$$

The limiting distribution of F_u as u goes to infinity is known: It belongs to the two-parameter family of *generalized Pareto distributions* (GPD) with

$$
F_{\xi,\mu,\beta}(x) = \begin{cases} 1 - \left(1 + \xi\dfrac{x-\mu}{\beta}\right)^{-1/\xi} & \text{for } \xi \neq 0, \\[2ex] 1 - e^{-\frac{x-\mu}{\beta}} & \text{for } \xi = 0, \end{cases}
$$

where $x \geq \mu$ if $\xi \geq 0$ and $\mu \leq x \leq \mu - \frac{\beta}{\xi}$ if $\xi < 0$; ξ, μ and β are the shape, location and scale parameters of the distribution.[1] The main point here is that even if the distribution F is unknown, we can use the GPD to get explicit functional form, at least as an approximation. From our data, we have an estimate of $1 - F(u)$, namely the proportion of observed losses above u, and, similarly, the parameters which characterize the variance and tail of the distribution can be estimated from data. This means that one can compute approximate quantiles of the distribution of F as well as mean excess $e(u) = \mathsf{E}[\widetilde{X} - u \mid \widetilde{X} > u]$.

It remains to choose the size of the threshold u. Because our use of the GPD presupposes that u is quite large, the number of cases where losses exceed the threshold will remain reasonably small, which, however, is unfortunate for purposes of estimating the tail. In practice, one uses the mean excess: For the GPD, one has

$$
e(u) = \frac{\beta}{1-\xi} + \frac{\xi}{1-\xi}u,
$$

which for $0 < \xi < 1$ and $\beta + \xi u > 0$ would give a straight line with positive slope, which, is steeper the closer ξ comes to 1. A rule of thumb for selecting the threshold is then to plot the mean excesses against different values of u and then select the value of u such that the plot is approximately linear above this value.

13.3 Value creation and operational risk

In the previous sections, we have discussed ways of modelling the operational loss process, the underlying purpose being that of finding the *economic capital* connected with operational risk, that is, the amount of capital that would be enough to prevent with high probability that the financial firm would not be able to cover its obligations. This economic capital is usually found as the VaR of the loss distribution, and therefore the search for a suitable model of the loss distribution is so important.

It may be argued, however (following Jarrow [2008]), that the approach taken so far is inappropriate when dealing with operational risk, because this is risk connected with the value process of the firm (here the banking firm), where value is created in a random way, with some negative events creating losses intervening. Therefore, economic capital should be found from a consideration of this net value creation, which in some cases may

---

[1] A random variable distributed according to GPD with parameters ξ, μ, β can be obtained as $\widetilde{X} = \mu + \frac{\beta}{\xi}(\widetilde{U}^{-\xi} - 1)$ for $\xi \neq 0$, $\widetilde{X} = \mu - \beta \ln \widetilde{U}$ for $\xi = 0$, where $\widetilde{U}$ is uniformly distributed in $[0, 1]$.

result in large negative values but in most cases would be positive, rather from an isolated consideration of a loss distribution.

In order to connect operational losses with the operation of the financial firm, one has to model the process of value creation. We consider a financial firm operating in an interval of time from 0 to T. Suppose that the financial firm has some assets, the value of which evolves according to a stochastic process S_t. We may think of the assets as securities, loans or even physical assets, and the composition may change over time as a result of trade. They can be traded in a market, and assuming that the market is arbitrage free, the time t value of these assets can be written as

$$S_t = \mathsf{E}_t \left[S_T \exp\left(-\int_t^T r_s \, ds\right) \right],$$

where r_s is the risk-free rate of interest at time s, and E_t denotes expectation given the information available at time t.[2] In particular, the firm may be liquidated of all assets which are sold at time t at the market value S_t. But buying the assets does not mean that the activities of the firm continue unimpaired; for this one has to add the specific competences of the financial firm, the workings of which give rise to a value V_t of the financial firm, which is also considered as an asset that can be traded in the market, so

$$V_t = \mathsf{E}_t \left[V_T \exp\left(-\int_t^T r_s \, ds\right) \right],$$

The specification of the value-creating process, by which S_t is transformed to V_t, is split into three parts. First of all, the firm's operating technology gives rise to a value creation, called the NPV process, by which the asset values S_t are transformed to

$$S_t \cdot \pi_t,$$

where π_t is a stochastic process taking values > 1. One may formulate π_t as a doubly stochastic process, giving rise to upwards jumps of size $1 + \alpha_t$, with α_t a non-negative random variable, occurring randomly governed by a Poisson process with time dependent or even stochastic intensity λ_t^0, so

$$\pi_t = \prod_{i=0}^{N_0(t)} (1 + \alpha_{t_i}),$$

where t_i are the dates at which a jump has occurred, and $N_0(t)$ is the number of jumps that have occurred before t.

Next, the result of value creation is modified by operational losses. To model this modification, it might seem most in line with the present approach to derive the loss process from details of the transactions of value creation (as in Leippold and Vanini [2005]), which

---

[2]Technically, E_t denotes conditional expectations taken with respect to the risk-adjusted martingale measure associated with the arbitrage-free market.

would make this a structural approach to operational risk, but because this would demand a more detailed description of the many different ways in which operational losses may occur, a reduced form specification will be used. Thus, losses are described by another stochastic process θ_t, modifying the value created. The process θ_t can be further specified as a doubly stochastic process, where loss events occur with some intensity λ_t^1, giving rise to jumps of size $1 - \delta_t$, so

$$\theta_t = \prod_{i=0}^{N_1(t)} (1 - \delta_{t_i}).$$

The value of the firm at date T can be written as

$$V_T = S_T \cdot \pi_T \cdot \theta_T$$

or, with the specifications of the NPV and the loss processes, as

$$V_t = \mathsf{E}_t \left[S_T \exp\left(-\int_t^T r_s \, ds \right) \prod_{i=0}^{N_0(t)} (1 + \alpha_{t_i}) \prod_{i=0}^{N_t^1} (1 - \delta_{t_i}) \right]. \tag{3}$$

It can be shown (cf. Jarrow [2008]) that (3) can be written as

$$V_t = \mathsf{E}_t \left[S_T \exp\left(-\int_t^T \left[r_s - \alpha_s \lambda_s^0 \mu_s^0 + \delta_s \lambda_s^1 \mu_s^1 \right] ds \right) \right], \tag{4}$$

where μ_t^0, μ_t^1 are correction terms for the intensities under the risk-neutral probability measures. The advantage of the representation in (4) is that the NPV and the operational loss processes can be treated as an adjustment of the discount rate in finding net present values. This in turn means that many well-known techniques from pricing of interest rate derivatives can be used when dealing with operational risk.

For the purpose of estimating the NPV and operational loss processes, one would need data for both asset values and firm values, and the latter may not be immediately observable. However, this problem can be circumvented in the same way as it was done in the structural approach to credit risk, and then standard methods for estimation of Cox processes can be used. The result is an operational loss function which is derived from the comprehensive economic activity of the financial firm rather than just fitted to suitably selected data.

13.4 Capital requirements for operational risk

The Basel rules for capital reserves against operational risk date back to Basel II. As with credit risk, there are several alternatives open to the banks, although it has been the intention that at some future point all banks would choose the more sophisticated approach, based on their own data collection.

13.4.1 The basic indicator approach

Because the bank has to carry out business even without knowing in detail where the losses due to operational risk are most likely to occur, it can act according to rules of prudent behaviour: It should set aside capital for operational risk. The *basic indicator* approach in Basel II specifies this as

$$C_t = \frac{1}{\sum_{i=1}^{3} I_{\{Y_{t-i}>0\}}} \sum_{i=1}^{3} \alpha \max\{Y_{t-i}, 0\},$$

where Y_{t-i} is gross income in year $t - i$, and I_A is the indicator function of A (being 1 when the event A happens and 0 otherwise; in plain words, the risk capital is found as a certain percentage of gross income (as a proxy for the activity level in the bank, assuming that losses are proportional to the activity), averaged over the last three years provided that income was non-negative. The suggestion for the percentage α is 15%.

13.4.2 The standardized approach

In Basel II, banks may choose to follow the standardized approach (S), relying on such percentages. For this, the activities of the bank are divided into eight distinct business lines, and the general formula is now modified to

$$C_t^S = \frac{1}{3} \sum_{i=1}^{3} \max \left\{ \sum_{j=1}^{8} \beta_j Y_{t-i}^j, 0 \right\}.$$

It is seen that the formula differs slightly from the first one, because negative income in one business line does not reduce the capital requirements from the other business lines. The reason for this asymmetry is that banks should be induced to move from the standardized approach to the so-called advanced management approach, to which we shall turn in the next section.

The lines of business and the associated percentages are given in Table 13.2.

In addition to the capital requirement rules, banks are expected to conform to the guidelines outlined in Pillars 2 and 3 of the Basel Accord, concerning public access to details which matter in connection with operational risk, but this part of Basel II is less elaborated than the capital rules and will presumably be implemented later.

13.4.3 Advanced management approaches

In accordance with the general approach of Basel II, banks are allowed to use their own internal risk measurement system to determine the capital requirement (as long as it satisfies general criteria). As already mentioned, there is no obvious single approach to risk measurement in the field of operational risk, and the Basel Committee did not specify either approach or assumptions on distributions, but demands that the methods used meet the standards which would be demanded of similar models for assessment of credit risk.

Typically, a method for assessing operational losses will assess a combination of event (Table 13.1) and business line (Table 13.2) separately, giving a total of 56 different cases.

Table 13.2 Lines of Business and Their Betas

j	**Business Line**	β_j (%)
1	Corporate finance	18
2	Trading & sales	18
3	Retail banking	12
4	Commercial banking	15
5	Payment & settlement	18
6	Agency services	15
7	Asset management	12
8	Retail brokerage	12

Source: Basel Committee on Banking Supervision [2001a].

For each, the banks will gather internal data on repetitive, high-frequency losses covering three to five years, as well as relevant external data on non-repetitive, low-frequency losses. There are three different methods for calculating the capital charges, and the bank must choose one of these.

The internal measurement approach: Here the bank should find for each of the 56 business line–event combinations the following quantities:

   (i) The exposure indicator, *EI* (which may be gross income);
  (ii) Probability of event, *PE*;
 (iii) Loss given the event, *LGE*.

The product of the three is the expected loss *EL* for each of the business line–event combinations. The computed value of *EL* is then multiplied by a constant γ_{jk} depending on business line j and event type k, set by the supervisor, to take into account that there can be a certain amount of *unexpected loss* on top of *EL*, and one reaches the total capital charges

$$K = \sum_{j=1}^{8} \sum_{k=1}^{7} \gamma_{jk} \times EI_{jk} \times PE_{jk} \times LGE_{jk}.$$

The values of PE_{jk} and LGE_{jk} are found using historical data, which must have been collected for each business line j and vent type k over a certain span of time.

The scorecard approach begins with the determination of an initial operational risk capital, either at firm or at business line level, using, for example, the basic indicator or the standardized approach. Then the initial values are modified on the basis of scorecards (cf. Section 7.6), relying on a number of indicators which should be proxies for particular risk types in the business lines. These scorecards are completed regularly, and then the capital charge is computed as

$$K = \sum_{j=1}^{8} K_j^0 \times \mathcal{R}_j,$$

where $\mathcal{R}_j$ is the risk score that rescales the initial capital charge K_j^0 to a new one for the business line j.

The loss distribution approach uses historical data on the operational loss frequency and severity. For each of the 56 business line–event combinations, the bank must estimate the loss severity and the loss frequency distributions. Using this, it can find the probability distribution of operational loss for this combination and the associated Value at Risk, VaR_{jk} (with confidence level at 99.9%).

Next, the operational capital charge is found as the sum of all the VaR_{ij}, that is,

$$K = \sum_{j=1}^{8} \sum_{k=1}^{7} \text{VaR}_{jk}.$$

The loss distribution approach has several advantages (as was to be expected because it follows the general methodology outlined in Chapter 3): First of all, it is risk sensitive, because it uses the internal loss data. Secondly, it is free of ad hoc assumptions such as the fixed proportion of unexpected losses used in the internal measurement approach. And finally, if the method of estimation is correct, it computes the exact capital charge needed to take care of the operational losses.

Even so, it is not perfect because it may be complicated to estimate loss distributions. The confidence level is also not universally agreed upon, and it may matter rather much in relation to the result. Finally, because it relies on past loss history, it may become outdated if something qualitatively new happens.

13.4.4 Pillars 2 and 3 and operational risk

Whereas the first pillar of Basel II deals with capital requirements (for credit, market and operational risk), Pillar 2 contains rules for supervision, and Pillar 3 deals with market discipline through public disclosure mechanisms. The idea is that the openness of banks with regard to their procedures as well as their actual capital charges in each business line should make it possible for the public to assess the risks of the bank and the ability of the bank to withstand pressures.

As with the other risk types, the belief in the market as a means of disciplining the banks was seriously weakened after the financial crisis of 2007–8. In the years that have followed, the emphasis has been on tighter regulation of market and credit risk, although the regulation of operational risk has remained largely the same.

13.5 Exercises

1. After a change in management, a bank adopts a new method of conducting business, where more emphasis is put on the personal relationship between customer and bank employee as well as on streamlining internal procedures. As a consequence, the bank has reduced the cost of dealing with customers' complaints, and it has been possible to open up some new fields of business without changes of staff.

The bank wants to reduce its capital charges in order to expand its credit sector, and for this it would like to exploit the reduction in operational losses. How should this be done?

2. A financial institution has specialized in a standardized asset management process. It has 3,000 customers, each of which pays a fee of €100 per week for this service. There are, however, some random losses connected with this service, with estimated monthly mean of €20 and standard derivation of €10.

Find the probability that the institution runs a loss in a given month.

3. After a series of acquisitions, a small local bank has grown to a medium-sized bank which not only serves the traditional local customers in the field of private banking, but in addition aims at increasing its business in ALM (asset and liability management) and trade in derivatives. Each of the former banks had a simple standardized risk management system, but the direction contemplates a change, mainly with the aim of reducing the capital charges.

Give a suggestion for the method of operational risk management of this bank.

13.6 Comments

There are several textbooks on operational risk, e.g. King [2001], Chernobai et al. [2007]. Texts on extreme value theory are e.g. Embrechts et al. [1997], de Haan and Ferreira [2006].

The approach to operational risk outlined in Section 13.4 has been followed up in Jarrow et al. [2010] for computation of the cost of operational loss insurance.

Chapter 14

Liquidity Shocks, Bank Runs and the Interbank Market

14.1 Bank runs in the liquidity insurance model

A bank run occurs when the depositors become worried about the possibility of getting their money back from the bank, so they take immediate action in order to save their deposits. The combined action of many worried depositors will make it impossible for the bank to honour all its obligations, and this may bring about the event that was feared by the depositors.

Because a bank run may start with subjective assessments by depositors, not necessarily founded in events related to the bank, and may have quite serious consequences, it is important to be able to prevent bank runs or to make sure that they will not have too big repercussions on the financial sector as a whole. A first step in this direction must be a closer investigation of the mechanisms leading to the bank run; even though based on expectations of depositors, it is, of course, related to the basic business model of a bank, which consists in financing illiquid investments by liquid (deposit) obligations. A reasonable point of departure for this investigation will be a further look at the liquidity insurance model [Diamond and Dybvig, 1983] of Section 1.2.

In this model, we had an investment project I giving rise to a payoff $R > 1$ per unit invested, which could be carried out by individuals or alternatively by the bank. The reason why individuals might not take on this investment on their own was that they were exposed to a random liquidity shock, so they might need cash after having undertaken the investment, something that happens with probability π, and liquidating this investment would entail a considerable loss, the liquidation value (per unit invested) was $L < 1$.

It was shown that from the point of view of society, the optimal arrangement would be a deposit contract, whereby the individuals hand over their endowment of 1 unit to the bank,

277

and the bank promises to deliver either c_1^0 at $t = 1$ or c_2^0 at $t = 2$, where (c_1^0, c_2^0) solves the utility maximization problem

$$\max_{c_1,c_2,I} \pi u(c_1) + (1 - \pi)u(c_2)$$

subject to constraints

$$\pi c_1 = 1 - I,$$

$$(1 - \pi)c_2 = RI.$$

The contract between bank and individual, according to which the individual can obtain the stipulated amount whenever presenting herself to the bank, is incentive compatible as long as $c_1^0 \leq c_2^0$, excluding the possibility that patient depositors could benefit by pretending to be impatient. The arrangement has overcome the problem of asymmetric information, in the sense that in the equilibrium, agents disclose their true type.

However (as was also noticed at our first acquaintance with the model), there is room for some reservations as to whether we solved the problem of liquidity insurance without any side effects. What may concern us is that if for some reason patient depositors become afraid that the bank will not fulfil its promises at $t = 2$, they will prefer to withdraw the smaller amount c_1 at $t = 1$. But then we have a *bank run*, and if all depositors want their money at $t = 1$, the bank cannot satisfy its obligations and goes bankrupt. Thus, the disadvantage of fractional reserve banking as developed here is the possibility of a bank run.

From a purely technical point of view, bank runs do not happen in our very simple model, at least when we assume rational behaviour of agents, because the amounts to be delivered to patient individuals are obtained with certainty through the investment. However, the model can easily be extended in such a way that bank runs occur as equilibrium outcomes. For this we need only to add a mechanism which produces a signal $s \in \{0, 1\}$. The signal has no connection with the investment technology or the bank, but if the depositors believe that they will get nothing at $t = 2$ and only L at $t = 1$ in the case of signal $s = 1$, then they will run the bank – and the result is that they indeed get nothing at $t = 2$ and L at $t = 1$, because the bank defaults and the investment is liquidated.

We have here a simple example of what is known in the literature as a *sunspot equilibrium*: Events which have no relation to the fundamentals of the economy do nevertheless influence the choices of the agents and thereby turn out to have an effect on the equilibrium outcomes. In our case, the sunspot equilibrium gives rise to a bank run: The individuals being afraid that the bank may collapse demand their money back and thereby cause the collapse which they believed to be coming.

14.1.1 Suspension of payment

Staying within the confines of our simple model, we can propose another, and surprisingly simple, cure of the problem of bank runs: If the bank announces officially that it will not pay out more than the total sum of πc_1^0 to depositors claiming to need liquidity, then the belief formation leading to a bank run will be suspended. Indeed, as long as the bank limits

---

Box 14.1

The run on Northern Rock. One of the more spectacular bank runs in recent times was the run on the English bank Northern Rock. This bank had its roots in building societies operating for more than one hundred years, but after mergers and reorganizations it had become an ordinary bank taking deposits and arranging loans, mainly in mortgages. In the course of August and the first part of September 2007, it was hit – together with many other banks – by the sharp increase in interbank rates occurring at this time, which made the position of several banks very strained. In this situation the Bank of England declared that it would provide emergency loans to banks which were getting into short-term difficulties due to the high interbank rates.

On 13 September, the BBC revealed that Northern Rock had asked for and been given emergency support from the Bank of England, and the news was commented with remarks pointing to the critical situation of the financial sector and its impact on the everyday life of ordinary citizens. On the next day, 14 September, the Bank of England, the Treasury and the financial inspection authority issued a statement saying that they believed Northern Rock to be solvent and that the funding facility had been given so as to help the bank through a period of financial turbulence. However, the shares of Northern Rock dropped by 32%, and queues began to form outside some Northern Rock branches. Also, the bank's website collapsed under the strain.

On 17 September, the shares had dropped by another 40%; the queues at all its 76 branches were not diminishing; and the Chancellor declared that no depositor would lose money (the deposit insurance did not provide full coverage of losses for depositors). This seemed to have some effect on the queues, which diminished over the following days. On 1 October, the deposit insurance scheme was revised so as to provide full coverage up to £35,000.

In the following months, attempts to find a buyer who would agree to take over the bank failed, and on 18 February 2008, the bank was nationalized. Subsequently, it was sold in 2012 to Virgin Money.

Although the background of financial unrest did contribute, it was not the main reason that a run occurred; several other banks had similar problems, but there were no runs on these banks. That it happened to Northern Rock was due to the public announcement of the emergency support from the Bank of England, which made the public aware of this particular bank. Depositors queuing for their money was only the last event in a long chain, and much of the trouble came not from depositors, but from Northern Rock's reliance on 'wholesale funding', short-term credit with a maturity of a few months, which had to be rolled over continuously for the bank to function properly. The general decline in the properties market meant that the short-term credit could not be renewed as expected, and when the troubles became known to the public, the bank had been strained for some time already [Shin, 2009].

---

its payments to this sum, it will be able to honour all obligations to the patient individuals, who were those causing the problems in the first place. This means that nobody is hurt by this measure which, on the face of it, looks as if the bank denies its contractual obligations to pay c_1^0 whenever an individual turns up and claims it.

The solution is, however, strongly dependent on the parameters of the model. If π is incorrectly estimated, then problems may arise, and indeed the exact way of specifying the limits on what can be paid will constitute a problem of its own as soon as we allow for banks with many different investment contracts and with inhomogeneous depositors.

A more robust way of achieving the same objective, namely the eradication of belief-induced bank runs, is *deposit insurance*. If the deposits are guaranteed by an independent institution, possibly backed by the government, then again there will be no reason for demanding the deposits back before time, and now the working of the deposit insurance is independent of any parameter estimation. The use of deposit insurance to prevent bank runs has been widespread in recent years, so both for theoretical and practical reasons, we need to consider this arrangement in further detail. This will be done in a separate chapter to follow.

14.1.2 Equity rather than deposits

Another workable method for avoiding bank runs was investigated in Jacklin [1987]. It consists in making the deposits transferable so that depositors can sell them in a market rather than having to convert them to cash at the bank. Technically, this means that the depositor gets equity with face value 1 and a prescribed dividend payment d to be paid at $t = 1$, giving the right to $R(1 - d)$ units of output at time 2. Each such share can be sold at $t = 1$ at a price p.

With this arrangement, an individual in need of cash at $t = 1$ can sell the share and get

$$c_1 = d + p,$$

and the individuals waiting to $t = 2$ buy $\dfrac{d}{p}$ shares, so they get

$$c_2 = \left(1 + \frac{d}{p}\right) R(1 - d).$$

The price p at which shares are traded is determined by supply and demand, so

$$\pi = (1 - \pi)\frac{d}{p} \text{ or } p = \frac{1 - \pi}{\pi} d,$$

and we therefore have that

$$c_1 = \frac{d}{\pi}, \quad c_2 = \frac{R(1 - d)}{1 - \pi}.$$

If the dividend payment can be specified initially, then it can be set so that $c_t = c_t^0$ for $t = 1, 2$, so optimal consumption can be achieved with this arrangement.

As was to be expected, the very neat results obtained here, according to which equity can achieve exactly the same as deposits, is to some extent dependent on the model. Adding some features to the model, the equivalence of equity and deposits will disappear, so deposits may give a higher payoff than equity, although they are susceptible to bank runs.

14.2 Narrow banking

Although bank runs occur with some frequency even in our time, the occurrence of bank runs was a much more usual event in the nineteenth century, and the discussion of the phenomenon as well as of means to prevent them from happening has a long history. Among the proposals being formulated at that time was one which has been revived recently, namely that of *narrow banking*, the essence of which is to demand that deposit-taking banks should invest only in securities which are very safe and can be sold at full value at any time, so that bank runs cannot occur.

The exact way of formulating narrow banking is subject to some variations in the literature. In Wallace [1996], who investigates the phenomenon in the framework of the Diamond-Dybvig model, it is interpreted as a demand that the bank must be able to satisfy all contractual obligations at each date. Then the bank must work under the constraints

$$c_1 \leq 1 - I$$
$$c_2 \leq RI,$$

and a solution which maximizes expected utility under these constraints is clearly inferior to the optimal solution considered above. Actually, it is even inferior to the case where investment is done on an individual basis, so narrow banking seems to be equivalent to the abandonment of any banking activity.

However, most proposals for narrow banking are less drastic. One way or another, they attempt to separate the deposit business from other financial transactions involving risk. This separation is not thought of as creating independent firms; rather, deposits should be taken care of by special subsidiaries, and the deposits should be placed in safe securities. What this means is also subject to some discussion, and some authors [Bryan, 1991] also allow lending activities by the narrow bank, provided that they take the form of safe mortgages.

The assessment of narrow banking in the literature has mainly been negative, cf. e.g. Wallace [1996], Kobayakawa and Nakamura [2000], arguing that the different risks arising from deposits and loans, respectively, are uncorrelated and that separating these activities will be damaging from the synergies created by having both. However, this argumentation might not be as convincing now as when it was put forward, years before the financial crisis around 2008. Also, the synergies created by having the many different financial activities in the same firm seem to be a matter of belief rather than evidence. And finally, although bank runs can be avoided by having a system of deposit insurance, the latter does not come for free, and its cost to society should be taken into consideration and weighed against the 'synergies'.

Not surprisingly, the ideas of separating some of the activities of the financial intermediaries are still alive, and they turn up even in contexts which seem rather far from the original background, such as Islamic banking (considered in Chapter 9) and proposals for another way of regulating financial intermediaries (to be dealt with in Chapter 18).

14.3 Liquidity risk management

Given the crucial importance of being able to satisfy liquidity needs of depositors, it comes as no surprise that banks must take particular care to control their own liquidity. A simple first approach consists in comparing the liquid assets and liabilities to see whether the bank is in need of additional liquid reserves. But such a simple comparison does not quite capture the nature of the problem, namely that depositors may require cash as a result of a random liquidity shock. Without explicitly involving the stochastic demand for liquidity, it is difficult to give an assessment of the needed liquidity reserve.

The problem of finding the appropriate size of this reserve is basically one of finding an optimal inventory (of cash), and consequently methods of inventory planning can be used. Following Ho and Saunders [1981], we apply the classical newsvendor model to the problem at hand.

Suppose that the bank gets the rate r_L on its loans but must pay a penalty rate r_p if it requires cash above the amount of its own reserves, possibly from the central bank. Depositors' demand for cash $\tilde{x}$ is assumed to be random, with a probability distribution function $F(x)$ and density function $f(x)$. If, for simplicity, we assume that the deposit rate is 0, then the expected profit of the bank, seen as a function of its reserves R takes the form

$$\pi(R) = (D - R)r_L + Rr - r_p \int_R^\infty (x - R)f(x)\,dx,$$

where the last member on the right-hand side is the expected penalty cost, to be paid whenever the demand for cash exceeds R.

First-order conditions for a maximum are found by differentiating w.r.t. R,

$$-r_L + r + r_p \int_R^\infty f(x)\,dx = 0,$$

or, using that $\int_R^\infty f(x)\,dx = 1 - F(R)$,

$$1 - F(R) = \mathrm{P}\{\tilde{x} \geq R\} = \frac{r_L - r}{r_p}.$$

We have thus determined the optimal reserve by a condition on the probability of having to use outside sources of liquidity. The result may look somewhat unrealistic in numerical examples: If for example $r_L - r = 4\%$ and $r_p = 20\%$, then the probability of being short of cash is $1/5$ in optimum, so this event should occur roughly once a week. Intuitively, this seems to be too high a probability, so the reserves may be greater in real life than what is prescribed by the optimal inventory theory, or, alternatively, there may be other costs of running short of cash than what is captured by the penalty rate of interest.

In the considerations above, we have not concentrated attention on the optimization of R, but the optimal reserve must be found together with other strategic variables of the bank.

This can be illustrated by looking at liquidity management in the Monti-Klein model of a monopolistic bank, as done by Prisman et al. [1986]. As in Chapter 11, the bank chooses r_L and r_D so as to maximize profits given that L depends on r_L and D on r_D. We abstract from administration cost but now include the penalty cost of running short of cash, so expected profit takes the form

$$(r_L - r)L(r_L) + (r - r_D)D(r_D) - r_p \int_R^\infty (x - (D(r_D) - L(r_L))f(x)dx$$

(where we have used that reserves equal the difference between deposits and loans). The first-order conditions are

$$(r_L - r)L'(r_L) + L(r_L) - r_p \left[\int_R^\infty f(x)\,dx \right] L'(r_L) = 0,$$

$$(r - r_D)D'(r_D) - D(r_D) + r_p \left[\int_R^\infty f(x)\,dx \right] D'(r_D) = 0,$$

which can be reformulated to yield the Amoroso-Robinson formula

$$r_L = \left(r + r_p P\{\tilde{x} \geq R\} \right) \frac{1}{1 - \dfrac{1}{\varepsilon_L}}$$

for the loan rate, and

$$r_D = \left(r + r_p P\{\tilde{x} \geq R\} \right) \frac{1}{1 + \dfrac{1}{\varepsilon_D}}$$

for the deposit rate. It is not surprising that the size of the optimal level of reserves matters for both rates, but what is more important, this introduces a dependence of loan and deposit rate on *both* loans and deposits, so the two departments cannot be seen as independent of each other, as would be the case in simpler versions of the Monti-Klein model.

14.4 Liquidity insurance with several banks: The interbank market

In the classical model of Diamond and Dybvig, we had only one bank serving a homogeneous population. In the present section, we look at a slight extension of this model, following Bhattacharya and Gale [1987], where we allow for several, say n, banks. Each bank j has a given set of potential customers, characterized by the probability π_j of being impatient. This probability may differ among banks, but for each bank it is the same for all its customers. Also, the utility function $u(c)$ is assumed to be identical for all individuals. There is only one investment, with the same characteristics as previously.

In the spirit of the model, each bank can propose a deposit contract for its customers, in which they deposit 1 unit, getting c_1^j in case of impatience and c_2^j otherwise, where (c_1^j, c_2^j) maximizes

$$\pi_j c_1 + (1 - \pi_j) c_2$$

over all (c_1, c_2) with

$$\pi_j c_1^j = 1 - I$$

$$\left(1 - \pi_j\right) c_2^j = RI,$$

$$0 \leq I \leq 1.$$

This is clearly the best that the bank can do for its customers, maximizing welfare if the customers are seen isolated from the remaining individuals. However, it is not necessarily a welfare maximum for society as a whole, the latter being defined as a family $(c_1^j, c_2^j)_{j=1}^n$ which maximizes

$$\frac{1}{n} \sum_{j=1}^{n} \left[\pi_j u\left(c_1^j\right) + \left(1 - \pi_j\right) u\left(c_2^j\right) \right]$$

under the constraints

$$\frac{1}{n} \sum_{j=1}^{n} \pi_j c_1^j = 1 - I,$$

$$\frac{1}{n} \sum_{j=1}^{n} \left(1 - \pi_j\right) c_2^j = RI,$$

$$0 \leq I \leq 1.$$

We first notice that in the solution to this maximization problem, all individuals get the same pair (c_1^*, c_2^*), independent of the bank to which they belong. Indeed, if $(c_1^1, \ldots, c_n^1)$ is not a vector with all coordinates identical, then

$$u\left(\sum_{j=1}^{n} \pi_j c_1^j \right) > \sum_{j=1}^{n} \pi_j u\left(c_1^j\right)$$

by concavity of u, showing that in optimum all consumptions at $t = 1$ are equal; the same argument holds for the consumptions at $t = 2$.

Now we take a closer look at the optimum (c_1^*, c_2^*). If I^* is the associated investment level, then we must have that

$$c_1^* = \frac{1 - I^*}{\overline{\pi}}, \quad c_2^* = \frac{RI^*}{1 - \overline{\pi}},$$

where $\bar{\pi} = \frac{1}{n}\sum_{j=1}^{n}\pi_j$ is the average probability of being impatient. Interpreting the π_j as the proportion of impatient customers among the customers of bank j, we see that in the optimum, the individuals are fully insured against the liquidity risk.

However, we now face the problem of designing bank contracts which implement this social optimum. Clearly, any bank in isolation cannot take on this task, because one of the constraints (either at $t = 1$ or at $t = 2$) will be violated. If the proportion of impatient customers π_j of bank j is above the average $\bar{\pi}$, then the bank will experience a need for liquidity at $t = 1$ of the size $D_j = \pi_j c_1^* - (1 - I^*)$, and for a bank k with $\pi_k \leq \bar{\pi}$, there is an excess of liquidity $C_k = (1 - I^*) - \bar{\pi}_k c_1^*$. We have that the average need for liquidity

$$\frac{1}{n}\sum_{j:\pi_j>\bar{\pi}} D_j = \frac{1}{n}\sum_{j:\pi_j>\bar{\pi}} \pi_j c_1^* - \frac{n_1}{n}(1 - I^*),$$

where n_1 is the number of banks with liquidity needs, and

$$\frac{1}{n}\sum_{j:\pi_j\leq\bar{\pi}} C_j = \frac{n_2}{n}(1 - I^*) - \frac{1}{n}\sum_{j:\pi_j\leq\bar{\pi}} \pi_j c_1^*,$$

where $n_2 = n - n_1$ is the number of banks with non-negative liquidity reserves, so

$$\frac{1}{n}\sum_{j:\pi_j>\bar{\pi}} D_j = \frac{1}{n}\sum_{j:\pi_j\leq\bar{\pi}} C_j$$

and the demand and supply for liquidity balances. Therefore, banks in need of liquidity may borrow from banks with excess liquidity. At $t = 2$, the loans should be paid back with an interbank interest rate r, so for banks k with excess liquidity at $t = 1$, the return of the loan together with interest payment can finance the difference between investment yield and demand for consumption of its customers,

$$(1 + r)\left(1 - I^* - \pi_k c_1^*\right) = (1 - \pi_k)c_2^* - RI^*,$$

and similarly for banks j which are borrowers in the interbank market, for which the repayment should correspond to the surplus at $t = 2$,

$$(1 + r)\left[\pi_j c_1^* - (1 - I^*)\right] = RI^* - \left(1 - \pi_j\right)c_2^*,$$

or equivalently

$$(1 + r)\left(1 - I^* - \pi_j c_1^*\right) = \left(1 - \pi_j\right)c_2^* - RI^*.$$

Inserting $1 - I^* = \bar{\pi}c_1^*$ and $RI^* = (1 - \bar{)}\pi c_2^*$, we get that

$$(1 + r)\left(\bar{\pi} - \pi_j\right)c_1^* = \left[\left(1 - \pi_j\right) - (1 - \bar{\pi})\right]c_2^* = \left(\bar{\pi} - \pi_j\right)c_2^*,$$

which gives us that

$$(1+r) = \frac{c_2^*}{c_1^*},$$

or, with the expressions for c_1^* and c_2^* inserted back,

$$(1+r) = \left(\frac{\overline{\pi}}{1-\overline{\pi}}\right)\left(\frac{I^*}{1-I^*}\right)R.$$

So far, we have assumed that for the purpose of the interbank market, the liquidity shocks are observable, so banks demanding loans are doing this because of a genuine lack of liquidity. If the liquidity shocks are no longer observable, then the interbank equilibrium considered above would break down, at least in the case where $R > r + 1$, because every bank would choose investment level $I = 1$ and rely on the interbank market to cover the need for liquidity arising at $t = 1$. In such cases, we need an incentive compatibility condition for the banks to prevent excessive lending, and with such an additional condition we can no longer obtain full equality of the contracts between banks, because now $c_1^j < c_1^k$ if $\pi_j < \overline{\pi} < \pi_k$.

14.5 Financial contagion

The bank runs considered previously in the context of the Diamond-Dybvig model were initiated by expectations about the fraction of impatient depositors, and as such they were related to the particular bank, and there would be no immediate reason that bank runs should occur in other banks. However, the contagious nature of bank runs and bank panics seems to be thoroughly supported by evidence, and therefore it would be useful to have a model where such a contagion may indeed occur. Models where contagion can occur have been proposed, e.g. in Diamond and Rajan [2005], which we follow in broad outline below.

In this model, the basic uncertainty is created not by depositor impatience but by the randomness of timing of the investment projects, because the projects may mature and produce an outcome either *early*, at $t = 1$, or *late*, at $t = 2$. We assume that projects are early with probability θ, in which case they yield the outcome at $t = 1$; or late, with probability $1 - \theta$, giving now an outcome only at $t = 2$. The type of any given object is revealed only after the investment decisions have been made at $t = 0$, but before the early projects yield their outcome. For this reason, we extend the number of dates so as to include also a date $t = \frac{1}{2}$. At this date, all can observe the type of projects.

Projects are initiated by entrepreneurs, who have specific skills for managing projects, which will result in the outcome R (either at date 1 or 2). To finance the project, they obtain a loan from the bank. Banks can also manage projects, but they are less skilled and therefore can obtain only γR. This is also what they demand from the entrepreneur as a repayment at date $t = 1$. We assume that at $t = \frac{1}{2}$, when it is revealed whether a project is early or late, projects may be *restructured* (roughly corresponding to the liquidation option in our previous model), whereby the investment is transformed into payments l_1 at $t = 1$ and l_2 at $t = 2$, subject to the condition

$$l_1 + l_2 < 1 < \gamma R.$$

EXAMPLE 14.2 Suppose that projects yield an outcome $R = 1.2$, that $\gamma R = 1.1$ and that $l_1 = 0.8, l_2 = 0.1$. If a fraction $3/10$ of the projects are late, then the bank receives only the outcome $0.7 \cdot 1.1 = 0.77$ at $t = 1$, and thus it lacks 0.23 for paying off the investor-depositors.

The late projects will give an outcome of $0.3 \cdot 1.1 = 0.33$ at $t = 2$, but the liquidity is needed now, so the bank needs the interbank market. If the repayment rate in the interbank market r is 1.2, then borrowing 0.23 units would entail a repayment of $0.23 \cdot 1.2 = 0.276$, which can be paid from the outcome obtained at $t = 2$, yielding a net profit of 0.054 to the bank at that date. Thus, the bank is solvent at this interbank rate, and there is no need for the investors to run the bank at $t = \frac{1}{2}$.

Alternatively, the bank could have restructured the late projects: Using 0.2875 of the project in this way, one obtains $0.2875 \cdot 0.8 = 0.23$ units at $t = 1$ and $0.2875 \cdot 0.1 = 0.02875$ units at $t = 2$. This suffices for paying off the depositors at $t = 1$ and gives a total outcome of

$$0.02875 + 0.0125 \cdot 1.1 = 0.0425$$

at $t = 2$. Alternatively the bank could restructure all late projects. This will give $0.3 \cdot 0.8 = 0.24$ units at $t = 1$, leaving 0.01 units for lending to other banks, and the total outcome at $t = 2$ will be

$$0.03 + 0.01 \cdot 1.2 = 0.042$$

at $t = 2$. This alternative is inferior to the previous one (and to borrowing in the interbank market), at least at the prevailing rate $r = 1.2$.

If the interbank rate had been higher, say $r = 1.5$, then borrowing the difference in the interbank market would not be a feasible option, whereas restructuring becomes even more profitable, leaving a surplus of

$$0.03 + 0.01 \cdot 1.5 = 0.045.$$

So far the interbank rate has been taken as given from outside, but its size will depend on whether there are few or many banks wanting to lend or wanting to borrow. The bank considered here turned from net borrowing to net lending when the interbank rate increased, so it is natural to look for an equilibrium rate. We return to this below.

Let us consider the equilibrium repayment rent in a particular state. We assume that there are three banks, which differ not only in the fractions of early or late projects but also in the way in which projects can be restructured. Bank 1 has 1 unit of deposits, and it has $4/10$ late projects. Its projects can be restructured with $l_1^1 = 0.85$, $l_2^1 = 0.05$. If the interbank rate is $r = 1.25$, then Bank 1 will prefer to restructure late projects. In this way it obtains $0.4 \cdot 0.85 = 0.34$ units, which together with the outcome 0.66 from early projects will suffice to pay off the debtors, leaving 0.02 as net profit at $t = 2$. Thus, Bank 1 is not present in the interbank market, and only its entrepreneurs will enter with a loanable fund of size 0.06.

Example 14.2 continued

Bank 2 also has 1 unit of deposits; it has again a fraction 4/10 of deposits, but restructuring projects takes place with $l_1^2 = 0.8$, $l_2^2 = 0.1$. Bank 2 again needs to find 0.34 units for repaying the depositors, and it may do so by borrowing in the interbank market at the rate 1.25. Again the entrepreneurs of early projects bring their gains of size 0.06 to the interbank market.

The third bank has a fraction 1/11 of late projects and a total of 2.42 in deposits. This bank will also break even because per unit of investment, the bank obtains

$$\frac{10}{11} \cdot 1.1 = 1$$

as the outcome of early projects, and this exactly covers the repayment of deposits. The projects in which this bank is engaged can be restructured with $c_1^3 = 0.65$, $c_2^3 = 0.25$. Because the bank breaks even, it is not forced to restructure, and at the interbank rate of 1.25, this would not be profitable. The entrepreneurs of early projects in this last bank each obtain 0.1 to be used for lending to banks, amounting to

$$\frac{10}{11} \cdot 2.42 \cdot 0.1 = 0.22,$$

so the available loanable funds $0.06 + 0.06 + 0.22 = 0.34$ cover the demand for funds. Consequently, we have an equilibrium in the interbank market at the rate $r = 1.25$.

Suppose now that Bank 1 gets 5/10 late projects instead of 4/10. Then the bank will need 0.45 units to repay the depositors. Restructuring late projects will yield at most $0.5 \cdot 0.85 = 0.425$ units, and borrowing this at a rate ≥ 1.25 will entail a repayment of at least $0.45 \cdot 1.25 = 0.5625$ units, which is more than the 0.55 available from the output. Thus, Bank 1 has become insolvent, and the projects are restructured at $t = \frac{1}{2}$.

As a consequence of the failure of Bank 1, none of its entrepreneurs will obtain profits. Therefore, the funds for lending to Bank 2 have decreased by 0.06 units. These funds can be provided only by Bank 3, but in order to do so, the bank must restructure late projects and use the proceeds for lending in the interbank market.

For this to be acceptable for Bank 2, the interbank rate must be at least such that

$$0.65 + \frac{0.25}{r} = \frac{1.1}{r},$$

or $r > 1.3$. But then the repayment will exceed the outcome 0.44 available at $t = 2$. Consequently, Bank 2 has become insolvent as well, although its fraction of late projects was unchanged. It falls victim to the events that happened in another bank.

Banks have no endowments and need to attract deposits from investor-depositors, who in their turn have no other option because only banks have the necessary skills to supervise entrepreneurs. We therefore get a system of *fractional reserve banking*: Banks take the deposits from investors and lend them to entrepreneurs, but because projects may turn out to be late, the banks do not keep the necessary liquidity to satisfy all depositor demand.

To make the system work, we also need an *interbank* loan market: At date $t = 1$, banks and entrepreneurs with excess liquidity may offer loans to banks in need of liquidity, with a repayment rate r. Thus, if the fraction of late projects of the bank is not too large, the deposits may be paid back using the outcome of early projects and loans obtained from entrepreneurs and banks with few late projects.

At date $t = 1$, the value of present and discounted future net payments to the bank can be found by maximizing

$$\theta\gamma R + \mu(1 - \theta)\left(l_1 + \frac{l_2}{r}\right) + (1 - \mu)(1 - \theta)\frac{\gamma R}{r} \tag{1}$$

in $\mu \in [0, 1]$, the fraction of late projects that are restructured, subject to the constraint. Because the expression to be maximized is linear in μ, the optimal value will be either 0, so no restructuring takes place, or 1, all the late projects are restructured.

It can be seen from (1) that the solvency of the bank at $t = \frac{1}{2}$, where the type of all projects is observable to all, depends on the interbank rate r, which in turn is determined by supply of and demand for loanable funds given all the types. But this means that in some states of the economy, the number of late projects of some banks may be so large that it upsets the interbank market, giving rise to higher repayment rates, so banks that would otherwise have been solvent cannot fulfil their obligations and will be subject to runs.

In order for this to occur in our simple model, we have to allow for participation in the interbank market by the entrepreneurs having obtained their outcome $(1 - \gamma)R$ from the early projects. As long as $r \geq 1$, the entrepreneurs will enter the market as lenders, and if

$$l_1 + \frac{l_2}{r} < \frac{\gamma R}{r},$$

the banks will prefer to be borrowers in this market. Suppose now that the fraction of late projects in one bank is increased so much that it becomes insolvent as measured by (1) and therefore is subject to a run. This will cause the project to be restructured at $t = \frac{1}{2}$, and, as a consequence, the entrepreneurs of early projects financed by this bank will lose their profits, causing a reduction of the supply of funds in the interbank market. This in its turn will change the solvency position of other banks, possibly causing some of them to restructure. Thus, the initial shock in a single bank is transmitted to other banks, and the bank run is *contagious*.

Strictly speaking, what we are considering in the model is not a sequence of events (one bank getting into trouble, other banks following); rather, it is a description of different states of the economy, depending on the randomness of the duration of projects. However, it seems more intuitive to see the difference between states of the economy as a chain of events, where initially one bank is in trouble, and when the interbank market adapts to the situation, it leads to further defaults.

It should be noted, that the present model of fractional banking and bank runs is very different from the one with which we began the chapter. In the Diamond-Dybvig model, bank runs are created by self-fulfilling depositor expectations, whereas in this model, they are caused by events in the productive sector which are correctly anticipated by depositors.

14.6 A model of the interbank market with counterparty risk

One of the most significant features of the financial crisis in 2008 was the breakdown of the interbank market. From a period of high activity in this market in previous years, during which many banks relied mainly on the interbank market for funding, this market almost dried up in the course of a few weeks, and it never recovered to its previous levels of activity. To see how this could happen, we shall use a simplified version of a model proposed by Heider et al. [2009], which expands on the ideas put forward in the Diamond model which we have used as our baseline approach to liquidity problems. However, because our focus has shifted from the relationship between a bank and its depositors to that between banks, having recourse to the interbank market to level out differences in liquidity needs of their customers, we concentrate on the banks and let the depositors play a secondary role.

As usual, we consider a situation which runs over three periods, for $t = 0, 1$ and 2. In accordance with our previous considerations, banks have made contracts with depositors, allowing them to claim either c_1 at $t = 1$ or c_2 at $t = 2$. As in the model at Section 14.3, the banks can have different fractions of their depositors claiming c_1 at $t = 1$; we shall assume that this fraction is either π_h or π_l, with $\pi_h > \pi_l$, so we will expect an interbank market to materialize at $t = 1$. As always, the investment can be liquidated at $t = 1$ at a value $L < 1$ per unit.

In the present model, we add another feature: The investment of the bank is now subject to uncertainty, so at $t = 2$, it will yield R with some probability u, and 0 otherwise. The probability of success u can take values u_s and u_r, with $u_s > u_r$. This probability is revealed only at $t = 1$; at $t = 0$, when the investment decision is made, neither the withdrawals at $t = 1$ nor the quality of the investment is known.

We assume throughout that all the random variables involved are independent, in the sense that size of withdrawals or quality of investment of one bank has no connection with those of other banks. To facilitate reasoning in the model, we assume that there are sufficiently many banks such that the probabilities π_j for $j = h, l$ and u_i, $i = s, r$ can be identified with the fraction of banks having the respective properties.

We make another simplifying assumption, namely that deposit contracts cannot be made dependent on the outcome of the random variables i and j. This seems reasonable enough with respect to the quality of the investments of the bank which may be observable to banks, but not to outsiders. It is less appealing that also the amount of withdrawals is an event which cannot be used when setting up deposit contracts, but it will make our argument much simpler.

Full information. Let us begin with the case where both size of withdrawal $j \in \{h, l\}$ and quality of investment $i \in \{r, s\}$ can be observed by all banks at $t = 1$. The banks will then be characterized by the pair (i, j), where i is quality of investment and j is size of withdrawals. Banks with low withdrawals will be potential lenders in the interbank market, whereas those with high withdrawals are borrowers. But the borrowers may have high- or low-quality investments, and because this is observable, it will influence the conditions at which credit can be obtained in the interbank market. Consequently, there will be two different interest rates, r_s and r_r, applying to the two types of borrowers.

The lenders have the option of getting the expected payoff $u_s(1 + r_s)$ per unit contracted with the s-borrowers and $u_r(1 + r_r)$ if lending to the r-borrowers, and if both types are served in the market at equilibrium, we must have that

$$u_s(1 + r_s) = u_r(1 + r_r). \tag{2}$$

As in the previous section, a bank with a large fraction π_h of depositors withdrawing needs a loan of size $\pi_h c_1 - (1 - I^*)$, where I^* is the optimal investment decided at $t = 0$ (to be considered later), whereas a bank with a small fraction of depositors withdrawing at $t = 1$ has $(1 - I^*) - \pi_l c_1$ at its disposal. If high and low fractions of customers withdrawing are equally probable, we have that the supply equals demand when

$$(1 - I^*) - \pi_l c_1 = \pi_h c_1 - (1 - I^*),$$

which is the case when

$$\frac{\pi_h + \pi_l}{2} c_1 = 1 - I^*.$$

The interbank rates r_r and r_s can then be found from the equations which determine the availability of funds for the claimants at $t = 2$; here θ is the probability of high quality, or equivalently (by the law of large numbers) the fraction of banks getting the signal u_s at $t = 1$:

$$(1 + r_i)(\pi_h c_1 - (1 - I^*)) = u_i R I^* - (1 - \pi_h)c_2, \ i = s, r,$$

for borrowers; taking the average over investment types and using notation $\hat{u} = \theta u_s + (1 - \theta)u_r$ for average quality of investment and $\rho_0 = \theta u_s(1 + r_s) + (1 - \theta)u_r(1 + r_r)$ for the average payoff per unit in the interbank market, we get that

$$\rho_0(\pi_h c_1 - (1 - I^*)) = \hat{u} R I^* - (1 - \pi_h)c_2.$$

Now we may proceed as in Section 15.4 and find the average interbank market payoff as

$$\rho_0 = \frac{\hat{\pi}}{1 - \hat{\pi}} \frac{I^*}{1 - I^*} \hat{u} R,$$

and using (2), we may find the market interest rates for each investment quality type.

The main outcome of our analysis is not so much the precise expressions for the interbank market rates, but rather the fact that the market can be set up and will function in our present context in exactly the same way as it did when there was no uncertainty. This should not come as a surprise, because we have assumed full information, and, under this assumption, risk can be fully insured through the market. But full information is not a realistic assumption, and the main reason for studying interbank markets under uncertainty is that asymmetric information may give rise to some dysfunctional phenomena.

Asymmetric information. When the quality of the banks' assets is private information, the interbank market cannot distinguish between risky and safe borrowers, but will have to use a single interest rate for both.

Let ρ_1 be the payoff per unit borrowed in the interbank market. A lender in this market cannot distinguish between safe and risky borrowers and therefore expected payoff is $u'\rho_1$, where u' is the average probability of succes of the borrowers. If $u'\rho_1 < 1$, the lenders will prefer to keep the liquidity reserve from $t = 1$ to $t = 2$, and there is no supply in the market.

If both (r, h)- and (s, h)-banks are in the market, then $u' = \hat{u}$; we can then proceed as above and find the interbank interest rate r from $r = \rho_1 - 1$, where

$$\rho_1 = \frac{\hat{\pi}}{1 - \hat{\pi}} \frac{I^*}{1 - I^*} \hat{u} R.$$

Thus, we get the same type of expressions as under full information, but with only one interest rate. This means that in certain cases, the equilibrium interest rate may be so high that some borrowers may look for alternative ways of meeting the depositors' claims.

Suppose therefore that $\hat{u}\rho_1 > 1$. For a borrower bank with probability of succes u, the expected profit after using the interbank market, as seen at $t = 1$ will be

$$u(RI^* - (1 - \pi_h)c_2 - \rho_1(\pi_h c_1 - (1 - I^*))) - (1 - I^*). \tag{3}$$

If the interbank market is *not* used, it will be

$$u\left(RI^* - \frac{1}{L}(\pi_h c_1 - (1 - I^*)) - (1 - \pi_h)c_2\right) - \pi_h c_1 \tag{4}$$

(here the bank liquidates some of its investments at the rate L in order to pay all the depositors that claim c_1 at $t = 1$). We now rewrite (3) as

$$u(RI^* - (1 - \pi_h)c_2) - u\rho_1(\pi_h c_1 - (1 - I^*)) - (1 - I^*) =$$
$$u(RI^* - (1 - \pi_h)c_2) - [u\rho_1 \pi_h c_1 + (1 - u\rho_1)(1 - I^*)] \tag{5}$$

and (4) as

$$u(RI^* - (1 - \pi_h)c_2) - \left[\left(1 + \frac{uR}{L}\right)\pi_h c_1 - \frac{uR}{L}(1 - I^*))\right]. \tag{6}$$

Consider a case where u_s is very close to 1, whereas u_r is small, say around 0.5. Then it may well be the case that the bank with safe investments will be better off *not* using the interbank market; indeed, in the case where only the risky banks participate in the equilibrium, the lenders will have anticipated this, so $u = u_r$ in (5). From the participation condition $u_r\rho_1 > 1$, we get that $\rho > 2$, and for $u_s \sim 1$ we can have that

$$u_r\rho_1 > 1 + u_s\frac{R}{L}$$

if R/L is also close to 1. In this case, there is adverse selection in the interbank market, only the risky banks will use it as borrowers.

Summing up, the interbank market presents some additional features under asymmetric information: There may be *adverse selection*, so the safer banks prefer to handle their liquidity problems without participation in the interbank market, meaning that only the more risky borrowers will be present. This risk bias may lead to complete absence of trade, namely if the probability of success on the borrower side is too small to allow for positive expected profits for lenders. In this case, we shall have what could be considered as an *interbank market freeze*: Although there are banks with surplus liquidity, these banks prefer to keep it rather than to make themselves vulnerable to *counterparty risk* by lending in the interbank market.

14.7 Runs on shadow banks: Repo runs

In previous chapters (2 and 8), we occasionally discussed *shadow banking*, where deposits are replaced by repo trades, so investors buy securities with an agreement that the bank will buy them back on a specified date and at a specified price. If at this date, the repo trade is renewed, then it works as a deposit that is kept with the bank, whereas a repo trade that is *not* renewed works as a withdrawal of the deposit. On the face of it, there is little difference between traditional banking based on deposits and shadow banking relying on repo trades. Nevertheless, the situations in which a run on the bank may occur are different. In the classical case considered above, otherwise patient depositors lose confidence in the bank and therefore want their deposits back. This loss of confidence may be caused by counterpart risk, in the sense that some of the assets of the bank have lost value, but the main focus will be on the bank. With repo trading, non-renewal is usually based on the loss of value of the particular security underlying the repo trade, which works as collateral for the deposit, and not so much on the bank itself. As a consequence, we may expect the shadow bank to avoid some liquidity problems which may threaten a classical bank, whereas it will be susceptible to runs in other situations.

14.7.1 A model of repo trading

To investigate this somewhat more closely, we follow the approach of Martin et al. [2010]. We are here considering an economy over an infinite number of time periods (rather than over three periods as in the Diamond-Dybvig framework). At each date t, an infinite number of investors enter the economy endowed with 1 unit of money, which they can invest. They live for three consecutive periods where they have no endowment; at the second date, they observe whether they are impatient or not, and a fraction π of this generation turns out to be impatient, in which case they want their investment back at $t + 1$. Otherwise, they wait until $t + 2$.

Money, which we may also think of as a single consumption good, may be stored, but there is also a technology which can transform input of money to output after two periods. It is assumed that it requires special skills to operate this technology, so only banks can operate it. The technology is one of constant returns to scale, but with a capacity constraint, so with input I_t at date t, output at date $t + 2$ is RI_t if $I_t \leq \bar{I}$ and $R\bar{I}$ if $I_t \geq \bar{I}$, with $R > 1$

and $\bar{I} > 1$. We may think of the bank as investing I_t at date t and simultaneously issuing securities for this investment. Banks may use their own money (we return later to the question of where this money comes from) or they may obtain money from investors through repo sales.

If at any date t the bank concludes a repo trade selling securities to the amount b_t from the young investors at date t, promising to buy back securities from impatient one-year-old investors at the price $r_{1,t}$ and from patient old investors at the price $r_{2,t}$, then the cash flow at date τ will be

$$\Pi_\tau = RI_{\tau-2} + b_\tau - \pi r_{1,\tau-1}b_{\tau-1} - (1-\alpha)r_{2,\tau-2}b_{\tau-2} - I_\tau. \tag{7}$$

We assume that the bank maximizes net present value of all future cash flows, $\sum_{\tau=1}^{\infty} \beta^\tau \Pi_\tau$, where $\beta < 1$ is the discount rate. It is assumed throughout that the long-term investment is profitable in the sense that $\beta^2 R > 1$ (otherwise storing the good would be a better option), and that liquidating assets is a less desirable option: We assume that investments can be transferred to a third party (not in the model) after one year at a discount γ, which is such that $\beta\gamma R < 1$ (investing and liquidating after one period is worse than storing).

14.7.2 The steady-state equilibrium

In our analysis of the model, which is dynamic and therefore somewhat more complex than what we are used to, we begin with a *steady state*, where the repo purchases $b_t = b$, the input into the long-term technology $I_t = I$ and the repurchase rates $(r_{1,t}, r_{2,t}) = (r_1, r_2)$ are constant over time. If the steady state is an equilibrium, so no agent can choose a better action, then the repurchase rates must satisfy

$$r_2 = r_1^2. \tag{8}$$

Indeed, if $r_2 < r_1^2$, then investors could do better by terminating the contract after one year and enter a new one-year repo contract. If, conversely, $r_2 > r_1^2$, then the investor could gain from rolling over the contract after one year but simultaneously borrow b' slightly greater than r_1 at the interest rate $r_1 - 1$ using the collateral that she has received in the original repo trade. After another year, this loan is repaid as $b'r_1$, which is less than r_1^2, leaving the investor with a profit, once again contradicting the equilibrium property.

As a consequence of (8), we may describe the steady-state equilibrium by the three variables r, I and b. Moreover, if $r > 0$, then we must have $b = 1$, because otherwise investors would lose profits from the unused endowments. Also, if the cash flow Π of the bank (which in the steady state is independent of t) is positive, then $I = \bar{I}$.

Turning now to the equilibrium conditions for the bank, we notice that borrowing 1 unit and paying back πr after one year, and $(1 - \pi)r$ after two years, will result in a return R at this second year. Discounted profits are therefore

$$\beta^2\left(R - (1-\pi)r^2\right) - \beta\pi r.$$

Investing instead its own money, the bank would obtain $\beta^2 R - 1$, and because this is not better than what was obtained through borrowing, we get that

$$\beta^2(1 - \pi)r^2 + \beta\pi r \leq 1.$$

If the inequality is strict, then investing with borrowed money is better than investing with their own money, and because $\bar{I} > 1$, so banks also use the latter option, they might increase profits by offering higher rates $r' > r$ to investors and thereby getting some additional investors. We conclude that

$$\beta^2(1 - \pi)r^2 + \beta\pi r = 1. \tag{9}$$

This equation has two real roots, one of which, however, is negative, so the relevant value is $r = \frac{1}{\beta}$. Using this equilibrium rate, we find the profits of the bank as

$$\Pi = (R - 1)\bar{I} + 1 - \pi r - (1 - \pi)r^2 = (R - 1)\bar{I} + 1 - \frac{\pi}{\beta} - \frac{1 - \pi}{\beta^2}, \tag{10}$$

showing that if β is close to 1, then profits in each period are positive.

14.7.3 Repo runs

We now use the model to analyse a bank run, which in this context becomes a *repo run*, happening in the steady-state equilibrium. Suppose that at date t, the fraction $1 - \pi$ of patient investors from $t - 1$, which under normal circumstances should be repaid at $t + 1$, decide not to continue their engagement, so the bank must also pay back the amount $(1-\pi)r$ (in addition to the planned payment πr due to the impatient investors of this generation). If current profits are large enough for this payment, then the run can be countered, and a return to the steady state may take place from the next period. More specifically, if

$$(R - 1)\bar{I} \geq r + (1 - \pi)r^2,$$

then all payments to previous generations can be made using current profits, and there is no reason for a run on the bank.

No new funding at runs. If the claims for liquidity exceed the current profit, then the steady-state investments cannot be upheld. Indeed, it seems reasonable to assume that if confidence in the shadow bank has crumbled to the extent that investors want their money back, then new investors will not be forthcoming. If no liquidity can be obtained by selling the assets (which are the investments initiated at $t - 1$), then the bank can avoid bankruptcy only if

$$R\bar{I} \geq r + (1 - \pi)r^2,$$

or, inserting $r = 1/\beta$,

$$\beta^2 R\bar{I} \geq 1 - \pi + \beta. \tag{11}$$

It is seen that the constraint on banking given by (11) is becoming more tight when the exposure is higher (and $\bar{I}$ is closer to 1, which is the amount obtained from investors), and it also depends on the size R of the payoff.

New funding also at runs. If new repo trades can be initiated even when previous investors call off their engagements, then the bank has a possibility of meeting the liquidity demand by reducing investment. If $\bar{I}$ is reduced by $\dfrac{\Pi}{R}$, then profits in $t + 2$ are

$$R\left(\bar{I} - \frac{\Pi}{R}\right) - \bar{I} + 1 - \pi r - (1 - \pi)r^2 = 0,$$

and the bank is back at the steady state after two rounds. The reduction in investment can then be used together with current profits to meet the liquidity demand at t. By exactly the same argument, the bank can reduce investment at t even more, namely to the extent that it needs $\frac{\Pi}{R}$ at $t + 2$, which will now give $\Pi = 0$ at $t + 4$. Repeating this argument, one gets that date t investment can be reduced by

$$\frac{1}{R}\Pi + \frac{1}{R^2}\Pi + \cdots = \frac{1}{R - 1}\Pi \tag{12}$$

while still allowing for a return towards the steady-state path. But also profits at $t + 1$ and the amount $(1 - \pi)r^2$, which are no longer needed because the patient investors were paid off at t, can be used at $t + 2$, so date t investment can also be reduced with this amount. Consequently, the unexpected liquidity demand can be met, and a run prevented, as long as

$$(1 - \pi)r \leq \frac{R + 1}{R - 1}\Pi + \frac{1}{R}(1 - \pi)r^2.$$

Otherwise, the bank cannot satisfy the demand of the depositors in the long run and must close down.

If assets can be sold at t, the above results are somewhat modified. However, the message remains the same: The bank is not altogether passive when it encounters a liquidity shock; rather, it can take several actions in order to meet the unexpected liquidity demand without compromising the future demands of depositors. Some of them depend on a future inflow of funds from new depositors, but even without these much can be achieved simply by postponing investment (under the assumption that business is resumed when the attempts at a run have been countered). There is, of course, a limit to what can be achieved in this way, as indeed was to be expected with a view to the collapse of repo trade connected with Lehman Brothers.

14.8 Exercises

1. In the liquidity insurance model of fractional banking, there is only one investment option. Assume that there is an additional investment possibility open to the agents, where funds have to be invested at $t = 1$ and yield a random payoff $\tilde{\rho}$ at $t = 2$. This payoff is unknown at $t = 0$ but is revealed to the agents at $t = 1$.

Describe how the availability of an additional investment option will upset the optimal contracts of the original Diamond-Dybvig model. How should the contracts proposed by the banks be extended so as to take this additional option into account? Can the banks provide full insurance against liquidity shocks?

2. In a situation with many defaults and rumours about banks in trouble, each bank experiences a growing frequency of customers wanting to transfer their deposits to other banks or alternative placements. It is argued that the trouble is caused by problems for the borrowers in servicing their debt, thus causing unexpected losses to the banks.

In order to restore confidence, the government tries to convince the banks to keep the amount of credit at the previous level. Give an assessment, with suitable theoretical background, of whether the banks can or should follow this advice.

3. In a region there is only one bank, which serves almost everybody. The bank has for some time been criticized for not holding sufficient liquid reserves to be able to serve the depositors if they want to withdraw their deposits. Other banks and the financial authorities see this as a problem and want the bank to reduce its risk of not holding sufficient liquid reserves.

What can be done in order to achieve this, when it is also taken into account that for political reasons the customers, borrowers or depositors, must not become worse off as a result of the regulation.

4. In order to provide a regulated way of liquidating banks with a large number of troubled loans, some countries have set up a government institution taking over all assets and liabilities of these banks and carrying out day-to-day business while seeking to sell suitable parts of the activities to other private banks.

It has been proposed that such an institution should take action as soon as the solvency rate of the bank falls below a certain limit. Give an assessment of such a mechanical rule for reconstructing troubled banks, taking into consideration the possibility of contagion. Can the activity of the government institution aggravate the banking crisis?

5. When determining the haircut (percentage of overcollateralization) in repo trades, the riskiness of the security matters, and when the assessment of risk changes, the percentage will be adjusted. Describe how this, taken together with the developments in the financial markets, can lead to *liquidity spirals* in the sense that still more securities are needed as collateral to secure the same amount of repo contracts.

14.9 Comments

The discussion of bank runs takes its point of departure as the Diamond-Dybvig model already known from Chapter 1, but now the emphasis is on the sunspot equilibrium involving bank runs; see also Huo and Yu [1994]. For another but related model, where there is a unique equilibrium which gives a bank run with positive probability, see Postlewaite and Vives [1987], and for a more general treatment, see Peck and Shell [2003].

Whereas the early contributions to the literature on interbank markets, such as Bhattacharya and Gale [1987], considered its beneficial effects, the events of the financial crisis have led to an increased interest in the causes of instability of those markets, as e.g. Ashcraft et al. [2011]. Financial contagion through the interbank market has been investigated empirically; see e.g. Allen and Gale [2000].

Chapter 15

Deposit Insurance

15.1 Who should pay and how much?

In the previous chapter, we saw that depositors fearing that the bank will not be able to fulfil their contracts may run the bank, thereby causing exactly what was feared. One of the ways in which this can be prevented is to insure the deposits: If an independent deposit insurance organization pays out what is promised to the depositor if the bank is not able to do so, then the causes of the bank run have been eliminated.

In the present chapter, we take a closer look at this arrangement. Although intuitively clear and consistent with the historical development, organizing deposit insurance as a matter between the bank and the insurer, whereby the bank pays a premium and the insurer reimburses the depositors if the bank cannot satisfy its obligations, is not the only possible solution, and even when arranging deposit insurance in this way, it may not be quite clear what the bank should pay.

Pricing of deposit insurance is clearly a matter of importance; the insurance of deposits serves several purposes, safeguarding depositors and thereby changing the risk structure of the bank, as we shall see in the following. But in principle, deposit insurance is an insurance contract, and its 'true' price might in principle be found in the same way as for other types of insurance contracts, by looking at the losses that the deposit insurance will reimburse. These losses are, however, somewhat more complicated than they would be in the case of ordinary loss insurance, because they are related to the loans which the bank has contracted with borrowers. This suggests that we need an approach similar to that used when assessing credit risk.

The structural approach to deposit insurance. Here we are concerned with the assets of the bank and derive the insured event (reimbursement of deposits by the deposit insurance) from the performance of the assets. Following Merton [1977], we can view the deposit insurance contract as a *put option* on the assets: The bank which at $t = 0$ has deposits D, all invested in random assets L, has obtained a right to sell its assets at date T to the insurance company at the strike price $De^{r_D T}$, where r_D is the deposit rate of interest. Although this option can be exercised at any date, we may simplify and consider it to be valid only at specific dates, and we let T be the first such date in the future. If the asset value $\tilde{L}$ follows a geometric Brownian motion,

$$\frac{d\tilde{L}}{\tilde{L}} = \mu dt + \sigma \, dZ,$$

where Z is standard Brownian motion, and if in addition we assume that the financial markets are sufficiently complete to allow complete simulation of $\tilde{L}$ by a suitable portfolio, then we may use Black-Scholes to assess the value of the deposit insurance as

$$P^* = De^{(r_D - r)T} N(d_2) - LN(d_1),$$

where

$$d_1 = \frac{\ln\left(\dfrac{De^{(r_D - r)T}}{L}\right) - \dfrac{1}{2}\sigma^2 T}{\sigma \sqrt{T}}, \; d_2 = d_1 + \sigma \sqrt{T},$$

and r, the risk-free rate of interest. It is seen that the ratio between premium and deposit (which gives the price of the insurance as a proportion of the potential loss to be covered by the insurance) is not a constant, but depends on the ratio between loans and deposits as well as on the volatility σ of the assets.

15.2 Deposit insurance and moral hazard

Although deposit insurance, which may be costly to the bank, appears as an unmixed blessing to the depositor, this is not altogether the case. The very fact that depositors are covered by the insurance may have as a side effect that the risk-taking behaviour of the bank will change. This can be illustrated by the following very simple example.

Consider a bank which operates in two consecutive periods, after which it is liquidated. At $t = 0$ it has equity E_0, receives deposits D, and contracts loans to the amount of L_0. The deposits are covered by insurance, and the bank pays the premium P at $t = 0$. In the following period, the value of the loans has changed to $\tilde{L}$ (assumed to be random). The liquidation value of the bank with deposit insurance must be

$$\tilde{E} = \tilde{L} - D + \max\{0, D - \tilde{L}\}, \tag{1}$$

where the last member on the right-hand side is the reimbursement of losses received from the deposit insurance. Because $D + E_0 = L_0 + P$, we can write (1) as

$$\tilde{E} = E_0 + \tilde{L} - L_0 + \max\{0, D - \tilde{L}\} - P,$$

so the (random) profit of the bank has the form

$$\tilde{\Pi} = \tilde{E} - E_0 = (\tilde{L} - L_0) + \left[\max\{0, D - \tilde{L}\} - P\right],$$

where we have added brackets to emphasize that profits arise from the change in value of equity *and* the workings of the deposit insurance.

To proceed, we specify the randomness of $\widetilde{L}$ in the simplest possible way, so $\widetilde{L}$ takes the value A with probability p and 0 otherwise. We can then find expected profit as

$$\mathsf{E}\widetilde{\Pi} = \mathsf{E}\left[\widetilde{E} - E_0\right] = (pA - L_0) + [(1 - p)D - P]. \tag{2}$$

Now it can be seen easily that expected profits are influenced by the deposit insurance: Assume that the bank has a choice between loans with different characteristics (p, A), but with the same expected payoff. In this case, the first member in (2) is constant, but the second member depends on p – indeed, expected profits are maximized when p is chosen as small as possible! This may sound strange, but it should be remembered that we have chosen among projects with the same expected payoff, so only the deposit insurance matters, and given that the premium has already been paid, the bank wants to get as much value for money as possible out of the insurance company.

This is a classical instance of *moral hazard*: Given that losses are reimbursed by an insurance company, the behaviour of the insured will necessarily change so as to take this into account. In our case of a deposit insurance, we must expect the banks to take greater risk than they would have done otherwise.

Clearly, the result obtained depended on the assumption of a fixed premium P, which did not depend on the choice of investment project, at least as long as the expected payoff remained constant. In practice, the premium must depend on the amount D of deposits to be insured as well as on the riskiness of these deposits, the probability p of repayment of the investments of the bank. With asymmetric information, p is private information of the bank. The following argument, due to Chan et al. [1992], shows that with asymmetric information, we cannot have fair pricing of deposit insurance.

Let $D(p)$ be the amount of deposits that are optimal given the investment choices of the bank (with repayment probability p). A pricing rule $P(D)$, assumed to be differentiable, would be actuarially fair if

$$P(D(p)) = (1 - p)D(p),$$

meaning that the payment for the insurance equals the expected loss. Because this equation is to hold for all p, we get, also assuming differentiability of $D(p)$ of both P and D, that

$$P'(D(p))D'(p) = (1 - p)D'(p) - D(p). \tag{3}$$

Because $D(p)$ maximizes profits

$$(pA - L_0) + (1 - p)D(p) - P(D(p))$$

over D, we also have the first-order condition

$$(1 - p) - P'(D(p)) = 0.$$

Multiplying this equation by $D'(p)$ and using (3) we get that

$$D(p) = 0$$

for all p, which is a contradiction. Thus, the presence of asymmetric information rules out fair pricing of deposit insurance.

15.3 Deposit insurance premium: Size and correlation of assets

15.3.1 A multiperiod model with bank failures

In the previous sections, we have treated deposit insurance as something which concerns only the individual bank, and the price to be paid for insurance was considered as something which should be derived from the situation of this bank alone. However, deposit insurance is largely justified from considerations of the banking system as a whole, because it prevents bank runs and liquidity crises, and therefore it might be useful to see deposit insurance in a somewhat larger context, which is what we do in this section, following Acharya et al. [2010].

Assume that there are two banks, doing business at dates $t = 0, 1, 2$. At dates $t = 0$ and $t = 1$, the banks can choose to finance investments, which in the next period yield R per unit invested with probability π and 0 with probability $1 - \pi$. The payoffs are independent over time, but they are industry dependent: We assume that each bank chooses a specific industry for its investments, and all investments in the same industry experience success and failure in the same way; but two banks may invest in the same or in different industries, and this will have an impact on the overall probability of losses. The investments are financed by deposits. We assume throughout that these deposits are fully insured and therefore risk-free, and with no discounting their values are 1 at each date.

A crucial feature of our model is that *banks have specific skills in monitoring investments*: When the investment is carried out by a bank, it will give a payoff R in the case of success, but if a non-bank investor is in charge, it will yield less, namely $R - \Delta$, where Δ measures the ability to use banking assets. This matters if an investment has to be sold to an outside investor (in connection with a liquidation of the bank), who then cannot be expected to pay full price.

15.3.2 Insurance premium when investment projects have a liquidation value

Setting the model to work, we first look at the situation at $t = 1$. To see what the actuarially fair premium would be, we need to compute the expected net outlays of the insurer. There are four possible states of the world, described by successes and failures of the two banks.

In the case FF of two failures, the banks must be sold to private investors, who will pay at most

$$\underline{p} = \pi(R - \Delta - 1)$$

for this investment opportunity (which now consists in investing 1 at date t and getting $R - \Delta$ at $t = 2$, subject to the probability π). If either SF or FS holds (one bank fails and the other succeeds), then there is another bank which can acquire the assets of the bank which failed, and the surviving bank can get the payoff

$$\overline{p} = \pi(R - 1)$$

from the project. However, we cannot be sure whether the surviving bank will actually buy the project at this price, because this depends on the bargaining powers of the regulator in charge of liquidation and the surviving bank, so we assume that it takes some intermediate value p^* with

$$\underline{p} < p^* < \overline{p}.$$

If SS obtains and both banks succeed, then there is no need for liquidation.

We can now find the insurance premium, which depends on the correlation between the investment projects of the bank. If the banks choose projects from the same industry, then the probability of FF at $t = 1$ is π (all projects in the industry will succeed or fail simultaneously), and the probability of FS or SF is 0, so the expected net outlays of the insurance can be found as

$$q_s = (1 - \pi)(1 - \underline{p}), \tag{4}$$

and if they invest in different industries, so the probability of FF is $(1 - \pi)^2$, whereas the probability of SF or FS is $\pi(1 - \pi)$, we get the expected net outlays

$$q_d = \pi(1 - \pi)(1 - p^*) + (1 - \pi)^2(1 - \underline{p}) = q_s - \pi(1 - \pi)(p^* - \underline{p}). \tag{5}$$

As an immediate consequence of (4) and (5), we get that the actuarially fair insurance premium depends on the correlation between banks' return and is higher when banks invest in the same industry than when they invest in different industries. This is in itself not too surprising because it fits well with intuition and traditional reservation about highly correlated investment policies. However, our model provides another insight which perhaps was less obvious from the start: The actuarially fair premium depends on the size of the bank even when the investment policy is uncorrelated.

Indeed, if bank 1 is small and bank 2 is large, then after a failure of the small bank, the large bank may take over the assets at some price p° with $\underline{p} < p^\circ < \overline{p}$, so, as above, we find that the expected net outlay of the insurance is

$$q^\circ = \pi(1 - \pi)(1 - p^\circ) + (1 - \pi)^2(1 - \underline{p}) < (1 - \pi)(1 - \underline{p}),$$

whereas if the large bank fails, the small bank is too small to take over its investments (except, of course, a small part of them, a possibility which we neglect here), and the actuarially fair premium for the large bank becomes $(1 - \pi)(1 - \underline{p})$. It follows that the fair premium must be smaller for the small than for the large bank.

15.3.3 Taking into account the possibility of bailout

Now we add some additional aspects of stylized reality: When a bank fails, and in particular when both banks fail, the regulator faces a choice of either liquidating and selling the assets to private investors or, alternatively, bailing out the bank by providing the necessary liquidity, in our case 1. We assume that financing a bank in trouble has some social cost of magnitude c per unit provided. Thus, bailing out two banks in the case where both fail would give the regulator an expected net benefit of $\pi R - 1 - c$ for each bank, whereas liquidating the banks would result in an expected loss to society to the amount of $\pi\Delta$ (the reduction of payoff due to private investment will occur only if the investment succeeds), so the regulator should bail out if $\pi\Delta > c$ and liquidate otherwise. As a consequence, expected profits of the bank in the next (second) period will be

$$E\left[\widetilde{\Pi}_2 \middle| FF\right] = \begin{cases} 0 & \pi\Delta \le c, \\ \underline{p} & \pi\Delta > c, \end{cases}$$

where $\widetilde{\Pi}_2$ is the (random) profit of the bank in period 2. In the case SF and FS, there is no welfare loss from liquidating the bank and selling it to the successful bank, so the regulator may choose this solution.

We can now find what could be called full-cost insurance premiums both for the case where banks choose the same industry,

$$\bar{q}_s = (1 - \pi)\left[\left(1 - \underline{p}\right) + \min\{\pi\Delta, c\}\right]$$

and for the case of different investments,

$$\bar{q}_d = \pi(1 - \pi)(1 - p^*) + (1 - \pi)^2\left[\left(1 - \underline{p}\right) + \min\{\pi\Delta, c\}\right].$$

It is easily seen that $\bar{q}_s > q_s$ and $\bar{q}_d > q_d$, not surprising because more cost items are taken into account, and that

$$\bar{q}_s > \bar{q}_d,$$

reflecting the higher probabilities of loss to society with correlated investments than with independent investments of banks. But it can also be seen that

$$\bar{q}_s - \bar{q}_d > q_s - q_d,$$

so the difference between premiums when choosing the same or different industries becomes greater when all costs are taken into consideration.

15.3.4 The incentive-compatible insurance premium

This leads to the logical next problem, namely whether the premiums can be designed in such a way that they induce the banks to choose uncorrelated investments. Suppose that

$\hat{q}_s$ and $\hat{q}_d$ are such that banks will make the right choices. If the banks invest in the same industry, their expected profit will be

$$\Pi_s = \pi\mathsf{E}\big[\widetilde{\Pi}_2\big|SS\big] + (1-\pi)\mathsf{E}\big[\widetilde{\Pi}_2|FF\big] - \hat{q}_s, \tag{6}$$

and when they invest in different industries, it will be

$$\Pi_d = \pi\mathsf{E}\big[\widetilde{\Pi}_2\big|SS\big] + \pi(1-\pi)\mathsf{E}\big[\widetilde{\Pi}_2\big|SF\big] + (1-\pi)^2\mathsf{E}\big[\widetilde{\Pi}_2\big|FF\big] - \hat{q}_d.$$

Here, $\mathsf{E}\big[\widetilde{\Pi}_2\big|SF\big]$ is the gain to a successful bank from taking over the assets of the other bank, which failed, and we have

$$\mathsf{E}\big[\widetilde{\Pi}_2\big|SF\big] = \mathsf{E}\big[\widetilde{\Pi}_2\big|SS\big] + (\bar{p} - p^*),$$

so

$$\Pi_d = \pi\mathsf{E}\big[\widetilde{\Pi}_2\big|SS\big] + \pi(1-\pi)(\bar{p} - p^*) + (1-\pi)^2\mathsf{E}\big[\widetilde{\Pi}_2\big|FF\big] - \hat{q}_d. \tag{7}$$

From (6) and (7), we now get that

$$\Pi_s - \Pi_d = \pi(1-\pi)\big[\mathsf{E}\big[\widetilde{\Pi}_2\big|FF\big] - (\bar{p} - p^*)\big] + \hat{q}_d - \hat{q}_s.$$

Now we can find the premium for the case where investments are in the same industry as

$$\hat{q}_s = \pi(1-\pi)\big[\mathsf{E}\big[\widetilde{\Pi}_2\big|FF\big] - (\bar{p} - p^*)\big] + \hat{q}_d.$$

As was to be expected, the surcharge on insurance with correlated investments depends on the subsidy that the bank receives in case of a bailout, namely $\mathsf{E}\big[\widetilde{\Pi}_2\big|FF\big]$, and on the discount given to the surviving bank in the case of only one failure. If the regulator chooses not to bail out, the first term disappears, and the full-cost premiums will be incentive compatible.

The incentive-compatible insurance premium will keep banks from deliberately choosing correlated investments when they expect to be bailed out by the regulator in case of a failure. Because the problem of correlated investment policies for banks seems to be a rather widespread phenomenon, there might indeed be a case for payment rules that would counteract such tendencies. The above discussion shows that the search for a right or fair insurance premium has no simple answer. As can be seen in the next section, it is also far from obvious that the premium should be paid by the banks.

15.4 Should deposit insurance be financed by general taxes?

In the previous discussion, we have considered deposit insurance as an arrangement made by and for the banks and involving only the banks and their depositors. It may, however, be argued that there are other interests involved, because the smooth working of financial intermediation matters for the long-term development of the economy. Therefore, it also matters for those not involved, either as bankers or as depositors, that funds are channelled towards investment in the best possible way, and it might make sense that everybody should contribute to this in the form of taxes.

In the following, we consider a model, proposed by Morrison and White [2004], where there are N households and μ banks, each endowed with 1 unit of money. There is a single investment technology available (to all), which gives a payoff $R > 0$ if it succeeds, something which happens with probability p_L. If it fails, then payoff is 0. Households may use this technology themselves, but alternatively, they may sign a deposit contract with a bank that then takes care of the investment. This may make a difference: Banks can be either sound, in which case the probability of success of the investment is $p_H = p_L + \triangle p > p_L$, an improvement which is achieved by active monitoring of the investment, something which comes at the cost of C per unit invested, or unsound, in which case the investment is no better than if carried out by the household. The households cannot observe whether a bank is sound or unsound.

We assume that banks are allowed to invest not only their own unit of money but also up to $k - 1$ units of money as deposits, carrying out a total of k investment projects. Alternatively (and more important in the sequel than at this point), we may see this as a capital requirement for the bank, which is demanded to keep $1/k$ of its assets as equity.

We assume that the banks demand a fee Q from the depositors (for taking care of their investment). Because the bank can decide whether to be sound or unsound, there is an incentive problem: Banks taking deposits k will monitor investment (and thus be sound) only if

$$[R + Q(k - 1)]p_H - Ck \geq [R + Q(k - 1)]p_L,$$

saying that income for sound banks (payoff of own investment plus fee from deposits minus cost of monitoring investment) should be at least as big as that for unsound banks (where there is no monitoring cost, but lower probability of success). This can also be written as a condition

$$Q \geq \frac{Ck - R\triangle p}{(k - 1)\triangle p} \tag{8}$$

on the depositors' fee.

Now, we turn to the households, which can either invest by themselves or use the banks, in which case they will get $R - Q$ with probability p_H. Assuming that the households believe that the probability of sound banks is g, we get that being a depositor is economically feasible only if

$$(R - Q)(p_L + g\triangle p) \geq Rp_L$$

or

$$Q \leq \frac{Rg\triangle p}{p_L + g\triangle p}. \tag{9}$$

The two inequalities (8) and (9) give rise to a region of feasible (k, Q)-pairs, as illustrated in Fig. 15.1. Depending on the parameters, we may have cases where arbitrary large k is possible, but such cases are less interesting from our point of view, so we have illustrated the case where there is a maximal size of investment which is compatible with sound banking. The two curves bounding the regions defined in (8) and (9) intersect at

$$k^* = \frac{R p_L \Delta p}{C(p_L + g\Delta p) - Rg(\Delta p)^2}, \tag{10}$$

which is the maximal investment size. Because the amount invested by the banks cannot exceed the amount initially available, we have that $\mu k^* \leq N + \mu$ or

$$k^* \leq 1 + \frac{N}{\mu}. \tag{11}$$

But because (10) and (11) involve different parameters, it may well be the case – and we shall assume this in the following – that k^* is strictly smaller than $1 + \frac{N}{\mu}$.

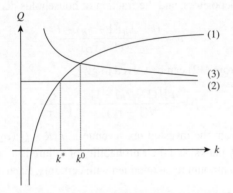

Figure 15.1 Maximal investment volume under different regimes: To avoid moral hazard in the banks, the combinations (k, Q) of investment volume and fee to the banks must be above the curve (1). With no taxation, households will find it worthwhile to let the banks do their investment only if (k, Q) is below (2), so maximal investment is k^*. With taxation, higher fee is compatible with investment through banks because the investors are then covered by deposit insurance, and as a result, more investment can be carried through.

Assuming that investment is in the interest of society, it is preferable that it is carried out by sound banks rather than by individuals. Therefore, it makes sense to investigate whether a higher investment level in banks could be obtained by using taxes to make the banking contract more attractive to the depositors, even if the deposit charges Q must remain high to secure bankers' incentives. This is where deposit insurance comes in: We assume that taxes are collected from banks, depositors and individual investors to make up for the losses of households in the case of failure of the investment. We shall assume that tax rates are announced initially; then deposit contracts are set up, and households decide whether to deposit their wealth with the banks. Now taxes are collected, and we assume that the tax revenue is deposited with the banks. Finally, investment payoffs are received and paid out, together with the insurance covering the losses, to the depositors.

Let τ_j, for $j = B, D, S$ be the tax rates for banks, depositors and individual investors. The tax revenue is then

$$T = \mu\tau_B + N\rho\tau_D + N(1 - \rho)\tau_S. \tag{12}$$

where ρ is the fraction of households choosing to be depositors. Each bank has a capital of $1 - \tau_B$ after tax, and with a capital requirement of $1/k$, it can initiate investments to the amount of $k(1 - \tau_B)$. Total investment is then $k\mu(1 - \tau_B)$, of which the banks themselves contribute with $\mu(1 - \tau_B)$, and the rest, $(k - 1)\mu(1 - \tau_B)$, comes from depositors and investment of the tax revenue T. We may assume that

$$T < (k - 1)\mu(1 - \tau_B)$$

because it makes no sense to collect more taxes than can be invested. Because the after-tax wealth of depositors is $N(1 - \tau_D)$ and the maximal to be invested is $(k - 1)\mu(1 - \tau_B)$, not all consumers can be depositors, and the fraction of households depositing is defined by

$$\rho = \frac{(k - 1)\mu(1 - \tau_B) - T}{N(1 - \tau_D)},$$

which after inserting from (12) can be solved to give

$$\rho = \frac{\mu[k(1 - \tau_B) - 1]}{N(1 - \tau_S)} - \frac{\tau_S}{1 - \tau_S}.$$

The expected return from the invested tax revenue is $T(R - Q)(p_L + g\triangle p)$, and because this is invested in many banks, and their probability of failure is assumed independent, we may consider this as an amount to be obtained with certainty. Each depositor can therefore expect to get

$$\frac{T}{\rho N}(R - Q)(p_L + g\triangle p) \tag{13}$$

in case of a failed investment.

Turning to incentives, it is seen that (8) is unaffected because it is a condition measured per unit invested, but (9) has to be replaced by the condition

$$\rho\left[\frac{T}{\rho N} + (1 - \tau_D)\right](R - Q)(p_L + g\triangle p) + (1 - \rho)(1 - \tau_S)Rp_L \geq Rp_L(1 - \tau_S). \tag{14}$$

On the left-hand side, we have the expected income to the household if it uses the bank and applies for a deposit contract. Because the bank is restricted in the number of investment projects that it can carry out, only a fraction ρ of the households or, alternatively, of the wealth of each household, is admitted for deposits. On the right-hand side, we have the expected income if the bank is not used.

The incentive condition (14) can be rearranged into

$$Q \leq R - \frac{Rp_L}{p_L + g\Delta p} \frac{\mu(k(1 - \tau_B) - 1) - N\tau_S}{\mu(k(1 - \tau_B) - 1) + \mu\tau_B}. \tag{15}$$

The fraction

$$\frac{\mu(k(1 - \tau_B) - 1) - N\tau_S}{\mu(k(1 - \tau_B) - 1) + \mu\tau_B} \tag{16}$$

on the right-hand side in (15) is ≤ 1 and increases in k towards 1, so the right-hand side decreases towards the quantity on the right-hand side in (9). In Fig. 15.1, we have inserted the curve which limits the region of pairs (k, Q) satisfying (15), and it is seen that the maximal amount of deposits possible has increased from k^* to k^0.

So far, we have obtained an increased investment volume using the tax-financed deposit insurance scheme. The logical next question is whether this approach may sustain the maximal investment volume $\mu + N$. We consider the case where $\tau_B = 0$, which seems a reasonable choice because we want the banks to carry out as many investments as possible. In this case the quantity in (16) reduces to $1 - \tau_S$, and equating the right-hand sides of (8) and (15) under this condition, we obtain the condition

$$\frac{Ck - R\Delta p}{(k - 1)\Delta p} = \frac{Rp_L\tau_S + Rg\Delta p}{p_L + g\Delta p},$$

and using that $k - 1 = N/\mu$ in the maximum, the equation can be solved for τ_S to give the value

$$\tau_S = \left(1 + \frac{\mu}{N}\right) \frac{C(p_L + g\Delta p) - Rg(\Delta p)^2}{Rp_L\Delta p} - \frac{\mu}{N},$$

which is the (non-zero) contribution of non-depositors to the deposit insurance. It can be shown that the two other tax rates, τ_B for banks and τ_D for depositors, matter only for the distribution of income between the two types of agents.

Although the results may at first sight seem counterintuitive, it should be remembered that the non-depositors in our model are bank costumers who were prevented from being depositors because of the rationing induced by the leverage restriction. Taxing the non-depositors makes it more attractive to use the bank, and if the rationing is such that every household deposits the share ρ of its wealth, then the tax can be considered as levied on bank users in general rather than on non-depositors in a discriminative way.

15.5 Exercises

1. In a proposal for reform of the financial sector, the institution of deposit insurance is abandoned. Instead, the banks are obliged to buy credit default swaps on their assets to an amount which corresponds to a repayment of all deposits less than or equal to €100,000. Comment on this proposal: If feasible, what will the cost be compared to ordinary deposit insurance, and will it improve or reduce the stability of the financial system?

2. In the simple model of moral hazard caused by deposit insurance in Section 15.2, it was found that the bank would choose maximal riskiness when all available projects had the same expected payoff. What happens when the set of available projects contains many different projects, varying in both expected payoff and probability of default?

3. In a proposal for a reform of deposit insurance, it is suggested that banks should be allowed to receive deposits for which no insurance is taken by the bank, and a separate institution should be established which would offer full insurance to the individual depositor against a premium also paid by the depositor. Banks accepting such uninsured deposits should accept a representative of the new insurance institution on their board of directors.

Comment on this arrangement. Can it be used to satisfy depositors' need for safety without creating moral hazard in the banks?

4. After a period of financial insecurity it has been decided that the deposit insurance of the country should be reorganized. As a main principle for the new arrangements, the deposit insurance should be self-financing, at least on average, but it has also been an important argument that the deposit insurance should reduce risk, not only for depositors but for the financial sector as a whole.

Give a brief survey of the alternative approaches towards financing deposit insurance, with suggestions for the particular one described above.

In the final phase of negotiation, representatives of the large banks argue that small banks have a higher risk of bank runs than large banks, so small banks should pay a higher premium relative to the size of their deposits than large banks. Can it be argued that size should matter when determining the premium?

5. An entrepreneur has a portfolio of government bonds and proposes deposit accounts to the general public with full collateral in government bonds. The deposits are used for investment in risky projects with high payoffs. Explain why this arrangement might be better than selling the original portfolio and investing the proceeds in risky projects.

The entrepreneur argues that she should not be obliged to pay for deposit insurance. Comment on this argument.

15.6 Comments

Deposit insurance was introduced in the 1930s, but not widely discussed until around 1980, where some of the negative effects were acknowledged, cf. e.g. Keeley [1990]. The options pricing approach to deposit insurance [Merton, 1977] has been elaborated by other authors, see e.g. [Duffie et al., 2003].

The moral hazard problem connected with deposit insurance is one of the persistent themes in the literature, and several proposals have been put forward to reform the financial system so as to get around this moral hazard problem, e.g. Martin [2006] (which will be used in the next chapter), Niinimäki [2010].

Chapter 16

Lenders of Last Resort and Central Banks

16.1 Bank runs and liquidity provision

In our treatment of bank runs and what to do to prevent them, we have so far put the emphasis on the individual level, discussing what the bank can do, either by itself, by using the interbank market, or by insuring its deposits. We have not yet considered the perhaps most well-known way of handling bank runs, namely by obtaining additional liquidity from a *lender of last resort*. It is now time to consider this alternative.

The attempt to prevent bank runs through deposit insurance, considered in the previous chapter, was successful insofar as bank runs can indeed be avoided, but it gave rise to moral hazard: Banks may take excessive risks when expecting to be bailed out by a lender of last resort. This phenomenon has been a recurrent theme in previous sections, and in the present section we consider it in a more direct way. Following Martin [2006], we consider a situation which is only slightly different from the standard liquidity insurance case, but where the risk taking of banks can be explicitly formulated.

As is by now usual, we have three dates, $t = 0, 1, 2$. There are two types of investment available: The first type of investment uses a storage technology, transforming 1 unit of input at $t = 0$ or $t = 1$ to 1 unit of output in the next period. The second type of investment exploits a risky technology, which transforms 1 unit at $t = 0$ to an outcome $\widetilde{R}$ at $t = 2$, taking the values $\frac{1}{q}R$ with probability q and 0 with probability $1 - q$, where $R > 1$ is a constant. The parameter q can be chosen by the bank; it is seen that the expected payoff of the investment is equal to R and independent of q, whereas its variance is

$$\sigma^2(\widetilde{R}) = q\left(R - \frac{1}{q}R\right)^2 + (1 - q)R^2 = \frac{1 - q}{q}R^2,$$

which is decreasing in q, becoming 0 when $q = 1$. Depositors can observe q only at date 2, and the outcomes of the projects are assumed to be independent between banks. As always, we assume that liquidating projects at $t = 1$ will yield only $L < 1$.

Households can be either impatient, with probability π, or patient, with probability $1-\pi$, where π is a given probability, and their expected utility is

$$U(c_1, c_2) = \pi u(c_1) + (1 - \pi)u(c_2). \tag{1}$$

Following our usual approach, we should look for the socially optimal investment policy, maximizing expected utility over the constraint given by technology and the demands for liquidity. However, there is an additional complication, because expectations must be taken not only with respect to patience/impatience, but also over the random outcome of the technology at date 2. Fortunately, if we assume that households are risk averse, then the safe project with $q = 1$ will be better than any risky one; indeed, for given investment I, if the consumptions of the depositor satisfy the standard constraints

$$\pi c_1 = 1 - I, \tag{2}$$

$$(1 - \pi)c_2 = I\widetilde{R}, \tag{3}$$

then we have that consumption at date 2 is $\dfrac{I}{1 - \pi}\dfrac{1}{q}R$ with probability q, and 0 with probability $1 - q$, and at date 2 expected utility is

$$qu\left(\frac{I}{1-\pi}\frac{1}{q}R\right) \leq u\left(q\frac{I}{1-\pi}\frac{1}{q}R\right) = u\left(\frac{I}{1-\pi}R\right)$$

by concavity of u, so the choice $q = 1$ is optimal for the consumer and thus for society. Therefore, the socially optimal investment policy is found by maximizing (1) subject to (2) and (3).

Now we turn to the problem of finding the optimal contracts between banks and depositors. To keep the model simple, we assume that banks maximize the utility of the representative consumer; this can be justified if we assume that there are many banks competing for deposit contracts. In particular, the contract will specify withdrawal c_E at date 1 and withdrawal c_L at date 2, and outcome risk must be absorbed by the bank. However, in the context of banks taking deposits, we know that there is a possibility of a bank run; we assume that this happens if depositors observe a signal (a 'sunspot') at $t = 1$, and that the probability of this signal is p. If the fraction of depositors observing the signal is μ, then the expected depositor utility to be maximized is

$$(1 - \mu p)[\pi u(c_E) + (1 - \pi)u(c_L)] + \mu p\hat{\pi}u(c_E). \tag{4}$$

Here $\hat{\pi}$ is the probability that the bank, which is subject to a run, will have the necessary funds to satisfy the fraction μ of depositors having observed the signal; it should satisfy $\hat{\pi}c_E = 1 - I + IL = 1 - I(1 - L)$ or

$$\hat{\pi} = \frac{1 - I(1 - L)}{c_E}. \tag{5}$$

Thus, (4) should be maximized subject to (2), (3) and (5).

As before, banks will have no incentive to choose risky projects because they compete for depositors having no interest in a risky outcome. This will change, however, if there is a deposit insurance promising a payment D to depositors in bankrupt banks. Then bank runs are prevented, at least if D is large enough, but a new problem arises because bankruptcy may occur not only as a result of a run but also if the bank has chosen a risky project which fails. The deposit insurance scheme has, of course, to be financed, and we assume that this is done by collecting taxes from depositors. In order to collect enough to pay all the patient consumers who may present themselves in a bank run, the tax T collected should satisfy

$$TR = (1 - \pi)\mu D.$$

If there is no bank run, or only a few banks experience runs, the surplus will be distributed equally among depositors in banks that have not been declared bankrupt; we denote this amount by B.

To see that the introduction of such a deposit insurance scheme will change the behaviour of the banks, we look at a case where all banks have chosen the safe project with $q = 1$. If a bank contemplates a deviation, choosing $q < 1$, then project outcome becomes random, and the deposit contract should be suitably revised. We assume that the deviating bank proposes a contract where the depositor gets a mark-up $1/q$ on the repayment at $t = 2$. The expected utility of a patient depositor will become

$$qu\left(\frac{1}{q}\left[c_L - \frac{TR}{1 - \pi}\right] + \frac{B}{1 - \pi}\right) + (1 - q)u(D). \tag{6}$$

The tax paid for the deposit insurance is considered as reduced outpayment at $t = 2$, but then the depositor also receives a share of the unused tax payments. Finally, the promised amount D is paid out in case of a default. Because we consider a deviation from $q = 1$, where bank runs do not occur, bankruptcy will occur only as a result of failed projects, that is, with probability $1 - q$. Also, because only a single (small) bank deviates, we have that $B = TR$.

Evaluating the partial derivative of expected utility as expressed in (6) with respect to q, we get that

$$\left.\frac{\partial U}{\partial q}\right|_{q=1} = -u'(c_L)[c_L - \mu D] - u(D) + u(c_L),$$

which is negative (so that expected utility increases when q is reduced below 1) when $\mu < 1$ and D is sufficiently close to c_L. This means that we cannot expect banks to choose the safe investment technology when there is deposit insurance, and $q = 1$ will not be an equilibrium choice for the bank.

Liquidity provision instead of deposit insurance. The fact that deposit insurance will upset the initial equilibrium, giving rise to moral hazard, is not new, but if we replace the deposit insurance by a lender of last resort, the situation changes quite remarkably: Suppose that in the model considered, there is a *central bank*, with a specific *liquidity provision policy*: At date 1, and before the depositors can withdraw whatever they are entitled to, the banks can borrow specially issued money at the central bank with their assets as collateral; at the end of this period, the banks can change back to their original assets. If it is not able to pay back the loan, it defaults. Depositors having obtained the specially issued money at $t = 1$ are entitled to goods (or usual money) at $t = 2$ at a specified rate.

With this liquidity provision policy, if a depositor asks for the amount c_E at $t = 1$, then banks must borrow $(1 - \pi)c_E$ from the central bank in order to cover all patient depositors. A depositor who receives c_E units of money at $t = 1$ will get m units of goods, with $c_E \leq m < c_L$, at date $t = 2$. This is indeed feasible because the central bank receives the collateral in the case that the bank is liquidated and therefore gets the payoff of the investment. As always, the depositors who may run the bank are those who turn out to be patient, and with the above liquidity provision rule, they will have no incentive to run, getting a better outcome if they wait, and knowing that the investment will be continued anyway, if not by the bank then by the central bank.

What is perhaps more interesting is that with liquidity provision the banks have no incentive to invest in the risky technology. With deposit insurance, the depositors would gain because they receive more in the case of success but are compensated in the case of loss. This asymmetry is no longer present if deposit insurance is replaced by liquidity provision.

This double advantage of the specially constructed system of liquidity provision seems to solve many problems – preventing bank runs and eradicating moral hazard. It should, of course, be emphasized that these advantages were obtained in a very simple model and might not carry over to more complex situations. Anyway, the case for a lender of last resort has been rather convincingly presented.

16.2 The decision to bail out a bank

In the following, we consider the central bank in its role as lender of last resort. As such it has the option of assisting a bank in trouble, bailing it out, or alternatively rejecting the request for assistance and letting the bank be liquidated. We shall have a closer look at this situation and the choices involved.

Consider a bank which has assets that will generate an interest income y with probability p, 0 otherwise. If y is obtained, the bank is solvent and has no need for assistance. However, with probability $1 - p$ (assumed to be small compared with p), the bank is in trouble and needs a bailout. If it receives assistance and therefore is able to continue in business, the value of its assets will be V_C. Otherwise, it will be liquidated at a value $V_L < V_C$. We assume that the bank has deposits D, so depositors have a claim of $D(1 + r_D)$, where r_D is the deposit rate. The premium for deposit insurance is fixed as

$$m = (1 - p)\max\{D(1 + r_D) - V_L, 0\}.$$

In addition to depositors, there are also uninsured debt holders in the bank to the amount B, who will get $B(1 + r_B)$ if the bank is successful or if the bank is bailed out, and $\max\{0, V_L - D(1 + r_D)\}$ otherwise. Because the market for such debt is competitive, we assume that expected return equals $1 + r$, where r is the interbank market rate.

At the start of the period, the assets A of the bank correspond to the value of debt plus equity E. Considering E as given, and also assuming that deposits cannot vary much, the volume of the bank's business may be taken to depend only on B, and the payoff is a function $y(B)$ of B.

In the case of a failure the lender of last resort must choose whether to bail out the bank, and we assume – as is standard in the literature – that there is social cost η per unit of money provided for such a bailout. If the bailout is chosen, then it amounts to a subsidy to the uninsured debt holders to the amount of

$$S = B(1 + r_B) - \max\{V_L - D(1 + r_D), 0\}. \tag{7}$$

Because the value of the assets will then be V_C rather than V_L, the cost to society is only $S - (V_C - V_L)$. The alternative, which is liquidation, is also costly because it involves administration, legal assistance, etc., to the amount $C(A)$, where we have assumed that it depends on A, the size of the banks' assets.

In this situation, the lender of last resort will decide to bailout if

$$\eta[B(1 + r_B) - \max\{V_L - D(1 + r_D), 0\}] - (1 + \eta)(V_C - V_L),$$

which is the cost of bailout, does not exceed the cost of liquidation, which is $(1 + \eta)C(A)$. Defining the net cost of bailout as

$$\Delta = \eta[B(1 + r_B) - \max\{V_L - D(1 + r_D), 0\}] - (1 + \eta)(V_C - V_L) - (1 + \eta)C(A), \tag{8}$$

we thus have that the bank will be bailed out if $\Delta < 0$ and liquidated if $\Delta > 0$.

If the bank is bailed out, then holders of uninsured debt can be sure of getting the promised payoff, so in this case $r_B = r$. In the general case, where the decision of the lender of last resort is given as a probability π of bailout (that is, the lender of last resort chooses a mixed strategy), the rate r_B is given by

$$(p + (1 - p)\pi)B(1 + r_B) + (1 - p)(1 - \pi)\max\{V_L - D(1 + r_D), 0\} = (1 + r)B. \tag{9}$$

Denoting by $r_B(\pi)$ the solution of (9), we can write the subsidy given to the bank as $pB(r_B(0) - r_B(\pi))$, and using (7) we get that

$$pB(r_B(0) - r_B(\pi)) = (1 - p)\eta S.$$

So far we have considered only the decisions of the lender of last resort, but also the bank will have to make decisions. In our simple model, only the amount of uninsured debt B can be varied in the short run, with resulting expected profit

$$\Pi = p[y(B) - B(1 + r_B) - D(1 + r_D)] - m.$$

The bank chooses B^* so as to maximize Π. Inserting the expression for m and using (9), we get that

$$\Pi = \Pi_0 + (1 - p)\eta S,$$

where

$$\Pi_0 = py(B) + (1 - p)V_L - B(1 + r) - D(1 + r_D)$$

is the expected profit to be obtained without any subsidy (which may well be negative). It is seen that the bailout implies a subsidy to the bank even though the bank's profit will be zero when it happens, because a commitment to bail the bank out results in lower rates for the uninsured debt.

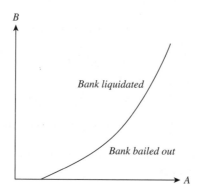

Figure 16.1 Combinations of assets A and uninsured debt B at which the lender of last resort will or will not bail out the bank in trouble. If assets are very large, then also banks with very large debt can expect to be bailed out.

If Δ is increasing in B (after inserting $A = B + D + E$ in (8)), we get that there is a unique $\hat{B}$ for which $\Delta = 0$, so the bank is bailed out when $B^* < \hat{B}$ and liquidated when $B^* > \hat{B}$. We thus obtain an equilibrium where the bank maximizes Π given the decision of the lender of last resort (bail out or liquidate) and the latter has chosen the least costly decision.

As we saw, the lender of last resort will prefer liquidation if B becomes larger at a given level of A. However, when the bank changes B, it will change A as well. In Fig. 16.1, we have illustrated the two regions of optimal decisions in (A, B) space, where the boundary is given by the equation $\Delta = 0$. It is seen that there are situations where B is very large but where the bank is still bailed out. This is due to the possibly high cost $C(A)$ to society of liquidating the bank, which may be steeply increasing in A, thus presenting a case where the bank has become 'too big to fail', in the sense that closing down the bank will be too costly for the financial sector or for society as a whole. We return to this problem in the next chapter.

16.3 Bank liquidity regulation and lenders of last resort

16.3.1 Lenders of last resort and bank behaviour

In the previous section, we saw that lenders of last resort fulfil an important role in offering a service to the banks, so important that the banks might create a lender of last resort if there was no such institution available. However, once the lender of last resort is in place, it may influence the behaviour of the banks, in the sense that they may take excessive risk knowing or anticipating that they will be bailed out by the central bank in the case of a failure. Because the central bank will not be willing (or able) to bail out troubled banks automatically, a balance must be found between the liquidity reserve kept by the bank and the policy of the lender of last resort. We shall have a closer look at this, following the work of Ratnovski [2009].

As usual, we consider a time span of three periods starting with $t = 0$, when decisions are made; over $t = 1$, where banks receive (private) signals on quality of their investment and may be subject to liquidity shocks; to $t = 2$, where the investments pay off.

There are two banks. At $t = 0$, each bank receives 1 unit of money from depositors, for which it has promised a return at $t = 2$. There is only one investment opportunity, which is risky with high return R_H or low return R_L at $t = 2$, each with probability $1/2$. The investment projects of the two banks are assumed to be independent.

At $t = 1$, a bank may be hit by a liquidity shock, so it needs an additional investment L with $R_L > L > R_L - 1$ to carry through its original investment project; without this additional investment, the project will yield return 0 at $t = 2$. We let p be the probability that this shock occurs. The bank has the possibility of keeping a *liquidity reserve* of size L, obtained by attracting additional funds which are placed in liquid assets (not related to the investment project).

We shall add an additional feature to the model, related to the *moral hazard* of banks: At $t = 1$, and after having observed the liquidity shock, the bank has the option of transferring its investment project to one of lower quality, giving the bank a payoff β but leaving nothing to the depositors. This opportunity will be exploited only in the case of a liquidity shock, because we assume that

$$(1 - p)R_L - 1 > \beta.$$

Here the first term on the left-hand side is the smallest possible expected repayment to depositors, and subtracting the deposit we get a lower bound to the expected profit of the bank, which is greater than what could be obtained through moral hazard.

If a liquidity shock occurs for a bank with low return, and the bank chooses additional investment, then the net worth of the bank is negative because

$$R_L < 1 + L,$$

and even though from the point of view of society the investment L should be carried out, this gives rise to insolvency for the bank, and the bank managers may prefer to engage in moral hazard. If the bank has high returns, we assume that net worth remains positive after the additional investment,

$$R_L > \frac{1+L}{1-p} + \beta.$$

Here the first term on the right-hand side is the maximal debt repayment.

16.3.2 Liquidity choice with no lender of last resort

If there is no possibility of bailout in the case of a liquidity shock, the bank must consider whether it wants to keep reserves to the amount L from the outset. If it chooses not to keep reserves, then assuming as above that its funding cost corresponds to expected repayment, we get that expected profit to the bank with no reserve is

$$\mathsf{E}\pi_1 = (1-p)\frac{R_H + R_L}{2} - 1.$$

If the bank also keeps a reserve of size L so that it collects ordinary deposits of size 1 and additional deposits L at $t = 0$, it can avoid bankruptcy in the case of a liquidity shock at $t = 1$. But if it has observed that repayment is R_L, it will prefer to choose the moral hazard solution, leaving it with profits β, rather than being closed down at $t = 2$ with a resulting loss of equity due to insolvency. Assuming that depositors can distinguish between banks collecting large $(1 + L)$ or small deposits (of size 1), they will demand a repayment of

$$\frac{1}{1 - \frac{p}{2}}$$

for the funding, and the expected payment is therefore

$$\mathsf{E}\pi_2 = (1-p)\frac{R_H + R_L}{2} + \frac{p}{2}(R_H - L) - \frac{p}{2}(L - \beta) - 1. \tag{10}$$

If $L \le L^*$, where

$$L^* = \frac{R_H + \beta}{2},$$

as we shall assume throughout, then $\mathsf{E}\pi_2 \ge \mathsf{E}\pi_1$, and banks will prefer to keep the liquid reserve.

16.3.3 Liquidity choices with a lender of last resort

We assume now that there is a central bank which will offer support if the banks are illiquid. However, the central bank will do this only if there is a systemic crisis under way. In our model, it means that the central bank intervenes only if *both* banks have experienced a liquidity shock. Because the central bank cannot risk that the supported bank engages in moral hazard, the equity value of this bank must be at least β after the support. Because the central bank cannot observe the returns of the supported bank, the bank with high returns will receive a rent of $\beta + (R_H - R_L)$ if supported.

We consider the expected payoff of a bank in this context. If the bank has chosen to be liquid, it will never need assistance, and net payoff is as above. But in the case that the bank chooses not to be liquid, its expected payoff will depend on the choice of the other bank, because the central bank supports only if *both* banks have liquidity problems, and this will happen only if the other bank has low asset value so that it becomes insolvent.

In this latter case, our bank will experience a liquidity shock with probability p. In the case of no liquidity shock, expected payoff is $\frac{R_H + R_L}{2} - \frac{1}{1-p}$, and in the case of the shock, it is assisted only with probability $\frac{p}{4}$, in which case it gets $\beta + \frac{R_H - R_L}{2}$. Adding the two terms and rewriting, we get

$$\mathsf{E}\pi_1^2 = (1 - p)\frac{R_H + R_L}{2} + \frac{p}{4}\left(\beta + \frac{R_H - R_L}{2}\right) - 1.$$

In the case that the other bank is illiquid as well, bailout will occur with probability $\frac{p}{2}$ instead of $\frac{p}{4}$, and we get the expression

$$\mathsf{E}\pi_1^1 = (1 - p)\frac{R_H + R_L}{2} + \frac{p}{2}\left(\beta + \frac{R_H - R_L}{2}\right) - 1.$$

We notice that $\mathsf{E}\pi_2 \geq \mathsf{E}\pi_1^2$ (being liquid is best response to the other bank being liquid) if

$$L \leq \frac{1}{8}(3R_H + R_L + 2\beta), \tag{11}$$

and we will have $\mathsf{E}\pi_2 \geq \mathsf{E}\pi_1^1$ (being liquid is best response to the other bank being illiquid) if

$$L \leq \frac{R_H + R_L}{4}. \tag{12}$$

Define L^1 as the quantity on the right-hand side of (12) and L^2 as that on the right-hand side of (11); clearly, $L^1 < L^2$. We may now characterize the Nash equilibria of the liquidity choice game, depending on the size of the liquidity shock L. If $L < L^1$, a bank will always choose to be liquid, and for $L > L^2$, it will always be illiquid. Finally, if $L^1 \leq L \leq L^2$, then the bank will prefer being liquid if the other bank is illiquid, but it is better for it to be illiquid when the other bank is illiquid. This means that both the strategy arrays (*liquid, liquid*) and (*illiquid, illiquid*) are Nash equilibria, something which can be interpreted as liquidity choices depending on the situation in the banking sector.[1]

It is easily checked that $L^1 < L^2 < L^*$, which means that for values of L between L^1 and L^2, the presence of a lender of last resort gives rise to suboptimal allocation in the banking sector, because banks may be illiquid (and for $L^2 < L < L^*$ definitely will be illiquid) instead of being liquid as was the first-best solution. The presence of a lender of last resort thus comes at a cost to society.

---

[1] In addition, there are equilibria in mixed strategies, leaving the choice between being liquid and illiquid to chance, with probabilities that depend on the shock L.

16.4 The emergence of central banking

In the preceding sections, we have dealt with the central bank as a provider of liquidity, a lender of last resort. The central bank may have many other roles, related to macroeconomic policy and exchange rate determination, but we shall be interested only in its role in connection with banks getting into trouble, either because of liquidity trouble or perhaps as a result of more deeply rooted difficulties. This particular role of central banks is actually a very important one, to the extent that if there were no central bank, the ordinary banks would be much worse off. As a way of introducing the central bank and its intercourse with the other banks, we consider below a simple model, taken from Gorton and Huang [2006], where a central bank is 'created' by the banks in order to cope with the problem of bank runs.

We consider banks taking deposits and investing either in storage or in an investment project with a random payoff rate. There are three periods of time, namely $t = 0$, when decisions on investment and storage (reserve) are taken by the banks. They all start with an initial capital E and receive deposits to the amount of 1 from the public. Out of this they decide on the amount M of reserves, and the rest is invested. Investment takes two periods and payoff comes at $t = 2$. The payoff rate has the form $\tilde{\pi} + \tilde{r}$, where $\tilde{\pi}$ is common for all banks (considered as a macroeconomic factor), whereas $\tilde{r}$ is specific for each bank and independent among banks. For simplicity, we assume that $\tilde{\pi}$ is uniformly distributed in an interval $[\tilde{\pi}_{\min}, \tilde{\pi}_{\max}]$, for simplicity assumed to have length 1, and that $\tilde{r}$ is uniformly distributed in $[0, 2\bar{r}]$, for $\bar{r} > 0$ a constant.

At $t = 1$, the value π of the random variable $\tilde{\pi}$ can be observed by everybody. The individual signal r can be observed but is not *verifiable* at $t = 1$, meaning that no legal action can be taken depending on the signal at this point of time (note that it becomes verifiable at $t = 2$ if the investment is carried through, because the size of the payoff will then reveal r). The depositors have a right to get their deposit back (which corresponds to a run on the bank) at this point. The bank can liquidate the investment at $t = 1$ at rate L.

The reason why depositors may want their deposits back is that banks may engage in fraudulent behaviour. This happens when investment has reached the final state but before paying back the deposits; instead, the bank can secure a fraction $f < 1$ of the investment $(\pi + r)(1 + E - M)$ to itself, leaving nothing for others. We assume that depositors are (very) risk averse, so they will claim their deposits back at $t = 1$ as soon as they see a possibility of fraud, that is, whenever the banker would be better off by engaging in fraud than by following the rules. For this to happen at least in some situations, we assume that the parameter values are such that

$$(1 + E)(\pi_{\min} + \bar{r}) - 1 < f(1 + E)(\pi_{\min} + \bar{r}). \tag{13}$$

On the right-hand side, we have the outcome for the banker with the lowest macroeconomic rate and average individual payoff rate (having put nothing aside as reserves), and on the right-hand side, the gain in the case of fraud. Thus, when payoff rates are low the bankers are tempted to avoid paying back the deposits.

We make some additional (and in most cases natural) assumptions on the parameters: First of all, carrying through investment even when rates are the smallest possible is better for society than liquidating, which again is better than fraud, even with the highest payoff rates,

$$\pi_{\min} > L > f(\pi_{\max} + 2\bar{r}), \tag{14}$$

and

$$\frac{\pi_{\min} + \pi_{\max}}{2} + \bar{r} > 1 > L, \tag{15}$$

investment at average rates is better than storage. Moreover, we assume that depositors can actually recover their deposits if the bank is liquidated,

$$(1 + E)L > 1. \tag{16}$$

This means that even in the case of a bank run, which results in termination and liquidation of the bank, the bank does not incur losses. This makes our treatment of such cases simpler, but the model could be adapted so as to allow for losses and limited liability. When liquidation happens, all of the project must be terminated; the bank cannot liquidate only part of the investment.

Independent small banks. We now consider the behaviour of banks in the situation where there are many small banks, each acting independently. The decision to be taken by the bank is the size of the investment, or equivalently – and more conveniently for the analysis – the amount of reserves. Holding large reserves means that some gains from investment (which considered ex ante is better than storage, cf. (15)) are foregone. On the other hand, the level of reserves has implications for whether there will be a run on the bank. This latter relationship comes from the behaviour of depositors: If at $t = 0$ they observe π, then they will infer that the banker will engage in fraud if

$$\pi f(1 + E - M) \geq \pi(1 + E - M) + M - 1,$$

where we have gains from fraud on the left-hand side and gains from carrying through investment on the other side; depositors are pessimistic, so they assume that the (hidden) individual payoff rate r is 0. The rate $\hat{\pi}(M)$ at which there is equality gives the critical value of the macroeconomic rate, which can be found as

$$\hat{\pi}(M) = \frac{1 - M}{(1 - f)(1 + E - M)}, \tag{17}$$

below which fraud will happen so that depositors make a run on the bank. Bankers therefore choose M so as to maximize expected payoff

$$\int_{\pi_{\min}}^{\hat{\pi}(M)} (M + (1 + E - M)L - 1)d\pi + \int_{\hat{\pi}(M)}^{\pi_{\max}} [M + (1 + E - M)(\pi + \bar{r}) - 1]d\pi.$$

Here the first integral is the average over all cases of bank run where the bank is liquidated and the banker gets what is left when depositors have got their money back (which is non-negative by (16)), and the second integral is average gain over the cases where the investment is carried through.

Maximizing expected payoff gives an optimal value of reserved M_{IB}^* for the case of individual banks. We shall use it mainly for comparison with alternative ways of organizing the banking sector. Because there is a level of reserves such that fraud does not pay, no matter which payoff rates will materialize, we have that some investment must be carried out, but on the other hand, low reserves increase the critical payoff rate and thereby the probability of a run.

Big banks. We now consider the opposite case of many independent banks, namely that of big banks. For our model, this means that the bank consists of many branches, each with one project, for which the individual payoff rate $\tilde{r}$ is still independent of other branches.

(a) The first advantage of the big bank is in the individual payoff rate: Because there are many independent branches, the bank as a whole realizes the average $\bar{r}$ (almost) with certainty, so there is no uncertainty on this rate.

(b) But the main advantage is elsewhere: The big bank can adopt a policy of closing down branches with too small an individual payoff rate, so as to prevent bank runs. Let x be a fraction of branches to be closed down, so liquidation of projects will occur when the realized r is below $x2\bar{r}$. Then the payoff from the investment projects actually carried out becomes

$$\pi + \frac{x2\bar{r} + 2\bar{r}}{2} = \pi + (1 + x)\bar{r},$$

and fraud is possible only if

$$M + (1 + E - M)xL + (1 + E - M)(1 - x)(\pi + (1 + x)\bar{r}) - 1 \tag{18}$$
$$\geq (1 - x)f(\pi + (1 + x)\bar{r})(1 + E - M).$$

Here the left-hand side is the gain to the bank when liquidating the fraction x of the projects with lowest local payoff and going through with the rest (the proceeds from liquidations, after depositors have been paid off, are assumed added to the reserves), whereas the right-hand side gives the gain upon fraud, where the banker leaves the obligations to the depositors but then also has to leave the reserves.

We can now repeat the previous steps: First we find the critical value $\hat{\pi}_{BB}(x, M)$ of the macroeconomic payoff rate π given the reserves M *and* the fraction x of branches to be liquidated as the value of π which gives equality in (18). This critical value now depends not only on the size of the reserves but also on the liquidation policy. Given this critical value, expected profits of the bank are

$$\int_{\pi_{min}}^{\hat{\pi}_{BB}(x,M)} [M + (1 + E - M)xL + (1 + E - M)(1 - x(M))(\pi + (1 + x)\bar{r}) - 1]d\pi$$

$$+ \int_{\hat{\pi}_{BB}(x,M)}^{\pi_{max}} [M + (1 + E - M)(\pi + \bar{r}) - 1]d\pi. \tag{19}$$

The bank chooses the values of M and x so as to maximize (19), and the solution to this problem is denoted M^*_{BB}.

Comparing the expressions used in deriving the optimal reserve in the two cases, we see that at any M, it is seen that the optimal reserve M^*_{BB} of the big bank is smaller than that of the individual small bank. The big bank has an advantage already from (a) because bank runs will occur less often. But in addition, it can prevent some bank runs (where all the investments of the bank are liquidated) by voluntary liquidation of the branches realizing the smallest local return on investment. We state this result as a proposition:

PROPOSITION 1: *The optimal reserve level is smaller for the big bank than for the individual small bank,* $M^*_{BB} < M^*_{IB}$.

The two ways of organizing the market for financial intermediation are different, as we have seen, and the big bank is better adapted to the situation than the small independent banks. The question which comes naturally at this point is whether there is any way in which the small banks could reap some of the benefits of size (which in the present model is not connected with market power, but rather with the ability of doing away with the individual risks). This is the situation to be considered next.

A coalition of small banks. If the banks are independent and do not share the payoffs of all investments (as does the big bank), they cannot take advantage of the law of large numbers as in (a) above. What remains is the possibility of liquidating banks with bad investments. For this, the banks can form a coalition which as far as possible should act as the big bank, closing down banks which are subject to a run while keeping the rest of the banks in the coalition going. To achieve this, they introduce a threshold value of r, liquidating banks with local payoff below this threshold. However, the coalition faces an incentive problem which was absent for the big bank: Banks which are not liquidated might still be tempted to engage in fraud, and this has to be prevented by a transfer of money from the high-payoff banks.

Thus, the coalition specifies *two rules*, namely a *liquidation rule*, specifying for the given value of π a fraction $x^*(\pi, M)$ of banks to be closed down, and a *transfer* or *debt restructuring rule* $T(\pi, M, r)$ specifying the transfer for a bank with $r \geq x^*(\pi, M)2\bar{r}$.

To see how it works, suppose that $\pi < \pi(M)$ has been observed. If the banks had been acting on their own, then depositors would run all the banks, because they pessimistically assume that $r = 0$. This is prevented by the coalition, which immediately liquidates all the banks with $r < x^*(\pi, M)2\bar{r}$. The liquidated banks get the payoff $M + (1 + E - M)L - 1$, and they cannot obtain anything better by withdrawing from the coalition, because in that case the depositors would run the bank, given the low value of π).

For the banks which are not liquidated, namely those with $r > x^*(\pi, M)2\bar{r}$, a transfer must be arranged to prevent the bank being better off doing fraud, so

$$f(1 + E - M)(\pi + r) \leq M + (1 + E - M)(\pi + r) - 1 + T(\pi, M, r), \qquad (20)$$

and $T(\pi, M, r)$ is determined so (20) is satisfied with equality,

$$T(\pi, M, r) = 1 - M + (f - 1)(1 + E - M)(\pi + r).$$

Because the coalition can arrange all systems of transfers between banks, this will work as long as

$$\mathsf{E}\left[T(\pi, M, \tilde{r})|\tilde{r} > x^* 2\tilde{r}\right] = 0$$

or

$$[1 - M + (f - 1)(1 + E - M)\pi] + (f - 1)(1 + E - M)(1 + x^*)\tilde{r} = 0,$$

which can be solved to give the value

$$x^*(\pi, M) = \frac{1 - M - \pi(1 - f)(1 + E - M)}{\tilde{r}(1 - f)(1 + E - M)} - 1. \tag{21}$$

Thus, the coalition can credibly announce that it will continue all banks with $r \geq x^*(\pi, M)$ and liquidate the others, because the remaining banks will have no incentive to commit fraud once they have obtained the transfer, and these transfers to banks with low r can be financed by banks with higher values of r.

For the relation to depositors, the arrangement may be interpreted as a replacement of the original deposits by loan certificates issued by the coalition; indeed, the behaviour of the depositors is guided by their confidence in the overall soundness of the coalition and its ability to prevent member banks committing fraud. Instead of a bank obtaining a payoff $\pi + r$, the depositor has to do with a bank having average payoff $\pi + (x^*(\pi, M) + 1)\tilde{r}$, and as long as this is large enough, the depositor has no incentive to run the bank.

We have now described the workings of the coalition at any given M. What remains is to find the optimal value M_C^* of reserves to be used in this case, namely that which maximizes ex ante expected gain of the bank, which is

$$\int_{\pi_{\min}}^{\pi(M)} [M + (1 + E - M)x^*(\pi, M)L + (1 - x^*(\pi, M))(\pi + (1 + x^*(\pi, M))\tilde{r}]dF(\pi)$$

$$+ \int_{\pi(M)}^{\pi_{\max}} [M + (1 + E - M)(\pi + \tilde{r})]dF(\pi) - 1.$$

Here $\pi(M)$ is determined by $x^*(\pi, M) = 0$; the first integral is expected gain when π is low, so some of the banks are liquidated, and the second integral is expectation over high π's where all the banks carry their investment through.

The main point of our analysis is to assess the outcome of the coalition in relation to the two previous benchmarks, individual banks or one big bank. Compared to the case of individual banks, there is an obvious gain because the coalition as a whole can go on working when π is small, even if it has to close down some of the member banks. Therefore, the level of reserves may be kept lower than if all the banks had been on their own. On the other hand, the big bank has the advantage that it can control its branches fully and decide whether to engage in fraud from the point of view of the totality, thereby keeping the fraction of banks to be liquidated low, whereas the coalition can go no further than what can be made incentive-compatible by debt reallocation. Because the big bank is less exposed at any level of reserves, the latter may be kept lower than in the case of a coalition. Summing up, we have the following:

PROPOSITION 2: *For the three ways of organizing the banking sector, we have that*

$$M^*_{BB} < M^*_C < M^*_{IB},$$

so optimal reserves are lowest for the big bank and highest for the individual banks, with coalition banking in between.

Looking at the result from society's point of view, we have that big banks are more efficient than coalition banking, which again is more efficient than individual banking. It should, of course, be remembered that we have been concerned only with the risk-sharing aspects of banking, not with problems of market power which would speak against the big bank solution.

Returning again to the coalition of banks, we may interpret this as a forerunner of a central bank, which is taking action in situations where a bank run is threatening. This action consistis in closing down some of the less promising banks but assisting other banks in preventing the run, arranging a debt restructuring which will convince the public about the safety of the bank in question. In our model, this did not take the form of a loan to the threatened bank, but with a suitable reformulation of the model it could take this classical form as well. Therefore, the model tells us that if there were no central bank, it would come into existence by the joint action of the banks themselves, much like what happened when the US Federal Reserve System was created.

16.5 Exercises

1. In an attempt to restore confidence in the financial sector, the central bank contemplates a new way of assisting banks with liquidity problems: The loans given by the central bank will be given as preferential debt, so no dividend can be paid on shares before these loans have been paid back. Comment on this proposal.

The proposed reform is supplemented by a rule which defines a maximal salary (including bonus) to bank management in the case that the bank has debt to the central bank. How can this be expected to influence risk taking in banks?

2. Consider a model of Diamond-Dybvig type, where an additional investment opportunity is introduced. This investment can be initiated only at $t = 1$ and gives a repayment $\tilde{r}$ at $t = 2$, which is uniformly distributed in the interval $[0, 2R]$; the realized value of r will be observed only at $t = 1$.

How should a deposit contract specifying the withdrawals of impatient and patient depositors be constructed in this case? Will bank runs be a possibility in this extended model, and can a lender of last resort resolve such problems?

3. In a new approach to the problem of assisting banks which are experiencing a bank run, it is proposed to offer loans not to the bank in trouble, but to other banks if they agree to buy the shares of the troubled bank and carry on their business. It is argued that because the assistance implies a change of ownership, banks will take care to avoid excessive risks which may provoke a run from its depositors.

Comment on this proposal.

16.6 Comments

The importance of a lender of last resort was first emphasized by Bagehot in his work 'Lombard Street' from 1873, which is widely quoted even today.

The model in Section 16.2 is based on Freixas [1999]; however, we use only the initial part of the work. The literature on bailout and its consequences is quite considerable; for contributions, see e.g. Diamond and Rajan [2002], Acharya and Yorulmazer [2008]. For another contribution which connects risk taking and the probability of being bailed out, see Hakenes and Schnabel [2010].

Chapter 17

Reorganization of Banks

17.1 Introduction

The possibility of bank runs and major systemic crises in the financial sector has brought with it the need for suitable institutions in society which can take action whenever a problem occurs. But in addition to this, it seems natural to consider the possibility of taking action even *before* the problems arise, thereby preventing bank runs or bank defaults from taking place. Indeed, such authorities have usually been created in most countries, and the legal prerequisites have been created so that suitable authorities may take action if a bank shows signs of moving towards a future crisis.

On the other hand, regulating banks, even when the formal tools are available, is not an altogether simple affair. First of all, the regulating authority may not have access to relevant information, so action, when taken, may come too late or may even be damaging. But secondly, regulating a bank will typically be costly, and considerations of cost may have as their effect that the regulator may refrain from taking action. And thirdly, in many countries several authorities may be involved, then posing the question of which of these should decide upon the action to be taken against a bank in trouble.

In the following, we consider some of these problems in more detail. To simplify the discussion, emphasis will be on a particular way of regulating, namely the ultimate regulation consisting in the forced closure of a bank, with subsequent liquidation of its activities. We begin with the most obvious line of defence against unwanted conduction of business, which would be the bank's own board of directors, which might act by reorganizing the bank and sacking the manager. Because in most cases this is not quite enough, other authorities need to be involved, and we then look at the possible division of labour by central banks and deposit insurance organizations. Finally, we consider a simple model of the basic bank-regulator conflict, where the regulator's threat of closing down the bank should act as a correcting force on the business choices of the bank; the model shows why this threat in many cases will turn out to be insufficient.

17.2 Shareholder control of banks

If a bank is run in an improper way, it has consequences for the survival of the bank, and because the shareholders are the first to lose their money in a default, they should be correspondingly concerned, so they would follow the business decisions of the bank management in detail, taking action in the case of an unsatisfactory record of the bank. This is not quite in accordance with real-life experience, where the bank's management will often be able to run the bank almost independently of shareholder interference.

To see why the owners do not control the bank to the extent expected, it is useful to look at the problems behind the delegation of power from ownership to management. The first problem here is that any particular shareholder will own at most a small fraction of the capital, so the influence on management cannot be direct, but should go through *rules* or incentive schemes for managers, so the latter will behave in a way which as far as possible is in the interest of the shareholders. Clearly, the rules – which may be thought of as a contract between shareholders and management – cannot be so detailed as to specify all possible events in the business life of the bank, but as a minimum they should specify the conditions under which the shareholders can intervene in the management of the bank, reorganizing the bank by firing the manager and setting up a new set of rules. In other words, it should deal with the *allocation of control rights* of the bank. The model of this to be considered below is taken from Dewatripont and Tirole [1994].

We consider a bank which conducts business over three periods, $t = 0, 1, 2$. At $t = 0$, it uses deposits D_0 and equity E_0 to finance loans L_0. The quality of these loans will depend on the effort e of the manager; effort can take values e_H and e_L, and there is a cost $h(e)$ of effort with $h(e_H) > h(e_L)$. We assume that it is desirable for the bank that the manager supplies effort e_H, and the task of the incentive scheme is to make sure that this will happen.

At date $t = 1$, a first repayment $\tilde{v}$ is made on the loan, and in addition, a signal $\tilde{u}$ is observed which has a relation to the value of the remainder of the loan $\tilde{\eta}$ at $t = 2$. The two random variables v and u are independent, but both are related to the effort e supplied by the manager. We assume that η obtained at $t = 1$ is reinvested at the risk-free rate of interest, which in the model is assumed to be 0, so the repayment at $t = 2$ is $v + \eta$. Having observed the values of $\tilde{u}$ and $\tilde{v}$, the shareholders can decide whether to close down the bank (the decision $d = 0$) or to continue ($d = 1$). The decision influences the probability distribution of $\tilde{\eta}$, which is written as $F_d(\eta \mid u)$, for $d = 0, 1$. It should be noticed that this distribution depends only on u, not on v.

Finally, at date $t = 2$ the value of $\tilde{\eta}$ is observed. The decision d as to whether the bank shall be reorganized or continued is to be taken by the controlling shareholders at $t = 1$ and cannot be written into the contract with the manager. Also, we assume that the only incentive structure that can be used is the threat of reorganizing the bank, whereby the manager who is fired will lose a benefit B which comes from running the bank.

Because $\tilde{u}$ and $\tilde{v}$ are independent, the future of the bank depends only on u, and the value of $\tilde{v}$ would be irrelevant under complete information. Expected profit from continuing rather than stopping, defined as

$$\Pi(u) = \mathsf{E}[\tilde{\eta} \mid \tilde{u} = u, d = 1] - \mathsf{E}[\tilde{\eta} \mid \tilde{u} = u, d = 0]$$

can then be written as

$$\Pi(u) = \int_0^\infty \eta \, dF_1(\eta|u) - \int_0^\infty \eta \, dF_0(\eta|u)$$

$$= \int_0^\infty [F_0(\eta|u) - F_1(\eta|u)] d\eta,$$

where we have used the formula for integration by parts,

$$\int_0^\infty \eta \, dF_d(\eta|u) = [\eta F_d(\eta|u)]_0^\infty - \int_0^\infty F_d(\eta|u) d\eta,$$

$d = 0, 1$, where the first member on the right-hand side vanishes. The decision $d = 1$ is advantageous for the shareholders if $\Pi(u) \geq 0$. Assuming that $\Pi(u)$ is increasing in u, there will be a threshold value $\hat{u}$ such that if the value of $\tilde{u}$ exceeds $\hat{u}$, then the bank is allowed to continue, and otherwise it is reorganized.

However, this decision has not taken management effort into consideration, or rather, it was assumed throughout that effort was e_H. But if the owners cannot observe e and act solely on the information from $\tilde{u}$, then it may not be in the interest of the manager to choose the high level of effort. Consequently, we need to add an incentive scheme. The particular one used here builds on the manager's fear of being fired and losing a bonus which would be obtained otherwise.

In this new context, we introduce a decision rule $x(u, v)$ which determines the probability of continuing given the values of $\tilde{u}$ and $\tilde{v}$. Although $\tilde{v}$ says nothing about the future outcome, it does say something about the effort level of the manager, and therefore it makes sense to condition the decision rule upon its value. Notice that we have introduced the decision rule as a mixed strategy, but it turns out that the optimal values of $x(u, v)$ are always either 0 or 1. We denote the distributions of $\tilde{u}$ and $\tilde{\eta}$, given effort level e, by $g(u|e)$ and $h(v|e)$, and we assume that

$$\frac{g(\cdot|e_H)}{g(\cdot|e_L)}, \quad \frac{h(\cdot|e_H)}{h(\cdot|e_L)}$$

are increasing functions.

To find the optimal decision rule for the owners, we need to maximize the expected profit, which now becomes

$$\int_{-\infty}^{\infty} \int_{-\infty}^{\infty} x(u,v)\Pi(u)g(u|e_H)h(v|e_H)\, du\, dv$$

under the management incentive constraint

$$B \int_{-\infty}^{\infty} \int_{-\infty}^{\infty} x(u,v)[g(u|e_H)h(v|e_H) - g(u|e_L)h(v|e_L)]\, du\, dv \geq h(e_H) - h(e_L),$$

saying that expected loss from being fired is greater than the cost of the high effort. The Lagrangian of this constrained maximization problem is

$$\int_{-\infty}^{\infty} \int_{-\infty}^{\infty} x(u,v)[(\Pi(u) + \mu B)g(u|e_H)h(v|e_H) - \mu Bg(u|e_L)h(v|e_L)]\, du\, dv - \mu H,$$

where $H = h(e_H) - h(e_L)$, and the maximum of this Lagrangian is attained by choosing

$$x(u,v) = 1 \text{ if } \Pi(u) + \mu B \geq \frac{g(u|e_H)h(v|e_H)}{g(u|e_L)h(v|e_L)},$$

$$x(u,v) = 0 \text{ otherwise.}$$

Rewriting the condition for continuing the bank, we see that continuation is optimal if

$$\frac{g(u|e_H)}{g(u|e_L)}\left[1 + \frac{\Pi(u)}{\mu B}\right] \geq \frac{h(v|e_L)}{h(u|e_H)}.$$

The limiting case of equality defines u as an implicit function u^0 of v, and it is easily seen that $u^0(\cdot)$ is decreasing. We let $\tilde{v}$ be the value of v such that $\hat{u} = u^0(\hat{v})$.

Comparing now the decision rule in the incomplete information framework with our first rule, where we assumed that the manager could be forced to choose e_H, we see that

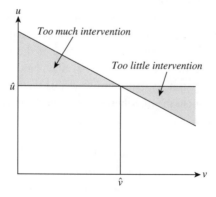

Figure 17.1 Decision rules in the management incentive problem. In order to keep management effort high, owners must allow continuation even when perspectives are not too good, given that previous results were satisfactory. Conversely, management will also be changed after bad results when outlook is rather good.

this decision rule is too active when $\tilde{v}$ takes small values (closing down the bank even when the information provided by u alone would point to a continuation), but too lenient when $\tilde{v}$ takes values above $\hat{v}$, cf. Fig. 17.1.

17.3 Who should decide upon the closure of a bank?

The model in this section deals with the problem of selecting the proper institution for determining whether a bank in trouble should be closed down. The formal setting of the model is inspired by that of the previous section (but the regulating authorities are different): The bank obtains deposits 1 at $t = 0$, which are invested over two periods. In the meantime, at time $t = 1$, two signals are received, namely v (which in this model is the amount of withdrawals that the depositors make at $t = 1$) and u, which is a signal on the quality of the investment. In the original formulation, u is the probability of success of the investment, which has a random payoff $\tilde{R}$ given by

$$\tilde{R} = \begin{cases} R & \text{with probability } u, \\ 0 & \text{with probability } 1 - u. \end{cases}$$

In addition, Repullo [2000] assumes liquidation value $L < 1$ and liquidation cost c.

From the point of view of society, the bank should be liquidated when the expected value of investment as seen at $t = 1$,

$$uR - (1 - u)c,$$

is smaller than the value if liquidated,

$$L - c.$$

This gives rise to a threshold value

$$u^* = \frac{L}{R + c}$$

below which liquidation should take place. However, society has to perform this through suitable institutions. Two such are considered:

The central bank. We assume that the central bank covers only fraction β of the liquidation costs. In this case, the central bank will assist the bank, giving a loan of v, if the cost of doing so, namely expected values of losses,

$$(1 - u)(v + \beta c),$$

does not exceed the losses from liquidating here and now, βc. Equating the two expressions, we get a threshold value of u (now depending on v),

$$\hat{u}(v) = \frac{v}{v + \beta c},$$

below which the central bank will close down the bank, as illustrated in Fig. 17.2.

The deposit insurer. Assuming that the deposit insurer covers a fraction γ of the liquidation cost, we get that closing down immediately costs

$$\gamma c + 1 - L$$

(the deposit insurer must reimburse the depositors fully but gets the liquidation value), whereas proceeding has an expected cost of

$$(1 - u)(1 + \gamma c).$$

This gives us a threshold value

$$\bar{u} = \frac{L}{1 + \gamma c},$$

below which the deposit insurer will liquidate the bank.

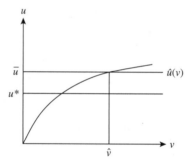

Figure 17.2 The regions where a troubled bank will be closed down. The central bank will deny support and close down the bank when the (v, u)-combinations are below the graph of $\hat{u}$, whereas the deposit insurer will decide for closure at all (v, u) with $u \leq \bar{u}$. Neither of these decision rules are in full accordance with what is best for society.

Collecting the expressions, we see that the central bank will be too lenient for small values of v and too tough at high values of v, whereas the deposit insurer is uniformly too tough. However, using the assumption that v is verifiable, the right to decide about bank closure may be made dependent on v, and an obvious choice would be to use the value $\hat{v}$, where

$$\hat{u}(\hat{v}) = \bar{u},$$

as the threshold below which the central bank should decide whether to assist the bank, whereas the decision is up to the deposit insurer if v is above this value.

Using this rule for assigning control, we get as near as possible to the socially optimal decision. The functioning of the rule does, however, depend on the availability of the (non-verifiable) information u. If, for example, only the central bank knows u and must communicate it to the deposit insurer if v is big, then the central bank may reduce losses by understating u, thereby replacing immediate cost βc by expected cost $(1 - u)\beta c$; this incentive to misrepresent will be present as long as $u > 0$. This shows that delegation of control rights must be supported by availability of information in order to work properly.

17.4 The regulatory game

As we have seen in the previous sections, it matters for the final outcome who is given the authority of closing a bank when its performance gives rise to serious doubts about its solvency in the future. This was due to the fact that a bank default will have different consequences for regulators of different types. This insight points to a logical next step in the analysis: If the bank, which is subject to regulation, knows about the costs of regulation to the regulator, it will adapt its choices accordingly. We shall consider a simple such case, taken from Mailath and Mester [1994].

In order to capture the idea of mutual dependence of actions, we consider a bank which receives a deposit of 1 unit. This unit is invested in a project which may be either safe (here denoted G) in the sense that it yields a payoff $1 + r$ with certainty, or risky (B), with random payoff $1 + \tilde{\rho}$, where

$$\tilde{\rho} = \begin{cases} \rho & \text{with probability } p, \\ 0 & \text{otherwise.} \end{cases}$$

Once the investment has been chosen by the bank, its type can be inspected by the regulator, who then has the option of closing the bank (C) or leaving it open (O). Then the outcome of the project is observed, and if the bank is left open, it chooses a second round of investment (so it is assumed that the bank has access to credit at this stage), after which the bank liquidates and pays whatever came out of the two projects.

It is assumed that the regulator will have to reimburse losses to the creditors of the bank and to pay additional cost C of liquidation. Also, it is assumed that $\rho > r$ but $p(1+\rho) < 1+r$, so the safe investment is best for society, and that $\rho < 1$, so one successful investment will yield too little to repay one failed investment.

The conflicting interests of bank and regulator can now be drawn up as a game in extensive form, as shown in Fig. 17.3. The payoff structure of the game is as follows: If the bank chooses G and the regulator C (not a very likely choice, but in principle a possibility), then the play results in the terminal node numbered (1) with a gain of r to the bank and a cost of C to the regulator. If the bank chose B and the regulator C (node (2)), then the payoff to the bank would be $p\rho$ and the cost to the regulator $C + (1 - p)$ (with probability $1 - p$, the investment fails and the regulator will have to compensate the depositors to the amount 1).

The payoffs of the remaining nodes can be assessed in a similar way: At node (3), where the bank has chosen G twice, the payoff to the bank is $2r$ and the cost to the regulator is 0. Node (4) actually consists of two nodes of the game tree, but the payoffs are identical because they arise when the regulator keeps the bank open and the latter chooses

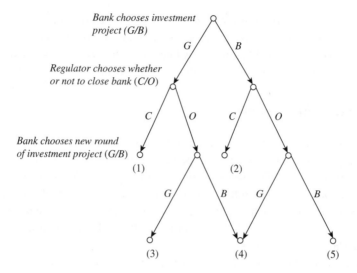

Figure 17.3 The bank-regulator game tree. The bank may be closed down by the regulator after the first round of investment decisions. Whether this will happen depends on the cost to the regulator of either stopping the bank after the first investment or letting it also go through with the second round.

one G and one B: The payoff to the bank is then $p(\rho + r)$ (in the case of at least one failure, the bank defaults and gets nothing), and the cost to the regulator is $(1 - p)[C + (1 - r)]$ (because there was one safe investment, the amount to be paid back to depositors is reduced by r). Finally, node (5) with two risky investments will give the bank a payoff of $p^2(2\rho)$, and the cost to the regulator is $(1 - p^2)C + (1 - p)^2 2 + 2p(1 - p)[1 - \rho]$ (cost of liquidation must be paid unless there are two successes, and reimbursement to depositors depends on whether there are one or no successes).

Having thus defined the game (or, to be precise, the game form, because we have not yet considered preferences over outcomes), we may proceed towards finding its Nash equilibria. What constitutes an equilibrium will depend on the the preferences of the bank, which again depends on the value of the parameters.

Consider first the case where the bank prefers one risky and one safe investment to two risky investments; this is clearly the case when $p(\rho + r) > 2p^2\rho$ (the outcome in (4) is better than that in (5)) or

$$p < \frac{\rho + r}{2\rho}. \tag{1}$$

If the regulator observes that the bank has chosen B, then she knows that if kept open, the bank will choose G next time, and a comparison of the cost incurred at nodes (2) and (4) shows that it is better for the bank to keep the bank open. If the bank initially chooses G, then again cost will be bigger if closing down immediately than if waiting, even though the bank must now be expected to choose B next time. Thus, for the parameters satisfying inequality (1) it will never be advantageous to close the bank.

It remains to consider the other case, where two risky investments are preferred to one risky and one safe. In this case, we must expect the bank to choose B if it gets to the second round, no matter what was chosen before. If the first choice was B, then the regulator will be better off by closing the bank if

$$C + (1 - p) < C\left(1 - p^2\right) + 2(1 - p)^2 + 2p(1 - p)(1 - \rho)$$

or, equivalently, if

$$C < \frac{(1 - p)(1 - 2p\rho)}{p^2}. \tag{2}$$

Otherwise, the regulator will keep the bank open after an initial choice of B. If, however, (2) is satisfied, then an initial choice of B by the bank will result in its being closed by the regulator, and therefore it will be better for the bank to choose G initially and then B. After an initial choice of G, the regulator will leave the bank open, even taking into consideration that B will be chosen next, unless

$$C < C(1 - p) + (1 - p)(1 - r),$$

which can also be stated as

$$C < \frac{1 - p}{p}(1 - r),$$

in which case closing the bank has a lower cost than letting it proceed to another round of investment.

We can see from the analysis that the regulator will refrain from closing the bank in quite a lot of cases, although the bank can be seen to have chosen an investment which is undesirable from a social point of view, the reason being that the cost of liquidating the bank and paying out the compensation will be higher than those following if not interfering. In Fig. 17.4, we have shown the different outcomes as depending on the parameters p and C.

The region to the left of

$$p_2 = \frac{1 + r}{1 + \rho}$$

constitutes all parameter combinations (p, C) such that expected payoff of the investment B is smaller than $1 + r$, the payoff of the safe investment, so B is socially undesirable. Nevertheless, for values of p smaller than

$$p_1 = \frac{\rho + r}{2\rho},$$

that is, in the region A in Fig. 17.4, the bank may choose B as its first investment, followed by G, and it will not be closed down. For $p > p_1$ the bank may still choose B in the first round without being closed by the regulator, namely in the region B where the

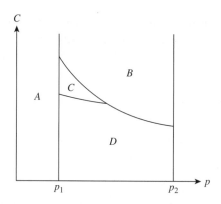

Figure 17.4 Regions in the parameter space where particular strategies are equilibria. For many combinations of the values p and C of the parameters, the regulator will prefer to let the bank continue operating even after having chosen the 'wrong' investment in the first round.

inequality (2) is violated. Even below the limiting curve, namely in region C, the bank is not closed down when choosing at least one B, but it has to choose G the first time. Finally, only in the remaining region D will the regulators close the bank.

17.5 Systemic risk and the too-big-to-fail problem

17.5.1 Systemic risk
Because the discussion so far has been centred on the problems of a single bank, we could reasonably assume that if these problems became too worrying, it would result in closing down and liquidating the bank. However, there are situations where this final option is not available, namely when the bank is considered as so important for the economy that a default must be avoided almost at any cost. The bank has become 'too big to fail' and must be kept going, not for its own sake, but for that of society as a whole.

It is rather clear that being to big to fail is not a question of size alone, or perhaps not at all. What matters is the consequence of a possible default of the bank for the financial system and the economy, so it is a question of the *systemic importance* of the bank. This in its turn has to do with the properties of the financial sector as a whole, its concentration, its interconnectedness and the degree to which the banks choose correlated risks. Consequently, the decision as to whether a bank is systemically important or not cannot be decided in an immediate way, but depends on the situation.

17.5.2 A simple model of systemically important banks
In order to analyse the way in which to approach a systemic crisis, we consider a situation with only two banks A and B, which we follow over two periods [Acharya and Yorulmazer, 2007]. Banks receive deposits and invest in a risky technology with payoff y obtained in the next period $t + 1$ with probability π_t, for $t = 0, 1$, and 0 otherwise. The returns are independent from one period to the next, but the probability of success may change.

There is a regulator which also manages deposit insurance in the first period. Because the second period is the last one, there is no deposit insurance.

If the bank succeeds in the first period, then it proceeds to the second period with a new investment. If the investment fails, the bank is in default at $t = 1$, and the regulator decides whether to sell it to the other bank not in default (if there is one) or to liquidate the bank and sell its assets to outside investors. We assume that there is a cost $C(x)$ of bailing out a bank in terms of resources needed in the process, which is linear in the amount of funds x provided.

There are four possible states of the system at $t = 1$, namely

  SS: Both banks had a success in the first period and operate in the second period;

  SF: Bank A had a success, but B had a failure, so bank B is either bailed out or acquired by bank A or liquidated;

  FS: The same situation, only with A having a failure and B a success;

  FF: Both banks fail and are either bailed out or liquidated.

We shall use some of the features of the model discussed in Section 15.3: Banks have specific skills in performing investments, so outside investors can obtain only $y - \Delta$ in case of success. Furthermore, the investment option comes in two versions, in the sense that banks can invest in different industries or in the same industry, and the outcome $\tilde{y}$ is determined by *industry* rather than by firms. Thus, if banks invest in the same industry, the joint probabilities of success or failure of the two banks will be

	Success for B	Failure for B
Success for A	π_t^2	$\pi_t(1 - \pi_t)$
Failure for A	$(1 - \pi_t)\pi_t$	$(1 - \pi_t)^2$

For later purposes, we introduce also a specific feature of bank ownership, namely that bank owners can realize only the outcome $y - \Delta_1$ in the case of choosing the same industry as that of the other bank. Bank managers are remunerated by a share θ of the profits of the bank, but in addition, they obtain a non-pecuniary benefit b in the case of investment in the same technology (a satisfaction connected with doing the same kind of business as the other bank); b is assumed to be smaller than Δ_1. In order for bank managers to choose investments from different industries, we must have

$$\pi_t \theta(y - r) \geq \pi_t[\theta((y - \Delta_1) - r) + b],$$

where r is the repayment to depositors, which depends on the date and for $t = 1$ also on the state at this date t. Equivalently, the share θ should satisfy

$$\theta > \bar{\theta} = \frac{b}{\Delta_1} \tag{3}$$

to prevent the moral hazard of bank managers. We assume that deposits are insured at $t = 0$, so depositors get their money back with certainty, meaning that $r_0 = 1$.

To analyse the model, we begin with the last date at which decisions are made, that is, at $t = 1$, and consider the situation in each of the four possible states.

SS: Here both banks have succeeded in the previous period, and they begin a new round. The expected payoff of the bank is

$$\mathsf{E}\big[\widetilde{\Pi}_2^{SS}\big] = \pi_1\big(y - r_1^{SS}\big),$$

and assuming that depositors are forthcoming as long as expected return on deposits equals 1 (keeping their wealth), so $\pi_1 r_1^{SS} = 1$, we get that $\mathsf{E}\big[\widetilde{\Pi}_2^{SS}\big] = \pi_1 y - 1$.

SF or FS: Here only one bank was successful; suppose that A succeeded while B failed. Bank A then has the option of buying the assets of bank B. The price to be paid must be such that outside investors would not step in, which means that it should be at least $P = (\pi_1(y - \Delta) - 1)$, corresponding to the profit to outside investors from paying out the depositors from $t = 0$ and starting a new round with new depositors. We assume also that selling to outside investors, which gives $(\pi_1(y - \Delta) - 1)$, will not be sufficient to cover the repayment of interest to period 0 depositors, so

$$(\pi_1(y - \Delta) - 1) < 1,$$

so selling to outside investors is costly to the regulator. This will occur only if Δ is large enough, so banks must have sufficiently high competence.

Under these assumptions, bank A has sufficient funds for buying the assets of bank B, because

$$y - r_0 > \pi_1(y - \Delta) - 1.$$

It will also want to do so, because it can borrow at the expected cost 1, and it gets a discount on the value to the amount of $\pi_1 \Delta$. We conclude that bank A buys bank B, whereby its value increases by $\pi_1 \Delta$.

FF: In this case, the assets of the banks can be sold only to outside investors. Alternatively, the banks can be bailed out. The latter action will give the regulator a share β in the bank, and in the case of success, which happens with probability π_2, the regulator gets back $\beta(y - r_1^{FF})$ at $t = 2$. If the share is greater than $1 - \bar{\theta}$, then the bank managers are forced into moral hazard, and because $\Delta_1 > \Delta$, we get from (3) that the regulator will take a share only as long as $\beta \le 1 - \bar{\theta}$.

If we assume that the regulator chooses to maximize the expected outcome of the banks minus the cost of either bailout or liquidation, which we denote by $\mathsf{E}\big[\widetilde{S}_2^{FF}\big]$, then there are three possibilities:

(a) Both banks are sold to outside investors, giving a result

$$\mathsf{E}\big[\widetilde{S}_2^{FF}\big] = 2[\pi_1(y - \Delta) - 1] - c(2r_0 - 2P), \tag{4}$$

where we have subtracted the cost of funds needed, and the latter are what must be paid by the deposit insurance minus the proceeds from selling the assets.

(b) One bank is bailed out and the other one sold to outside investors, giving a payoff of

$$\mathsf{E}\!\left[\widetilde{S}_2^{FF}\right] = (\pi_1 y - 1) + [\pi_1(y - \Delta) - 1] - c(2r_0 - P) = 2(\pi_1(y - 1) + \pi_1\Delta - c(2r_0 - P). \tag{5}$$

(c) Both banks are bailed out, in which case payoff becomes

$$\mathsf{E}\!\left[\widetilde{S}_2^{FF}\right] = 2(\pi_1 y - 1) - 2cr_0. \tag{6}$$

Comparing the three cases, it can be seen that what matters is whether the loss connected with liquidation, $\pi_1\Delta$, is big compared to the loss connected with bailout, cP. Indeed, define a break-even value of Δ as

$$\Delta^* = \frac{c(\pi_1 y - 1)}{\pi_1(1 + c)}.$$

Then the following holds:

PROPOSITION 1: *If $\Delta > \Delta^*$, then the regulator bails out both banks, and if $\Delta \leq \Delta^*$, then the banks are liquidated. When bailing out the banks, the regulator chooses a share $\beta < 1 - \bar{\theta}$.*

PROOF: The second part of the proposition was shown above. To show that the first part holds, we notice that by liquidating a bank instead of bailing it out, the regulator loses $\pi_1\Delta$ in terms of payoff foregone but saves cP in terms of resource cost of financing the regulation. Equating the two terms, we get that the two options are of equal value if

$$\pi_1\Delta = c(\pi_1(y - \Delta) - 1)$$

or $\Delta = \Delta^*$, and that bailing out is best when $\Delta > \Delta^*$, liquidating best for $\Delta \leq \Delta^*$. It is easily seen that if bailing out one bank is better than liquidating it, then bailing out both is even better. □

The result in Proposition 1 shows that the regulator will have to step in if both banks are in trouble. Thus the model displays a phenomenon which might be called *too many to fail*, in the sense that the banks can rely on being bailed out in case of trouble if this trouble is shared by sufficiently many banks.

We may now conclude our treatment of the case FF, and thus of the decisions made at $t = 1$, by stating the payoff of the bank in this situation, which is

$$\mathsf{E}\!\left[\widetilde{\Pi}^{FF}\right] = \begin{cases} 0 & \Delta \leq \Delta^*, \\ (1 - \beta)(\pi_1 y - 1) & \Delta > \Delta^*. \end{cases}$$

Having analysed the second period, we may turn to the first period. A bank can choose investment in an industry different from that chosen by the other bank (we identify this as $\rho = 0$, zero correlation between banks) or in the same industry ($\rho = 1$). The expected payoff of the first round is $\pi_0(y - r_0)$ independent of the choice of ρ, but the second period payoff matters. If $\rho = 1$, then SF does not occur, and second period expected payoff is

$$\mathsf{E}\left[\widetilde{\Pi}_2(1)\right] = \pi_0 \mathsf{E}\left[\widetilde{\Pi}_2^{SS}\right] + (1 - \pi_0)\mathsf{E}\left[\widetilde{\Pi}_2^{FF}\right].$$

If $\rho = 0$, then

$$\mathsf{E}\left[\widetilde{\Pi}_2(0)\right] = \pi_0^2 \mathsf{E}\left[\widetilde{\Pi}_2^{SS}(0)\right] + \pi_0(1 - \pi_0)\mathsf{E}\left[\widetilde{\Pi}_2^{SF}(0)\right] + (1 - \pi_0)^2 \mathsf{E}\left[\widetilde{\Pi}_2^{FF}(0)\right].$$

Here $\mathsf{E}\left[\widetilde{\Pi}_2^{SF}(0)\right] = \pi_1 \Delta$, because bank A buys the assets of bank B. Therefore, we have that

$$\mathsf{E}\left[\widetilde{\Pi}_2(0)\right] = \pi_0^2 \mathsf{E}\left[\widetilde{\Pi}_2^{SS}(0)\right] + \pi_0(1 - \pi_0)\pi_1 \Delta + (1 - \pi_0)^2 \mathsf{E}\left[\widetilde{\Pi}_2^{FF}(0)\right],$$

and

$$\mathsf{E}\left[\widetilde{\Pi}_2(1)\right] - \mathsf{E}\left[\widetilde{\Pi}_2(0)\right] = \pi_0(1 - \pi_0)\left(\mathsf{E}\left[\widetilde{\Pi}_2^{FF}(0)\right] - \pi_1 \Delta\right). \tag{7}$$

It follows that the bank will choose $\rho = 1$ when the right-hand side of (7) is positive and $\rho = 0$ otherwise. Defining

$$\beta^* = 1 - \frac{\pi_1 \Delta}{\pi_1 y - 1} \tag{8}$$

as the value of β for which this right-hand side is 0, we may state the full result of the model:

PROPOSITION 2: *Let β^* be given by (8).*

If $\Delta \leq \Delta^*$, so the regulator liquidates both banks in state FF, then banks choose uncorrelated investments, $\rho = 0$.

If $\Delta > \Delta^*$ and the regulator bails out the banks in state FF, then

(i) *for $\beta \leq 1 - \bar{\theta}$, bailout strategies with share β satisfying $\beta^* \leq \beta \leq 1 - \bar{\theta}$ result in uncorrelated investment choices, $\rho = 0$, whereas banks choose $\rho = 1$ for $\beta < \beta^*$;*

(ii) *for $\beta^* > 1 - \bar{\theta}$, then for any bailout strategy with $0 \leq \beta \leq 1 - \bar{\theta}$, the banks will choose correlated investment, $\rho = 1$.*

It may be noticed that β was left undetermined in the equilibrium as described above. Because the choice of β matters for the equilibrium, the regulator might announce a policy which will result in this choice, thereby influencing the investment choices of the bank and reducing the risk that the banks must be bailed out.

The way of treating the too-big-to-fail problem in practice has been by increased capital requirements for banks singled out as *systemically important* rather than by direct participation of the regulator in the case of a bailout, even though government assistance in the form of capital injection was used widely in the financial crisis of 2007–8 and its aftermath.

17.5.3 Measuring systemic importance

Once it has been accepted that some banks have a size or an impact on the financial system which makes it undesirable to close them down after a failure, the logical next step would be to introduce specific policies or regulations on such systemically important banks. This presupposes that the systemically important banks can be identified, something which may be less easy in practice than might be expected.

Suppose that the banking system has n banks and that the state of each bank i is described by a random variable $\tilde{x}_i$, which may be losses on total assets or possibly on some other crucial positions. To describe a crisis level of the variable, it seems reasonable to use Value at Risk (VaR), so

$$\hat{x}_i = \text{VaR}_{1-p}(\tilde{x}_i),$$

for p either 1% or 0.1% describes a threshold value above which bank i is in trouble.

Given that crisis is indicated by a value of $\tilde{x}_i$ greater than $\text{VaR}_{1-p}(\tilde{x}_i)$, we get an indicator of the systemic importance of bank i, using the conditional probability that some other bank fails given that i is in trouble,

$$\text{PO}_i(p) = \mathsf{P}\big\{\exists j \neq i : \tilde{x}_j > \text{VaR}_{1-p}(\tilde{x}_j) \,\big|\, \tilde{x}_i > \text{VaR}_{1-p}(\tilde{x}_i)\big\}. \tag{9}$$

This measure, proposed in Segoviano and Goodhart [2009], does give an indication of the extent to which bank i influences the state of other banks, but it might be insufficient for other reasons, as pointed out by Zhou [2010]: Banks may influence each other in many ways, and it may be the case that bank i has a considerable influence on the state of bank j, but that the two banks i and j influence all the other banks only marginally. Thus, PO_i measures only the probability that a failure of i creates trouble for some other bank, not the systemic impact. For this, we would also need to know how many of the other banks that could get into trouble.

A measure of systemic importance which takes this latter aspect into account is the *systemic impact index* (SII) proposed by Zhou [2010],

$$\text{SII}_i(p) = \mathsf{E}\left[\sum_{j=1}^{n} 1_{\tilde{x}_j > \text{VaR}_{1-p}(\tilde{x}_j)} \,\bigg|\, \tilde{x}_i > \text{VaR}_{1-p}(\tilde{x}_i)\right],$$

which gives the expected number of banks that will fail as a consequence of the failure of bank i.

Finally, we may also consider the dependence of banks from the opposite angle and define the *vulnerability index* VI for bank i,

$$\text{VI}_i(p) = \mathsf{P}\big\{\tilde{x}_i > \text{VaR}_{1-p}(\tilde{x}_i) \,\big|\, \exists j \neq i : \tilde{x}_j > \text{VaR}_{1-p}(\tilde{x}_j)\big\},$$

as the conditional probability that i gets into trouble given that some other bank is in crisis.

For a further – and more technical – analysis of the SII measure, we turn to *extreme value theory* (cf. Section 13.2.5). To assess the co-movement of extreme events, one introduces the function L defined for threshold levels $(z_1, \ldots, z_n)$ as

$$L(z_1, \ldots, z_n) = \lim_{p \to \infty} \frac{\mathsf{P}\{\tilde{x}_1 > \mathrm{VaR}_{1-z_1 p}(\tilde{x}_1) \wedge \cdots \wedge \tilde{x}_n > \mathrm{VaR}_{1-z_n p}(\tilde{x}_n)\}}{p}$$

(assuming that the limit exists). Here the numbers $(z_1, \ldots, z_n)$ are used to define the thresholds; in our case they can be set to 1, so we get

$$L(1, \ldots, 1) = \lim_{p \to \infty} \frac{\mathsf{P}\{\tilde{x}_1 > \mathrm{VaR}_{1-p}(\tilde{x}_1) \wedge \cdots \wedge \tilde{x}_n > \mathrm{VaR}_{1-p}(\tilde{x}_n)\}}{p}, \tag{10}$$

which for small p is the ratio between the probability of at least one bank in trouble and the tail probability p used in defining a crisis.

The probability that at least one bank is in trouble can also be expressed as $1 - F(\mathrm{VaR}_{1-p}(\tilde{x}_1), \ldots, \mathrm{VaR}_{1-p}(\tilde{x}_n))$, where F is the joint distribution function of $(\tilde{x}_1, \ldots, \tilde{x}_n)$. We may now use the *copula* approach (cf. Section 3.6) to separate marginal distributions and dependence structure: By Sklar's theorem, there is a unique distribution function C on $[0, 1]^n$ such that

$$F(x_1, \ldots, x_n) = C(F_1(x_1), \ldots, F_n(x_n)),$$

where F_i is the marginal distribution of $\tilde{x}_i$. Consequently, we have that

$$\frac{\mathsf{P}\{\tilde{x}_1 > \mathrm{VaR}_{1-z_1 p}(\tilde{x}_1) \wedge \cdots \wedge \tilde{x}_n > \mathrm{VaR}_{1-z_n p}(\tilde{x}_n)\}}{p}$$

$$= \frac{1 - C(1 - z_1 p, \ldots, 1 - z_n p)}{p} \to L(z_1, \ldots, z_n),$$

so L gives the limit behaviour of C around the point $(1, \ldots, 1)$ (which corresponds to the tail of the distribution). It should be noticed that using copulas we have eliminated the marginal distributions from the expression, thus concentrating on dependence, which seems to be reasonable in the present context.

Some of the measures introduced above have simple limiting expressions using the copula. If we define

$$PO_i = \lim_{p \to 0} PO_i(p),$$

then

$$PO_i = L(1, \ldots, 1) + 1 - L_{-i}(1, \ldots, 1), \tag{11}$$

where L_{-i} is the L-function defined on $\mathbb{R}^{n-1}$ using the joint distribution of $(\tilde{x}_1, \ldots, \tilde{x}_{i-1}, \tilde{x}_{i+1}, \ldots, x_n)$ (so $L_{-i}(1, \ldots, 1) = L(1, \ldots, 1, 0, 1, \ldots, 1)$). Indeed, rewriting (9) we get that

$$PO_i(p) = \frac{1}{p}\mathsf{P}\{\exists j \neq i : \tilde{x}_j > \mathrm{VaR}_{1-p}(\tilde{x}_j) \text{ or } \tilde{x}_i > \mathrm{VaR}_{1-p}(\tilde{x}_i)\}$$

$$+ 1 - \frac{1}{p}\left[\mathsf{P}\{\exists j \neq i : \tilde{x}_j > \mathrm{VaR}_{1-p}(\tilde{x}_j)\}\right],$$

where we have used that $P(A) + P(B) = P(A \cup B) + P(A \cap B)$ or equivalently $P(A \cap B) = P(A) + P(B) - P(A \cup B)$ for arbitrary events A and B. Using the definition of L, we get the expression in (11).

Also the vulnerability index can be expressed through the function L: Defining VI_i as the limit of $\mathrm{VI}_i(p)$ for $p \to 0$, we have that

$$\mathrm{VI}_i = \frac{L_{-i}(1,\ldots,1) + 1 - L(1,\ldots,1)}{L_{-i}(1,\ldots,1)},$$

so $\mathrm{PO}_i = \mathrm{VI}_i L_{-i}(1,\ldots 1)$.

Finally, for the systemic impact index SII_i defined as $\lim_{p \to 0} \mathrm{SII}_i(p)$, we have that

$$\mathrm{SII}_i = \sum_{j=1}^{n} \left[2 - L_{i,j}(1,1)\right], \tag{12}$$

where $L_{i,j}(1,1) = L(0,\ldots,0,1,0,\ldots,0,1,0,\ldots,0)$ is the L-function defined on the joint distribution of $\tilde{x}_i$ and $\tilde{x}_j$. To see this, we notice that

$$\mathrm{SII}_i(p) = \sum_{j=1}^{n} \mathsf{E}\left[1_{\tilde{x}_j > \mathrm{VaR}_{1-p}(\tilde{x}_j)}\Big|\tilde{x}_i > \mathrm{VaR}_{1-p}(\tilde{x}_i)\right]$$

$$= \sum_{j=1}^{n} \mathsf{P}\left\{\tilde{x}_j > \mathrm{VaR}_{1-p}(\tilde{x}_j)\Big|\tilde{x}_i > \mathrm{VaR}_{1-p}(\tilde{x}_i)\right\}$$

$$= \sum_{j=1}^{n} \frac{\mathsf{P}\left\{\tilde{x}_j > \mathrm{VaR}_{1-p}(\tilde{x}_j) \wedge \tilde{x}_i > \mathrm{VaR}_{1-p}(\tilde{x}_i)\right\}}{\mathsf{P}\left\{\tilde{x}_j > \mathrm{VaR}_{1-p}(\tilde{x}_j)\right\}}.$$

Using the same expression for the probability of a joint event as above, and inserting $\mathsf{P}\{\tilde{x}_j > \mathrm{VaR}_{1-p}(\tilde{x}_j)\} = \mathsf{P}\{\tilde{x}_i > \mathrm{VaR}_{1-p}(\tilde{x}_i)\} = p$, we get that

$$\mathrm{SII}_i(p) = \sum_{j=1}^{n} \left[2 - \frac{\mathsf{P}\left\{\tilde{x}_j > \mathrm{VaR}_{1-p}(\tilde{x}_j) \text{ or } \tilde{x}_i > \mathrm{VaR}_{1-p}(\tilde{x}_i)\right\}}{p}\right].$$

Letting p go to 0 and using the definition of $L_{i,j}$, we obtain (12).

The advantage of using the L-function, apart from the fact that the measures of systemic impact considered above can be expressed through L, is that it can be estimated from historical data.

As can be seen, in the approach to measuring systemic importance, the latter is identified with the feature that failures in the given bank come together with failures in other banks. This captures some but not all aspects of the too-big-to-fail problem: A bank may have assets which are uncorrelated with those of other banks, but a failure of the bank may nevertheless cause problems for other – non-financial – sectors of the economy. This can happen if the loans of the defaulted bank are called in or not renewed, leading possibly to liquidity crises and defaults. Problems of this type may very well be more serious than those of correlated bank assets.

17.6 Exercises

1. A country has an independent organization taking care of deposit insurance, thus securing the short-term deposits of ordinary bank customers, and a central bank which is entitled to assist in the case that a bank experiences a run. In addition, there is an established practice according to which the private banks solve their problems collectively, either by offering short-term loans or by mergers and takeovers of banks in trouble.

When a bank has liquidity problems, this may be a sign of more fundamental problems in the bank, so it might be relevant to terminate the activities of the bank and liquidate its assets and liabilities. Discuss, from the point of view of society, whether it is best to let the decision on liquidation of a bank be taken by (1) the central bank, (2) the deposit insurer or (3) the other private banks.

Does the solution depend on whether one of the three mentioned parties has better access to information about the situation of the troubled bank, and if so, how?

2. In a country which has experienced several bank runs, it is decided to reconsider the problem of deciding whether to assist a troubled bank with a loan or whether to liquidate the bank. The information available is the size of the loan asked for by the bank and the information about the bank's assets which can be obtained from a two-day audit of the bank. The decision may be taken either by the central bank as lender of last resort or by the deposit insurance organization.

Give a theory-based suggestion for the solution of this problem: Who should take the decision? It is argued from several sides, including the banks themselves, that banks experiencing runs should be assisted in the first place by the other banks by a reconstruction and possibly takeover and that the central bank or deposit insurer should only act in the case that the banking sector cannot solve the problem itself. How does this argument fit into the theoretical model used above?

3. A bank has recently come out with results which are above average, but its forecasts for the future are not too promising. A group of new shareholders argue that past performance is irrelevant, and with the available forecasts the bank should not be allowed to continue in this form, but should be reorganized with a new management.

Give an assessment of this statement. Is it correct or could there be circumstances not taken into account by the new shareholders which point to another conclusion, and, if so, what is the other conclusion?

4. A small country has only recently opened up for private banks, and there are now a number of privatized former state banks as well as some newly founded banks, most of which are subsidiaries of foreign banks. The level of interest rates is high, and many of the projects financed by the banks are characterized as very risky.

The financial regulators of the country can demand that a bank be subjected to additional control or even liquidated if its loan portfolio contains too many risky loans. Give an assessment of whether the authorities can use these rights to reduce overall riskiness in the banking sector.

It now turns out that a large number of the banks which are subsidiaries of foreign banks close down or are liquidated as a consequence of failed investments, but at the same time several new banks of this type are opened. What can the authorities do to prevent this, given that they must avoid creating too many difficulties for the domestic banks?

17.7 Comments

The problems of bank management and their incentives has its background in the literature on control rights and agency, cf. e.g. Banks and Sundaram [1998]. The model of Repullo [2000] has been elaborated upon by Kahn and Santos [2006]. For further contributions on the regulatory game, see e.g. Park [1997].

The idea of a special regulation for SIFIs (systemically important financial institutions) was introduced in Basel III, but it has not been easy to identify the SIFIs, and the precise definition has been left to the individual countries. A list of global SIFIs (G-SIFIs) is published annually by the Financial Stability Board.

Chapter 18

Capital Regulation and the Basel Accords

18.1 Why capital regulation?

18.1.1 Introduction

We have been concerned with capital regulation all through this book, and this final chapter summarizes some of the points made earlier, adding some new ones as we proceed. Because the banks are subject to capital regulation, it matters for their decision making, and the measurement and management of risk has become a very important part of their activity. On the other hand, the Basel regulations, introducing capital requirements and basing itself almost exclusively on capital regulation, did not prevent the 2007–8 financial crisis, and to some extent perhaps even aggravated it. It is therefore not surprising that the capital regulation has been subject to considerable debate and that alternatives to the methods of regulation represented by Basel I–III are being proposed.

In this chapter, we consider several models showing that straightforward intuitive views on capital regulation, that banks are required to hold more capital than they would otherwise have done as a buffer against the losses that may arise due to the riskiness of its assets, must be taken with a pinch of salt, because such a regulation is not always called for, and it may in some cases even increase the riskiness of a bank. We then consider the Basel regulations in some detail as well as some of the theoretical issues involved. At the end of the chapter, we consider a proposal for a regulation which does away with the need for supervision and regulatory actions.

18.1.2 A model where banks have equity in excess of regulatory demand

There is some empirical evidence that banks choose a composition of funding where the share of equity is larger than what is demanded by regulators. Below we consider a simple model of largely competitive financial markets, as per Allen, Carletti and Marquez (2011), where this is the case.

We consider a one-period economy with firms having access to a risky investment and in need of financing, and banks that lend to the investors and monitor them. An investment requires 1 unit of funds, and its payoff is y if successful, 0 if not. The loan contract specifies a repayment r_L, and the loan market is assumed to be competitive, so the firm receives any surplus arising from the project. The bank chooses an amount k of capital which costs $r_E \geq 1$ per unit, and an amount $1 - k$ of deposits, for which they pay a deposit rate r_D. We assume that the deposit market is also competitive, so the deposit rate r_D will be such that depositors maintain the value of their deposits.

In addition, the bank chooses a level q of monitoring the borrower, here measured as the probability of success of the investment, at a cost $q^2/2$ to the bank. This is indeed the key ingredient of the model. We have assumed that monitoring cost has decreasing returns to scale (hence the quadratic functional form), and it is not observable to other agents than the bank. The role of monitoring should be that banks have experience in financial matters and thereby can help investors to achieve a higher expected value.

We begin by considering the *market* case with no regulation. Here the bank chooses k and then sets the deposit and loan rates (subject to the conditions given by the market). The level of monitoring is set so as to maximize expected profit

$$\Pi = q(r_L - (1 - k)r_D) - kr_E - \frac{1}{2}q^2,$$

and the first-order conditions for a maximum gives us the optimal level of q as

$$q = \min\{r_L - (1 - k)r_D, 1\}.$$

It is seen that monitoring effort is increasing in both loan rate r_L and capital ratio k, but it decreases in r_D. This suggests that there may be a moral hazard problem, given that monitoring is costly for the bank and cannot be observed by the other agents in the market, so the bank must be given incentives to monitor in the proper way.

This, of course, presupposes that there is some interconnection between monitoring and competitive loan rates, so we assume that there is no deposit insurance. If the depositors expect the probability of success of investments to be q, then $qr_D = 1$. In the case of no regulation of k, if competition assures that all surplus goes to the borrower, we find the values of k and the loan rates by maximizing borrower expected profits

$$B = q(y - r_L)$$

subject to

$$q = \min\{r_L - (1 - k)r_D, 1\},$$

$$qr_D = 1,$$

together with the constraints that B and Π should be non-negative and $0 \leq k \leq 1$.

If $r_E \geq 1$ is kept fixed, we can find the solution to this problem. Clearly, as long as $q \neq 0$, we have that $r_L \leq y$. If $q < 1$, then an increase in q will increase Π without decreasing B, so it may be accompanied by a decrease in r_L giving a larger B. We conclude that $q = 1$ in the optimum. It follows that $r_D = 1$, so the participation constraint for the bank becomes

$$r_L - 1 + k - kr_E - \frac{1}{2} \geq 0. \tag{1}$$

Also, from

$$1 = q \leq r_L - (1 - k)$$

we get that $r_L \geq 2 - k$, and inserting this into (1), we get that $k \geq \dfrac{1}{2r_E}$.

The above result is formally derived under an assumption of perfect competition, so the conclusions of the model tell us that the market by itself will discipline banks so as to hold capital above a certain level. However, the distinctive feature is that k is determined so as to maximize borrowers' expected profits hence the lower bound on k: Too small a value of k would mean that the bank might settle down with $q < 1$, which would reduce borrowers' profits. If this is a result of market forces, it must be a market where all bargaining power is left with the borrowers and none with the banks. Therefore, it may be questioned whether the result can be seen as a decision by banks to hold more than the minimal capital required.

If instead we introduce a regulator, determining k so as to maximize a social welfare function defined as

$$B + \Pi = q(y - r_L) + q(r_L - (1 - k)r_D) - kr_E - \frac{1}{2}q^2 = q(y - (1 - k)r_D) - kr_E - \frac{1}{2}q^2,$$

while otherwise everything is as before; then for large enough y (namely $y \geq 2$), the capital ratio k may be chosen as 0, because the banks' gain with $r_E = 2$ is large enough to give incentives for $q = 1$. If $y < 2$, the capital ratio must be positive, whereas q may be less than 1. We have thereby displayed a case where the market will force a higher capital ratio on the banks than that determined by a welfare maximizing regulator.

18.1.3 A model where capital regulation may increase risk

To see that capital regulation may work in ways that run counter to intuition, we look at a simple model proposed by Hakenes and Schnabel [2011], which resembles those considered in the discussion of competition and risk (Chapter 11). We assume that there are N banks which are financed either by deposits D_j or by equity E_j, $j = 1, \ldots, N$. The banks compete for depositors and for loans.

Borrowers are entrepreneurs, who may choose risky projects, all of equal size 1, characterized by a payoff s in case of success, which comes with probability $p(s)$ and 0 otherwise; the success probability is assumed to be a decreasing function of the success payoff s. The banks cannot observe the project choices of the borrowers; they can only see whether they were a success or a failure. The demand for loans is given by an inverse demand curve $r_L(L)$ giving the loan rate at which the total amount L of loans are taken by entrepreneurs.

The banks consider equity as costly, because shareholders demand a payoff r_E which is greater than r_D, the deposit rate. We shall assume that banks are subject to capital regulation in the sense that $E_j > kL_j$ for each j, for some $k > 0$.

In order to create a situation where an increase in k leads to increased risk, we introduce another feature: Entrepreneurs may have a preference for a particular sector in the economy, and if the risk is sector specific, then choosing all borrowers as belonging to the same sector, the bank has arranged loans that are perfectly correlated. Choosing all borrowers from different sectors, the loans become uncorrelated by the law of large numbers.

We assume that a bank can choose the extent to which the loans are correlated. For simplicity, this is formalized as the choice of a parameter ρ, which is the probability that the loan portfolio is uncorrelated, whereas it is perfectly correlated with probability $1 - \rho$; the expected payoff is unaffected by the choice of ρ. There is a cost $c(\rho_j)$ connected with this choice, and c is assumed to be convex, attaining a minimum at some 'normal' level ρ_0 of ρ.

Entrepreneurs choose s so as to maximize expected payoff at the loan rate r_L, giving the first-order condition

$$s + \frac{p(s)}{p'(s)} = r_L, \tag{2}$$

which gives s as an increasing function of r_L. Bank j chooses the values of the correlation parameter ρ_j (share of uncorrelated loans), loans L_j, deposits D_j *and* equity E_j such that profit

$$\Pi_j = p(s)r_L(\overline{L})L_j - \left[\rho_j + (1 - \rho_j)p(s)\right]\left(r_D(\overline{D}) + \alpha\right)D_j - r_E E_j - c(\rho_j)L_j,$$

with $\overline{L} = \sum_{i=1}^{N} L_i$, $\overline{D} = \sum_{i=1}^{N} D_i$ are maximal. Here the quantity $[\rho_j + (1 - \rho_j)p(s)]$ is the probability of survival of the bank, which defaults if loans are perfectly correlated and the investment fails. The quantity α is the premium for the deposit insurance, assumed fixed. Taking first-order conditions w.r.t. ρ_j, we obtain

$$c'(\rho_j)L_j = -(1 - p(s))\left(r_D(\overline{D}) + \alpha\right)D_j. \tag{3}$$

We now add that equity is chosen such that $E_j = kL_j$ (the bank will keep this funding at its minimal level because it is more expensive than deposits), and that $D_j = (1 - k)L_j$ by the overall funding constraint of the bank. Then we get that the bank must choose L_j so as to maximize

$$L_j\left[p(s)r_L(\overline{L}) - (1 - k)\left(\rho_j + (1 - \rho_j)p(s)\right)\left(r_D((1 - k)\overline{L}) + \alpha\right) - kr_E - c(\rho_j)\right] \tag{4}$$

under the constraints given by (2) with $r_L = r_L(\overline{L})$ and (3).

We may now check how a change in the capital ratio k affects the equilibrium. Because we are looking at symmetric equilibria, we skip the reference to bank j from now on. At the outset, a change in k decreases the profits of the banks by increasing the funding cost, and the banks adapt to this by lowering the deposit and loan volumes. This, in its turn, results in a rise in the loan rate, which by (2) forces the entrepreneurs into choosing more risky investments.

To capture the overall effects, we must also track the changes in correlation. We may rewrite (3) as

$$c'(\rho)L = (1 - k)\big[r_D\big((1 - k)\overline{L}\big) + \alpha\big]\big[p\big(s(\overline{L})\big) - 1\big],\tag{5}$$

and considering (5) as an equation determining ρ once k is given, we may use implicit function theorem to determine how k influences ρ. Using the notational convention

$$\Phi = \big[r_D\big((1 - k)\overline{L}\big) + \alpha\big]\big[1 - p\big(s(\overline{L})\big)\big]$$

we get that

$$\frac{d\rho}{dk} = -\frac{1}{c''(\rho)}\left[-\Phi + (1 - k)\left(\frac{\partial\Phi}{\partial\overline{L}}\frac{\partial\overline{L}}{\partial k} + \frac{\partial\Phi}{\partial k}\right)\right].$$

We have $c''(\rho) > 0$ because $c(\cdot)$ is a convex function, and we obtain that stricter capital regulation in the form of an increase in k will increase ρ and thereby decrease the correlation of the loan portfolio if the expression in the bracket is negative, that is, if

$$(1 - k)\left(\frac{\partial\Phi}{\partial\overline{L}}\frac{\partial\overline{L}}{\partial k} + \frac{\partial\Phi}{\partial k}\right) < \Phi$$

Intuitively, the change of k has several different effects, pointing in opposite directions. The effect of higher capital ratio on loan rates and indirectly on riskiness of investments was mentioned above, and taken in isolation this will lead to more correlation because it makes risk taking more profitable for the bank. However, the more standard effects of increased capital ratios are also at work: A larger proportion of equity reduces the advantages of limited liability, and it will decrease the deposit rate, thereby increasing the interest margin, which would speak for a lower ρ. The total effect is ambiguous and will depend on the parameter values and the functions $r_D(\cdot)$ and $p(\cdot)$, but the main point is that it is indeed possible that increased capital ratios may lead to higher correlation of bank portfolios, with the ensuing higher risk for the financial sector as a whole.

18.2 The Basel Accords

In previous chapters, we have repeatedly referred to regulations following from Basel II. Below we give a brief account of the history of Basel II and an outline of the agreement.

18.2.1 The Basel Committee

After two major international bank failures in 1974 (see e.g. Heffernan [2005] for an account of some conspicuous bank failures), a standing committee of bank supervisory authorities in the G-10 countries (Belgium, Canada, France, Germany, Italy, Japan, Netherlands, Sweden, the United Kingdom and the United States) was created, with a permanent secretariat in Basel and meetings three times a year. The secretariat is located at the *Bank for International Settlements*, which is owned by the central banks, formerly only Western countries, but now comprising also some central banks from the emerging economies.

The role of the committee has changed somewhat over the years. At the outset, its main purpose was to assure that international banks did not escape the supervisory authority which typically is restricted to a particular country, and to ensure that foreign branches and subsidiaries were adequately regulated, because there had been cases where a subsidiary experienced a bank run, but the central bank of the country in which the main bank was situated refused to assist. The initial agreements ('concordats') which were approved by the committee did not, however, solve the problems of international banking and financial stability, and this led to a new approach as witnessed by the Basel accords.

18.2.2 Basel I

The first Basel Accord from 1988 marked the beginning of a new style for supervision and regulation of banking because it established a single system of capital adequacy standards for the international banks of the participating countries, which was to come into effect from January 1993. The main principle was that banks should have to set aside reserves based on the Basel risk assets ratio

$$\frac{\text{capital}}{\text{weighted risk assets}}$$

(a principle taken from the regulation used in the United Kingdom and the United States, where the risk assets ratio was known as the Cooke Ratio). Here 'capital' should be understood as consisting of tier 1 and tier 2 capital, where

- tier 1, or core capital, consists of equity, disclosed reserves and retained earnings, less goodwill and other deductions; and
- tier 2, or supplementary capital, are loan loss allowances, undisclosed reserves, general loss reserves, etc.

The risk-weighted assets are found by sorting the assets by credit type and assigning lower weights to more creditworthy assets:

- 0%:   cash, gold, bonds issued by OECD governments
- 20%:   bonds issued by agencies of OECD governments (as e.g. export credit guarantee agencies), local (municipal) governments and insured mortgages
- 50%:   uninsured mortgages
- 100%:   all corporate loans and claims by non-OECD banks or government debts, equity and property.

Off-balance items (letters of credit, futures, swaps, forex agreements) were converted into 'credit risk equivalents' (a method later abandoned) and weighted by the type of counterparty.

The Basel Accord requires that banks set aside a *minimum* of 8% capital and 4% for core capital. But in practice, the ratios have been higher.

Basel I was criticized on several accounts. The rules did not account for the many differences among banks in different countries, where the way of measuring capital might differ quite substantially. This also holds for the determination of tier 1 and tier 2 capital where the rules in one country may result in another classification than those of another country. The off-balance items were considered in a too simplistic way when translated to ordinary assets, because this translation did not take into account the risk in market price, concentrating on default risk. Finally, the weighting used in Basel I is simplistic, because corporate loans with rating AAA still count as 100%, whereas loans to Italian banks can be weighted 20%, even though the rating of these banks varies from A+ to AA−. Such shortcomings of the regulation may be used by the banks to reduce capital requirements without a corresponding risk reduction. Moreover, the rules fail to encourage risk reduction by diversification, and the same amount of capital has to be set aside against one big loan and two smaller loans with the same total amount.

18.2.3 The 1996 amendment

The lack of consideration of price risk led to the incorporation of *market risk* in the additions to the Basel Accord made in 1996. A third type of capital, tier 3 capital, was introduced for the computation of the capital charge for market risk. This is defined as short-time subordinated debt (maturity less than two years) which satisfies a number of requirements, among which is that neither interest nor principal can be repaid if thereby the bank falls below the minimal capital requirement.

Another new aspect of the Basel amendment was the introduction of the internal model approach for computing the amount of capital set aside for market risk. The bank now has a choice between a standardized and the internal model approach. To use the latter, the banks must meet the following requirements:

1. Bank models must compute Value at Risk (VaR) on a daily basis.

2. The four risk factors to be used are interest rates, exchange rates, equity prices and commodity prices.

3. A one-sided confidence interval of 99% should be used.

4. The choice of period should depend on the objective: Banks with liquid trading books should consider daily returns, whereas pension and investment funds may use one-month periods for price changes.

5. There is no requirement of type of distribution, but if a variance-covariance approach is used, then the banks should make allowances for non-linearities, in particular in connection with option positions.

Once the VaR is computed using the internal model, the capital charge is found as

$$\mu_1[\text{10-day market risk VaR}] + \mu_2[\text{10-day specific risk VaR}]\frac{\tau}{8},$$

where μ_1 is a market risk multiplier, taking the value 3 or 4 after a decision by the regulator, indicating the quality of the model for detecting systemic risk, and μ_2 similarly takes values either 4 or 5. The quantity τ, known as the trigger, is assigned based on the quality of the bank's control processes and can vary between 8 and 25.

In addition to the above, the amendment introduced limitations on the total concentration of risk: If a risky asset contributes to more than 10% of the bank's total capital, the regulator must be informed, and advance permission must be obtained for a risk exceeding 25% of the capital.

The standardized approach uses fixed percentages, and there are precise instructions for computing capital charge on equity risk, foreign exchange risk, interest rate risk and commodities risk.

18.2.4 Basel II: The three pillars

In response to the criticism of Basel I and its amendment, a number of changes were made, and all this was collected into the new proposal for an amendment finally adopted in 2004. The standardized approach was to be adopted by all G-10 countries by 2006, and the advanced approach by 2007. Although some of the US banks did not follow the timetable, the rules have obtained widespread acceptance, also by countries which are not formally members of the Bank for International Settlements.

The overall structure of the new accord can be summarized in the table below, showing the three pillars of the Basel Accord.

Table 18.1 The Three Pillars of the Basel Accord

Pillar 1 **Risk Assets Ratio**	Pillar 2 **Supervisors**	Pillar 3 **Market Discipline**
New measurement of credit risk	Encourage banks to develop internal methods to assess capital	Disclose methods for computing capital adequacy
Measurement of market risk		
Measurement of operational risk	Setting capital targets	

In the first pillar, we find the rules for risk capital ratios, which now cover not only credit and market risk but also operational risk. The choice between a standardized and a more sophisticated approach is outlined in Table 18.2.

The fundamental ratio to be computed in Basel II for the minimum capital requirements is

$$\frac{\text{Capital (tier 1 and 2)}}{\text{Amended credit risk} + \text{market risk} + \text{operational risk}},$$

Table 18.2 Basel II, Pillar 1: Summary of Approaches

Credit Risk	Market Risk	Operational Risk
(1) Standardized approach	(1) Standardized approach	(1) Basic indicator approach
(2) Foundation internal ratings–based (IRB) approach	(2) Internal model	(2) Standardized approach
(3) Advanced IRB approach		(3) Advanced measurement approaches

and the requirements themselves are unchanged, 4% for tier 1 and 8% for tier 2. The details of the risk capital ratio computations have been given in previous chapters.

In Pillar 2, dealing with the role of the national supervisors, there are four principles of supervisory review:

1. Supervisors should ensure that banks use appropriate methodology to determine Basel II ratios, and have a strategy to maintain capital requirements.

2. Supervisors should review banks' internal assessment procedures and strategies, taking appropriate action if they fall below standards.

3. Banks should be encouraged by supervisors to hold capital above the minimum requirement.

4. Supervisors are expected to intervene as early as possible to ask a bank to restore its capital levels if they fall below the minimum.

There are no details in the Basel Accord about the precise way in which supervisors should behave, but the formulations suggest that the supervisory authorities should have the staff and competences to engage in an ongoing dialogue with the banks about the best way to secure that adequate capital is available.

Pillar 3, which deals with market discipline, is meant to be a reinforcement of the first two pillars. It underlines the availability of timely and transparent information, which should make it possible for the market to discipline the banks. Participating banks are expected to disclose their risk exposure and capital adequacy, but also their methods for computing capital adequacy, as well as all information which, if omitted or misstated, could affect the decisions of agents using the information. This disclosure should take place every half year, and more often if the bank engages in global activities. It is the plan that the Committee will set up special forms for this disclosure of information.

18.2.5 Some criticisms against Basel II

Some reservations against the proposed changes from Basel I to Basel II were formulated in Danielsson et al. [2001]. The authors pointed to inherent weaknesses in Basel II as well as possible inconsistencies in the general approach, summarized as follows:

Risk is endogenous. The introduction of the internal ratings approach for the computation of regulatory capital in the bank was introduced in order to make the reserve requirements respond in a more flexible way to the risk profile of the bank, in particular with regard to credit risk. However, the approach to forecasting risk, based on VaR, neglects crucial aspects of risk in the financial markets. In particular, it is assumed that the bank's own actions, based on its forecast of future volatility, do not affect this volatility.

This is, however, not the case. Unlike weather forecasts, where the action taken on the basis of the forecast does not change this forecast, financial risk is created by the market behaviour of all agents, including the banks which are forecasting their risk. This leads to the contagion phenomena known from financial crises, where expectation of falling prices triggers more sales, with an increased downturn of prices as a result. Similarly, during financial crises some specific financial markets, typically for derivatives such as futures or credit default swaps, may cease to function due to the fact that all traders are in the same side of the market, so the pricing breaks down and volatility is increased drastically.

In this context, a regulation based on VaR can have unwanted consequences, in particular in a context where the traders in the market are very different with respect to their risk aversion. Here VaR-based regulation will reduce the possibility of the almost risk-neutral financial institutions (such as hedge funds) to take risk, and therefore the overall willingness of taking risks is reduced; if risk-averse banks want to get rid of risky assets in a downturn, then there are no buyers, and the downturn is therefore aggravated. What goes wrong here is not that there is some form of regulation, but rather that the regulation works through VaR, which fails to recognize the endogeneity of risk *and* demands that all financial institutions use the same approach.

A possible remedy might be found in the improvement of the information streams, calling for sufficient transparency in the market so that banks are aware of the state of the financial system. The third pillar indeed contains proposals to this effect, but more information does not necessarily solve all problems. It can be shown (cf. Morris and Shin [2004]) that disclosing aggregate positions in financial markets to its participants can have negative as well as positive effects, so openness is not a general answer to such problems. On the other hand, increased information from banks to regulators may give the latter improved conditions for regulating in the proper way.

VaR neglects some crucial information. The use of VaR-based risk measurement is in accordance with practice, but it has some flaws, as was mentioned during the discussion of risk measures in Chapter 3. Using a point estimate to describe a probability distribution will by necessity induce some loss of information, but in the case of VaR this is aggravated by the fact that VaR is insensitive to distribution of the tail. To this should be added that in practical computations, one often uses methods which implicitly assume that the underlying probability distribution is normal, which is known not to be the case.

Reliance on ratings. Because both the standardized and to some extent the internal ratings–based approaches rely on credit ratings of borrowers, such ratings should be widespread, which they are in the United States, but not in Europe. The Basel rules take this into account by setting a specific weight for unrated firms, but this again gives rise to some unwanted effects, because it may then be in the interest of the bank to transfer firms with a low rating to the general group of unrated firms. But what is much more important, ratings are only reliable if they are consistent across agencies and through time; many ratings agencies have provided notoriously inconsistent ratings over time for one and the same firm. Consequently, the use of ratings presupposes that supervisors have the possibility of checking the use of the system by the banks and preventing ratings shopping.

Another drawback of the ratings approach is that although ratings may provide some assessment of a company's riskiness, this usually comes after the developments in the market because the ratings agencies rely on accounting data they observe only at intervals. Therefore, they are generally reluctant to change their assessments if there is a possibility that they will have to change them back again shortly afterwards, and all this points towards slow reaction to market developments.

Why operational risk? The introduction of capital charges against operational risk was a novelty of Basel II, but it can be argued that this constitutes a break with the very purpose of the Basel Accords. Capital adequacy regulations are there to prevent systemic bank failures through contagion. Market and credit risk are risks shared by all the market participants with many common exposures, so the failure of one bank can spread to another bank because their background is shocks which are common to both. But operational risk is quite different; it is in most cases idiosyncratic risk, that is, risk which pertains to a particular bank and does not involve other banks. Losses due to operational risk hit the shareholders, management, bondholders, etc. of this bank, but they do not spread to other banks. It may therefore be speculated that the addition of capital charges for operational risk was rather meant as a corrective to the tendency observed after introduction of internal ratings–based market and credit charges, where the capital set aside might otherwise become rather too small.

Procyclicality. Riskiness of assets vary over the business cycle, and risk assessments reflect this procyclicality, presumably more so with the internal ratings–based approaches than with the standardized approach. Consequently, one will experience a similar procyclicality of the capital charges, so banks set less aside at the top of the cycle, meaning that they are overlending in the late phase of the upturn, and more at the bottom of the cycle. In this way, the regulation makes the banks more, rather than less, vulnerable to failures and can destabilize the economy as a whole. The recent financial crisis lends some additional credence to this argument. However, there is no easy remedy for this problem: Allowing regulators to adjust the capital charges to the business cycle moves the problem elsewhere, rather than presenting a solution, because the phases of the business cycle are typically very hard to detect. It may be the reliance on capital charges as the one and only instrument of regulation that has to be revised.

18.2.6 Basel III

The events of the financial crisis of 2007–8 pointed to several shortcomings of previous regulation, and this gave rise to several additions to the existing framework, appearing in 2010 and known as Basel III. In general, the rules in Basel III can be seen as a strengthening of those in Basel II, with higher capital requirements as well as more precise rules for what constitutes capital of tier 1 and tier 2. There are, however, also some new features.

The main points of Basel III can be summarized as follows:

(i) *Increased capital reserves:* In addition to the existing system of capital regulation, two new items are added, namely a mandatory *capital conservation buffer* of 2.5%, which comes into force in cases where the activities of the bank increase rapidly, and a discretionary *countercyclical buffer*, of a size up to another 2.5%, to be enforced by national regulators when considered necessary, so as to prevent the tendency that capital reserves according to the existing rules will be small during booms and large in slumps.

(ii) *Leverage rule:* This is a rule which is aimed to prevent too small capital reserves, even in cases where assets have low risk and therefore would not give rise to building up reserves by using the existing rules. The rule demands that capital should constitute at least 3% of total (not risk-weighted) assets.

(iii) *Liquidity rules:* Here Basel III introduces the *liquidity coverage ratio*: High quality assets should be large enough to cover one month net cash outflow. In addition, Basel III introduces the notion of *net stable funding*, which are deposits, long-term loans and equity. When fully implemented (according to the plans, this will happen in 2019) the *net stable funding ratio* will establish a ratio between long-term assets, suitably risk weighted, and the net stable funding.

The new rules are clearly intended to take care of the specific problems that became visible during the financial crisis of 2007–8. However, they still leave some problems open, in particular in relation to the phenomenon of shadow banking (because there are financial institutions not covered by the Basel rules), and the idea of incorporating liquidity problems into the Basel framework may be criticized.

As pointed out in Blundell-Wignall and Atkinson [2010], the liquidity rules were introduced under the impression of the bank runs occurring during the crisis, notably that of Northern Rock in 2007, and the subsequent drying up of the interbank market as a source of funding. However, it is questionable whether financial supervisors are the right institutions for dealing with questions of liquidity, where we already have a well-functioning institution in the form of a lender of last resort.

18.2.7 The need for a leverage rule

One of the new items in Basel III was the leverage regulation, supplementing the by now very elaborate rules of risk-weighted capital charges. Intuitively, this rule can be explained as a consequence of the increasing lack of confidence in the banks' own risk assessments; bank supervisors have little if any chance of discovering too risky behaviour before it is too late. The model below, by Blum [2008], shows that in this case a leverage ratio may be useful.

We consider a very simple world with banks of two types, *safe* and *risky*. All banks have total assets 1, and they are funded by deposits D and capital E. We assume that deposits

---

Box 18.1

Regulatory arbitrage in Basel III. As pointed out by Blundell-Wignall and Atkinson [2010], banks can arrange to get away with substantially smaller capital than was intended by the Basel rules. This can happen if assets are transferred between banks and in particular if institutions not subject to the Basel regulations are involved, for example if risky engagements which are initiated by banks are eventually transferred to insurance companies:

Suppose that bank A lends €100 to a company buying a bond issued by this company, for which the risk weight is 100%, and with a capital ratio of 8% the bank must hold additional capital to the amount of €8.

Next, bank A transfers the risk to another bank B by shortselling the bond and buying a CDS (credit default swap) from B. The asset, seen as a promise to pay the €100, has been transferred from the original firm to a bank, and its risk weight is now 20%, so the capital charge for A is reduced from €8 to €2.

The smaller capital charge would in principle have to be offset by bank B, but if this bank chooses to reinsure its CDS outside the banking sector, then the charge reduces to 8% of the spread price of the CDS (and if the spread is 700 bps, then this price is €7) plus a surcharge of 1.5% of the bond, all multiplied by 50% weighing for off-balance commitments, resulting in a total of €0.08 · (7 + 1.5) · 0.5 = €0.34.

In total, the arrangement has reduced the capital requirement for basically the same asset from originally €8 to €2.34. The possibility of such transactions indicates that the regulations must provide for capital reserve in any case and also when the transacting parties are not banks.

---

are insured, so the deposit rate is equal to the risk-free rate, which is set to 1. Capital has a cost c_e per unit, and we assume that capital is more expensive than deposits, $c_e > 1$.

The safe banks have a return of $1 + r$ with safety, whereas the return of the risky bank is random,

$$\widetilde{R} = \begin{cases} 1 + r & \text{with probability } p, \\ 1 - r & \text{with probability } 1 - p, \end{cases}$$

where $p > \frac{1}{2}$, so both types of bank are profitable on average, meaning that they are acceptable from the point of view of society. The bank supervisors cannot observe the type of the bank, whereas the banks themselves know their type. If the bank has return $1 + r$, then it is not revealed whether the bank is safe or risky. If it defaults, there is a social cost C connected with the bankruptcy.

From the point of view of society, safe banks should hold no capital at all, because it is more expensive than deposits. For the risky banks, matters are different, however. With no capital, society will have expected bankruptcy costs $(1 - p)C$, but bankruptcy may be avoided if banks hold exactly enough capital to remain solvent, which is the amount r; the cost of which is $c_e r$. Thus, for large enough C, namely if

$$C > \frac{(c_e - 1)r}{1 - p},$$

then risky banks should hold a fraction r of assets as capital.

Suppose now that the banks are not restricted by capital regulation in any way. If the bank managers are profit maximizers then, the safe banks should maximize

$$\Pi_s = (1 + r)(D + E) - D - c_e E$$

in E subject to the constraint $D = 1 - E$, or, after inserting the constraint,

$$\Pi_s = r - (c_e - 1)E,$$

which means that, as before, $E = 0$. For the risky bank, expected profits are

$$\text{E}\Pi_s = p[(1 + r)(D + E) - D] + (1 - p) \max\{(1 - r)(D + E) - D, 0\} - c_e E = (2p - c_e)r. \tag{6}$$

In the case of the bad outcome, the bank may either default, in which case the payoff is 0, or it may cover the losses from its capital, given that the latter is big enough. Clearly, the risky bank also wants to hold as little capital as possible, in this case 0.

The obvious way of regulating the banks is to impose a minimal amount of capital, in our case

$$E_{min} = r. \tag{7}$$

Because total assets have been normalized to 1, it can be seen as a minimal *leverage ratio*, prescribing the size of capital in relation to total (not risk-weighted) assets. Introducing this rule will allow society to avoid the bankruptcy cost, but it entails an efficiency loss because it must be imposed for *all* banks, whether safe or risky.

A first step towards an improvement of this inefficient regulation would be to allow banks to signal their type, followed by an assignment of capital ratio depending on the signal. Clearly, safe banks should be allowed a capital ratio of 0, but if there is no possibility of control, then also risky banks would signal 'safe', and the regulation would not work as intended. So, in order to get a truthful signal from the bank, the supervisor must have some additional possibilities of action: We assume that the regulator may inspect the bank, and if the bank is risky, this will be detected with probability q. A risky bank which is caught misinforming the supervisor may be fined by an amount F which is assumed to correspond to a fraction s of its profits.

For the safe banks, the optimal message is, of course, 'safe', and it incurs no risk of being fined. The risky bank may signal 'risky', in which case it must hold capital according to (7), and expected profit will be

$$\text{E}\Pi_r(\text{risky}) = (2p - c_e)r \tag{8}$$

as in (6). If it signals 'safe', then it may get away with capital 0 but incurs a risk of being fined (something which happens only if it survives), so expected profit is

$$\text{E}\Pi_r(\text{safe}) = p[(1 + r)D - D - qs((1 + r)D - D)] = p(1 - qs)r.$$

Truthful reporting is incentive compatible only if $\text{E}\Pi_r(\text{risky}) \geq \text{E}\Pi_r(\text{safe})$ or

$$qs \geq \frac{c_e - p}{p}. \tag{9}$$

It is seen that if the supervisor detects untruthful reporting only with small probability or if the penalty for untruthful reporting is low, so (9) will not be satisfied, then, again, the more sophisticated methods will not work.

There is, however, a further possibility of regulating the banks, even when the regulator is not very powerful. This can be achieved by adding another constraint, namely a leverage constraint $k_{min} \leq r$. For the safe banks, this represents an additional cost, but otherwise nothing is changed. The same holds for the risky banks in the case of truthful reporting because the bank will then be subject to a more strict capital regulation, and expected profit is as before in (8). But for the risky bank sending the message 'safe', expected profit will now be

$$E\Pi_r(\text{safe}) = p[1 + r - (1 - k_{min})](1 - qs) - c_e k_{min} = p(1 - qs)(r + k_{min}) - c_e k_{min}.$$

To induce truthful reporting, this result should be no better than that of (8), and the break-even condition reduces to

$$k_{min} = \frac{p(1 - qs) - (2p - c_e)}{c_e - p(1 - qs)} r,$$

which may serve as a rule for determining the minimal leverage ratio that will induce truthful reporting by banks.

It is seen that the leverage ratio acts as a substitute for penalizing the banks by detecting false reports and collecting fines. When qs, the average amount paid for false reporting, becomes small, the leverage ratio approaches r. Although this policy induces truthful reporting, it does so at the cost of the risky banks, which pay the cost of holding more capital than what is necessary from the point of view of society.

18.3 Bank reaction to changes in capital regulation

18.3.1 Consequences of capital regulation

The intuitive justification for capital regulation – banks should set aside some equity so losses on their assets will not hurt their creditors unless they surpass a certain limit – has long ago been supplemented by several other arguments pointing to disadvantages of capital regulation, in particular when this regulation has been tightened, as was the case at least with Basel III. Following the discussion in Admati et al. [2010], we review briefly some of these arguments.

(i) *Increased equity requirements means that banks must 'set aside' funds that could otherwise be used for lending.* This argument confuses capital requirements with liquidity requirements, because capital requirements pertain only to the relation between debt and equity in the funding of the bank. No capital is 'set aside' as it would have been in the case of liquidity requirements.

(ii) *Increased equity requirements will increase the banks' cost of funding.* Here it is assumed that equity requires a higher return than debt, but the argument forgets the risk premium. Changing the composition of capital between equity and debt also means that the risk premium is changed.

(iii) *Increased equity requirements lower the bank's return on equity (ROE), which means a loss in value.* This argument is another version of the previous one. The first part of the statement is true, but the second is not, because shareholder value depends both on return and on risk.

(iv) *Increased equity requirements will increase banks' funding cost because banks cannot borrow as much as previously with taxation subsidies.* This is actually true, but the problem is not so much capital regulation as the fact that banks are encouraged by tax subsidies on debt to increase leverage, which is not a suitable way of supporting activities which are considered socially desirable.

(v) *Increased equity requirements are counterproductive because debt is necessary for providing 'market discipline' to bank managers.* It may indeed be argued that debt may play this role, but on the other hand, high leverage creates incentives to take excessive risks, and the evidence of the disciplining role of the markets in the years preceding the financial crisis of 2007–8 is weak.

(vi) *Increased equity requirements will force the banks to reduce lending.* This is not necessarily true, in the sense that there is no mechanical connection between capital ratio and assets. Banks may maintain all their activities by issuing new equity, keeping all assets and liabilities as they were. Banks may not want to do so, because this may be interpreted as a negative signal on the situation of the bank, and instead they would prefer not to exploit lending opportunities, but regulators might require new equity issuance to prevent this.

(vii) *The way banks fund themselves with debt and equity is the optimal way of funding bank activities.* There is no theoretical basis for this statement, because the banking industry is subject to frictions, incomplete competition and asymmetric information.

Summing up, the reservations against capital regulation seem to lack a solid theoretical basis. On the other hand, this reservation is manifest, and banks are putting up much effort to reduce the reported riskiness of assets. Also, it may be argued that strengthening capital regulation does not by itself create a less risky banking sector, as is shown in the model considered below.

18.3.2 A model where stricter capital regulation does not increase capital

When banks are regulated by capital requirements, there are two possible responses to increases in these requirements, namely (1) increase of capital and (2) reduction of assets, that is, of loans. The latter option is often socially undesirable, because stricter regulation often comes in periods of economic downturn, so the regulator would prefer that banks issue new equity rather than reduce their activities. However, as shown in the following simple model taken from Hyun and Rhee [2011], this may not happen, even in cases where there is no cost of issuing new equity.

There are – as usual – three periods of time in our model. At $t = 0$, an entrepreneur opens a firm at cost C_0, which is borrowed from the bank as a loan which is repaid with interest at $t = 2$. The results to be obtained from the activity of the firm, once it is opened, depends on a random variable $\tilde{e}$ which may be interpreted as effort or competence of the entrepreneur, for simplicity it is assumed, to be uniformly distributed in $[0, 1]$. Because the value of e is drawn independently and is uniformly distributed, there will be (approximately) the same amount of entrepreneurs with any particular value of e. We shall normalize this amount so it corresponds to the interval $[0, 1]$.

Production occurs at $t = 1$ and $t = 2$, and in order to carry out business, the firm needs additional working capital C_t for $t = 1, 2$. The firms then produce outcome $y_t(e)$ which is random and given by

$$y_t(e) = \begin{cases} y & \text{with probability } p(e), \\ 0 & \text{with probability } 1 - p(e), \end{cases}$$

where $y > C_t$ for $t = 1, 2$, and the probability $p(e)$ is given by $p(e) = eA + (1 - A)$ for $0 < A < 1$ (so there is a lower limit $1 - A$ to the probability of non-zero outcome). We assume independence between outcomes in the two periods, so firms surviving at $t = 1$ have the same probability of defaulting at $t = 2$ as they had at $t = 1$.

A bank is now established at $t = 0$ with a capital of the size $K > 0$. We assume that the cost of establishing the bank is equal to K, so an increase of capital requirements means that the bank must sell shares to the public. The bank obtains deposits, which are assumed to be fixed and normalized to 1. The assets of the bank are either loans to enterprises or government bonds. The deposit interest rate is r_D and the loan rate is r_L. The government offers bonds for banks' investment purposes, and it determines the capital adequacy ratio, which is defined as the ratio of capital to risk-weighted assets. Here government bonds have weight 0 and loans have risk weight 1.

In this context, the firms maximize profit by borrowing C_t from the bank in each period. If it cannot borrow at some t, it cannot produce in that period. If a firm had output y at $t = 1$, it has a profit of

$$\pi_1 = y - (r_L C_0 + (1 + r_L) C_1)$$

in this period, and π_1 is assumed to be consumed by the entrepreneur. If outcome was 0, the firm tells the bank that it cannot pay, but they retain the business and wait for the next period. To make the model work smoothly, we assume that the bank accepts the loss of C_1 upon a default, but that the firm remains active, possibly with a new owner. At the end of period 2, the firm sells the factory at scrap value, which is assumed to be C_0, and pays interest on the loan of C_0.

The bank observes the value of e for each entrepreneur, and it uses the observation as a credit rating for the firm. At $t = 0$, all firms apply for loans, and the remaining amount $1 + K - C_0$ is placed in government bonds. At $t = 1$, firms apply for working capital, and the expected period 1 profit obtained from a loan to a firm with credit rating e is

$$p(e) r_L (C_0 + C_1) - (1 - p(e)) C_1,$$

so the bank will offer loans to all firms with $e \geq e_1$, where e_1 satisfies the break-even condition

$$p(e_1)r_L(C_0 + C_1) - (1 - p(e_1))C_1 = r_G C_1,$$

where r_G is the interest rate on government bonds. We may think of r_G as the discount rate in the economy, which for simplicity is set to 0, and assuming that also depositors may invest in government bonds, we have that $r_D = r_G = 0$, and the break-even condition can be written as

$$p(e_1)r_L(C_0 + C_1) - (1 - p(e_1))C_1 = 0. \tag{10}$$

To find the expected profit of the bank at $t = 1$, we first integrate over all firms (s, e) with a fixed credit rating $e \geq e_1$, for which the proportion of successful firms equals $eA + (1 - A)$, and then over all such e. The overall successful firms are easily found as all (s, e) with $e \geq e_1$ and $s \leq eA + 1 - A$, which amounts to the fraction

$$(1 - e_1)(Ae_1 + 1 - A) + \frac{1}{2}(1 - e_1)(1 - (Ae_1 + 1 - A)) = (1 - e_1)\left(\frac{2 - (1 - e_1)A}{2}\right),$$

and the fraction of unsuccessful firms is

$$\frac{1}{2}(1 - e_1)(1 - (Ae_1 + 1 - A)) = \frac{A}{2}(1 - e_1)^2,$$

giving an expected profit on the loan transaction of

$$\pi(e_1) = (1 - e_1)\left(\frac{2 - (1 - e_1)A}{2}\right)r_L(C_0 + C_1) - \frac{A}{2}(1 - e_1)^2 C_1. \tag{11}$$

Now we introduce capital adequacy into the model. Let k be the ratio determined by the government; then the fraction of entrepreneurs that can obtain credit must be restricted by $e \geq e_2$, where e_2 is given by

$$\frac{K}{C_0 + (1 - e_2)C_1} = k. \tag{12}$$

The value e_2 can be greater or smaller than e_1 determined by (10), in the following we assume that $e_1 \leq e_2$. The bank then grants credit to firms with $e \geq e_2$ and uses the remainder, $1 - K - C_0 - (1 - e_2)C_1$, on government bonds, and profits are as in (11), with e_1 replaced by e_2,

$$\pi(e_2) = (1 - e_2)\left(\frac{2 - (1 - e_2)A}{2}\right)r_L(C_0 + C_1) - \frac{A}{2}(1 - e_2)^2 C_1. \tag{13}$$

In period 2, everything is repeated, and because credit rating is unchanged, the bank will grant credit on the same conditions as at $t = 1$, unless some of the parameters have been changed. At the end of period 2, the long-term loans C_0 are repaid.

Now we assume that the capital adequacy ratio is changed from k to $k' > k$. If K remains unchanged, e_2 must change upwards, and from (12) we get that

$$\frac{de_2}{dk'} = \frac{K}{C_1(k')^2}. \tag{14}$$

Differentiating (13) and using (14) we get that

$$\frac{d\pi(e_2)}{dk'} = [((1 - e_2)A - 1) r_L(C_0 + C_1) + A(1 - e_2)C_1] \frac{K}{C_1(k')^2}. \tag{15}$$

On the other hand, extending the capital means that profit may be kept unchanged, but the existing shareholders now get only the fraction $v = \dfrac{k}{k'}$ of the profit, and we get that profit changes by

$$\pi(e_2)\frac{dv}{dk'} = \left[(1 - e_2)\left(\frac{2 - (1 - e_2)A}{2}\right)r_L(C_0 + C_1) - \frac{A}{2}(1 - e_2)^2 C_1\right]\left(-\frac{k}{(k')^2}\right).$$

If we assume that C_0 is small, then

$$k \sim \frac{K}{(1 - e_2)C_1},$$

and then

$$\pi(e_2)\frac{dv}{dk'} \sim \left[\left(\frac{2 - (1 - e_2)A}{2}\right)r_L(C_0 + C_1) - \frac{A}{2}(1 - e_2)C_1\right]\left(-\frac{K}{C_1(k')^2}\right).$$

Comparing this expression with (15), we see that for small values of C_0, profits of incumbent shareholders are reduced less by cutting back loans than by issuing new shares. We have shown that it is a rational decision for the banks' shareholders to tighten credit as a response to changes in the capital adequacy ratio.

18.4 Bank regulation without regulators?

The regulation of banks as embodied in the Basel rules is not perfect, and it is being revised continually; in the debate following Basel III, many contributors have announced that they expect a Basel IV before long, containing a strengthening of the leverage rule and possibly simplification of the rules for internally based risk assessments. Such revisions do not change the fundamental structure of the regulation with some of its characteristic features: Internal methods have become so complicated that supervisors cannot monitor the riskiness of the banks under supervision, and many rules have a discretionary nature, depending on the actions of national regulators.

An alternative to this regulation is an increased reliance on self-regulating market forces, but this in turn demands a very fundamental restructuring of banking business. Indeed, market signals proved themselves quite inefficient as a method of assessing risks in the years preceding the financial crisis of 2007–8. The following is a brief outline of the proposal in Bulow and Klemperer [2013].

One of the main reasons for regulating banks is that in the case of a default, the owners should suffer considerable losses before any other creditor is hit. However, regulation cannot always secure that this will be the case, and therefore it might be worthwhile considering a system where creditors either have guarantees in form of collateral, or they will be converted to owners rather than creditors in time to prevent a default from happening.

In the proposed system, the *assets* to which bank creditors may turn in the case of a default should be of the following three types:

- assets posted as collateral,
- equity, and
- unsecured debt which can be converted to equity.

Corresponding to this, the *debt* of a bank is either

- deposits or other debts guaranteed by government, such debt must be backed by government securities, or
- unsecured debt to be fully financed by *equity recourse notes*, or ERNs, securities which are transformed to equity if their value falls to a certain level.

The proposed new organization of banking business points both to *narrow banking*, in the sense that deposits should be backed by government securities, and to *securitization* with regard to commercial banking. However, the basic new aspect here is that debtors become shareholders automatically, thereby preventing bankruptcy; clearly, the possible change of role from debtor to shareholder is taken into account when the notes issued by the bank are absorbed by the market.

Let us take a closer look at ERNs. Consider a bank which has both equity and a number N of issues of ERNs. In the kth issue of ERNs, the total number of bonds have face value D_k, and by the rules for the issue, they can be converted to S_k shares, which means that the price at which conversion takes place is D_k/S_k. We assume that the issues (which may correspond to N different loan contracts) are numbered in such a way that

$$\frac{D_1}{S_1} > \cdots > \frac{D_k}{S_k} > \frac{D_{k+1}}{S_{k+1}} > \cdots > \frac{D_N}{S_N}.$$

This means that issue 1 is the first to be converted, then issue 2, etc. By S_0 we denote the number of original shares of the bank. Let V be the value of the bank and denote by $V_k(V)$ the market value of the bonds from the kth issue when the bank has value V.

The bank converts debt to shares when this will increase the value of its shares, which again is the value of the bank divided by the number of shares, and taking into account the possibility of converting debt to shares, conversion is made so as to maximize

$$\frac{1}{\sum_{i=0}^{j} S_i}\left(V - \sum_{i=j+1}^{N} D_i\right)$$

over the issues $j = 1,\ldots,N$. We can find the value to the owners of the kth security as

$$V_k(V) = \min\left\{D_k, \max_j\left\{\frac{S_k}{\sum_{i=0}^{j} S_i}\left(V - \sum_{i=j+1}^{N} D_i\right)\right\}\right\}, \tag{16}$$

because they either receive the face value of their debt, D_k, or their bonds have been converted to shares so they obtain the value corresponding to the S_k shares.

The expression in (16) can be used to find X_k, the value of V at which the kth issue is converted, by the condition

$$\frac{D_k}{S_k} = \frac{1}{\sum_{i=0}^{k} S_i}\left(X_k - \sum_{i=k+1}^{N} D_i\right),$$

from which we get that

$$X_k = \frac{D_k}{S_k}\sum_{i=0}^{k} S_i + \sum_{i=k+1}^{N} D_i.$$

Using this, one may find the value of the bonds of issue k, given that the firm has value V, as

$$V_k(V) = S_k\left[\frac{V}{\sum_{i=0}^{N} S_i} + \sum_{j=k+1}^{N} \frac{S_j}{\sum_{i=0}^{j} S_i} \frac{E(V,X_j)}{\sum_{i=0}^{j-1} S_i} - \frac{E(V,X_k)}{\sum_{i=0}^{k} S_i}\right]. \tag{17}$$

Here $E(V,X)$ is the value of the option to buy the firm at price X (at the end of the period considered) when the value is V, cf. Section 7.3). To see why (17) holds, we notice that the first term in the bracket on the right-hand side is the value per share in the kth issue of the ownership of the firm. The last term, which is subtracted from the other terms, is the value per share of the call option that issuers with a lower index than k have of paying out the shares of issue k, an option which will be exercised when the value of the firm is greater than X_k. Now the sum in the middle term is made up of elements which are similar to the last one, only they represent the options for shareholders of issue k together with shareholders of lower issues to buy out those of any issue $j > k$. Starting from the top, the shareholders of issues $0,1,\ldots,N-1$ can buy out shareholders of issue k, so each share gets a fraction $S_N / \sum_{i=0}^{N} S_i$ of the proceeds, which would be $E(V, X_N) / \sum_{i=0}^{N-1} S_i$, so each share of issue k retains an option value of

$$\frac{S_N}{\sum_{i=0}^{N} S_i} \frac{E(V, X_N)}{\sum_{i=0}^{N-1} S_i}.$$

Then the shareholders of issue $j = N - 2$ may buy out those of issue $N - 1$, and repeating the argument with issue $N - 1$ being the last one, we get a term

$$\frac{S_{N-1}}{\sum_{i=0}^{N-1} S_i} \frac{E(V, X_{N-1})}{\sum_{i=0}^{N-2} S_i}.$$

Collecting all the terms from $j = N$ and downwards to $j = k + 1$, we get the middle term in (17).

The main point of our finding the explicit expression (17) is that the ERN bonds have a fairly transparent valuation, so it seems reasonable that ERNs can be absorbed by the market at prices which reflect their value. Because the conversion to equity is a built-in feature of the securities, the liquidity crises which have been seen in connection with securitization and repo markets cannot occur with the ERNs, because bondholders know that they are transformed into shareholders when the firm value changes unexpectedly.

A bank which functions according to this plan will need no capital requirements; indeed, there is always enough equity to cover the losses of the debtors. This, of course, does not mean that losses will not occur, but debtors will not be hit as such, but as shareholders, and they know this before entering into relationship with the bank. The proposed system therefore goes a long way in the direction of replacing a system which must be monitored by regulators who often are less well equipped for this task than the banks are to exploit the rules to their own advantage, with a system that largely disciplines itself.

18.5 Exercises

1. In the Allen-Carletti-Marquez model of Section 18.1, banks may choose to keep a larger capital ratio than what is socially desirable. Show that this voluntary capital ratio may increase if the cost of equity is reduced.

Discuss the means by which a social planner could achieve that the capital ratio chosen by banks is more in line with what is socially desirable.

2. To ensure a quick recovery after a major financial crisis, the banks in a country have been exempted from taxation. There has been a change in management in the banks, and the new managers are committed to running the banks in such a way that the market values of the banks are kept as large as possible.

It is argued (with reference to the Modigliani-Miller theorem [Prop. 1 in Chapter 9]) that in this situation it is possible to abolish the leverage rule of Basel III, and possibly even the whole system of capital regulation.

Comment on this argument. What kind of additional assumptions must be made?

3. Operational risk and capital charges: Suppose that banks are regulated according to the standardized approach (cf. Chapter 13). Discuss whether a change in the capital charges can result in a shift in the business profile of the bank, so it will accept greater risks than hitherto.

4. A country has adapted its financial supervision authority (FSA) to the Basel regulations, and the financial institutions are continuously supervised. After the financial crisis, the government decides that additional effort is needed to guarantee the stability of the country's financial institutions, and they introduce an increase by 2% in all capital ratios. The FSA is entitled to close down a bank whenever it fails to comply with these rules.

Comment on whether a rule of this type has the desired effect, in particular in situations where the authorities can inspect the balances and loan portfolios of a bank but are less informed about the borrowers and their probabilities of success than is the bank.

Assume now that information about borrower quality is observable but not verifiable. What are the consequences?

5. Suppose that the financial sector of a country is transferred from traditional capital regulation to funding through equity recourse notes as described in Section 18.4. Give an assessment of the impact of the reform on

(i) Risk taking of banks: Will the banks be more or less open to moral hazard?

(ii) Willingness to offer credits: How will the credit rationing problems change as a result of the reform?

(iii) Risk-management efforts: Will the banks use more or less resources on risk management?

18.6 Comments

The present chapter collects many different models and ideas, connected by the common theme of capital regulation. The idea that banks should have a sufficient amount of risk capital, so losses are taken by owners rather than depositors, is so intuitively obvious that it would seem almost impossible to argue against it. Because self-evident ideas often turn out to have weaknesses, we consider models where capital regulation may have some effects which are not expected and even not wanted.

The Basel rules have been a recurring theme in this book, and much of what is in Section 18.3 has been mentioned at earlier stages. More space has been devoted to Basel I and (in particular) II than to the newest of them, Basel III, because most of the principal ideas of the Basel rules were introduced in the earlier accords, whereas Basel III can be considered as an update and a response to the widespread argumentation that Basel I and II had not been good enough to prevent the financial crisis of 2007–8.

It has been argued that the revisions included in Basel III are not sufficient to guarantee financial stability, so a Basel IV is needed, but what it should contain remains as yet debatable. The proposal in Section 18.4 for a fundamentally new way of regulating the financial sector, relying on self-correcting forces rather than on legal rules and supervision, can be taken as an indication that capital regulation as the backbone of financial security may have passed its prime.

References

V.V. Acharya and T. Yorulmazer. Too many to fail – an analysis of time-inconsistency in bank closure policies. *Journal of Financial Intermediation*, 16:1–31, 2007.

V.V. Acharya and T. Yorulmazer. Cash-in-the-market pricing and optimal resolution of bank failures. *Review of Financial Studies*, 21:2705–2742, 2008.

V.V. Acharya, J.A.C. Santos and T. Yorulmazer. Systemic risk and deposit insurance premiums. *FRBNY Economic Policy Reviews*, 16:89–99, 2010.

A.R. Admati, P.M. DeMarzo, M. Hellwig and P. Pfleiderer. Fallacies, irrelevant facts, and myths in the discussion of capital regulation: why bank equity is not expensive. Technical Report 42, Max Planck Institute for Research in Collective Goods, 2010.

P. Aghion and P. Bolton. An 'incomplete contracts' approach to financial contracting. *Review of Economic Studies*, 59:473–479, 1992.

G.A. Akerlof and P.M. Romer. Looting: the economic underworld of bankruptcy for profit. *Brookings Papers on Economic Activity*, 2:1–73, 1993.

C. Alexander. *Market risk analysis, Vol. IV, Value at Risk models*. Wiley, New Jersey, 2009.

F. Allen. Credit rationing and payment incentives. *Review of Economic Studies*, 50:639–646, 1983.

F. Allen and D. Gale. Innovations in financial services, relationships, and risk sharing. *Management Science*, 45:239–1253, 1999.

F. Allen and D. Gale. Financial contagion. *Journal of Political Economy*, 108:1–33, 2000.

E.I. Altman. Financial ratios, discriminant analysis and the prediction of corporate bankruptcy. *Journal of Finance*, 23:189–209, 1968.

B. Armendáriz and R. Morduch. *The economics of microfinance*. The MIT Press, Cambridge, Massachusetts, 2005.

L.G. Arnold and J.G. Riley. On the possibility of credit rationing in the Stiglitz-Weiss model. *American Economic Review*, 99:2012–2021, 2009.

K.J. Arrow. Uncertainty and the welfare economics of medical care. *American Economic Review*, 53:941–973, 1963.

P. Artzner, F. Delbaen, J.-M. Eber and D. Heath. Coherent measures of risk. *Mathematical Finance*, 3:203–228, 1999.

A. Ashcraft, J. McAndrews and D. Skeie. Precautionary reserves and the interbank market. *Journal of Money, Credit and Banking*, 43:311–348, 2011.

369

B. Baesens and T. Van Gestel. *Credit risk management*. Oxford University Press, Oxford, 2009.

E. Baltensperger. Alternative approaches to the theory of the banking firm. *Journal of Monetary Economics*, 6:1–37, 1980.

S. Banerji, J. Bhattacharya and N.V. Long. Can financial intermediation induce endogenous fluctuations. *Journal of Economic Dynamics and Control*, 28:2215–2238, 2004.

J.S. Banks and R.K. Sundaram. Optimal retention in agency problems. *Journal of Economic Theory*, 82:293–323, 1998.

J.R. Barro. The loan market, collateral, and rates of interest. *Journal of Money, Credit and Banking*, 8:439–456, 1976.

J.R. Barth, C. Lin, P. Lin and F.M. Song. Corruption in bank lending to firms: Cross-country micro evidence on the beneficial role of competition and information sharing. *Journal of Financial Economics*, 91:361–388, 2009.

Basel Committee on Banking Supervision. Operational risk. Technical report, Bank for International Settlements, January 2001a.

Basel Committee on Banking Supervision. The new Basel capital accord. Technical report, Bank for International Settlements, January 2001b.

Basel Committee on Banking Supervision. Sound practices for the management and supervision of operational risk. Technical report, Bank for International Settlements, February 2003.

M. Bech and R. Garratt. The intraday liquidity management game. *Journal of Economic Theory*, 109:198–219, 2003.

T. Beck, A. Demirguc-Kunt and R. Levine. Bank supervision and corruption in lending. *Journal of Monetary Economics*, 53:2131–2163, 2006.

D. Besanko and A.V. Thakor. Collateral and rationing: sorting equilibria in monopolistic and competitive credit markets. *International Economic Review*, 28:671–689, 1987.

D. Besanko and A.V. Thakor. Relationship banking, deposit insurance and bank portfolio choice. Technical report, Discussion Paper 0411046, EconWPA, Finance, 2004.

J. Bessis. *Risk management in banking*. Wiley, Chichester, England, 2nd edition, 2002.

H. Bester. Screening vs. rationing in credit markets with imperfect information. *American Economic Review*, 75:850–855, 1985.

S. Bhattacharya and D. Gale. Preference shocks, liquidity and central bank policy. In W. Barnett and K. Singleton, editors, *New approaches to monetary economics*, Cambridge University Press, Cambridge, 1987.

S. Bhattacharya and A.V. Thakor. Contemporary banking theory. *Journal of Financial Intermediation*, 3:2–50, 1993.

F. Black and M. Scholes. The pricing of options and corporate liabilities. *Journal of Political Economy*, 81:637–654, 1973.

J.M. Blum. Why 'Basel II' may need a leverage ratio restriction. *Journal of Banking and Finance*, 32:1699–1707, 2008.

A. Blundell-Wignall and P. Atkinson. Thinking beyond Basel III: necessary solutions for capital and liquidity. *OECD Journal: Financial Market Trends*, 1, 2010.

P. Bolton and D. Scharfstein. A theory of predation based on agency problems in financial contracting. *American Economic Review*, 80:93–106, 1990.

A.W.A. Boot. Relationship banking: What do we know? *Journal of Financial Intermediation*, 9:7–25, 2000.

W.A. Boot, A.V. Thakor and G.F. Udell. Secured lending and default risk: equilibrium analysis, policy implications and empirical results. *Economic Journal*, 101:458–472, 1991.

J.H. Boyd and G. de Nicoló. The theory of bank risk taking and competition revisited. *The Journal of Finance*, 60:1329–1343, 2005.

S.J. Brown and O.W. Steenbeek. Doubling: Nick Leeson's trading strategy. *Pacific-Basin Finance Journal*, 9:83–99, 2001.

R. Bruner. Where M&A pays and where it strays: a survey of the research. *Journal of Applied Corporate Finance*, 16:63–77, 2004.

L. Bryan. Core banking. *McKinsey Quarterly*, 1, 1991.

S. Buckle and E. Campbell. Settlement bank behaviour and throughput rules in an RTGS payment system with collateralised intraday credit. Working Paper 209, Bank of England, 2003.

J. Bulow and P. Klemperer. Market-based bank capital regulation, 2013. URL http://163.1.40.43/economics/papers/2013/MBBCRFinalpaperSept.pdf

Y.S. Chan, S.I. Greenbaum and A.V. Thakor. Is fairly priced deposit insurance possible? *Journal of Finance*, 47:227–245, 1992.

T.J. Chemmanur and P. Fulghieri. Reputation, renegotiaton, and the choice between bank loans and publicly traded debt. *Review of Financial Studies*, 7:475–506, 1994.

T.J. Chemmanur and J. He. IPO waves, product market competition, and the going public decision: theory and evidence. *Journal of Financial Economics*, 101:382–412, 2011.

A.S. Chernobai, S.T. Rachev and F.J. Fabozzi. *Operational risk, a guide to Basel II capital requirements, models and analysis*. Wiley, New Jersey, 2007.

K. Cuthbertson and D. Nitzsche. *Quantitative financial economics*. Wiley, Chichester, England, 2005.

J. Danielsson, P. Embrechts, C. Goodhart, C. Keating, F. Muennich, O. Renault and H.S. Shin. An academic response to Basel II. Technical Report 130, LSE Financial Markets Group, 2001.

M. Da Rin, T. Hellmann and M. Puri. A survey of venture capital research. In G.M. Constantinides, M. Harris and R.M. Stulz, editors, *Handbook of the Economics of Finance*, volume 2A, pages 573–648. Elsevier, Amsterdam, 2013.

A. Davidson, A. Sanders, L.-L. Wolff and A. Ching. *Securitization: structuring and investment analysis*. Wiley, New Jersey, 2003.

F.W.M. de Andrade and L.C. Thomas. Structural models in consumer credit. *European Journal of Operational Research*, 183:1569–1581, 2007.

L. de Haan and A. Ferreira. *Extreme value theory*. Springer, Amsterdam, 2006.

J.A. de Matos. *Theoretical foundations of corporate finance*. Princeton University Press, Princeton, New Jersey, 2001.

D. de Meza and D.C. Webb. Too much investment: a problem of asymmetric information. *The Quarterly Journal of Economics*, 102:281–292, 1987.

G. Dell'Ariccia. Asymmetric information and the structure of the banking industry. *European Economic Review*, 45:1957–1980, 2001.

M. Dewatripont and J. Tirole. *The prudential regulation of banks*. The MIT Press, Cambridge, Massachusetts, 1994.

J. Dhaene, R.J.A. Laeven, S. Vanduffel, G. Darkiewics and M.J. Goovaerts. Can a coherent risk measure be too subadditive? *Journal of Risk and Insurance*, 75:365–386, 2008.

D.W. Diamond. Financial intermediation and delegated monitoring. *Review of Economic Studies*, 51:393–414, 1984.

D.W. Diamond and P.H. Dybvig. Bank runs, deposit insurance, and liquidity. *Journal of Political Economy*, 91:401–419, 1983.

D.W. Diamond and R.G. Rajan. Bank bailouts and aggregate liquidity. *American Economic Review*, 92:38–41, 2002.

K. Dowd. *Measuring market risk*. Wiley, New Jersey, 2002.

D. Duffie. *Measuring corporate default risk*. Oxford University Press, Oxford, 2011.

D. Duffie and K.J. Singleton. *Credit risk: pricing, measurement and management*. Princeton University Press, Princeton, New Jersey, 2003.

D. Duffie, R. Jarrow and A. Purnanandam. Market pricing of deposit insurance. *Journal of Financial Services Research*, 24:93–119, 2003.

P. Embrechts, C. Klüppenberg and T. Mikosch. *Modelling extremal events for insurance and finance*. Springer Verlag, Berlin, 1997.

P. Embrechts, R. Frey and A.J. McNeil. *Quantitative risk management: concepts, techniques, and tools*. Princeton University Press, Princeton, New Jersey, 2005.

M. Everett, J. McNeill and G. Phelan. Measuring the value added of the financial sector in Ireland. *Bank of Ireland Quarterly Bulletin*, pages 85–93, 2013.

G. Favarel-Garrigues, T. Godefroy and P. Lascoumes. Reluctant partners? Banks in the fight against money laundering and terrorism financing in France. *Security Dialogue*, 42:179–196, 2011.

S. Finlay. *The management of consumer credit: theory and practice*. Palgrave Macmillan, Basingstoke, Hampshire, 2010.

D. Fixler and K. Zieschang. Deconstructing FISIM: Should financial risk affect GDP? Technical report, U.S. Bureau of Economic Analysis and International Monetary Fund, July 2010.

S. Freeman. The payments system, liquidity, and rediscounting. *American Economic Review*, 86:1126–1138, 1996.

X. Freixas. Optimal bail out policy, conditionality and constructive ambiguity. Discussion Paper 237, LSE Financial Markets Group, 1999.

X. Freixas. Deconstructing relationship banking. *Investigaciones Económicas*, 29:3–31, 2005.

X. Freixas and J.-C. Rochet. *Microeconomics of banking*. The MIT Press, Cambridge, Massachusetts, 2nd edition, 2008.

D. Gale and M. Hellwig. Incentive-compatible debt contracts: the one-period problem. *Review of Economic Studies*, 52:647–663, 1985.

V.F. García, V.F. Cibils and R. Maino. Remedy for banking crisis: what Chicago and Islam have in common. *Islamic Economic Studies*, 11:1–22, 2004.

J. Geanakoplos. The levarage cycle. Paper 1304, Cowles Foundation, 2010.

N. Gennaioli, A. Shleifer and R.W. Vishny. A model of shadow banking. *Journal of Finance*, 68:1331–1363, 2013.

M. Gertler and N. Kiyotaki. Financial intermediation and credit policy in business cycle analysis. In B.J. Friedman and M. Woodford, editors, *Handbook of Monetary Economics*, volume 3, pages 547–599. Elsevier, Amsterdam, 2010.

G. Gorton and L. Huang. Bank panics and the endogeneity of central banking. *Journal of Monetary Economics*, 53:1613–1629, 2006.

G. Gorton and A. Metrick. Regulating the shadow banking system. *Brookings Papers on Economic Activity (Fall 2010)*, pages 261–312, 2011.

S.I. Greenbaum and A.V. Thakor. *Contemporary financial intermediation*. Academic Press, Amsterdam, 2007.

S.J. Grossman and O.D. Hart. Takeover bids, the free-rider problem and the theory of the corporation. *Bell Journal of Economics*, 11:42–64, 1980.

H. Hakenes and I. Schnabel. Banks without parachutes: competitive effects of bailout policies. *Journal of Financial Stability*, 6:156–168, 2010.

H. Hakenes and I. Schnabel. Capital regulation, bank competition, and financial stability. *Economics Letters*, 113:256–258, 2011.

A. Haldane, S. Brennan and V. Madouros. What is the contribution of the financial sector: miracle or mirage? In *The future of finance: the LSE report*, pages 87–110. LSE, 2010.

R.G. Hansen. A theory for the choice of exchange medium in mergers and acquisitions. *Journal of Business*, 60:75–95, 1987.

S. Heffernan. *Modern Banking*. Wiley, London, 2005.

F. Heider, M. Hoerova and C. Holthausen. Liquidity hoarding and interbank market spreads: the role of counterparty risk. Discussion Paper 2009-40S, CentER, 2009.

T. Ho and A. Saunders. The determinants of bank interest margins: theory and empirical evidence. *Journal of Financial and Quantitative Analysis*, 16:581–600, 1981.

N. Houy. The economics of bitcoin transaction fees. WP 1407, Groupe d'analyse et de théorie économique Lyon Saint-Étienne, February 2004.

J.C. Hull. *Options, futures and other derivatives*. Prentice Hall, New Jersey, 1997.

T.-M. Huo and M.T. Yu. Do bank runs exist in the Diamond-Dybvig model? *Journal of Institutional and Theoretical Economics*, 150:537–542, 1994.

J. Hwang, N. Jiang and P. Wang. Collusion and overlending. *Economic Inquiry*, 45:691–707, 2007.

J.-S. Hyun and B.-K. Rhee. Bank capital regulation and credit supply. *Journal of Banking and Finance*, 35:323–330, 2011.

R.D. Innes. Limited liability and incentive contracting with ex-ante action choices. *Journal of Economic Theory*, 52:45–67, 1990.

C.J. Jacklin. Demand deposits, trading restrictions and risk sharing. In E. Prescott and N. Wallace, editors, *Contractual arrangements for intertemporal trade*. University of Minnesota Press, Minneapolis, 1987.

R.A. Jarrow. Operational risk. *Journal of Banking and Finance*, 32:870–879, 2008.

R.A. Jarrow, J. Oxman and Y. Yildirim. The cost of operational loss insurance. *Review of Derivatives Research*, 13:273–295, 2010.

D. Jones. Emerging problems with the Basel Capital Accord: regulatory capital arbitrage and related issues. *Journal of Banking and Finance*, 24:35–58, 2000.

P. Jorion. *Value at Risk: the new benchmark for managing financial risk*. McGraw-Hill, New York, 3rd edition, 2006.

Ciby Joseph. *Advanced credit risk: analysis and management*. Wiley, Chichester, 2013.

C.M. Kahn and J.A.C. Santos. Who should act as a lender of last resort? An incomplete contracts model: a comment. *Journal of Money, Credit and Banking*, 38:1111–1118, 2006.

M.C. Keeley. Deposit insurance, risk, and market power in banking. *American Economic Review*, 80:1183–1200, 1990.

F. Khan. How 'Islamic' is Islamic banking? *Journal of Economic Behavior and Organization*, 76:805–820, 2010.

M.S. Khan. Islamic interest-free banking: a theoretical analysis. *Staff Papers – International Monetary Fund*, 33:1–27, 1986.

J.L. King. *Operational risk: measurement and modelling*. Wiley, Chichester, England, 2001.

N. Kiyotaki and J. Moore. Credit cycles. *Journal of Political Economy*, 105:211–248, 1997.

N. Kiyotaki and J. Moore. Evil is the root of all money. *American Economic Review*, 92:62–66, 2002.

M. Klein. A theory of the banking firm. *Journal of Money, Credit and Banking*, 3:205–218, 1971.

S. Kobayakawa and H. Nakamura. A theoretical analysis of narrow banking proposals. *Bank of Japan Monetary and Economic Studies*, May:105–118, 2000.

D. Lando. *Credit risk modeling*. Princeton University Press, Princeton, New Jersey, 2004.

M. Leippold and P. Vanini. The quantification of operational risk. *The Journal of Risk*, 8:59–65, 2005.

H.E. Leland and D.H. Pyle. Informational asymmetries, financial structure and financial intermediation. *Journal of Finance*, 32:371–387, 1977.

J. Lintner. The valuation of risk assets and the selection of risky investments in stock portfolios and capital budgets. *Review of Economics and Statistics*, 47:13–37, 1965.

L. Maer and N. Broughton. Financial services: contribution to the UK economy. SN06193, House of Commons, 2012.

G. Mailath and L. Mester. A positive analysis of bank closure. *Journal of Financial Intermediation*, 3:272–299, 1994.

A. Martin. Liquidity provision vs. deposit insurance: preventing bank panics without moral hazard. *Economic Theory*, 28:197–211, 2006.

A. Martin and J. McAndrews. Liquidity-saving mechanisms. *Journal of Monetary Economics*, 55:554–567, 2008.

A. Martin, D. Skeie and E.-L. von Thadden. Repo runs. Staff Report 444, Federal Reserve Bank of New York, 2010.

D. Martinez-Miera and R. Repullo. Does competition reduce the risk of bank failure? *Review of Financial Studies*, 23:3638–3664, 2010.

D. Masciandaro. Money laundering: the economics of regulation. *European Journal of Law and Economics*, 7:225–240, 1999.

J. Mathis, J. McAndrews and J.-C. Rochet. Rating the raters: Are reputation concerns powerful enough to discipline rating agencies? *Journal of Monetary Economics*, 56:657–674, 2009.

C. Matutes and X. Vives. Competition for deposits, fragility, and insurance. *Journal of Financial Intermediation*, 5:184–216, 1996.

R.C. Merton. On the pricing of corporate debt: the risk structure of interest rates. *The Journal of Finance*, 29:449–470, 1974.

R.C. Merton. On the analytical derivation of the cost of deposit insurance and loan guarantees: an application of modern option pricing theory. *Journal of Banking and Finance*, 1:3–11, 1977.

D.C. Mills. Alternative central bank credit policies for liquidity provision in a model of payments. *Journal of Monetary Economics*, 53:1593–1611, 2006.

F. Modigliani and M. Miller. The cost of capital, corporation finance and the theory of investment. *American Economic Review*, 48:261–297, 1958.

F. Modigliani and M. Miller. Corporate income taxes and the cost of capital: a correction. *American Economic Review*, 53:433–443, 1963.

M. Monti. Deposit, credit, and interest rate determination under alternative bank objectives. In G.P. Szégö and K. Shell, editors, *Mathematical methods in investment and finance*, pages 431–454. North-Holland, Amsterdam, 1972.

S. Morris and H. Shin. Coordination risk and the price of debt, *European Economic Review*, 48: 133–153, 2004.

A.D. Morrison and L. White. Is deposit insurance a good thing, and who should pay for it. Discussion Paper 4424, CEPR, 2004.

S. Nakamoto. Bitcoin: a peer-to-peer electronic cash system, 2008. URL https://bitcoin.org/bitcoin.pdf

J.-P. Niinimäki. Evergreening in banking. *Journal of Financial Stability*, 3:368–393, 2007.

J.-P. Niinimäki. Liquidity creation without bank panics and deposit insurance. *Journal of Institutional and Theoretical Economics*, 166:521–547, 2010.

J. Ostroy and R. Starr. The transactions role of money. In B. Friedman and F. Hahn, editors, *Handbook of Monetary Economics*, volume I, pages 3–62. North-Holland, New York, 1990.

S. Park. Risk-taking behaviour of banks under regulation. *Journal of Banking and Finance*, 21:491–507, 1997.

A. Pavlov and S. Wachter. Robbing the bank: non-recourse lending and asset prices. *Journal of Real Estate Finance and Economics*, 28:147–160, 2004.

A. Pavlov and S. Wachter. Subprime lending and real estate prices. *Real Estate Economics*, 39:1–17, 2011.

J. Peck and K. Shell. Equilibrium bank runs. *Journal of Political Economy*, 111:103–123, 2003.

R. Peñaloza. A duality system of payment systems. *Journal of Mathematical Economics*, 45:679–692, 2009.

A. Postlewaite and X. Vives. Bank runs as an equilibrium phenomenon. *Journal of Political Economy*, 95:485–491, 1987.

Z. Pozsar, T. Adrian, A. Ashcraft and H. Boesky. Shadow banking. Staff Report 458, Federal Reserve Bank of New York, July 2010.

E. Prisman, M. Slovin and M. Sushka. A general model of the banking firm under conditions of monopoly, uncertainty and recourse. *Journal of Monetary Economics*, 17:737–747, 1986.

L. Ratnovski. Bank liquidity regulation and the lender of last resort. *Journal of Financial Intermediation*, 18:541–558, 2009.

R. Repullo. Who should act as a lender of last resort? An incomplete contracts model. *Journal of Money, Credit and Banking*, 32:580–605, 2000.

R. Repullo. Capital requirements, market power, and risk-taking in banking. *Journal of Financial Intermediation*, 13:156–182, 2002.

J.R. Ritter. The long-run performance of initial public offerings. *Journal of Finance*, 46:3–37, 1991.

J.R. Ritter and I. Welch. A review of IPO activity, pricing, and allocation. *The Journal of Finance*, 57:1795–1828, 2002.

J.-C. Rochet and J. Tirole. Cooperation among competitors: some economics of payment card associations. *Rand Journal of Economics*, 33:549–570, 2002.

J.-C. Rochet and J. Tirole. Two-sided markets: a progress report. *Rand Journal of Economics*, 37:645–667, 2006.

K. Rock. Why new issues are underpriced. *Journal of Financial Economics*, 15:187–212, 1986.

M. Rothschild and J.E. Stiglitz. Increasing risk I: a definition. *Journal of Economic Theory*, 2:225–283, 1970.

M. Rothschild and J.E. Stiglitz. Equilibrium in competitive insurance markets: an essay on the economics of imperfect information. *The Quarterly Journal of Economics*, 90:629–649, 1976.

S. Salop. Monopolistic competition with outside goods. *Bell Journal of Economics*, 10:131–156, 1979.

P.A. Samuelson. An exact consumption-loan model of interest with or without the social contrivance of money. *Journal of Political Economy*, 66:467–482, 1958.

M. Sarr, E. Bulte, C. Meissner and T. Swanson. On the looting of nations. *Public Choice*, 148:353–380, 2011.

F. Schneider. Turnover of organized crime and money laundering: some preliminary empirical findings. *Public Choice*, 144:473–486, 2010.

M. Segoviano and C. Goodhart. Banking stability measures. Working Paper 09/04, IMF, 2009.

W.F. Sharpe. Capital asset prices: a theory of market equilibrium under conditions of risk. *Journal of Finance*, 19:425–442, 1964.

H.S. Shin. Reflections on Northern Rock: the bank run that heralded the global financial crisis. *Journal of Economic Perspectives*, 23:101–119, 2009.

A. Shleifer and R.W. Vishny. A survey of corporate governance. *Journal of Finance*, 52:737–783, 1997.

A. Shleifer and R.W. Vishny. Unstable banking. *Journal of Financial Economics*, 97:306–318, 2010.

V. Skreta and L. Veldkamp. Ratings shopping and asset complexity: a theory of ratings inflation. *Journal of Monetary Economics*, 56:678–695, 2009.

K. Soramäki, M.L. Bech, J. Arnold, R.J. Glass and W.E. Beyeler. The topology of interbank payment flows. *Physica A: Statistical Mechanics and its Applications*, 379:317–333, 2007.

J.E. Stiglitz. Peer monitoring and credit markets. *The World Bank Economic Review*, 4:351–366, 1990.

J.E. Stiglitz and A. Weiss. Credit rationing in markets with imperfect information. *American Economic Review*, 71:393–410, 1981.

E. Takáts. A theory of 'crying wolf': the economics of money laundering enforcement. *Journal of Law, Economics, and Organization*, 27:32–78, 2011.

J. Tirole. *The theory of corporate finance*. Princeton University Press, Princeton, New Jersey, 2006.

R. Townsend. Optimal contracts and competitive markets with costly state verification. *Journal of Economic Theory*, 21:265–293, 1979.

N. Wallace. Narrow banking meets the Diamond-Dybvig model. *Federal Reserve Bank of Minneapolis Quarterly Review*, pages 3–13, Winter 1996.

W. Watanabe. Does a large loss of bank capital cause *evergreening*? Evidence from Japan. *Journal of the Japanese and International Economies*, 24:116–136, 2010.

L.J. White. The credit-rating agencies and the subprime debacle. *Critical Review: A Journal of Politics and Society*, 21:389–399, 2009.

S.D. Williamson. Costly monitoring, financial intermediation, and equilibrium credit rationing. *Journal of Monetary Economics*, 18:159–179, 1986.

C. Wilson. The nature of equilibrium in markets with adverse selection. *The Bell Journal of Economics*, 11:108–130, 1980.

T.C. Wilson. Plugging the gap. *Risk*, 7:74–80, 1994.

C. Zhou. Are banks too big to fail? Measuring systemic importance of financial institutions. *International Journal of Central Banking*, 6:205–250, 2010.

Index